Exploring the Impact of the Dissertation in Practice

Exploring the Impact of the Dissertation in Practice

Edited by

Valerie A. Storey

INFORMATION AGE PUBLISHING, INC.
Charlotte, NC • www.infoagepub.com

Library of Congress Cataloging-in-Publication Data

The CIP data for this book can be found on the Library of Congress website (loc.gov).

Paperback: 9781681238999
Hardcover: 9781681239002
E-Book: 9781681239019

Printed in the United States of America

CONTENTS

S E C T I O N T W O

ACKNOWLEDGEMENTS

This timely and needed book examines the significance of Dissertations in Practice on post-doctoral scholars, whose narratives transport us across wide-ranging fields of inquiry. In doing so, authors critically examine their personal transition from practitioner to scholar practitioner and change agent.

I am grateful to all chapter contributors who as EdD program graduates have dug deep in their psyche in an effort to articulate to readers the transforming impact of their Dissertation in Practice on education reform to the betterment of schooling.

——*Valerie Anne Storey*

FOREWORD

The editor of *Exploring the Impact of the Dissertation in Practice* takes up a central problem in graduate education today; i.e., the nature of the Dissertation in Practice, and the connection between dissertation models, rigor, change agency, and impact to the field of practice.

In the autobiographical chapters that follow, numerous professional practice program graduates (1) describe their personal experience of the professional practice doctoral program; (2) explain important lessons they learnt from the professional practice doctoral program; (3) describe the impact of their research and the Dissertation in Practice on their professional life; and (4) offer insights on their transformational journey from excellent practitioner to scholar practitioner.

Chapter authors are to be commended for their reflection, analysis, and honesty in undertaking this assignment. Individually and collectively, they spotlight material that is useful for program construction, implementation, delivery, and evaluation. In short, they assist the reader in developing needed architecture for the construction of powerful end-of-program doctoral work that dynamically impacts our professional domain of practice.

SECTION ONE

CHAPTER 1

IMPACT FACTORS OF THE DISSERTATION IN PRACTICE

A 21st Century Model

Valerie A. Storey

A dissertation is "a spoken or written discourse upon or treatment of a subject, in which it is discussed at length; a treatise, sermon, or the like."

—*Oxford English Dictionary*

A Dissertation in Practice (DiP) is the culminating experience that demonstrates a scholarly practitioner's ability to solve a problem of practice, or "to think, to perform, and to act with integrity."

—*Shulman, 2005*

INTRODUCTION

A current and ongoing international dialogue is focused on the nature of the doctorate and the impact of doctoral education (Gilbert, 2009; Halse & Mowbray, 2011; Kot & Hendel 2012; Tennant 2004). Conversations focus on doctorate program differentiation, rigor, and relevance depending on the lens applied. From

Exploring the Impact of the Dissertation in Practice, pages 3–15.
Copyright © 2017 by Information Age Publishing
All rights of reproduction in any form reserved.

a traditionalist perspective, the emphasis is on research methodology and validity, whereas advocates of professional practice doctorates (PPD) focus on program impact, and educational change. PPD programs in a variety of professional domains advocate for individualized capstone products rather than a "one size meets all," approach which focuses on a specific professional topic or problem of practice from the field. The intent being to transition from the traditional five-chapter research doctoral dissertation model, which has been fixed by centuries of tradition (Archbald, 2008; Murphy, 2014;), to a Dissertation in Practice (DiP), a non-traditional more varied model (ProDEL, 2012; Shulman, 2010; Storey & Maughan, 2014) that demonstrates and communicates the candidate's multifaceted abilities, skills, and talents over a variety of performance tasks. Essentially, the new DiP model must bridge the academia and practice gap, through a design that manifestly serves functions of stakeholders i.e., rigorous in the creation of new practitioner knowledge; value to a wide community; and represents craftsmanship (Storey & Maughan, 2014).

The impact of an EdD DiP that encompasses discipline-based coursework and scholarship as well as practice-embedded research is discussed in this chapter in the context of the larger debate surrounding the development, definition, and measurement of value and impact of doctoral programs capstone.

BACKGROUND

In considering a doctoral program's capstone, faculty is required to backward map to ensure that the capstone reflects the doctoral program's stewardship of academia, practice and the professions. Such conversations are difficult particularly if capstone products are pitted against each other in relation to rigor, relevance, process, supervision, etc. Rather, the conversation should first be individualized to the doctoral program, and second to the context being served. Thus, when discussing the PhD capstone, the conversation needs to focus on what is best for the candidate and research in the 21st Century whereas in the PPD programs the focus is what is best for candidate's professional practice in the 21st Century. In both doctoral programs, candidates continue to be "examined," requiring the dissertation model to meet specific graduate school criteria. However, there is now evidence that this traditional approach necessitating an overall argument or problem of practice from the field, contextualized with reference to theory and methodology, summarized with data and findings does not necessarily entail being written up in a five-chapter dissertation model. In fact, it has been argued that the traditional PhD dissertation model is inappropriate for the modern world.

PRACTICAL USABILITY OF ADVANCED KNOWLEDGE

Traditionally, the relationship between research producer and practitioner application has been tenuous (Chu, 2007; Love, 1985). Practitioners' use of research-based information is rarely a significant part of school practice (Dagenais et al.,

2012). As a consequence policies and programs may be developed and introduced by practitioners, which intuitively seem beneficial but have been found to be ineffective or of little value by empirical research. Clearly, this is an issue that needs to be addressed. Bridges need to be built, links developed, strategies and structures introduced to support the knowledge transfer process from researchers to practitioners in the field.

PPD graduates make a personal and professional difference to a specific community (Bourner et al., 2001) resulting in the major products of the PPD research process providing useful and innovative contributions to professional work. Closely allied to this is the focus on individual practitioners and their experience as the starting point (Costley, 2014).

Strategies such as high-quality communication between researchers and practitioners, (Lafleur, 1995), direct involvement in research by practitioners (Lafleur, 1995; Simons et al., 2003), and organizational support for the research to be conducted and used, all support knowledge transference and are foundational to PPD programs. In fact, PPD graduates are "taught to decipher, debate, and design studies as tools for confronting daily problems in education" (Perry, 2016, p. 304) . Furthermore, practitioners are in the enviable position of first being able to conduct in-depth research in the field, and second, generating and applying knowledge in the field.

THE PROFESSIONAL PRACTICE DOCTORATE (PPD)

Professional Practice Doctorates (PPD) have been designed and implemented in Australia, the United Kingdom, and the United States and mainly target adult professional practitioners who wish to further develop their qualifications and skills. The purposes of PPDs are usually to research and develop an original contribution to practice through practitioner-research thus giving greater primacy to practice knowledge (Costley, 2014).

Their distinctive trait is an emphasis on applied research in order to contribute to the development of skills in a certain sector in addition to critical and independent thinking, strong communication skills, a depth of knowledge related to the discipline, and the ability to generate and apply new knowledge (Costley, 2014; Nerad & Heggelund, 2008). More recently identified traits include the need for translational or soft skills, and the ability to work as part of a team (Holley, 2016).

In PPD programs, doctoral students work on research embedded in their field of practice with the final aim of further strengthening collaboration between academia and the organization they serve, while enhancing their career development. By establishing close cooperation between universities and organizations, and by combining work, learning, and research, these forms of modern doctorates have a three-fold added value. For PPD students, it means developing research where theory and practice are combined. For organizations, it translates into a unique opportunity to foster research and innovation and increase the level of skills and knowledge of its personnel.

PPDs range from doctorates that structure coursework and a discipline-specific dissertation to doctorates that are designed in collaboration with employers and include research that is conducted in the workplace and supervised by university faculty (Kumar & Dawson, 2014). Students who enroll in PPDs already possess many years of professional expertise in their discipline or area of specialization and usually have professional goals that drive them to enroll in a doctoral program (Dawson & Kumar, 2016).

THE CONTINENTAL DISSERTATION MODEL

Many European countries and Australia have introduced an "integrated format" for a PhD dissertation sometimes known as the "continental model" which allows the submission of previously published papers and other artifacts that evidence research which has been conducted soundly, securely, ethically and with a robust methodology (UK Council for Graduate Education, 2016). An appendage to the published papers usually includes an introduction, setting out the context in which the papers fit, and a critical summary at the end, bringing all the strands together (Christianson, Eliot, & Massey, 2015). As a consequence, the amount of material candidates have to write under the integrated format is about a fifth of that required for a traditional thesis. The continental model (integrated format) encourages communication of research through publication in journals appropriate to research development and application. Thereby, reaching a wider audience whether in the academy or the professional domain.

Artifacts such as novels, paintings, and musical scores are permitted by a number of arts doctoral programs as part of their PhD submission, provided they can show how the artifacts relate to the thesis and its defense.

Whilst there is general acceptance that the integrated format is not appropriate for all PhD programs and that the traditional thesis still has its merits a substantial number of institutions expect the integrated format to become more common over the next five years (UK Council for Graduate Education, 2016).

SCHOLAR-CHANGE AGENT

As awareness increases as to available dissertation options, the traditional model consisting of five chapters, including the introduction, literature review, research methodology, results, conclusions, and/or recommendations (Glatthorn, Joyner, & Glatthorn, 2005) is likely to become less common. The replacement being a capstone model that is an active and ongoing process of individual professional development, improvement, organizational impact, and change rather than a finished outcome. Such a dissertation becomes a dynamic instrument for transformative development and development of an identity change and commitment to making a difference or effecting change," (Kochar-Bryant, 2016, p. 37). The dissertation process, therefore should:

1. Provide a challenging opportunity to express one's values and talents and thus to actualize one's identity as a skilled professional;
2. Offer an opportunity to define and reflect on personal and professional transformations that contribute to one's identity as a change agent and commitment to a larger community project;
3. Provide an opportunity to construct a theory which is grounded in theory and understanding of the history of previous interventions into the problem in the past;
4. Offer the opportunity to develop a sense of mastering a challenging situation and, through this, to feel a sense of responsibility for future outcomes;
5. Provide a deep sense of commitment to a research problem that is compelling for the individual and the community or organization in which it occurs;
6. Provide an opportunity to envision solutions to problems within organizations and the community as they identify significant problems n the field. (Kochar-Bryant, 2016.)

Kochar-Bryant (2016) suggests that the dissertation process described above enables the doctoral student to embrace the "scholar-change agent's doctrine- impact the world and be in the community. This interactive relationship is immediately evident in the growing number of programs that are adopting non-traditional dissertation models commonly known as a Dissertation in Practice (DiP). The function of the DiP being to demonstrate understanding of core professional knowledge and the application of this knowledge to complex problems of practice (Perry & Imig, 2008) with a resulting change within the workplace (Maxwell, 2003).

GUIDING FRAMEWORKS AND PRINCIPLES FOR PROFESSIONAL PRACTICE DISSERTATION DESIGN

In the United States, Europe, and Australia, a growing literature is questioning the appropriateness of a traditional five-chapter research dissertation for practitioners in PPD programs. In the educational leadership domain, Andrews and Grogan (2005) argue that the traditional dissertation does not serve well those who seek to advance their professional practice by managing change and promoting renewal in educational settings. Rather, there is a need for the education doctorate dissertation or DiP to demonstrate "developmental efficacy" and "community benefit," as well as the preservation of "intellectual stewardship" (Archbald, 2008, p. 704). Essentially, an EdD student's focus comes from a need to make improvements in a specific educational context. This will also mean that its value will be judged more in terms of its potential to solve local and specific problems than in its capacity to generate generalizable findings (Belzer & Ryan, 2013). In the last decade there has been evidence of a movement away from the traditional dissertation model in an attempt to address localized specific problems as highlighted by Belzer and Ryan (2013) and to produce an artifact that communicates findings effectively with involved stakeholders. Notably, there has been the emergence of group-authored or group collaborations, group thematic dissertations, group consultation and evaluations for a client, film and video production, policy papers, technical reports, and three research articles unified by an introduction and conclusion (Storey & Maughan, 2014).

A search of the literature characterizes the DiP as a culminating capstone product conceptualized as a scholarly document that demonstrates: (1) a student's ability to conduct research on a complex problem of practice within a local context (Murphy, 2014; Storey & Maughan, 2014); (2) application of relevant academic theory to a complex problem of practice; (3) a resulting change within the workplace (Maxwell, 2003; Perry & Imig, 2008; Storey & Maughan, 2014); (4) a recognition that real-world problems inhabit a space, which is dynamic, multi-faceted and complex (Fulton, Kuitt, Sanders, & Smith, 2013); (5) rigorous creation of new practitioner knowledge; (6) stewardship of doctoral values (Perry & Imig, 2008); and (7) state of the art in professional practice (Maxwell, 2003; Murphy, 2014; Perry & Imig, 2008; Storey & Maughan, 2014).

Additionally, DiPs must bridge the existing gap between academia and practice, through a design that manifestly serves functions of stakeholders (i.e., rigorous in the creation of new practitioner knowledge and value to a wide community). Foremost, the DiP product must be a form that manifestly serves functions of the PPD (i.e. stewardship of doctoral values; rigorous in the creation of new practitioner knowledge; demonstrates ability to conceptualize, define, analyze, and frame a problem in practice that warrants academic rigor to find solutions; demonstrates ability to translate analytical data into normative solutions; and systematic) enabling PPD students to pursue questions that are of pragmatic importance (Archbald, 2008; Willis et al., 2010; Zambo, 2011) with the express intention of making improvements in practice settings (Maxwell, 2009). Archbald (2008) proposes that a practitioner-scholar study highlights:

- Pragmatic problem, not a theoretical question;
- Multiple questions, not a single "hypothesis" or research question;
- Persuasion, not proof;
- Recommended actions, not conclusions.

Dana, Bondy, Kennedy-Lewis, Adams, and Ma (2016) view the DiP as an instrument for transformative development and the completion process as a catalyst for practitioner-scholars to become a change agent in the community in which they serve. Their DiP framework: (a) focuses on a pragmatic problem in the student's local context; (b) describes the ways in which the student studied the problem; (c) reports on what the student learned from studying the problem; and (d) describes specific actions to be taken as a result of what the student has learned.

Dawson and Kumar (2016) completed an extensive literature review on the development and design of professional practice dissertations, and analyzed DiPs completed in their own program to develop guiding principles for professional practice dissertations:

Guiding Principle #1: The dissertation is embedded in the student's professional practice or context.

Guiding Principle #2: The dissertation addresses a problem in the student's professional practice and is related to the discipline.

Guiding Principle #3: Relevant literature is used to rationalize the problem, frame the study, and when applicable, support design of interventions.

Guiding Principle #4: The problem is framed with relevant research questions that are addressed using appropriate methods.

Guiding Principle #5: The dissertation demonstrates adequate rigor.

Guiding Principle #6: The dissertation discusses implications for professional practice at three levels: the student, the immediate context, and the field.

The Archbald DiP framework (2008), Dana et al. framework (2016), and Dawson and Kumar (2016) guiding principles all highlight the need to: (1) address a complex problem of practice from the practitioner's field; (2) demonstrate research rigor skills grounded on theory and inquiry; and (3) demonstrate the impact of the research

NOMENCLATURE

Dissertation, Dissertation in Practice, Dissertation of Practice, project, product, thesis, are subtle changes of nomenclature for a doctoral program's final capstone, which may possibly reflect the wider emerging trend of the adaptation of doctoral study to meet contemporary needs. Changing and varied nomenclature though ultimately leads to product comparison, currency, confusion, and anecdotal ranking as faculty assert one product and program superior to another.

MEASURES OF PROGRAM VALUE AND QUALITY

Programs that provide high value clearly define quality, and ensure that individual expenses (time and money) advance individual value and meets professional demand. In order to achieve this, programs must develop dynamic scholar-practitioner partnerships to collectively advance scholarly practitioner research that addresses complex problems of practice as opposed to a gap in the literature. Quality, however, is an elusive concept. Definitions tend to be vague e.g. the totality of characteristics of an entity that bear on its ability to satisfy stated and implied need (International Organization for Standardization, Technical Committee, 2015) or we regurgitate the mantra "I know it when I see it." For decades educators have struggled with the challenge of demonstrating the quality of programs they deliver. Increasing demand for accountability, greater transparency, and cost effectiveness place a premium on objective approaches, externalized from the graduate program.

A useful quality surrogate is that of impact. Traditionally, doctoral program impact is measured at the end of the program and is widely perceived to be scholarly placements, productivity, professional involvement and the acquisition of external funding (Halse & Mowbray, 2011). But the PPD can be viewed "as both a process and a product" (Halse & Mowbray, 2011, p. 514) where students remain embedded in their practice (Kumar & Dawson, 2012).

Currently, there is no agreed common definition of impact or metrics that can be used to measure PPD program impact (Halse & Mowbray, 2011; Murphy, 2014). Contributing to the complexity is that the DiP remains opaque without clear operational definitions (Murphy, Keynote Speech, CPED Spring Convening, Denver, Colorado, 2014). Some groups have made inroads in developing definitions as suggested by Murphy. For example, 86 institutional members of the Carnegie Project on the Education Doctorate (CPED) in the United States, Canada, and New Zealand (Perry, 2015) recognize the DiP as "a scholarly endeavor that identifies and addresses a complex and persistent problem of practice in the work of a professional practitioner, the addressing of which has the potential to result in improved understanding, experience, and outcomes," (Carnegie Project on the Education Doctorate, 2010). CPED-influenced programs seek to ensure that the capstone demonstrates understanding of core professional knowledge, application of this knowledge to complex problems of practice (Perry & Imig, 2008), and changes in participant learning and behavior.

COLLECTIVE IMPACT: TRANSFORMATIONAL CHANGE

A goal of the PPD dissertation is to be impactful. First, to make improvements in a practice setting, which requires modes of communication appropriate to the community of practice, it is designed to assist (Maxwell, 2009). Second, to transform PPD graduates' into stewards of the profession, i.e. practitioner and scholar (Perry, 2016). Whilst DiP artifacts such as group-authored or group collaborations, group thematic dissertations, group consultation and evaluations for a client, film and video production, policy papers, technical reports, and research articles (Storey & Maughan, 2014) are to be welcomed, measuring or assessing quality becomes particularly complex.

Golde (2006) and the Council of Graduate Schools (2007) advise against one specific definition for impact arguing that impact can refer to either the individual and/or the organization (i.e., individual application of scholarly practitioner acquired knowledge, skills, and research findings; and organizational changes in practice). Fox and Slade (2014) also warned that simple causal links between PPD programs and organizational impact were difficult to establish due to the complexity and messiness of the professional learning process. They also questioned the input–output model of impact currently used. They found that PPD program graduates themselves gave accounts of disruption, subversion, and challenge that they attributed to their new knowledge and understandings. Additionally, they reported increased personal and professional confidence; enhanced engagement within and beyond their organizations; and new capabilities and forms of interaction to facilitate the building of improved networks.

In PPD programs and EdD programs specifically, DiP impact will vary depending on the researched complex problem of practice, objectives, the clientele affected, the time frame, and to whom the results will be communicated. Individual impact data can be gained from survey and interview data whilst organizational impact data can be gathered from the clientele in several different ways: (1) ask them; (2) test them; or (3) observe them.

Lester and Costley (2010) suggest that when measuring dissertation and program impact, the locus should be impact for the learner and for the organization because dissertation research often takes place in a professional organization where the doctoral candidate is employed and is aimed at contributing or improving some aspect of practice. In contrast, many scholars (Costa & Kallick, 2008; Dawson & Kumar, 2014; Tennant, 2004) argue that skills demonstrated; knowledge acquired, developed, and generated; problem-solving skills developed; and generalizable habits of mind; need not necessarily be visible and measurable.

To date, PPD graduates have claimed personal growth such as increased expertise, skills, confidence, reflection; and professional growth. Additionally, many graduates report increased recognition, responsibility, and stature in their workplace as a result of participation in PPD programs (Costley & Stephenson, 2008; Lester & Costley, 2010; Nixon et al., 2008; Rhodes & Shiel, 2007). Two recent studies involving graduates from Carnegie Project on the Educational Doctorate-influenced EdD programs identified intellectual transformation as both personally and professionally impactful (Dawson & Kumar, 2016; Perry, 2016).

Kumar and Dawson, (2012), identified four initial areas of PPD impact, the application of learning in professional practice, enculturation into the professional community, professional growth, and the impact of the dissertation process. Additionally, Kumar and Dawson (2014) highlighted four other areas in their online technology EdD program that impacted student practice—a) that the program revolves around problems of practice, where students are encouraged to identify "what keeps them up at night" b) that they are encouraged to connect major assignments to their practice c) that they were required to reflect on their professional goals and trajectory d) transparent program goals. In summation Kumar and Dawson (2014) suggest that the flexibility to connect program learning with professional practice and to explore themes relevant to individual discipline and goals appears to have contributed to the resulting impact.

Perry's study (2016) explains how EdD graduates had transitioned from decision-making based on intuition to decision-making based on theory, research, and data. Interviewees expressed confidence in their ability to communicate research in a variety of ways depending on the audience. Overall, interviewees felt they had become change leaders, "impactful on their communities and students" (Perry, 2016, p. 309).

Currently, organizations such as American Education Research Association (AERA) and the Carnegie Project on the Education Doctorate (CPED) maintain databases as to DiPs nominated by institutions as being impactful and worthy of award recognition. Criteria used by CPED to select the annual DiP award include the requirement to show "evidence of scholarly endeavors in impacting a complex problem of practice, and aligns with CPED Working Principles" (CPED, 2016). Submission guidelines specifically reference impact on practice.

Determined impact on practice such as:
- What generative impact will this work have on practice, policy, and/or future research?
- What impact does this work have on the future work and agendas of the schol-ar-practitioner?
- How does this work demonstrate the scholarly practitioner's ability to solve or contribute to the solution of problems of practice?
- What, if any, action pieces have been generated? (http://www.cpedinitiative. org/page/dissertation)

Measuring how personal, professional development impacts on the organization in which a PPD program graduate works is challenging and isolating the impact of the DiP is messy. We do know that undertaking a PPD and an EdD specifically has profound effects on graduates at personal and professional levels (Fox & Slade, 2014). It is difficult to articulate these alterations in terms of 'impact,' where a simple input–output model of learning is employed.

CONCLUSION

This chapter has situated DiP impact in the context of the larger debate surrounding the development, definition, and measurement of value and impact of doctoral programs' capstone; highlighted the continual need to give attention to theorizing DiP impact; and identified frameworks for ways of measuring impact beyond the personal benefits accrued. DiP models cultivated to bridge the research-practitioner gap and develop meaningful knowledge to inform change; varying methods for measuring impact; and the need for exploring definitions of impact through a variety of lens have also been discussed. The continual gathering of hard data will help to frame scholarly conversations focused on the impact of DiPs, thereby contributing to our knowledge and thinking about professional practice doctorates.

REFERENCES

Andrews. R.. & Grogan. M. (2005, Spring). Form should follow function: Removing the EdD. dissertation from the Ph.D. straight jacket. *UCEA Review, XLVI* (2), 10–12.

Archbald, D. (2008). Research versus problem solving for the education leadership doctoral thesis: Implications for form and function. *Educational Administration Quarterly, 44*(5), 704–739.

Belzer, A., & Ryan, S. (2013). Defining the problem of practice dissertation: Where's the practice, what's the problem? *Planning & Changing, 44*(3/4), 195– 207.

Bourner, T., Bowden, R., & Laing, S. (2001). Professional Doctorates in England. *Studies in Higher Education, 26*(1), 65– 83.

Carnegie Project on the Education Doctorate (CPED). (2010). *Design concept definitions.* College Park, MD: Author. Retrieved from http://cpedinitiative.org/

Carnegie Project on the Education Doctorate. (CPED, 2016). *Dissertation in practice of the year award.* Retrieved from http://www.cpedinitiative.org/page/dissertation

Christianson, B., Eliot, M., & Massey, B., (2015). *The role of publications and artifacts in submission for the UK PhD.* Lichfield, UK: UK Council for Graduate Education.

Chu, F. T. (2007, June). Bridging the LIS-practitioner gap: Some frames for research. *Library Philosophy and Practice*, 1–8.

Costa, A. L., & Kallick, B. (2008). *Learning and leading with habits of mind: 16 essential characteristics for success.* Alexandria, VA: ASCD.

Costley, C. (2014). *Professional doctorates in the UK.* Retrieved from www.adaptinternational.it, @ADAPT_bulletin

Costley, C., & Stephenson, J. (2008). Building doctorates around individual candidates' professional experience. In D. Boud & A. Lee (Eds.), *Changing practices of doctoral education* (pp. 171–186). London: Routledge.

Council of Graduate Schools. (2007). *Task force on the professional doctorate.* Author.

Dagenais, C., Lysenko, L., Abrami, P. C., Bernard, R. M., Ramde, J., & Janosz, M. (2012). Use of research-based information by school practitioners and determinants of use: A review of empirical research. *Evidence and Policy, 8*(3), 285–309.

Dana, N. F., Bondy, E., Kennedy-Lewis, B., Adams, A., & Ma, V. W. (2016). Exemplifying the Dissertation in Practice. *CPED White Paper 1*(1). Retrieved from http://www.cpedinitiative.org/research-resources

Dawson, K., & Kumar, S. (2014). An analysis of professional practice Ed.D. Dissertations in Educational Technology. *Techtrends: Linking Research & Practice to Improve Learning, 58*(4), 62–72.

Dawson, K., & Kumar, S. (2016). Guiding principles for quality professional practice dissertations. In V. A. Storey & K. A. Hesbol (Eds.), *Contemporary approaches to dissertation development and research methods* (pp. 133–146). Hershey, PA: Information Science Reference.

Fox, A., & Slade, B. (2014). What impact can organizations expect from professional doctorates? *Professional Development in Education 40*(4), 546–560.

Fulton, J., Kuit, J., Sanders, G., & Smith, P. (2013). *The professional doctorate: A practical guide.* New York, NY: Palgrave Macmillan.

Gilbert, R. (2009). The doctorate as curriculum: A perspective on goals and outcomes of doctoral education. In D. Boud & A. Lees (Eds.), *Changing practice of doctoral education* (pp. 54–68). New York, NY: Routledge.

Glatthorn, A. A., Joyner, R. L., & Glatthorn, A. A. (2005). *Writing the winning thesis or dissertation: A step-by-step guide.* Thousand Oaks, CA: Corwin Press.

Golde, C. M. (2006). Preparing stewards of the discipline. In C. M. Golde & G. E. Walker (Eds.), *Envisioning the future of doctoral education* (pp. 3–23). San Francisco, CA: Jossey-Bass.

Halse, C., & Mowbray, S. (2011). The impact of the doctorate. *Studies in Higher Education 36*(5), 513–525.

Holley, K. (2016). Epilogue. In V. A. Storey, (Ed.), *International perspectives on designing professional practice doctorates: Applying the critical friends approach to the EdD and beyond* (pp.269–277). New York, NY: Palgrave Macmillan.

Kochhar-Bryant, C. A. (2016). Identity, commitment and change agency: Bedrock for bridging theory and practice in doctoral education. In V. A. Storey & K. A. Hesbol (Eds.), *Contemporary approaches to dissertation development and research methods,* (pp. 29–43). Hershey, PA: IGI Global.

Kot, F. C., & Hendel, D. D. (2012). Emergence and growth of professional doctorates in the United States, United Kingdom, Canada and Australia: A comparative analysis. *Studies in Higher Education 37*(3), 345–364.

Kumar, S. (2014). Signature pedagogy, implementation and evaluation of an online program that impacts educational practice. *Internet and Higher Education. 21*, 60–67.

Kumar, S., & Dawson, K. (2012). Exploring the impact of a professional practice education doctorate in educational environments. *Studies in Continuing Education, 35*(2), 165–178.

Kumar, S., & Dawson, K. (2014). The impact factor: Measuring student professional growth in an online doctoral program. *TechTrends (58)*4, 89–97.

International Organization for Standardization, Technical Committee. (2015). *ISO 9000:2015 quality management and quality assurance.* Geneva: ISO. Retrieved from http://www.iso.org/iso/home/store/catalogue_tc/catalogue_detail.htm?csnumber=45481

Lafleur, C. (1995). A participatory approach to district level program evaluation: The dynamics of internal evaluations. In J. B. Cousins & L. M. Earl (Eds.), *Participatory evaluation in education* (pp. 33–54). London: Falmer Press.

Lester, S., & Costley, C. (2010). Work-based learning at higher education level: Value, practice and critique. *Studies in Higher Education 35*(5), 561–575.

Love, J. M. (1985). Knowledge transfer and utilization in education. *Review of Research in Education. 12*, 337–386.

Maxwell, T. W. K. (2003). From the first to second generation professional doctorate. *Studies in Higher Education 28*(3), 279–291.

Maxwell, T. W. K. (2009). Producing the professional doctorate: The portfolio as a legitimate alternative to the dissertation. *Innovations in Education & Teaching International, 46*(2), 135–145. Doi: 10.1080/14703290902843760

Murphy, J. (2014). *Keynote speech.* CPED Spring Convening, Denver, Colorado.

Nerad, M., & Heggelund, M. (2008). *Toward a global PhD?: Forces and forms in doctoral education worldwide.* Seattle, WA: University of Washington Press.

Nixon, I., Willis, K., Major, D., Young, D., Tongue, A., Costley, C., Abukari, A. (2008). *Work-based learning impact study.* York, UK: Higher Education Academy.

Oxford English Dictionary Online. Preview citation in "dissertation, n." OED Online. Oxford University Press, March 2017. Web. 11 April 2017.

Perry, J. A. (2015). The EdD and the scholarly practitioner. *School Administrator Magazine.*

Perry, J. A. (2016). The scholar practitioner as steward of practice. In Storey, V. A. & Hesbol K. A. (Eds.), *Contemporary approaches to dissertation development and research methods*. Hershey, PA: IGI Global.

Perry, J. A., & Imig, D. G. (2008 November/December). A stewardship of practice in education. *Change Magazine, 40*(6), 42–48.

Professional Doctorate in Educational Leadership (ProDEL). (2012). *Dissertation in practice guidelines* (DP-2.2-Fa12). Duquesne University. Pittsburgh, PA: Author.

Rhodes, G., & Shiel, G. (2007.) Meeting the needs of the workplace and the learner through work-based learning. *Journal of Workplace Learning 18(*3), 173–187.

Shulman, L. S. (2010). Doctoral education shouldn't be a marathon. *The Chronicle of Higher Education, 56*(30), B9–B12.

Simons, H., Kushner, S., Jones, K., & James, D. (2003). From evidence-based practice to practice-based evidence: The idea of situated generalization. *Research Papers in Education 18*(4), 347–364.

Storey, V. A., & Maughan, B. D. (2014). *Beyond a definition: Designing and specifying Dissertation in Practice (DiP) models.* The Carnegie Project on the Education Doctorate. Retrieved from http://www.cpedinitiative.org/professional-practice-doctorate-dissertation-practice-definition-and-discourse

Tennant, M. (2004). Doctoring the knowledge worker. *Studies in Continuing Education 26* (3), 431–441.

UK Council for Graduate Education (2016). *The Oxford statement.* Retrieved from http://www.ukcge.ac.uk/article/the-oxford-statement-222.aspx.

Willis, J. W., Inman, D., & Valenti, R. (2010). *Completing a professional practice dissertation: A guide for doctoral students and faculty.* Charlotte, NC: Information Age Publishing.

Zambo, D. (2011). Action research as signature pedagogy in an education doctorate program: The reality and hope. *Innovative Higher Education, 36*(4), 261–271. doi: 10.1007/s10755-010-9171-.

CHAPTER 2

THROUGH A PROFESSOR'S LENS

A Narrative from the Field

Denver J. Fowler

INTRODUCTION

The Dissertation in Practice (DiP) is a relatively new concept in the higher education setting. Several of the initial Doctor of Education (EdD) programs in the United States have required students to complete the traditional dissertation model. That is, the traditional monographic five-chapter dissertation. In fact, I myself completed an EdD program in which I was required to complete a traditional dissertation versus a DiP. However, in recent years, there seems to have been a shift to the DiP model as it relates to EdD programs. Organizations such as The Carnegie Project on the Education Doctorate (CPED), established in 2007, and the American Educational Research Association are continually investigating effective strategies that focus on preparing individuals to become stewards of their professional practice through scholarship. In more recent years, specifically as it relates to EdD programs, rethinking and reimagining the type of scholarship that is required in EdD programs has been a topic of conversation, research, and in some arenas, much

Exploring the Impact of the Dissertation in Practice, pages 17–30.

debate. For this chapter, it is my hope to highlight some of the challenges (and advantages) associated with the DiP. More specifically, as it relates to my own experiences as a professor teaching in an EdD program where our program requires our students to complete a DiP. Finally, I offer both proven and suggested strategies for overcoming the challenges as well as methods to cultivate the advantages. In keeping theme with this book, I have broken down this chapter into three main sections: (1) How has the dissertation in practice become a dynamic document guiding change to help resolve complex problems in the educational setting?; (2) How has the redesign of Doctor of Education programs supported innovative Dissertation in Practice models?; and (3) What Dissertation in Practice issues have I personally encountered and addressed in my scholarly practice? In addition, several subsections are included within each of the three main sections guiding this chapter.

HOW HAS THE DISSERTATION IN PRACTICE (DIP) BECOME A DYNAMIC DOCUMENT GUIDING CHANGE TO HELP RESOLVE COMPLEX PROBLEMS IN THE EDUCATIONAL SETTING?

Perhaps at no other time in history have so many doctoral students been conducting and focusing their dissertation research on specific school site problems in the PreK–12 educational setting. Both national and international EdD programs have been redesigned, many of which have been strongly influenced by and/or are a member of CPED (Maughan & Storey, 2015). Several of these programs have adopted the DiP model as the capstone product, a design that both supports and aims at completing scholarly research on a problem within the local context (Dawson & Kumar, 2014). Although this type of research demonstrates the students' ability to conduct research on a problem, perhaps more importantly, this type of research allows for the opportunity and possibility of determining solutions to critical and often complex problems faced by practitioners in the PreK–12 educational setting; solutions of which many are transferable and can be applied in similar settings across the globe.

Problems that exist in the PreK–12 educational setting are often very complex and context related as well as unique to the setting in which the problem exists. It goes without saying that each school is unique and that school building and school district characteristics often change building to building (even within the same district) and district to district. In referencing my own research, I have found that school leader demographics also play a role in particular problems commonly faced by schools (and school leaders) and are correlated with school district characteristics such as student achievement (Fowler & Johnson, 2014). Nonetheless, one could argue that the solution to a similar problem may be applied elsewhere in similar settings, in some way, shape or form. However, I strongly believe the key to effective application is to understand the last part of the previous sentence, that is "in some way, shape, or form." This approach and mindset will be the crucial to using the DiP to effectively grapple with, research, and fix many of the problems and issues existing in the PreK–12 educational setting.

For example, years ago, I was able to effectively turn around a school through the implementation of a data team. In short, I (along with my staff) turned the school around from a school building receiving B's, C's and D's on the state report card, to a school building report card with all A's. In more recent years, I have had the opportunity to travel across the nation and around the globe presenting on this particular topic, that is, creating a data team to help close the achievement gap in a given school district/school building. However, it would be a disservice to the audience members not to note that their particular data team, and furthermore, the processes associated with it, may look somewhat different than mine in their particular setting. That is, "what worked for me, may not work for you," with regards to certain aspects of the process I shared with them in my presentation. Due to an array of microcosms, direct application of my plan without consideration to items specific to a particular school setting, such as cultural norms, what content is state tested, demographics of the students, and what other assessments are currently in place (i.e., formative, benchmark, common, etc.) etc., could and very well would be detrimental to the school turn around process. If one were to ignore such things, we might argue that this fact alone would most likely be the strongest predictor of whether or not my original plan would work in another school district/building. As more and more research is conducted, specifically in the school setting through the completion of DiP's, we must remain cognizant that there is no such thing as a "magic bullet" one size fits all model for solving often complex and context related problems, that vary school to school, state to state, nation to nation. Although this innovative research will be helpful in solving many of the complex problems faced by educators, we must apply the solutions with great care and even greater intentions. To do so without perspicacity, will surely do more harm than good.

HOW HAS THE REDESIGN OF DOCTOR OF EDUCATION PROGRAMS SUPPORTED INNOVATIVE DISSERTATION IN PRACTICE (DIP) MODELS?

With respect to innovative DiP models, we have seen an array of different prototypes for the DiP. This area particularly, in my own experience, has been an area of increasing debate amongst my colleagues, professors from a variety of disciplines, and even individuals outside of the education setting. With the redesign of both national and international EdD programs, several innovative DiP models have been proposed, developed and supported, many of which are considered to be non-traditional (Maughan & Storey, 2015; Shulman, 2010). Such models include both individual and collaborative models (i.e., teams or groups), problem-based investigations, and projects to address specific needs, to name a few. These models are certainly innovative in that many (if not most) dissertations historically are completed by a single individual (versus collaborative), that is, some DiP program models allow for collaboration among several doctoral students focusing on the same research/problem. Furthermore, as previously mentioned, such models are innovative in that many DiP are problem-based investigations aimed at possibly solving a problem while also improving practice/identifying promising practice, oftentimes producing documents, processes, and products that lead to improvements in the PreK–12 educational setting. Perhaps the most innovative model is the collaborative DiP. However, this is perhaps the most debated model as well. Traditionally, a doctoral student completes his/her dissertation individually. In recent years, we have seen several colleges and universities adopt a DiP model that allows, encourages, and supports collaborative dissertations to be completed. In fact, at Vanderbilt University, often ranked and considered the number one EdD program in the nation, doctoral candidates spend their third and final year completing an EdD capstone project. This capstone project is a group project in which each of the group members will receive a doctoral degree upon completion (Vanderbilt University, 2016). In more recent years, we have seen more EdD programs adopt this collaborative model with regards to the dissertation process. However, when discussing this particular topic with colleagues near and far, frequent, and often heated, debates arise. Having listened to several of my colleagues debate (both for and against) as to whether or not this is an appropriate model, I will share what I have found to be two main topics of debate with regards to this model, as well as reporting both sides of the debate(s).

The first, is quite simply, how does an individual receive a doctoral degree for a group project? This seems to be a major concern for many of the individuals I have spoken to with regards to this particular topic. In layman's terms, the question often posed is: How does one receive a terminal degree for group work? That is, my colleagues argue that the individuals completing their DiP in the collaborative model do not have the same experience (rigor) as those individuals completing the DiP process individually. Furthermore, my colleagues do not believe such collaboration models require the same amount of effort, and quite frankly, the same amount of work, and strongly believe such models are not equal to that of an individual completing a dissertation.

The second is, how could one (dissertation chair/committee) possibly ensure each group member in the collaborative model does his/her part. In layman's terms, the question often posed is: How would a dissertation chair know for a fact that each individual equally contributed to the entire DiP? That is, how would a dissertation chair and/or committee ensure individuals completing their dissertation in the collaborative model were equally contributing to the process as a whole. Furthermore, how might a dissertation chair and/or committee member ensure all students in the collaborative model are fully immersed in all portions of the dissertation process. This is complicated indeed, as you may have certain students who are strong in certain aspects of the DiP. For example, students (on their collaborative team) may be strong in research methods, thus, focusing on only this aspect of the DiP, while allowing and/or encouraging other team members to focus on other aspects of the DiP—aspects where they may feel less confident in their abilities to help with and/or complete. Whereas a traditional model requires the individual to fully immerse themselves in all aspects of the dissertation process, in a collaborative model, there may be an opportunity to avoid certain aspects of the dissertation while successfully completing it.

These two topics of debate are certainly areas of concerns not only for faculty teaching in EdD programs who require a DiP, but also for many of my colleagues in higher education who cannot fathom nor willing to accept this concept of a group dissertation (collaborative model). Furthermore, some believe it reinforces the old thought that an EdD is inferior to the Doctor of Philosophy degree (PhD). That is, throughout history, traditionally, the EdD has been regarded as inferior to the PhD by all higher education stakeholders including university administrators, faculty, and students (Coorough & Nelson, 1994; Spurr, 1970). When in fact, research has shown little or no differences in the two degrees aside from the fact that: (1) the field of education tends to be primarily an applied field of study; and (2) the differences mainly deals with research characteristics with regards to design, analyses, and the targeted populations (Borg & Gall, 1989; Coorough & Nelson, 1994; Gay, 1992). Furthermore, a bulk of research on doctoral programs spanning across the past six decades would suggest the main difference between the two (EdD and PhD) terminal degrees pertains to the use (or lack thereof) of advanced inferential statistics (Anderson, 1983; Browne-Ferrigno & Jensen, 2012; Deering, 1998; McCarthy & Forsythe, 2009; Osguthorpe & Wong, 1993). Nevertheless, amongst individuals in the higher education setting, as well as practitioners in the field, the EdD is referred to as the practitioner degree, whereas the PhD is often refereed to as the research degree (Brown, 1990; Browne-Feerigno & Jensen, 2012; Golde & Dore, 2001; Guthrie, 2009).

Although other items of the collaborative model are widely debated, the two topics reported seem to be the two most commonly debated in my own experiences. Just the mention of a collaborative model dissertation is often met with and garners heated debate among professors, scholars, researchers, and doctoral students (who themselves are completing their dissertation in the traditional model). Even those individuals outside of academia, such as my own family members, when discussing this model exclaimed "That's not fair!" in relation to what they know I experienced in my own dissertation process/experience (individually). Although this collaborative model will continue to be debated, I can see both sides of the debate, and I believe it to be reckless of me if I were not to report or mention the other side of this debate with regard to these two particular topics. I must note here, as the author of this chapter, that I take no sides in this debate, I am only here to report on them. That being said, the collaborative model allows the opportunity for our students to solve more complex and large scale problems and issues in the PreK–12 educational setting. With a team of researchers (versus one researcher in the individual model), one would argue that perhaps more could be accomplished, and furthermore, one might argue that more should be accomplished. In thinking of some of our nations largest school districts such as New York City, Los Angeles Unified, Chicago, Miami-Dade (American School & University, 2015), and others, the collaborative model might give us more insight into solving problems particular to districts of such vast size. For example, New York City serves over one million children alone. Such large scale research efforts would need to be conducted by a team of researchers, such as seen in the collaborative model. Secondly, EdD programs that utilize collaborative models with regard to the DiP, should and could have programmatic items in place to ensure that equal effort was contributed to the DiP. That is, there would be specific policies and procedures in place to ensure equal effort and contribution by all members completing the DiP in the collaborative model. Such policies and procedures would most likely deal directly with doctoral programmatic items such as the comprehensive exams, proposal/prospectus[1], and defense. This is certainly easier said then implemented, but being mindful of this particular concern is where we might start. We must have a system of checks and balances in place to ensure equal effort was bequeathed by all members of the group of doctoral candidates completing a given dissertation in the collaborative model.

WHAT DISSERTATION IN PRACTICE (DIP) ISSUES HAVE I PERSONALLY ENCOUNTERED AND ADDRESSED IN MY SCHOLARLY PRACTICE?

As a professor who teaches doctoral courses at a Research I institution within both a traditional PhD program and a CPED influenced EdD program that requires the DiP as the capstone project, I have personally encountered some of the issues that may arise within EdD programs using the DiP model. The most pressing issues I have encountered are: (1) level of writing ability and lack of clear understanding of research methods; (2) lack of knowledge regarding the use of current and innovative technology to both conduct research and locate extant research; (3) change of employment during program; (4) learning environment: classroom dynamics; (5) DiP prospectus (proposal) and comprehensive exams; (6) committee service; and (7) matriculation and completion of program. It is clear to me that many of these issues arise from the fact that often our students tend to be both practitioner and non-traditional[2] doctoral students. Nonetheless, these issues and concerns are worth highlighting and revisiting as we continue to analyze the myriad and often unique characteristics associated with the DiP.

---

[1] The University of Mississippi, School of Education, Department of Leadership and Counselor Education, refers to the dissertation proposal as the prospectus.

[2] The term non-traditional, as used in this text, is meant to describe my personal experience with an EdD program and what type of students are in such a program. Many of our EdD students are employed full-time in building and district level school administrative positions (i.e., principal, superintendent, etc.). Students of this nature tend to be the rule versus the exception in that our EdD program admission requirements requires such experience/employment.

LEVEL OF WRITING ABILITY AND LACK OF CLEAR
UNDERSTANDING OF RESEARCH METHODS

In my experience teaching within both PhD and EdD programs, I have found that the PhD and EdD programs differ in that students in the EdD program tend to have less time to develop their writing and research skills. Students in a traditional PhD program oftentimes have ample amount of courses to both develop and hone their writing and research skills before fully immersing themselves into the dissertation process. Whereas EdD students often are building the plane as it takes off, so to speak. That is, in my experience, EdD students are taking the course work alongside the DiP courses (i.e., DiP 1 [chapter 1], DiP 2 [chapter 2], DiP 3 [chapter 3], etc.) that are set up in such a way that the students are completing their DiP courses/dissertation while also completing their coursework (i.e., courses to develop their writing and research skills). I have addressed this problem by focusing on providing rich, intentional, and meaningful assignments within both the regular courses and DiP courses that are focused on ensuring the necessary skills and dispositions are developed with regards to writing and research. Additionally, we have an advanced individual study course focused on advanced writing skills that we offer our students (or encourage/require our students to complete as needed). This is certainly an area that needs to be well thought out with regards to the course sequencing throughout a given EdD program as well as the course content included in each course, especially as it pertains to writing and research methods. Professors teaching in such programs must be cognizant of these particular dilemmas and how they might adjust their own teaching to accommodate what the students need most, which is very often, writing instruction and a clear understanding of research methods. This is of particular importance because of the nature of such EdD programs, that is, students are often writing their dissertation and conducting research alongside the coursework they very well need to fully understand these very concepts.

LACK OF KNOWLEDGE REGARDING THE USE OF CURRENT
AND INNOVATIVE TECHNOLOGY TO BOTH CONDUCT
RESEARCH AND LOCATE EXTANT RESEARCH

Another problem that I have personally experienced with my EdD students is the lack of knowledge regarding the use of current and innovative technology to both conduct research and locate extant research. Many of my EdD students are practitioners and are several years removed from their last completed degree in higher education. Thus, I have found it exceedingly beneficial to spend time with my doctoral students at the university library reviewing how to use the technology our university has available to them such as Qualtrics, ProQuest, Google Scholar, EBSCO, Catalog, RefWorks, and Zotero, just to name a few. With new and innovative technology being created daily, many students in our EdD program are unfamiliar with the latest and most innovative technology that will help them in the process of conducting their research and locating existing literature on their DiP topics. As professors, we must be cognizant of this possible issue existing and address it by working with individuals at the library in order to bring our students up to speed.

In addition, it is worth noting that many new presentation software exists. I nudge (and often require) my students to present using the latest technology and presentation software. That is, for course presentations, proposals/prospectus, defenses, etc., I require my students to complete Prezi's versus PowerPoints. For audience engagement, I require my students to incorporate items such as Plickers, PollEverywhere, and Kahoot to both engage the audience as well as to be used as a formative assessment (before or after their presentations). This has proven to be beneficial as many of our EdD students choose to stay in the PreK–12 educational setting. Thus, they bring these new technologies back their schools and the use of such technology often spreads throughout the district. As professors, we must be lifelong learners willing to keep up to date with the latest technology as well as how it can be effectively utilized within our courses.

CHANGE OF EMPLOYMENT OR UNEMPLOYMENT DURING PROGRAM

Changing of employment can be a concern as well. This has been prevalent in our EdD program. I have found that many issues can arise from students changing employment during the duration of the program. For example, a student may start the EdD program employed in school district A, but in the middle of the program, accept a new job in school district B. Subsequently, our DiP is focused on applied problem based learning, that is, solving a problem at their local school site, many issues can arise from this change in employment. It goes without saying that school district A may be somewhat/very different from school district B as far as school district characteristics (i.e., district locale, student demographics, etc.) and perhaps more importantly to the DiP process, problems that need to be solved. For example, I recently had a student that accepted a new position in the middle of the EdD program. The students' topic was originally focused on the English Language Learner (ELL) population at the previous school site. However, at the new employer/school district, no ELL students existed. Thus, with both chapter one and two close to complete, this student had to make major edits/revisions/adjustments to their DiP with regards to selecting a new topic and rewriting chapters one and two. Furthermore, the length of time it takes for school districts to both approve and release data can be problematic in this given situation. Since many of our EdD students are practitioners, this concern is always prevalent. In such cases, I have found it advantageous to spend ample amounts of time with students in this particular situation in order to help them: (1) quickly decide on a new topic within their new school setting; (2) efficiently re-write chapters as needed, all with a focus of keeping them moving forward in the DiP process while having the highest expectations for both the topic they choose and the quality of their DiP; and (3) ensure they are completing the necessary paperwork and communication to gain approval for the research to be conducted in the new school district including (but not limited to) the data to be collected.

Along these same lines is the issue of unemployment. That is, students who start the program employed in a school district, but at some point in the program become unemployed due to a variety of reasons (i.e., terminated, resignations, etc.). Furthermore, said students may or may not regain employment the following academic school year. This can be especially problematic as the DiP often requires regular access to a school district files and data in order to both identify and solve a problem at a specific school site. These situations are difficult in that in order to complete the DiP, in our EdD program, one must be employed in a school district. The DiP (at least for our program) is supposed to be focused on a problem at a student's school site. Thus, when a student becomes unemployed, it can be difficult to determine how to handle a student's status in the program.

Program directors of such programs where a student's success is profoundly tied to remaining employed, and more so, if possible, and perhaps more beneficial, remaining employed in the district in which they start their program in, must be cognizant of this potential issue and possibly create innovative ways for trying to determine the status and/or intentions of a student with regards to their current and future employment. However, regardless of the intentions of a student, unforeseen things happen, and in my experience, many of the causes of such vicissitudes in employment are often unforeseen and hard to predict. Nonetheless, this aspect of the DiP can be problematic and detrimental to a student's success (or failure) in a doctoral program where the DiP relies heavily upon a students' employment/employer, as well as access to school district/building files, data, etc. Such models are effective in that students are solving problems front and center in their respective school districts. However, one could argue that such models become ineffective if a student becomes unemployed or takes a new job in different school district. In the first scenario (changing employment), at the very least, they are identifying a new problem to be solved and rewriting several chapters, often derailing them from maintaining normal matriculation in program with regards to the progress of the DiP, with regards to their classmates/cohort. In the second scenario (unemployment), their very livelihood in the program may be at stake. Both scenarios make it much more difficult to matriculate through the program, complete the DiP, as well as be successful in the completion of their EdD program.

LEARNING ENVIRONMENT: CLASSROOM DYNAMICS

The learning environment and classroom dynamics can be a concern as well. Again, at my institution, all of our EdD students are practitioners, many of which are employed by the same school district and oftentimes are in supervisory positions above (or below) their classmates. This can have a negative effect on the learning environment and classroom dynamics. For example, I have found that students in such situations tend to be less open about real problems facing their respective school districts as they want to exercise some political sensibility in how they discuss their school district/building in front of their supervisors—who are also in the classroom. Secondly, I have found that in other classroom discussions, these same students tend to be less than forthcoming in offering opinions one way or the other, and often choose not to engage in and/or participate in such discussions, especially what I consider to be hot-button topics regarding their schools. In addition, I have experienced these same reservations on the discussion forum assignments in which students are often required to answer a questions about their district, reply to a classmate's post, and then respond to at least one classmates comment on their post. Thus, I have experienced this phenomenon in both the classroom environment and the virtual world, through online assignments requiring discussion posts. In order to deter this type of dynamic, I have been both proactive and innovative in creating an excellent classroom learning environment. Although it is hard to measure the effectiveness of such strategies, at the first seminar I have given the "what happens in Vegas, stays in Vegas" speech, that is "what we talk about in here, stays in here." Likewise, I have been cognizant of this dynamic when assigning group work both in class and out of class. That is, ensuring such individuals are in separate groups. Both have proved to be beneficial, but exactly how beneficial is hard to determine without a real measure. Nonetheless, as professors, we should be cognizant of this possible portent existing within our programs.

DISSERTATION IN PRACTICE (DIP) PROSPECTUS (PROPOSAL) AND COMPREHENSIVE EXAMS

Another dilemma of the DiP model is the difficulties in determining exactly when the DiP prospectus (proposal) should take place as well as when the comprehensive exams will be administered. This is certainly a topic of debate amongst program directors and faculty members within such programs. Because of the non-traditional aspects of a DiP, such as completing the DiP throughout the program alongside the required coursework, it can be difficult to determine when it makes sense to allow students to schedule their prospectus (proposal). Furthermore, it becomes difficult to determine when to administer comprehensive exams. In a traditional doctoral program, comprehensive exams take place after all required coursework is completed. Although the format of comprehensive exams can differ from program to program, traditionally the comprehensive exams are administered after a doctoral student has successfully completed all required coursework in their respective doctoral program. Again, in the traditional model, students start taking dissertation hours and progressing in the dissertation process only after successfully passing the comprehensive exams. Because of the uniqueness of a EdD program that utilizes the DiP model alongside the required coursework, program directors and faculty members must make an informed decision with regards to the most apposite time to conduct the DiP prospectus (proposal) and administer the comprehensive exams. Because of the differing of doctoral programs that utilize the DiP, it is hard to make strong recommendations that are applicable to all such programs. That being said, all items unique to a respective doctoral program must be considered when determining the best window of time for both (prospectus [proposal] and comprehensive exams). Nonetheless, items such as course sequence, especially that of the DiP courses, must surely be considered, and taken into account, when making such decisions and doing so with the best interest of our students in mind.

COMMITTEE SERVICE

Committee service within a doctoral program utilizing the DiP can be a difficult task to navigate. For example, this can be especially difficult when deciding how to cover cohorts of 15 or more students starting each fall, especially if students (or entire cohorts) are not matriculating and completing the program on time (this particular aspect will be covered in the next section). Hypothetically, let's say you are a faculty team of four to five professors in an educational leadership program kicking off the fourth year of your EdD program. In this particular program, students complete a DiP alongside the completion of their coursework. Theoretically, each cohort of students will have successfully completed their coursework and DiP in three years. Entering year four, you have 30–45 DiP in progress with an anticipated 15 more starting in the fall. When fall semester begins, with the DiP I course right around the corner, you will soon have an estimated 60 DiP's in progress, minus those individuals from the first cohort that completed their DiP and coursework on schedule. Let's say 10 of the first cohort did just that. Now you are at 50 DiP's in progress. Of course it should be noted that this number excludes your traditional PhD students who are also working on their traditional dissertation. As you can see in this authentic scenario, the committee service becomes an area of concern. Furthermore, and worth noting, one might also argue that students completing the DiP alongside their coursework should have an opportunity to work with a dissertation committee throughout the DiP process—as they are completing/writing their dissertations. For example, without a committee in place, who should students complete the proposal (prospectus) process with before starting work on their research. These are all items to consider when determining how the committee service (as well as the chairing of dissertations) of faculty members will be evenly divided and equally distributed in EdD programs with the DiP. Furthermore, it reminds us and perhaps, even encourages us, to ensure our students are matriculating through and completing the program on schedule without sacrificing the rigor associated with the program.

MATRICULATION AND COMPLETION OF PROGRAM

Building off of the previous sections (i.e., change of employment or unemployment during program, level of writing ability and lack of clear understanding of research methods, etc.) one might be able to hypothesize what problems could arise in order to keep students from seamlessly matriculating through such a program, and furthermore, problems that could arise when several cohorts of students are not matriculating and completing the program on schedule (i.e., committee service). In a perfect scenario, each cohort of students would matriculate through and complete the program on schedule. In the scenario given in the committee service section of this chapter, this would be every three years. The reality is, students are going to progress through the program at varying alacrities with regard to the coursework completed, completion of the DiP, and in the end, completion of the program. The question is not whether or not all students will matriculate through the program and complete the program on schedule, because they will not. The question is, how will we continue to work with, accommodate, and support the students who do not seamlessly matriculate through the program and complete the program on schedule. This becomes especially difficult as we continue to take on more and more cohorts of students. As professors who teach and prepare students in such programs, we must be cognizant of the fact that this will be an issue. Furthermore, by understanding this, we can begin to strategize on how we might properly navigate such problems in a way that is best for our students, our programs, and our colleagues. Unfortunately, for many of us professors, this means going above and beyond the call of duty and cutting out time that we often do not have in our schedules, all in an effort to help our students finish.

SUMMARY

In this chapter, I attempted to provide valuable insight into the nature of the DiP through the lens of a professor who currently teaches in both a PhD program with the traditional dissertation model as well as an EdD program with the DiP model. Written in mostly narrative form, through a lens focused on the EdD program and DiP, it is my hope that I clearly articulated and highlighted many of the issues and problems I have personally experienced as a professor in the field. Someone once told me that proposing a problem without proposing a solution is called whining. Thus, in addition to identifying problems associated with the DiP, I also attempted to offer up some ideas for overcoming, anticipating, and effectively working through such issues as they arise. In addition, I attempted to highlight some of the advantages of the DiP in helping support more research towards solving many of the complex problems found in the PreK–12 educational setting.

Due to the continued pressure mounting in the PreK–12 educational arena from both federal and state legislation, and the fact that school leaders are feeling increasing pressure from the very stakeholders in which they serve, including students, staff, parents, and community members, perhaps now more than ever, I believe we will see more practitioners who obtain the EdD (who have completed a DiP) matriculating into higher education full-time versus staying in the PreK–12 educational setting. Although we might contend that such students should consider the PhD program with the traditional dissertation model, the reality is, many students do not make such decisions until long after they complete their doctoral degree, and spend a few more years in the PreK–12 educational setting. Because of this possibility, some have suggested that we reboot EdD programs to "represent continued scholarship into practice" (Wergin, 2011, p. 119). Thus, I propose that we ensure that our students who complete the DiP are just as prepared for the higher education setting as students who complete traditional model dissertations in PhD programs. That is, EdD programs utilizing the DiP should incorporate rigorous research training as part of the curriculum. If not, I strongly believe we are doing a disservice to both our students and our profession.

REFERENCES

American School & University. (2015). *2014 AS&U 100: Largest school districts in the U.S. by enrollment, 2012–2013* [Data file]. Retrieved from http://asumag.com/research/2014-asu-100-largest-school-districts-us-enrollment-2012-13Anderson, D.G. (1983). Differentiation of the Ed.D. and Ph.D. in education. *Journal of Teacher Education, 34*(3), 55–58.

Borg, W. R., & Gall, M. D. (1989). Educational research (5th ed.). New York: Longman.

Brown, L. D. (1990, April). *A perspective on Ph.D.-Ed.D. discussion in schools of education.* Paper presented at the annual meeting of the American Educational Research Association, Boston, MA.

Browne-Ferrigno, T., & Jensen, J. (2012). Preparing Ed.D. students to conduct group dissertations. *Innovative Higher Education, 37*(5), 407–421.

Coorough, C., & Nelson, J. (1994). Content analysis of the PhD versus the EdD dissertation. *Journal of Experimental Education, 62*(2), 158–169.

Dawson, K., & Kumar, S. (2014). An analysis of professional practice Ed.D. dissertations in educational technology. *TechTrends, 60*(1), 48–55.

Deering, T. E. (1998). Eliminating the doctor of education degree: It's the right thing to do. *Educational Forum, 62*(3), 243–248.

Fowler, D., & Johnson, J. (2014). An investigation of ethical leadership perspectives among Ohio school district superintendents. *Education Leadership Review of Doctoral Research. 1*(2), 96–112.

Gay, L. R. (1992). Educational research competencies for analysis and application (4th ed.). New York: Merrill.

Golde, C. M., & Dore, T. M. (2001). *At cross purposes: What the experiences of today's doctoral students reveal about doctoral education.* Philadelphia, PA: Pew Charitable Trusts.

Guthrie, J. W. (2009). The case for a modern doctor of education degree (Ed.D.): Multipurpose education doctorates no longer appropriate. *Peabody Journal of Education, 84*(1), 3–8.

Maughan, B., & Storey, V. (2015). Beyond a definition: Designing and specifying dissertation in practice (DiP) models. *The Carnegie Project on the Education Doctorate.*

McCarthy, M. M., & Forsythe, P. B. (2009). Research and development activities pertaining to the preparation of school leaders. In M. D. Young, G. Crow, J. Murphy, & R. Ogawa (Eds.), *Handbook of research on the education of school leaders* (pp. 85–128). New York, NY: Routledge.

Osguthorpe, R. T., & Wong, M. J. (1993). The Ph.D. versus the Ed.D.: Time for a decision. *Innovative Higher Education, 18*(1), 47–63.

Shulman, L. S. (2010). Doctoral education shouldn't be a marathon. *The Chronicle of Higher Education, 56*(30), B9–B12.

Spurr, S. H. (1970). Academic degree structures: Innovative approaches. San Francisco, CA: McGraw-Hill.

Vanderbilt University. (2016). *Ed.D. program.* Retrieved from http://peabody.vanderbilt.edu/departments/lpo/graduate_and_professional_programs/edd/

Wergin, J. (2011). Rebooting the EdD. *Harvard Educational Review, 81*(1), 119-140.

CHAPTER 3

THE COURAGE TO INTERVENE IN THE WORLD

The Power of the Dissertation in Practice

Carol A. Kochhar-Bryant

What we think, or what we know, or what we believe, is in
the end, of little consequence. The only thing of consequence
is what we do.

—John Ruskin (1866)

Today's educational leaders require extraordinary preparation. Beyond skill-building, leaders require courage, vision, and sustained commitment to *changing* the world. They are conscious of their identity as change agents and the depth of their commitment to their communities. They possess a deep understanding and appreciation that they cannot be interveners in the world without reciprocal relationships with those they seek to impact. Programs that commit to preparing doctoral candidates who can impact their world do so as a deliberate investment in the creation of extraordinary talent. Such programs require an interweaving of elements that nurture both the development of the individual as a committed person *and* as an effective professional. Both the program and the dissertation, therefore,

Exploring the Impact of the Dissertation in Practice, pages 31–50.

must be structured for such amalgamation. Grounded in theories of civic courage and critical pedagogy (Freire, 1998), educational identity (Nissan & Pekarsky, 2009), communities of practice (Wenger-Traynor, 2014), and pedagogies of engagement (Shulman, 2005), this chapter discusses the interweaving of theory and practice, and the impact of program and processes on doctoral candidates' personal and professional journeys. It presents exemplars of emerging scholars who are challenging educational orthodoxy and making an impact, the nature of the challenges faced when implementing innovation, and the dimensions of their impact. A rubric will be presented that assesses candidates' development on personal and professional scales.

FOUNDATION THEORIES: DESIGNING FOR IMPACT

The works of several educational philosophers are highlighted here as their ideas interconnect around the constructs of identity, commitment to change, and reciprocity with the community.

Educational Identity

Tikkun Olam is a Jewish concept that refers to acts of kindness performed to perfect or 'repair the world' and is found in the Mishnah, a collection of classical rabbinic teachings. It has come to connote social action and the pursuit of social justice, or an obligation to work toward the betterment of one's own existence as well as the lives of future generations. Tikkun Olam compels people to take ownership of their world (Fine, 2004) and is often used when discussing issues of social policy, particularly concerning those who may be at a disadvantage.

Mordecai Nisan and Daniel Pekarsky (2009) articulated the core philosophy of the internationally renowned Mandel School for Educational Leadership (2014) in Jerusalem, Israel, which develops influential leaders with the vision to advance education in Israel and work toward the betterment of society. Nisan and Pekarsky contend that 'educational identity' is an essential characteristic of an educational leader. The "identity view" of educational leadership emphasizes the development of a system of goals, values, and self-definition to which a person commits (p. 6). This view is not given adequate expression in the field of leadership training, but rather it is eclipsed by an opposite view, the *training view,* which focuses on the instruments and tools of management.

The *identity view*, which places goals and values at the focus of the development of educational leadership, along with the opportunity to actualize them through self-realization, is the basis for developing personal commitment and educational leadership.

> Such leaders' commitment to their profession is built upon their self-definition as people involved in education, their view of education's goals and values, their vision of the good person and the good society, their perception of the area in which they are meant to act in this regard, and their self-perception—the beliefs, feelings, plans

and abilities connected with their work that they have developed over the course of their lives…"educational identity (Nisan & Pekarsky, 2009, p. 32)."

Leaders learn what it means to carry out decisions by their value-based educational identity rather than on outside pressures or self-interests. The identity construct is viewed as essential to the development of the change agent because it connects self-definition with the aspiration to contribute to positive change in the real world.

Civic Courage and Critical Pedagogy

Paulo Freire (1921–1997) a Brazilian educator, philosopher, and leading advocate of critical pedagogy, argued that education cannot be neutral, but rather demands that the educator address issues of values, beliefs, and commitments (Freire, 1998). The teacher or educational leader is by his or her presence an *intervener* in the world and is destined to choose among alternative courses of action. Freire's term "intervention" refers to the aspiration for radical changes in society in areas such as health, education, economics, employment, and others. Freire speaks to the political nature of that intervention, proposing that "education cannot be neutral or indifferent in regard to the reproduction of the dominant ideology or the interrogation of it" (p. 91). He criticizes modern leadership development as including technical and scientific preparation but failing to address their "human and ethical presence in the world" (p. 92). The leader, therefore, needs to engage in the process of becoming a citizen, which does not happen as a consequence of 'technical efficiency,' but is a result of a political struggle to create a society that is humane and just. Freire's construct of *civic courage* (2009) connects learning and activism, which he views as the essence of human life. The educational leader takes a public stance, with integrity and at some personal risk, to challenge prevailing conditions and conventional ideas in pursuit of the common good.

Pedagogies of Engagement

Lee Shulman's (2005) proposition of the 'pedagogies of engagement' intersects with the constructs of identity and critical pedagogy. A family of problem-based pedagogies, first defined by Edgerton (1997), was expanded by Shulman to include six features or claims—the pedagogies of engagement, understanding, performance, reflection, generativity, and commitment. These pedagogies begin with real problems that *engage* students and deepen *understanding* of research-based and practical knowledge. They lead to *performance*—knowledge of how to act—which requires decision, judgment, and action. Performance must also be interrupted or disrupted to allow for *reflection* upon performance (e.g., How did I reach this decision? What did I do that makes this performance effective?) Active performance, then, must be balanced with strategic and intentional reflection (meaning making) on one's performance.

The pedagogies create a *generativity*, or powerful desire to know more and to value engagement in order to learn. Finally, *commitment* encompasses the affective and moral component of learning and development, a commitment not just to cognitive growth but also to *new dispositions*, habits, and values (Shulman, 2005, pp. 55–56). These pedagogies assist the emerging leader continuously to forge new connections between ideas and effective practice, and to perform with a sense of personal and social responsibility. The performances of practice must be skilled and theoretically grounded and also characterized by integrity and a commitment to responsible, ethical service (Shulman, 2005, p. 2).

Communities of Practice

A community of practice involves people who have much more than the technical knowledge or skill associated with undertaking some task. Members are involved in a set of relationships over time (Lave & Wenger, 1991) and communities develop around things that matter to people (Wenger, 1998). Work that is organized around a particular area of knowledge and activity provides group members a sense of common enterprise and identity. A community of practice functions effectively when it creates a shared repertoire of ideas, commitments, and memories. The community develops various resources such as tools, documents, routines, vocabulary, and symbols that carry the accumulated knowledge of the community (Wenger, 1998).

The interactions involved, and the ability to undertake larger or more complex activities and projects through cooperation, bind people together and help to facilitate relationship and trust.

A cross-stakeholder approach is believed to be essential for exploring complex problems (Mason & Mitroff, 1981). Community members see a clearer order through the complexity of today's social problems by coming together around the problem. It is the "pull" of the problem, rather than the "push" of a pre-determined solution that draws these diverse groups together to learn more about the dimensions of the problems (Wenger, McDermott, & Snyder, 2002). A researcher's lens on a problem, a method of study, and interpretation of findings and recommendations for improvement could all be considered a 'predetermined solution' if not done in collaboration. Solving complex problems in education requires a community of learners that span roles and settings, bringing all the important aspects of the problem to the forefront and creating a context for shared inquiry.

These theories and philosophies interconnect to form an intellectual framework for reevaluating the assumptions upon which our traditional EdD Programs are predicated.

DEVELOPING AN IDENTITY FOR CHANGE: CONSOLIDATING THE PERSONAL AND THE PROFESSIONAL

Professional skill-building for scholars is the 'first floor' in their preparation and serves as the foundation for the more challenging personal development. The personal journey involves dispositions of mind and character within the individual that are difficult to measure and to cultivate. Such scholar-practitioners are conscious of their identity as change agents and their depth of commitment to their communities. They recognize that they cannot be interveners without reciprocal relationships with those they seek to impact. The dual aspects of development demand that a Professional Practice Doctorate (PPD) program includes experiences that interweave both the development of the individual as a committed person and as an effective professional.

PPD programs that are designed for impact encompass a set of transformative developmental skills that reach beyond the aims and capacities of most traditional research oriented programs. These transformative skills enable scholar-leaders to harness their creativity to solve highly complex social problems. Transformative programs create scholar-pioneers who can redraw or expand the boundaries of practice and policy because they challenge intellectual and practical orthodoxy. They have developed the commitment and identity of a change agent, are guided by a powerful vision of the future, and can translate that vision into reality regardless of the environment (Nisan & Pekarsky, 2009). Transformative scholar-practitioners are those who envision in the field of education what has never been and then does whatever it takes to make it happen. In short, they are prepared for high impact action in the world.

Challenging Orthodoxy

Cultivating leaders with a strong identity for change means that their curriculum and research experiences prepare them for critical thinking that challenges prevailing assumptions and traditions—intellectual and practical 'orthodoxy.' They are skilled in 'assumption hunting' (Brandenburg, 2008) which refers to the identification of commonly held beliefs or dogmas, or dominant paradigms that shape our practice and policy—not for the sake of challenge alone, but for the purpose of close examination of such assumptions. Critical thinking occurs when the individual tries to uncover the assumptions that influence how he or she thinks and acts. It is profoundly important to introduce complexity to students, to open their minds to many perspectives on a problem, many shades of gray, and the needs of many different stakeholders in any given situation (Perry, 1999). Assumptions frame how we make decisions and take actions because they undergird how problems are defined (Brookfield, 2011):

- Causal assumptions or how we understand cause and effect (if I do A then B will happen).

- Prescriptive assumptions are assumptions we hold about what are desirable ways of thinking or acting ('shoulds').
- Paradigmatic assumptions (deeply held assumptions that frame how we look at the world. They lie deep within us (for example, they may influence how we view the etiology of problems).

As Brookfield advises, as soon as one understands critical thinking to be linked to action, they enter the realm of values, because you have to ask the questions 'action for what?' and 'whose actions' do we want to support? (Brookfield, 2011).

Paradigmatic Assumptions and Relational Leadership

Emerging scholars are typically also leaders working in a variety of contexts, and the effectiveness of their research depends on the relationships they build. Traditional views of leadership hold biases about women in such roles. The contemporary, post-heroic (masculine) models of leadership present it as 'a collaborative and relational process, dependent on social networks of influence' (Fletcher, 2004). Relational leadership refers to a model or perspective that leadership effectiveness is not gendered, but has to do with the ability of the leader to create positive relationships within the organization. Leadership is always dependent on the context, but the context is established by the relationships we value (Gergen, 2010; Wheatley, 1992). The relationship model is inclusive, empowering, purposeful, ethical, and process oriented (DeRue, Ashford, & Cotton, 2009; Komives & McMahon, 1998; Komives, Owen, Longerbeam, Mainella, & Osteen, 2006). The practice of leadership is therefore shared and distributed throughout the organization, creating an environment in which the positional leader is supported by 'a network of personal leadership practices distributed throughout the organization' (Komives & McMahon, 1998, p. 648). The relational nature of leadership in post-heroic models encourages a view of leadership as a social process that is less hierarchical than earlier models. Leadership is portrayed as 'an emergent process' and 'as something that occurs in and through relationships and networks of influence' (Eliott & Stead, 2008, p. 649). Leadership, therefore, is not just about leading people, but is often pioneering and can include the leadership of ideas, communities, and the representation of issues (Eliott & Stead, 2008). Emerging scholar-practitioners, prepared for impact, must necessarily become relational leaders who can develop *reciprocity* within the context in which they seek to intervene.

Reciprocity in Research and Practice

The scholar as 'intervener' forms reciprocal relationships with those they seek to impact. This orientation often conflicts with the dominant quantitative, positivist paradigm in traditional doctoral education. It offers alternative traditions in the development of scholarship—open dialogue with the subjects of research and critical reflection on personal identity and self as an instrument of research. Tensions among faculty of different traditions are often expressed either in mild tolerance of differences in orientation toward research to open hostility and ridicule in faculty meetings. As students bear witness to these tensions, they reflect such polarization as they classify faculty as 'stat' and 'non-stat.'

Problems of practice require intense, in-depth study to understand very complex phenomena in living contexts, for which there may be no, or totally ineffective, practical interventions. The practical interventions may not exist because we do not understand the underlying phenomena needing study, are not asking the right questions, or are oversimplifying the problem (Fowler & Hobbs, 2009). In over 30 years in doctoral education, I have heard from hundreds of students who describe harrowing experiences in their institutions of higher education as they seek to follow trails that depart from the traditional methodological pathways. Research faculty typically instructs doctoral students that the selection of the research paradigm and design depends on the nature of the question being asked. Yet, the process of choosing the right question involves more than matching questions to methods as it is influenced profoundly when the researcher believes that the path to understanding complex phenomena lies in the rich contexts in which they occur. It is influenced by stakeholders within the contexts, cultural factors and beliefs, and their perspective on the problem of interest. Defining the problem of interest, therefore, is a shared endeavor.

Research mentoring requires faculty and students to move far beyond the traditional process of naming the problem, then attaching an appropriate methodology, and then pursuing 'access' to data. Rather, it turns that process upside down, beginning with the context and those who 'hold' the data, how stakeholders view the problem and past attempts at solutions, the potential barriers to solutions, and what the community would view as positive outcomes. Scholars are urged not to look upon their produced findings as a culminating contribution, but to engage more fully with participants, negotiating work in progress to achieve results that the community finds beneficial (Subedi, 2006).

Powerful Mentorship

Challenging research orthodoxy requires mentors who can cultivate committed leaders. Powerful mentorship is based on the assumption that significant learning takes place at the intra-personal level and therefore every learning experience and input has an effect and contributes to the formation of the candidate's personal and professional path. Mentors support candidates on their journeys to integrating their personal-professional identities as they plan and carry out change and innovation initiatives (Storey & Richard, 2013).

IMPACT OF THE PROGRAM AND PROCESSES ON DOCTORAL CANDIDATES' PERSONAL AND PROFESSIONAL JOURNEY

The dissertation development process can be viewed as achieving a greater goal than the emerging scholar's professional development. Rather, it becomes an instrument for transformative development and development of an identity for change, deepening the intellectual skills of the individual and their ability to create reciprocal relationships with the community in which they want to intervene (Kochhar-Bryant, 2016). A special kind of intellectual cultivation is needed to affect the transformation required for doctoral scholars to move beyond translation of theory to practice to the next step of conceptualizing and catalyzing change. Scholars become conscious of the depth of their commitment to their communities and understand that they cannot be interveners without reciprocal relationships in the environment they seek to impact. They step outside the narrow band of advancing their self-interests as scholars. The negotiated process of research in the community becomes an enriching aspect of the dissertation for the researcher, and an ethical act on the part of the researcher as he or she develops a shared relationship with the researched.

Disrupting Our Doctoral Tradition

Over the past two years, our participation in the Carnegie Project on the Education Doctorate (CPED) has stimulated a comprehensive analysis of our product or EdD programs—their intellectual content, relevance to our consumers, and most of all, relevance for preparing our consumers to face the dominant challenges in American education today and internationally. While our leadership doctoral programs have undergone considerable change over the past two decades, we have recently found ourselves in a crucible of sorts. A faculty learning community was formed in 2011 to examine the literature on leadership training programs and identify core features of effective programs. Since then, faculty members have worked toward purposeful transformation through a process of "disruptive creativity" (Linker, 2014, p. 2) in rethinking the foundations of our program. Such transformation has not meant reinvention for the sake of change, but faculty recognized the need to nurture a new generation of courageous educational scholar-practitioners who can harness their creativity to solve crucial social problems. The professional practice program and dissertation can serve as a powerful tool for preparing the next generation of educational leaders.

Challenge to Program Ideology of the Traditional EdD and PhD

Our redesign is challenging the well-established ideology of some faculty. For example, many faculty have deep-seated beliefs that the doctorate is appropriate only for those whose career goals include research and academic roles. Advanced research courses should be a central part of the program as well as extensive research apprenticeships with faculty. The program should take five years or longer. Other faculty are open to the creation of the professional practice doctorate designed for applied research, field-based apprenticeships that prepare students for leadership roles, and can be completed in 3–1/2 years. It was vital to the success of the professional practice model to support those faculty who were excited by change and willing to 'suspend disbelief' and work actively to create new programs. They came to represent a new 'force' within the School and received special attention from the administration.

We asked—are we incorporating the pedagogies of *engagement, understanding, performance, reflection, generativity, and commitment* (Shulman, 2005)? Are we addressing the affective and moral component of learning and development, and not just cognitive growth? We examined the strategies we were using to help student crystallize an 'educational identity' (Nissan & Pekarsky, 2009), a 'civic courage' (Freire, 1998), and to engender an aspiration for courageous change in society and an ability to challenge prevailing conditions and conventional ideas in pursuit of the common good (Freire, 1998). This self-interrogation led to another set of questions related to the assumptions, content, and processes of our curriculum and pedagogy:

1. How can an EdD program cultivate a sense of 'identity' for social commitment to the community and help students clarify values associated with their identity?
2. What is the developmental and transformative process for crystallizing a leadership identity and how does it deepen over time?
3. What are the pedagogical strategies and instructional environments for creating committed leaders who can contribute to sustainable change?

Perspectives on the Co-existence of the EdD and PhD

Concerns about creating and sustaining quality and rigor represent the greatest challenge in the new design process and for the co-existence of the professional practice EdD and PhD programs. In traditional PhD programs quality is judged in terms of intensity of course work, high level of critical thinking, a key set of disciplinary concepts that all students should master, advanced knowledge of the major research methodologies of the discipline, original research contributions that build on current research available in the field of study, and stature of the journal or other media for publication. It is generally understood that a student who completes a doctoral degree, either PhD or professional practice EdD, should demonstrate the following skills:

*   broad and advanced knowledge within the discipline;
*   successful use of a range of methodologies of the discipline;
*   independent performance of original or applied research;
*   effective communication;
*   performance as a professional in the discipline.

Faculty, however, have raised questions about the meaning of rigor in a practitioner-oriented doctoral program. What is it? Who decides? Is it subjective, or can it be measured? What does 'relevance' have to do with it? Is it the determinant or litmus test for quality and stature in comparison to the PhD? Can a practitioner-oriented program achieve the same level of 'rigor' as a traditional research doctoral program or should the construct be redefined? Does 'rigor encompass a special set of skills that are associated with problem-solving and field impact? Program 'rigor' as defined within a practitioner-oriented program affects matters of program status and value within the school culture, faculty identity, student identity, resources, student performance expectations and experiences, and program content.

CPED held a discussion about this topic in its November 2012 UCEA meeting in Pittsburgh, offering the following observation:

> Because the professional practice doctorate in education prepares graduates to engage in a type of work fundamentally different from a research-heavy PhD, CPED asserts that the standards for the two degrees should display strikingly different definitions of excellence and quality. Reframing the question of what constitutes rigor, based on a criterion unique to the EdD, rather than a standard borrowed from the PhD offers an important opportunity for the development and longevity of a true professional practice degree in education. To that end, perhaps we should be asking—What is the impact of our programs? (Perry, 2012).

Other discussants suggested that quality should be defined as the impact our programs have on the profession that we serve. The challenge is, however, reaching consensus on how quality should be defined and how impact should be determined (Zambo et al., 2014; Zusman, 2013). How do we measure the impact of the program on candidates' educational identity, commitment, and vision? How do we measure the significance of the leadership performance of our graduates? Such measures of skill attainment should be grounded in the following program strategies:

1. Provide opportunities to examine the moral implications of social justice.
2. Provide opportunities to explore global perspectives on local issues.
3. Combine experiential and critical analytic learning to address actions and choices in educational leadership. Since the leader's value-commitments deeply affect and guide his or her actions and choices in the education policy arena, the program challenges leaders to reflect on the use of power and position to influence the quality of education in their domain of authority.
4. Prepare leaders to identify and explore ethical complexities in policy formation and important values underlie policy choices and the manner of their implementation.
5. Provide opportunities to participate in organizational change activities led by a skilled leader.
6. Work with a new change management tool and get feedback from mentors and stakeholders on what went well and what changes were needed.
7. Interview individuals who have successfully led an organizational change.

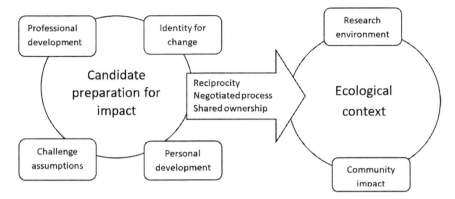

FIGURE 3.1.   Ecology for Impact of the Dissertation in Practice (Note: The Arrow in the Diagram Should Go in Two Directions.

8.   Provide opportunities early in the program to work in 'laboratories of practice' as authentic field-based settings in which theory and practice inform and enrich each other and allow students to address complex problems of policy and practice (Shulman, 2005).

9.   Build skills for the design of innovative solutions to address the problems of policy and practice.

10.   Deepen students' skills in using data to understand the effects of innovation, and prepare them to gather, organize, judge, and analyze situations, literature, and data through a critical lens (Shulman, 2005).

11.   Prepare students to target social change through their professional and applied research activities to improve social conditions within the community, particularly for vulnerable populations.

The faculty reinvention team at GW recognizes the potential power of our commitment to engage actively with the social and economic challenges facing the communities of which we are a part, and with the global community.

A VIGNETTE: RESEARCH RECIPROCITY AND IMPACT ON THE DOCTORAL CANDIDATE

The following vignette illustrates the process of interweaving professional and personal development through the curriculum, experiential activities, development experiences, and dissertation. This vignette is a composite of several that reflect actual students' experiences as doctoral candidates.

The choice. Angela H had examined several doctoral programs that offered PhDs. However, she was concerned about a 'traditional' program in which she may have to fit into existing research orthodoxy and faculty agendas rather than forge her unique path. She believed that research should be done in collaboration with the 'researched' and in real world settings. She was inspired by the proposition that solving complex problems required a community of learners that span roles and settings, bringing all the important aspects of the problem to the forefront by creating a context for shared inquiry. When she was interviewed for the program, she was asked—how do you want to make a difference in the world? She had never been asked this question and was intrigued with the idea of having the freedom to envision what has never been and then do whatever it took to make it happen. Faculty knew that Angela was self-motivated, inspired and committed, and could be guided to translate vision to practice.

The preparation. Angela was well prepared for the dissertation stage as a result of her coursework and related development experiences. She had completed all her coursework, which combined special education leadership courses, systemic change and consultation, qualitative and quantitative research tools, legal issues and public policy, preparation for the professorship, and course work that bridged neuroscience (brain science), child development, and education. She had also participated in two field-based internships in which she conducted various "research" projects under the direction of faculty leaders. For example, one of the projects engaged her, along with other doctoral students, in collaborative design of a program to prepare teachers in a school for adolescents with complex and multiple disabilities to deepen their knowledge and test their skills with students with severe communication disorders. She was in the school, assessing needs, meeting with staff and teachers, and collaborating in the design. She learned that this needed to be a transactional process, though, guided by faculty mentors. During these field experiences, Angela was challenged to think deeply about the kind of impact she wanted to prepare for and to create.

The mentoring process. Angela's program also included mentoring and guided processes in which students clarified their personal and professional identity, examined their motivations for their commitment to change, and reflected on the importance of culture and diversity in their own decisions and actions. They conducted and in-depth theoretical study, deepened their understanding of the complexity of the field of education, planned an educational undertaking, and created a set of meaningful personal and professional contacts. An important part of the curriculum and research preparation was the practice of 'assumption hunting' (Brandenburg, 2008) in which students examined the complexity of a program and examined the beliefs and assumptions at the root of the problems.

Doctoral studies that seek high-impact require intensive faculty time devoted to directing the study design, student advising, and supervision of the field negotiation and implementation. Angela and her mentor viewed the dissertation as having the aim of achieving a goal that is much greater than her individual's personal and professional development. Rather, it became an instrument for the transformative development of an identity for change and commitment to making a difference in her community. She and her peers had become aware that they had stepped outside the narrow band of advancing their self-interests as scholars and have embraced the scholar-change agent's doctrine—impact the world and be in the community.

In summary, Angela was oriented early to a critical interrogation of current practices and her beliefs. She strengthened her ability to express her values and talents and thus to actualize her identity as a skilled professional. She reflected on her value-commitments and how they guide her actions. She came to view cultural and linguistic diversity as an asset. She reflected on the personal and professional transformations that contributed to her identity as a change agent and commitment to the larger community. Finally, she learned what it meant to construct a *theory of change* that is grounded in an understanding of the history of previous interventions into the problem of interest. Angela believed she was ready for the dissertation, and she recalled the words in the very first brochure she saw on the program—seeking strong intellectual capabilities, visionary leaders who have the passion, commitment and practical wisdom to change society for the better.

The Dissertation in Practice (DiP). The Individuals with Disabilities Education Improvement Act (2004) mandates that teachers collaborate closely with the parents of children with disabilities to ensure that they participate in making decisions about educational services (Trainor & Bouchard, 2013). In many schools across the U.S. poor collaboration and communication leads to increased grievances and legal action from parents. Doctoral student Angela was interested in such collaborative relationships between teachers and parents within the individualized educational team (IEP team) that made decisions about services for children. She believed that processes could be improved. She interviewed parents, teachers, and administrators about the relationships, the services, the experiences in the IEP team meetings, and parents' sense of 'voice' in the meetings. These interviews deepened her understanding of the complexity of the problem and allowed her to become familiar with different perspectives. Angela made a concerted effort from the beginning of her research to identify shared interests with community members and to be mindful of them in her research design, implementation, and communication with her participants. She worked with district and school administrators to identify what they needed or expected from her research and learned of their interest in using the results of her study to improve practice and meet state educational requirements for data collection. In return, they agreed to help Angela to gain access to potential participants. She also asked parents and teachers what they believe needed to be explored and how they might contribute to the study. These perspectives were then shared with teachers and administrators, thus bringing their concerns to audiences who they might not have reached.

Lessons about stakeholder beliefs and perspectives. Acting on the ethic of reciprocity, Angela considered how the different groups in the study would use the work. She explored cultural issues that might shape the perspective on the problem and the solution. She asked the parents, teachers, and administrators what they were interested in seeing as a result of their participation, and she provided a thorough report of results, including information from parents on instances in which their children's rights were violated. This report resulted in the development of professional development materials for teachers, recommendations for data collection, processes for connecting parents with administrators when there were concerns, and the establishment of a parent liaison.

Angela worked continuously to adjust her study to ensure that she was exploring questions that were important to the community she was studying. In the process, she became an advocate for the groups of participants, representing their interests. Collaboration and reciprocity meant viewing research as a relational endeavor, asking questions that mattered to the community and engaging them in interpreting the meaning and importance of the results.

Lessons about reciprocity in research. The notion of reciprocity regarding the dissertation begged provocative questions from Angela about who owns a research project. For example, if the research is contextual, engages multiple stakeholders, is dependent upon these relationships, and the interpretation is context-sensitive, then who ultimately owns the work (Kochhar-Bryant, 2016). She learned that this is not a dichotomy, but it is both-and. She also learned that the Dissertation in Practice (DiP) embraces reciprocity, leads education researchers to a broader conceptualization of evidence, and expands the transformative potential of our collective work (Trainor & Bouchard, 2013).

Reflecting on barriers and threats in the process. Angela reflected on many barriers in the process of preparing for and negotiating the research project in an authentic setting. Echoing Schein (2004) she learned that for a culture to effectively change within an organization, the staff not only had to learn something new, but they also had to 'unlearn' something as well. Additionally, Angela realized that for transformative change to occur there needed to be 'discomfirming data' that suggested the inadequacy of the former strategies. It was important that she gathered and presented that data. Third Angela learned that the school culture was perpetuated through a process of socialization that involved the transmission of values and information. It was, therefore, important to ensure that the senior staff receives continued training, and be able to communicate and reinforce these concepts effectively with new staff (Van Maanen & Schein, 1979). Angela came to understand that the perfect reform initiative does not exist and that the focus on reform distracts educational leaders from focusing on the school culture and the elements of that culture that must be understood and nurtured for the reform to succeed (Ross, 2010).

A fourth serious threat to the successful implementation of the initiative was that there never seemed to be adequate time for planning, sharing information, and working through implementation problems. Fifth, the shrinking pool of financial resources available for staff training and for implementation required creative thinking about sustaining the project through alternative funding.

ASSESSING CANDIDATES' PERSONAL AND PROFESSIONAL DEVELOPMENT IN THE PROGRAM AND DISSERTATION IN PRACTICE (DIP)

Concerns with our educational leadership program centered on the strength of our curriculum and our field experiences to prepare leaders for a new paradigm of leadership, and to make a difference in contributing to the "common good" (Komives, Lucas, & McMahon, 1998; Morgeson, DeRue, & Karam, 2010). We asked—are we incorporating the pedagogies of engagement, understanding, performance, reflection, generativity, and commitment? Commitment encompasses the affective and moral component of learning and development, and means a commitment not just to cognitive growth but also to new dispositions, habits, and values (Shulman, 2004, pp. 55–56). We asked what strategies are we using to help student crystallize an 'educational identity,' develop 'civic courage,' engender an aspiration for radical changes in society, and develop an ability to challenge prevailing conditions and conventional ideas in pursuit of the common good (Freire, 1998). This self-interrogation led to another set of questions related to the content and processes of our curriculum and pedagogy and its potential to impact doctoral candidates from the time they enter the program to the dissertation:

1. How can an EdD program cultivate a sense of 'identity' for social commitment to the community and help students clarify values associated with their identity?
2. What is the developmental and transformative process for crystallizing a leadership identity and how does it deepen over time?
3. What are the pedagogical strategies and instructional environments for creating committed leaders?
4. What candidate assessment criteria should we focus on to appraise the socialization process?

We reviewed the curricula from 20 U.S. News top-ranked executive leadership doctoral programs and identified elements that they articulated as core features:

- Employs inquiry as practice in authentic settings in which students face uncertainty
- Attends to compelling issues in education policy and practice
- Challenges students to reflect on their capacity to attack complex education policies
- Facilitates the development, implementation, and stewardship of a school or district vision of learning supported by the school community.
- Is focused on managing the organization, operations, and resources in a way that promotes a safe, efficient, and effective learning environment.
- Collaborates with families and other community members.
- Promotes understanding, responding to, and influencing the larger political, social, economic, legal and cultural context.
- Promotes skills in the use of information and information technologies to enhance the effective utilization and practice of educational research.

None of the programs, however, spoke specifically to the shaping of an *educational identity* and the conditions that promote it—what we believe to be essential to socialization to creating impact. Table 3.1 presents the socialization criteria for

TABLE 3.1. Assessment of Doctoral Candidates' Development

Scale: 5 = exceeds expectations and serves as role model for others; 4 = exceeds expectations; 3 = meets expectations; 2 = approaches expectations for needs further development; 1 = needs considerable development and additional support

PHASE	PERSONAL DEVELOPMENT	PROFESSIONAL DEVELOPMENT
Curriculum for personal and professional development	• Is self-motivated, inspired and committed. • Conscious of their own identity as change agents, the depth of their commitment to their communities. • Interested in redrawing or expanding the boundaries of practice and policy. • Critical orientation and questions current practices and one's own beliefs; • Reflects on value-commitments and how they guide one's actions; • Views cultural and linguistic diversity as an asset. • Can move freely between different ways of seeing and understanding reality; and to uses these different perspectives to examine complex situations. • Expresses own values and talents and thus to actualize one's identity as a skilled professional; • Defines and reflects on personal and professional transformations that contribute to one's identity as a change agent and commitment to a larger community impact; • Possesses stamina in the face of failure, in order to embark on a "rocky path of translation from vision to practice"	• Demonstrates fluency in research-based and experiential knowledge and can maneuver between the theoretical and the practical worlds. • Make sound, defensible, research-based judgments regarding how current practices can be undertaken more effectively and efficiently. • Constructs a theory of change which is grounded in theory and an understanding of the history of previous interventions into the problem in the past. • Demonstrates interest in and capacity to design innovative solutions to address the problems of policy and practice. • Demonstrates skill in using data to understand the effects of innovation. • Can operate in complex situations, in an effort to translate ideas into reality. • Chooses among alternative courses of action and accepts responsibility.
Practice	• Reflects on mastering a challenging situation and the development of a sense of responsibility for future outcomes. • Articulates how value-commitments deeply affect and guide one's actions and choices. • Reflects on the use of power and position to effect change and influence the quality of education. • Considers problems of practice from perspectives other than those derived from their own experience. • Takes into consideration the needs, culture and characteristics of particular contexts.	• Identifies and explores ethical complexities in policy formation and important values that underlie policy choices and how they are implemented. • Applies skills of practical inquiry in a rigorous and systematic way to address problems of practice (including, but not be limited to, locating and framing problems; acquiring, organizing, and analyzing information; and planning, implementing, evaluating decisions).

(continues)

TABLE 3.1. Continued

PHASE	PERSONAL DEVELOPMENT	PROFESSIONAL DEVELOPMENT
Dissertation and dimensions of impact	• Develops and articulates a deep appreciation for the principle that they cannot be interveners in the world without reciprocal relationships with those they seek to impact. • Develops visions of the future related to particular educational problem and solution. • Reflects on actions and choices and the use of power and position in the context of research. • Identifies value-commitments that guide such actions and choices in the educational context. • Demonstrates ability to establish relationships with stakeholders in the negotiation of the dissertation project. • Demonstrates concern about application of research to improve social conditions within the community, particularly for vulnerable populations.	• Conducts a literature review to determine previous interventions and analyzes factors that have served as barriers to solutions. • Engages with a researchable, complex problem of practice. • Develops a problem-based thesis which involves change in practices and improved organizational performance. • Develops a theory of change or action in association with the dissertation. • Defines and gathers a community of learners who are stakeholders/beneficiaries of the intervention and appraises their concerns. • Develops steps for testing assumptions and achieving the solution within the environment of interest (e.g., preschool, K-12 school, community and non-profit organizations). • Demonstrates positive impact on the identified complex problem of practice. • Effectively communicates the results to appropriate audiences.

doctoral candidates that address curricular, personal development and identity, practice, and dissertation.

DEVELOPING AN EDUCATIONAL IDENTITY FOR IMPACT

Doctoral candidates immersed in the lexicon and ideology of identity formation as they become change agents. Curricular exercises require them to:

- study a problem of interest to them,
- conduct a literature review to determine previous interventions and to analyze factors that have served as barriers to solutions,
- based on this background understanding, develop visions of the future related to particular educational problem and solution,
- translate that vision into a theory of action,
- develop steps for testing assumptions and achieving the solution within the environment of concern (e.g., preschool, K–12 school, community, and non-profit organizations),

- define and gather a community of learners who are stakeholders/beneficia-ries of the intervention and appraise their concerns about the innovation and their participation.
- reflect on actions and choices and the use of power and position in the con-text of research, and identify value-commitments that guide such actions and choices in the educational context.

Cultivating leaders with a strong identity for change means that their curriculum and research experiences prepare them for critical thinking that challenges pre-vailing assumptions and traditions—the intellectual and practical 'orthodoxy.

We believe that the foundations for effective scholar-practitioners who wish to learn about and to contribute to a thriving educational system are courage, vision, and sustained commitment to *changing* the world. Our program, like many who are engaged in the building of professional practice doctoral programs, is commit-ted to strengthening the educational enterprise in the U.S. and around the world by preparing committed, vision-guided leaders who are equipped with innovative ideas that will enrich education and society. We believe that committed individu-als, endowed with passion, stamina, and inspiration can improve any environment in which they live. The preparation of doctoral candidates who can impact their world is an intentional and far-sighted investment in the creation of extraordinary national talent.

REFERENCES

Brandenburg, R. (2008). *Self study of a teacher educator's practice.* New York, NY: Springer Publishing Company.

Brookfield, S. (2011). *Teaching for critical thinking: Tools and techniques to help students question their assumptions.* San Francisco, CA: Jossey-Bass.

DeRue D. S., Ashford, S. J., & Cotton N. (2009). Assuming the mantle: Unpacking the process by which individuals internalize a leader identity. In L. M. Roberts & J. E. Dutton (Eds.), *Exploring positive identities and organizations: Building a theoreti-cal and research foundation* (pp. 213–232). New York, NY: Taylor & Francis.

Edgerton, R. (1997). *Higher Education* (unpublished white paper). Philadelphia, PA: The Pew Charitable Trusts Education Program.

Eliott, C., & Stead, V. (2008). Learning from leading women's experience: Towards a socio-logical understanding. *Leadership, 4(*2), 159–180. doi: 10.1177/1742715008089636

Fine, L. (2004). Tikkun: A Lurianic motif in contemporary Jewish thought. In J. Neusner et al (Ed.), *From ancient Israel to modern Judaism: Intellect in quest of understand-ing—Essays in Honor of Marvin Fox, Vol.* 4. Singapore: Scholars Press. REtrieved on 6/30/16 from http://www.myjewishlearning.com/daily_life/GemilutHasadim/TO_TikkunOlam/Contemp_Tikkun_Thought.htm.

Fletcher, J. K. (2004). The paradox of postheroic leadership: An essay on gender, power, and transformational change. *The Leadership Quarterly, 15* (2004) 647–661.

Fowler, G. W., & Hobbs, L. (2009). *Are we asking the right questions in Science and man-agement?* U.S. Department of Commerce. Retrieved on 6/15/16 from http://www.afsc.noaa.gov/Publications/AFSC-TM/NOAA-TM-AFSC-202.pdf

Fox, S., Scheffler, I., & Marom, D. (2003). *Visions of Jewish education*. New York, NY: Cambridge University Press.

Freire, P. (1998). *Pedagogy of freedom: Ethics, democracy and civic courage.* Lanham, MD: Rowman & Littlefield Publishers.

Gergen, K. (2010). *Relational being*. Oxford, UK: Oxford University Press.

Individuals with Disabilities Education Improvement Act, 20 U.S.C. § 1400 (2004).

Kochhar-Bryant, C. A. (2016). Identity, commitment and change agency: Bedrock for bridging theory and practice in doctoral education. In V. Storey & K. Hesbol, *Contemporary approaches to dissertation development and research methods* (pp. 29–42). Hershey, PA: IGI Global.

Komives, S., Lucas, N., & McMahon, T. (1998). *Exploring leadership for college students who want to make a difference*. San Francisco, CA: Jossey-Bass.

Komives, S. R., Owen, J. E., Longerbeam, S., Mainella, F. C., & Osteen, L. (2006). A leadership identity development modal: Applications from a grounded theory. *Journal of College Student Development, 47*(4), 401–418.

Lave, J., & Wenger, E. (1991). *Situated learning: Legitimate peripheral participation.* Cambridge, UK: Cambridge University Press.

Linker, J. (2014). *The road to reinvention: How to drive disruption and accelerate transformation.* San Francisco, CA: Jossey-Bass.

Mandel Leadership Institute. (2016). *Jerusalem*. Retrieved on 6/15/16 from http://www.mli.org.il/english/ MhlLeadership/Pages/HarediLeadershipPrograms.aspx

Mason, R. O., & Mitroff, I. I. (1981). *Challenging strategic planning assumptions: Theory, cases and techniques.* New York, NY: Wiley.

Morgeson, F. P., DeRue, D. S., Karam, E. P. (2010). Leadership in teams: A functional approach to understanding leadership structures and processes. *Journal of Management, 36*, 5–39.

Nissan, M., & Pekarsky, D. (2009). *Educational identity as a major factor in the development of educational leadership.* Mandel Institute. Jerusalem, Israel: Hebrew University.

Perry, J. (2012). *Discussion extended-Feb 10th: Rigor, consensus or impact? What is the CPED measure of high-quality?* Accessed 6/7/16 from http://cpedinitiative.org/forum-topic/discussion-extended-feb-10th-rigor-consensus-or-impact-what-cped-measure-high-quality

Perry, W. G. (1999). *Forms of ethical and intellectual development in the college years: A scheme* (2nd ed.). San Francisco, CA: Jossey-Bass.

Ross, C. (2010). *Changing your school? First, work on culture.* Southfield, MI: Education Partnerships, Inc. Retrieved from http://www.educationpartnerships.org.

Ruskin, J. (1866). The crown of wild olive, lecture IV: The future of England, section 151. In E. T. Cook & A. Wedderburn (Eds.), *The works of John Ruskin,* 1905. New York, NY: Longmans, Green & Co.

Schein, E. H. (1992). *Organizational culture and leadership* (3rd ed.). San Francisco, CA: Jossey-Bass.

Shulman, L. (2004). *Teaching as community property: Essays on higher education.* San Francisco, CA: Jossey-Bass.

Shulman, L. (Spring, 2005). Pedagogies of uncertainty. *Liberal Education, 91*(2). Online publication: https://www.aacu.org/publications-research/periodicals/pedagogies-uncertainty.

Storey, V. A., & Richard, B. M. (2013). Critical friends groups: Moving beyond mentoring. In V. A. Storey (Ed.), *Redesigning professional education doctorates: Applications of critical friendship theory to the Ed.D.* London: Palgrave McMillan.

Subedi, B. S. (2006, June). Cultural factors and beliefs influencing transfer of training. *International Journal of Training and Development, 10(2),* 88–97.

Trainor, A., & Bouchard, K. S. (2013). Exploring and developing reciprocity in research design. *International Journal of Qualitative Studies in Education, 26*(8), 986–1003. doi: 10.1080/09518398.2012.724467

Van Maanen, J., & E. H. Schein (1979). Toward of theory of organizational socialization. *Research in Organizational Behavior, 1,* 209–264.

Wenger, E. (1998). *Communities of practice: Learning, meaning, and identity (Learning in doing: Social, cognitive and computational perspectives).* Cambridge, UK: Cambridge University Press.

Wenger, E., McDermott, R., & Snyder, W. (2002). *Cultivating communities of practice: a guide to managing knowledge.* Cambridge, MA: Harvard Business School Press.

Wenger-Trayner, E., Fenton-O'Creevy, M., Hutchinson, S., Kubiak, C., & Wenger-Trayner, B. (Eds.). (2014). *Learning in landscapes of practice: Boundaries, identity, and knowledgeability in practice-based learning.* Abingdon on Thames, UK: Routledge.

Wheatley, M. J. (1992). *Leadership and the new science: Learning about organization from an orderly universe.* San Francisco, CA: Berrett-Kohler Publishers.

Zambo, R., Zambo, D., Buss, R. R., Perry, J. A., & Williams, T. R. (2014). Seven years after the call: students' and graduates' perceptions of the re-envisioned EdD. *Innovative Higher Education (39)*2, 123–137.

Zusman, A. (2013). *Degrees of change: How new kinds of professional doctorates are changing higher education institutions.* Research and Occasional Paper Series, CSHE 8–13. Center for Studies in Higher Education. Berkeley, CA: University of California.

CHAPTER 4

THE EdD PROGRAM

Context and Dilemmas in the Development of the Dissertation in Practice

Virginia Montero-Hernandez and Anysia Mayer

In this chapter we analyze the contextual factors that underlie graduate faculty and students' pursuit of the Dissertation in Practice (DiP). We take a macro-sociological perspective to understand the conditions that both constrain and allow faculty and students to work together in the completion of a capstone project or dissertation (Gumport, 1997; Gumport & Snydman, 2002; Honan & Teferra, 2001; Slaughter & Rhoades, 2004). We argue that graduate faculty in the EdD program experience tensions or dilemmas when guiding students through the writing and defense of the DiP. These faculty dilemmas derive from various factors including the origins of EdD programs, changes in the academic profession, and the complexity of an educational system that has to respond to local and national demands.

Three broad sections structure this chapter. In the first section, we discuss the authorization of professional doctorates in the higher education system in California and the implications of this new institutional agreement for the actors involved. In the second part of the chapter, we discuss who graduate faculty and working professionals in EdD programs are. We analyze graduate faculty as

Exploring the Impact of the Dissertation in Practice, pages 51–71.

members of a changing academic profession that has been dramatically affected by the economic and socio-cultural context in which higher education institutions operate. The discussion is followed by an examination of graduate students in the EdD program as adult learners and working professionals who aspire to become scholar-practitioners. The third section of the chapter develops the specific dilemmas that graduate faculty experience when working with students in the development of the DiP. By reflecting on our personal practice at an EdD in the California State System, we first analyze the ways in which the basic-applied distinction in research continues to create ambiguity in the definition of instructional formats and final products that EdD students need to achieve. The second dilemma refers to the ways in which attention to graduation rates distract actors from searching for meaningful learning experiences. Conclusions are drawn at the end of the chapter.

PART I. THE EDD PROGRAM IN CALIFORNIA: INNOVATION IN A COMPETING MARKET

Three conditions make the state of California an interesting case for the analysis of the EdD program. First, California's definition of educational structures has a significant influence upon the definition of other higher education institutions in the U.S. Second, during the 1970s, public higher education in California entered a period of instability that led to the public scrutiny of the organizational effectiveness of the University of California, California State University, and California community colleges (Almond, 1974; Callan, 2009). Third, and finally, the California higher education structure has undergone extreme, rapid expansion [i.e., economic and demographic changes, proliferation of faculty and managerial professionals, and the establishment of new campuses post-1970] (Callan, 2009), which has been different not in kind but in intensity from the process of growth in other states in the U.S.

Higher education institutions that prepare future leaders through EdD programs in California play a sizable role due to the complexity and structure of the education system in California. Managing and leading the nation's largest educational system demand the availability of professionals who can respond to the conditions of cultural and linguistic diversity that characterize the state. However, compared to other states, California's licensure requirements for administrators are minimal. Whereas 70% of states require a special license for the superintendent and 52% of states require a master's degree, California requires only three years of school-related work experience and has only one license for all pre-K–12 administrative jobs, including that of superintendent (Davis, 2010). Within this context, the expansion of EdD programs aims to respond to the demands of educational leaders in the region.

Over the past decade, higher education faculty responsible for preparing educational leaders endeavored to define the EdD and its boundaries in relation to the PhD conferred by schools of education. Since 2007, the Carnegie Project on the

Education Doctorate (CPED) has worked with over 80 colleges and schools of education to undertake a critical examination of the doctorate in education (EdD). The role of CPED has been to provide a conceptual framework and acknowledge promising practices in the implementation of EdD programs. The EdD degree at California State Universities (CSU) is attentive to the principles crafted by CPED members and emphasizes the urgency to develop educational leadership in local regions. In 2005, as an amendment to the 1960 California Master Plan, CSU campuses were authorized to grant doctoral degrees (EdD). By describing ongoing community partnerships and direct preparation for work in schools and community colleges, the Executive Order issued by the Chancellor's suggests that the purpose of the EdD degree is to directly impact the work of professionals through applied research.

Prior to 2005, there were approximately five joint CSU/UC doctoral programs in education. The implementation of the independent EdD programs at the CSU campuses was guided by Senate Bill 724 and Executive Order 991 issued by the system's Chancellor's Office. These two documents define the number of units, program goals, milestones, and faculty roles within the program. Although the first decade of the 21st century was a difficult time to start offering new programs at the CSUs (Orfield[1], 2011), within two years seven campuses began offering the EdD and today there are fourteen programs across the system. Despite the level of outside guidance, EdD programs at CSU campuses took fairly independent implementation paths by building on local strengths (Normore & Cook, 2011).

The creation of the EdD degree at CSUs had significant implications for the organizational identity of schools of education and the professional identity of graduate faculty in higher education institutions in California. The 1960 California Master Plan for Higher Education (CMPHE), which sought to coordinate the growth of higher education during a 15-year period to promote access in the state (Callan, 2009), asked for the University of California, The California State University, and Community Colleges to act as partners each performing a specific role in meeting the educational needs of state. However, with the authorization to offer EdD degrees, the CSU and the University of California system (UC) ceased to be partners and became competitors. Whereas the definition of the CMPHE was less than an effective solution to respond to the needs of the context (Kerr, 2001), the authorization of the EdD program at CSU) contributed to an increased sense of ambiguity and added to the complexity of the educational system in the state. Clark Kerr (2001), former UC president and co-author of the CMPHE, noted,

> The [Master Plan] looked to us who participated in its development more like a desperate attempt to prepare for a tidal wave of students, to escape state legislative domination, and to contain escalating warfare among its separate segments...[A]

[1] California went through a drastic drop in state income between 2007 and 2010, the CSU system saw a 625 million dollar drop in revenue between 2007-2010 which resulted in increased faculty workloads and reductions in course offerings

nd the preparation, the escape and the containment in each case was barely on time and barely succeeded. The Master Plan was a product of stark necessity, of political calculations, and of pragmatic transactions" (p. 173)

The 2005 authorization of the EdD programs at CSU brought concerns about the disruption of the roles that the CMPHE had attached to each type of institution (UC, CSU, and CC); additionally, there was a shared fear that "SB 724 could begin to spread California's resources for graduate education too thinly and dilute quality" (Arditti, 2005, p. 3). The 2005 authorization of the EdD program in CSU offered an alternative pathway for students; however, it blurred the boundaries between the PhD in education at the UCs and the EdD degree at the CSUs (Boyce, 2012). Another source of concern was the public perception of basic and applied research as being the exclusive domain of either the EdD or PhD, when in practice there is a continuum between basic and applied in the work of students at both degrees (Nelson & Coorough, 1994). Whereas the development of the EdD in California was viewed as a programmatic innovation, its authorization came with a series of challenges that demand the redefinition or actualization of functions and concepts that guide graduate education and the shaping of the scholar-practitioner in particular (Normore & Cook, 2011). We also need to understand faculty and student development of the DiP as an event defined by not only the pedagogical approach that faculty use but also the historical setting that defined the conditions of the faculty-student interaction and potential outcomes.

PART II. GRADUATE FACULTY AND DOCTORAL STUDENTS: LIVES IN INTERSECTION

While pursuing a doctoral degree, both graduate students and faculty share the challenges of building a professional identity. Faculty members invest an enormous amount of mental energy, time, and physical health to nurture and guide the careers of students at the same time that they navigate and survive a stressful workplace (Orfield, 2011). At the same time, doctoral students also sacrifice personal life and health to survive the demands of graduate school. Life conditions and the ways in which both faculty and graduate students in EdD programs respond to contextual demands will affect the quality of their relationship and the outcomes they can pursue together. The understanding of faculty and students' development of the DiP depends on a critical examination of the roles they play and the contextual challenges that each one of them experiences on a daily basis. The following sections explore who graduate faculty and students in the EdD program are. We explore features of the contemporary context of higher education that can create a problematical situation that affect the ways in which academics engage in their work and interactions with students (Clark, 2001).

Faculty in Professional Doctoral Programs: Redefined Roles in a Changing Profession

The mentoring of EdD students, as any other educational process, does not occur in a vacuum but in a context where certain opportunities are allowed and others are restricted by the cultural aspects that define the social context (Levinson & Holland, 1996). We argue that the changes in the academic profession define the characteristics and conditions for faculty and students' engagement in the DiP. Every time that the faculty meets with EdD students to guide them through the writing and defense of a DiP, there are two simultaneous processes taking place: Faculty's construction of an (1) academic identity that guarantees membership to the academia and job security and (2) an instructional relationship that allows students to become scholar-practitioners. The faculty and student engagement in the DiP is more than the development of a document but a shared effort to define professional identities and future career goals in a changing, demanding, ambiguous higher education context. Therefore, to understand how and why graduate faculty engage in mentoring a student through the DiP, we need to examine the ways in which faculty's membership to a professional community shapes who they are and what they can do with a student.

The academic identity and practice of university professors have undergone continual adjustment in order to respond to contextual changes and the re-imagination of institutions and programs. During the nineteen century, at research-based universities in the United States, faculty gained recognition for their expertise, specialization in intellectual disciplines, and their participation in the advancement of knowledge (Lane, 1985; Taylor, 1999). However, by the 1940s, the general education movement[2] in the U.S. modified the understating of faculty as professionals: Academics were expected to be not experts in a specialized body of knowledge but general practitioners in command of broad areas of knowledge and dedicated to teach and interact with students (Alpert, 1980). Since then, faculty members have started to experience role dilemmas that derive from the changes in the social, political, and economic landscape (Massey, 1997). Additionally, during the years following War World II and through the 1980s, faculty lost status and public esteem as a result of the low levels of academic performance in higher education institutions, the incorporation of professionals holding a managerial perspective, and the exclusion of faculty members from the decision-making processes aimed to organize academic life (Altbach, 2001; Massey, 1997).

In the last three decades faculty work has changed in response to the consolidation of three contemporary discourses shaping higher education across nations (Montero-Hernandez, 2010): The discourse of reform and university restructuring

---

[2] General education is opposed to specialization, research, and pre-professional training as defining elements of undergraduate education. As a movement, it argued instead for a liberal art program that would provide students with a broad learning experience and would treat them as whole persons (Alpert, 1980).

which emphasizes the necessity of structural change to address existing deficiencies and foster progress and economic productivity for a nation, the discourse of accountability and quality assurance which is based on accountability principles and the use of standardized means to assess outcomes; and the discourse of commodification and marketization of knowledge which emphasizes the implementation of a business-like institutional logic to regulate academic practices in higher education. These three discourses have created institutional regulations and organizational processes to define how universities and faculty should engage in research and how students in doctoral programs, both EdD and PhD, need to be educated.

In the last three decades, academic functions have become more complex and faculty's workload greater as a result of the following conditions: growing role of government in university control, reduced university budgets, decline of salaries and increase in the use of part-timers, the incorporation of managerial principles and accountability, technology integration, student diversity, and the development of bureaucratic structures, both inside and outside institutions, to exert mechanism of regulation, supervision, and control (Everett & Entrekin, 1994; Honan & Teferra, 2001; Jacobs & Winslow, 2004; Lane, 1985; Martin, 1999; Orfield, 2011). Changes in the academic profession and a climate of constantly evolving demands has caused faculty to experience a sense of loss and anxiety (Taylor, 1999). Academics at universities experience emotional distress as they feel undervalued and overworked (Martin, 1999). Since the 1990s, there is a clear tendency towards diminished job satisfaction and an increase in the levels of occupational stress across countries (Eagan & Garvey, 2015; Jacobs & Winslow, 2004; Neumann & Finaly-Neumann, 1990; Olsen, 1993; Perlberg & Keinan, 1986; Thompson & Dey, 1998; Thorsen, 1996).

Along with the changes in the academic profession, reward systems at universities have become both more critical for the definition of the educational process (Dundar & Lewis, 1998; Fairweather, 2002; Rhoades, 2001; Tien & Blackburn, 1996). Although the U.S. higher education adheres to the merit principle (i.e., technical competency and productivity) to assess faculty work; university administrators and officers often use ambiguous strategies and reductionist interpretations of academic productivity to dismiss, retard, or promote academic members (Fairweather, 1989, 2002; Taylor, 1999; Taylor, Fender, & Burke, 2006). Taylor's (1999) investigation of tenure policies since the 1960s and 1970s reveals a lack of systematic attention to the development of coherent appraisal standards and the evaluation of faculty services and productivity, which has created confusion and conflicting demands among academic faculty concerning the primary criteria for promotion and retention. Additionally, there is a tendency to view scholarly productivity (i.e., publications) as the primary symbol of both individual and institutional visibility, prestige, and value in the academic community both at the local, national, and international levels (Burgess, 1996; Deem, 2001; Fairweather, 1989, 2002; Gappa, Austin, & Trice, 2007; Taylor, 1999). It is widely acknowledged that the academic community tends to value research over teaching and mentoring (Grubb et al., 1999; Lane, 1985), even when teaching is also central to university's basic function (Boyer, 1990, 1991; Fairweather, 1989, 2002; Rhode, 2006). Additionally, reward systems continue to perpetuate the basic-applied distinction in research when they allocate a higher value to academic practices and outcomes that derived from engagement on basic research and that culminate with peer review publications. Although there have been efforts to acknowledge faculty engagement in community work, industry, and other social-oriented forms of productivity (Baez, 2000; Creamer, 1999; Lomnitz & Chazaro, 1999), basic research continues the priority in faculty workload (Braxton, 1983; Creamer, 1999; Fox & Mohapatra, 2007; Goodwin & Sauer, 1995).

Faculty working in EdD programs also function within the academic culture described in the previous section. They must mentor students through the capstone process while they maintain their research agenda and try to keep themselves up to date with the demands of prestige and professional survival in academia. Faculty have to find sources of support and motivation within a political and economic climate that calls for increased control and assessment, reduced funding, low salaries, and decreased job security and public esteem (Orfield, 2011). The ways in which university faculty decide to mentor students in an EdD program, pursue a specific dissertation topic, the number of mentoring session that they hold, the amount of time they can invest in students' fieldwork and writing process is strongly associated with the context in which faculty members work and the demands they finds as members of a professional community. Different from some faculty in PhD programs, who may have full-time students that are starting their career and can work as research assistants across multiple years, faculty in EdD programs work with students who have full-time jobs and do not have time, individually or in their program, to engage in work with faculty mentors that will result in peer-reviewed publications. Therefore, faculty in EdD programs often find it more challenging to work with students who are also working professionals as colleagues in the development of publications or research projects.

To summarize, faculty who advise EdD students engage in a continual process of negotiation of their professional identity. At the same time that faculty help EdD students to become scholar-practitioners, faculty had to negotiate their previous educational background and training (e.g., faculty who are holders of PhD degrees) and the ways and styles through which they establish their membership to the professional community. Faculty who learned to become primarily researchers as part of their graduate studies (i.e., PhD holders) will have to learn to interact and guide EdD students according to the particular principles that EdD programs and the dissertation in practice entail. Faculty who graduated from EdD programs may be already familiar with the principles and practices that the DiP entails and the commitment to educate scholar-practitioners. However, regardless of their educational background, whether EdD and PhD holders, faculty in EdD programs have to guarantee their membership to an academic profession that pays no significant attention to contextual differences and demands the same type of productivity and excellence from its members if they want to attain job security and prestige.

Adult Graduate Students: Becoming the Scholar-Practitioner

In the same way that faculty members have to manage the demands imposed on the academic profession, graduate students in the EdD programs have to navigate the specific conditions of their personal life and work. Adult students in professional doctorate programs are individuals who chose to continue their education to gain new professional skills even when they often remain in their original sites of practice (Lisi, 2013). Working professionals in EdD programs tend to be individuals in their thirties and older who do not complete traditional, full-time enrollment and do not actively participate in campus activities outside the classroom (Kuipers, 2011). Adult practitioners, who have already established themselves professionally, are characterized by a desire to continue their professional learning (Kuipers, 2011); they have an approach to learning characterized by (a) increased capacity for individual introspection and self-awareness, (b) intrinsic motivation, (c) a self-directed learning style, (d) involvement in off-campus activities, and (e) educational goal selection (Montero-Hernandez & Cerven, 2012).

As adult learners, who are also working professionals, students in EdD programs can experience three major challenges: Role conflicts, lack of confidence or self-doubt, and fixed belief structures that derive from their previous life experiences (Belzer, 2004; Crossan, Field, Gallacher, & Merrill, 2003; Giancola, Grawitch, & Borchert, 2009). Adult students also enact multiple roles and life demands such as work, marriage, and supporting dependents other than their spouse (Kasworm, 2003). As adult students struggle to meet multiple demands, their attention is divided between attending college and other activities that are not related to coursework (Kasworm, 1990, 1993, 2010; Ponton, Derrick, & Carr, 2005). The multiple role requirements that adults have to fulfill compete for a finite amount of energy and attention, this creates emotional distress and can influence their academic performance in classroom negatively (Prins, Toso, & Schafft, 2009; Vaccaro & Lovell, 2010). Female, minority, and economically disadvantaged adults tend to experience higher levels of stress and competing life demands (Prins, Toso, & Schafft, 2009; Vaccaro & Lovell, 2010).

Adult students who come back to school after a long period of time also experience self-doubt and lack of confidence (Chen, Kim, Moon, & Merriam, 2008; Donaldson & Townsend, 2007; Kasworm, 1990). The structure of educational programs can increase feelings of alienation among adult students who struggle to adopt fixed class schedules, full-time enrollment, and participate in campus life (Chaves, 2006; Sissel, Birdsong, & Silaski, 1997; Sissel, Hansman, & Kasworm, 2001). Adults often choose to become evening, weekend, and distance learners as this type of format fits their personal life better; however, these non-traditional schedules often deprive these students of necessary social and academic support services (Sissel, Hansman, & Kasworm, 2001). When adult students cannot meet traditional educational formats, it may cause them to question their ability to adapt to the academic culture (Donaldson & Townsend, 2007; Kasworm, 2005). Adult students can take longer periods of time to adjust their perspectives and belief systems on the basis of new knowledge, however the accelerated nature of EdD programs often does not afford students this time (Belzer, 2004; Crossan, Field, Gallacher, & Merrill, 2003; Sheckley, Donaldson, Mayer, & Lemons, 2010). However, adult students can incorporate new ways of thinking when they engage in stimulating interactions and dialogue with instructors, counselors, and classmates (Belzer, 2004).

Because of the student population that EdD programs receive, there is a critical demand to consider the specific demands of the working professionals. EdD programs seek to respond to the needs of their applicants by designing time-accelerated programs during afternoons, nights, or even weekends (Kuipers, 2011; Lisi, 2013; Sawyer, 2013). The purpose of the EdD programs' customized schedules and andragogy-based approach is to help working professionals to become scholar-practitioners who can contribute to and change practice by applying theory and knowledge to specific problems (Boyce, 2012; Kuipers, 2011; Sawyer, 2013). The process of becoming a scholar-practitioner is similar to that of other graduate students in that it is also a stressful and uncertain experience through which the student has to develop scholarship-oriented competencies and independence as thinkers (Gardner, 2008). Contrary to the isolating experiences that some graduate students describe, the development of the scholar-practitioner in many EdD programs is based on a cohort model to complete a capstone assignment and develop a scholarly community whose main goal is the solution of specific problems of practice (Lisi, 2013; Olson & Clark, 2009). In addition to sustained mentoring, learning in a community of practice is critical in the development of the scholar-practitioners. Students in EdD programs have emphasized that membership to a community of practice helped them persist and achieve their educational goals because the group provided a "family feeling" based on a sense of safety, trust, and connection (Olson & Clark, 2009).

PART III. DILEMMAS GRADUATE FACULTY AND STUDENTS LIVE BY: TENSIONS AND NEGOTIATIONS

The dilemmas we present in this section derive from the intersection of multiple contextual factors described above. We emphasize that faculty and students' engagement in the DiP is a process defined by the negotiation of multiple tensions. We define dilemmas as perplexing situations that involve (a) sequential rather than single decisions, (b) uncertainty about what the consequences of one's decision alternatives might be, and (c) a clash of competing objectives and interests (Vaupel, 1975). The occurrence of a dilemma can be associated with the characteristics of the context and the existence of conflicting roles and interests. Individuals' management of a dilemma depends on the contextual and psychological resources at hand (e.g., Ball, 1993; Cuban, 1984, 1992; Volkmann & Anderson, 1998). The contextual factors shaping the academic profession and the lives of adult practitioners contribute to the creation of dilemmas that graduate faculty in EdD programs experience. An accountability climate, rampant professional competition, cultural constructions of prestige and success, financial instability, and increased institutional differentiation contribute to the construction of challenging and stressful scenarios in which graduate faculty and students are expected to work together.

In this section, we discuss two critical dilemmas we identified as part of our practice in a professional doctorate in educational leadership in the California State University system. We realized these dilemmas as part of the weekly program meetings with colleagues who also teach in the EdD program. During these meetings, we discussed student performance, program structure, mentoring challenges, students' skills, graduation rates, graduation timelines, workloads, as well as personal struggles and frustrations. Every year core EdD faculty work with a cohort of fifteen students on average. The program is designed to take three years to complete. Our students come from various cultural backgrounds. Cultural and linguistic diversity is a salient characteristic of our student population. Similar to other graduate programs, our students often exhibit problems to engage in critical reading, academic writing, and conceptual abstraction. Each dilemma represents a perplexing situation in which competing values and options emerge. The characteristics of each dilemma are summarized in a series of personal questions that were not only validated but also shared by other colleagues. We introduce each dilemma by listing two competing values, ideas, or dimensions; however, we do not imply that the solution of the dilemma involves the selection of one dimension over the other. We realize that educational practices call for a continuum between seeming dichotomies.

Dilemma One: Basic versus Applied Research

How do I mentor my students to become experts in the use of theory and research methodology and at the same time help them learn to solve practical problems in their current job? How do I help my students to attain conceptual understanding of educational issues and develop problem-solving skills? Is one of these two learning goals more relevant or prestigious? Should my students engage in either basic or applied research? Should we, as faculty, focus on generalizable knowledge or on context-specific impact?

This dilemma is associated to a long-standing, critical conflict that is not unique to the field of education: At the core of this issue is the competing value of basic versus applied research. Historically, core arts and science departments at universities have been responsible for supporting and promoting basic research, whereas professional schools tend to take a more applied focus and solve practical problems (Bendor, 1994; McElroy, 1977). The field of education is primarily seen as an applied field of study; however, even within the educational field there is a tendency to perceive PhD programs as more basic- and EdD programs more applied-research oriented, which allocates more prestige to the former than the latter (Nelson & Coorough, 1994). EdD programs are often expected to prepare students in the dissemination and application of knowledge whereas the PhD is expected to prepare students in the generation and integration of knowledge (Boyce, 2012; Lisi, 2013). Although educational doctorates have emerged as an institutional effort to support applied research and the resolution of practical problems in education; we suggest that the orientation and identity of EdD programs continue to be a contested terrain. Faculty and students often perceive pursuing theory-based work must come at the cost of pursuing practical-oriented work.

At its core, our EdD program, like others across the nation, aims to educate scholar-practitioners through their engagement in the scholarship of practice, which involves reflection in action and "refers not only to the applied aspect of one's work, but also includes underlying theory, intellectual framings and processes, habits of mind, knowledge of method, knowledge of self, and reflection for improvement" (Sawyer, 2013, p. 210). Engagement in the scholarship of practice involves the use of action research to address problems of practice in local school settings, build capacity among educational leaders, and promote small-scale innovations in local educational practices (Olson & Clark, 2009). A problem of practice is defined as, "A persistent, contextualized, and specific issue embedded in the work of a professional practitioner, the addressing of which has the potential to result in improved understanding, experience, and outcomes" (Storey & Maughan, 2014, p. 10).

Over decades, the basic-applied distinction in research has become a source of continual debate in multiple disciplinary fields (Foote, 1965; Kuhn, 1977; McElroy, 1977; Nafstad, 1982; Reagan, 1967; Spurr, 1970). Although it seems arbitrary to establish a clear demarcation between basic and applied research, there is a strong symbolic value attached to each type of research (Reagan, 1967). In the history of science, theory has been regarded with superior status whereas practice has been perceived as having lower prestige (McElroy, 1977). For decades, the notion of basic research has had a strong presence and value within the political and scientific discourses (Pielke, 2012). However, lately there has been a significant impetus to support and increase the value of applied research and technological development; at times, in detriment of fundamental, creative research (Foote, 1965; McElroy, 1977; Pielke, 2012). As part of the debate, it is usually noted that basic researchers tend to identify an area of inquiry based on their individual theoretical profile or specialization whereas the applied researcher frames his work from the need to solve specific practical problems (Nafstad, 1982). Whereas some scholars try to exalt the differences between basic and applied research; others endeavored to create a bridge between the two types of research and point out that there is a continuum between basic and applied research and that both types of research can supplement each other (Davison, 1997; Joyner, 2003; McElroy, 1977; Nafstad, 1982; Niiniluoto, 1993; Schwebel, Plumert, & Pick, 2000).

At universities, one of the critical consequences of this ongoing debate about the basic-applied distinction in research is related to the confusing demands forced upon faculty members and consequently upon students. Traditional university reward systems are usually structured to emphasize faculty participation in basic research that will result in peer-reviewed publications; as a result, faculty find it problematic to engage in applied and industry-related research without risking denial of tenure (Boardman & Ponomariov, 2007). Faculty who become interested in specific types of applied research that emphasize community-based work are often questioned with regards to the rigor and academic value of their social-justice oriented initiatives (Barlow, 2007; Nyden, 2003; Schoorman, 2014). The ongoing debate about the basic-applied distinction in research is not an irrelevant issue since this debate has been critical in the negotiation of the DiP. The ways in which faculty chose to guide their students depends on the values and symbols of prestige in their academic community and disciplinary traditions they choose to follow. The faculty-student relationship in professional doctorates in education is shaped, among other factors, by the ways in which the academic profession and universities have embraced, resisted, or innovated the basic-applied distinction in research. The professional doctorate is part of the efforts to validate the status of applied research and the necessity of universities and faculty members who are able to create bridges between theory and practice through the resolution of problems of practice. Faculty and students in the EdD program continue to work in the definition of boundaries as part of the everyday work.

Second Dilemma: Meaningful Learning versus Doctoral Completion Rates

> How can I work with my students to help them develop refined research skills, change their epistemological skills, and become effective scholar-practitioners simultaneously and guarantee they attain a degree in three years? How do I create meaningful learning experiences for adult practitioners who have saturated agendas and limited time to read or to engage in deep reflection?

This dilemma derives from the pressures for accountability and the commodification of knowledge in higher education institutions. Faculty at graduate programs have to search for meaningful learning experiences at the same time that they manage to graduate students within expected timelines. The speed to attain a credential has become an important value in the educational market not only for students but also for institutions. Ideally, graduate students in our EdD program are expected to start and finish their program in three years. The financial and personal cost that earning an EdD entails motivates students to try to finish their graduate degree as soon as possible. Additionally, for faculty and program directors in EdD programs, it is important to guarantee that students do not take more than three years to graduate in order to maintain healthy faculty workloads[3] and positive community perceptions of the program (Lisi, 2013). In addition to the interests and concerns of graduate faculty and students, professional programs undergo processes of accreditation in order to attain external recognition and national positioning. As a result, doctoral completion rates become a valuable commodity for all actors involved.

After the 80s, educational accountability in higher education became a series of institutional practices through which students, faculty, and university officers were forced to fulfill specific performance indicators (e.g., graduation rates) to guarantee that universities are competitive in the global market (Alexander, 2000; Huisman & Currie, 2004; Kearns, 1998; Torres & Schugurensky, 2002). Educational accountability is based on an increased use of "technologies of assessment" such as self-study and evaluation of academic units and institutions, peer review by expert panels, audit by semi-autonomous agencies, performance indicators that are quantifiable, surveys of "client" groups, and public reporting (Mollis & Marginson, 2002; Tierney & Rhoads, 1995). The purpose of making universities accountable for their performance is to respond to public demands for access, high-quality research, engagement of institutions with surrounding communities, and the economic development of a nation (Gappa et al., 2007; Kearns, 1998; Neave, 1980). In a context of educational accountability and efficiency, the pursuit of meaningful learning and personal human development tends to become subordinated to the attainment of specific benchmarks. Both graduate faculty and students have to define their professional and educational goals between two competing agendas: meeting indicators and engaging in learning experiences that lead to human and professional development.

In opposition to concerns with the accomplishment of accountability measures, faculty are concerned about the development of learning opportunities that allow our EdD students to become a scholar-practitioner committed to enacting an equity-based leadership. The appropriation of new knowledge, the development of high-order thinking, and the ability to address social problems are not processes that can be accelerated at will (Danielson et al., 2007; Gorman & Carlson, 1990; King, 2009; Novak, 1990). The development of effective educational leaders who can alter the status quo in our local regions demands faculty and students in EdD programs to engage in experiences through which they can redefine who they are and their forms of intervention in their social context. According to critical multiculturalist perspectives (Kincheloe & Steinberg, 1997; Ladson-Billings & Tate, 1995; Lipsitz, 1995), transforming the larger social structure only becomes possible when individuals learn about themselves by engaging in dialogue and research.

On the one hand, dialogue in communities of practice allows individuals to develop a critical sense of themselves and the world around them by analyzing top-

---

[3] Mainly when there are programs that only have three full time faculty members

ics such as: social positions and access (or lack of it) to power (Rodriguez, 1998), the apparent neutrality and goodness of public instruments of instruction (Ladson-Billings & Tate, 1995), the nature of subjugated knowledge (Kincheloe & Steinberg, 1997), the attributes and purposes of the western cannon (Willinsky, 1998), the racialized nature of society and it intersection with class, gender discrimination, and oppression (Ladson-Billings & Tate, 1995), the structural inequality of capitalism and the centrality of property (Lipsitz, 1995), and the nature of curriculum as an intellectual property (Ladson-Billings & Tate, 1995). On the other hand, students' applied research becomes an instrument for self-transformation. As students engage in critical inquiry in their own workplace they not only learn to foster intellectual virtues but also to address social problems. Critical inquiry aims to question the role played by cultural practices in creating and sustaining certain discourses and social structures (Lipsitz, 1995). According to Willinsky (1998), research experiences afford students a critical distance from their own assumptions and previous education. By developing research skills, students are able to "understand their own education and the education of others as a worthy object of inquiry" (Willinsky, 1998; p. 18).

In EdD programs, instruction that emphasizes dialogue, collaboration, and critical inquiry is required for students to successfully complete the DiP. One of the signature pedagogies that incorporates the elements pointed out by the critical multiculturalist perspective is the Leader-scholar Community (LSC) designed by the College of Teacher Education and Leadership at Arizona State University (Olson & Clark, 2009). The purpose of this pedagogical approach "is to build capacity among leaders in education to introduce small-scale innovations into their practices through action research, to study the consequences, and to make evidence-supported arguments for improvements in local education contexts" (p. 216). The LSC is based on having students working as members of a community of practice. After the first year, students work in four or five-team groups who, during two years, engage in action research under the guidance of two faculty members (the advisor and a committee member) and an accomplished professional outside the university. Graduate students write their DiP on the basis of their experiences conducting action research in local schools, organizations, and communities. The pedagogical approach delineated by faculty in Arizona resembles the practices of other doctoral programs such as ours. We have implemented similar pedagogical approaches aimed to provide continual group support to students (Inquiry seminars), allow students to engage in practical problems that are meaningful to them (problems of practice and displacement experiences), collaborative learning experiences (learning communities). The development of meaningful learning experiences is a highly demanding process since faculty and students have to work around the logics of implementation. Students' tight agendas and faculty' workloads make challenging to deal with two competing realities: Demands for accountability and the need for social impact in local communities and individuals' self-actualization.

CONCLUSIONS

This chapter used a macro-sociological perspective to analyze the context in which graduate faculty and student engage in the DiP. We argue that preparing students to complete the DiP is a process that occurs at the intersection of multiple factors shaping higher education institutions, the academic profession, and the lives of students themselves. When faculty and students work together they have to negotiate various tensions that define the social context they navigate. We emphasize that these tensions are historical, political, and economically driven. In the case of California, the authorization of the EdD programs in the CSU system created an institutional scenario where both faculty and students have to compete for resources, prestige, and job opportunities since the PhD and EdD degrees are, implicit or explicitly, viewed as competing options in the professional marketplace

We emphasize that an authentic understanding of the faculty-student relationship in the EdD program is only possible when we take the time to consider the larger factors that both constrain and encourage the appropriation and construction of knowledge through research-based education. We identify two major dilemmas that faculty and students have to address while developing the DiP. These two dilemmas represent the intersection of the various factors we discuss through the chapter. The first dilemma, research versus applied research, derives from historical and organizational factors shaping the origins of the EdD program and the field of education as an applied-oriented profession. This dilemma involves the negotiation of the curriculum and pedagogical approach to shape the professional identity of the scholar-professional. We emphasize that the negotiation of this dilemma is based on the acknowledgment of a continuum between research and applied research. The second dilemma, meaningful learning versus accountability, derives from the exaltation of accountability principles and the culture of assessment that frames the learning experiences in higher education institutions. This dilemma demands faculty and students to work within challenging time constraints and to engage in dialogue and research in order to build their professional identity. We emphasize that the negotiation of this dilemma is based on the development of signature pedagogies that seek to integrate authentic, socially just research opportunities at the same time that encourage degree completion.

This chapter emphasizes that the development of the EdD DiP is a process for the negotiation of professional, disciplinary, organizational, historical, economic, and personal factors. Faculty work in an EdD program demands individuals' creativity, social skills, and emotional endurance to find strategies to learn in the midst of a changing and demanding work environment. The future development of effective pedagogical approaches for the EdD program requires a critical understanding of the practical conditions that graduate faculty and students navigate on a daily basis as members of a professional community.

REFERENCES

Alexander, F. K. (2000). The changing face of accountability: Monitoring and assessing institutional performance in higher education. *The Journal of Higher Education, 71*(4), 411–431.

Almond, G. (1974). Public higher education in California:1950–1970. *Bulletin of the American Academy of Arts and Sciences, 27*(6), 7–15.

Alpert, R. M. (1980). Professionalism and educational reform: The case of Hampshire College. *The Journal of Higher Education, 51*(5), 497–518.

Altbach, P. G. (2001). The international crisis? The American professoriate in comparative perspective. In S. R. Graubard (Ed.), *The American academic profession* (pp. 315–338). New Brunswick, NJ: Transactions Publisher.

Arditti, S. (2005). *SB 724 (Scott), As amended on April 5, 2005. Scheduled for hearing in the Senate Education Committee on April 13, 2005 Position: Opposed.* Retrieved from http://www.ucop.edu/acadinit/mastplan/edd/sb724_uc_position2.pdf

Baez, B. (2000). Race-related service and faculty of color: Conceptualizing critical agency in academe. *Higher Education, 39*(3), 363–391.

Ball, D. L. (1993). With an eye on the mathematical horizon: Dilemmas of teaching elementary school mathematics. *The Elementary School Journal, 93*(4), 373–397.

Barlow, A. L. (2007). *Collaborations for social justice: Professionals, publics, and policy change.* Lanham, MD: Rowman & Littlefield.

Belzer, A. (2004). "It's not like normal school": The role of prior learning contexts in adult learning. *Adult Education Quarterly, 55*(1), 41–59.

Bendor, J. (1994). The fields of bureaucracy and public administration: Basic and applied research. *Journal of Public Administration Research and Theory, 4*(1), 27–39.

Boardman, P. C., & Ponomariov, B. L. (2007). Reward systems and NSF university research centers: The Impact of tenure on university scientists' valuation of applied and commercially relevant research. *The Journal of Higher Education, 78*(1), 51–70.

Boyce, B. A. (2012). Redefining the EdD: Seeking a separate identity. *Quest, 64*(1), 24–33.

Boyer, E. L. (1990). *Scholarship reconsidered: Priorities of the Professorate* San Francisco, CA: Jossey-Bass.

Boyer, E. L. (1991). Highlights of the Carnegie Report: The scholarship of teaching from "Scholarship reconsidered: Priorities of the professoriate." *College Teaching, 39*(1), 11–13.

Braxton, J. M. (1983). Department colleagues and individual faculty publication productivity. *Review of Higher Education, 6*(2), 115.

Burgess, T. F. (1996). Planning the academic's workload: Different approaches to allocating work to University academics. *Higher Education, 32*(1), 63–75.

Callan, P. M. (2009). *California higher education: The Master Plan, and the erosion of college opportunity* (National Center Report #09-1). San Jose, CA. Retrieved from http://www.highereducation.org/reports/cal_highered/

Chaves, C. (2006). Involvement, development, and retention: Theoretical foundations and potential extensions for adult community college students. *Community College Review, 34*(2), 139–152.

Chen, L.-K., Kim, Y. S., Moon, P., & Merriam, S. B. (2008). A review and critique of the portrayal of older adult learners in adult education journals, 1980–2006. *Adult Education Quarterly, 59*(1), 3–21.

Clark, B. R. (2001). Small worlds, different worlds: The uniquenesses and troubles of American academic professions In S. R. Graubard (Ed.), *The American academic profession* (pp. 21–42). New Brunswick, NJ: Transactions.

Creamer, E. G. (1999). Knowledge production, publication productivity, and intimate academic partnerships. *The Journal of Higher Education, 70*(3), 261–277.

Crossan, B., Field, J., Gallacher, J., & Merrill, B. (2003). Understanding participation in learning for non-traditional adult learners: Learning careers and the construction of learning identities. *British Journal of Sociology of Education, 24*(1), 55–67.

Cuban, L. (1984). Policy and research dilemmas in the teaching of reasoning: Unplanned design. *Review of Educational Research, 54*(4), 655–681.

Cuban, L. (1992). Managing dilemmas while building professional communities. *Educational Researcher, 21*(1), 4–11.

Danielson, J. A., Mills, E. M., Vermeer, P. J., Preast, V. A., Young, K. M., Christopher, M. M., & Bender, H. S. (2007). Characteristics of a cognitive tool that helps students learn diagnostic problem solving. *Education Tech Research Dev, 55*, 499–520.

Davis, S. H. (2010). *Analysis of site-level administrator and superintendent certification requirements in the USA*. Paper presented at the Administrative Services Credential Advisory Panel, Pomona, California. Retrieved from http://www.ctc.ca.gov/educator-prep/asc/asc-analysis-of-usa-requirements.pdf

Davison, G. C. (1997). The mutual enrichment of basic and applied research in psychological science and practice. *Psychological Science, 8*(3), 194–197.

Deem, R. (2001). Globalisation, new managerialism, academic capitalism and entrepreneurialism in universities: Is the local dimension still important? *Comparative Education, 37*(1), 7–20.

Donaldson, J. F., & Townsend, B. K. (2007). Higher education journals' discourse about adult undergraduate students. *The Journal of Higher Education, 78*(1), 27–50.

Dundar, H., & Lewis, D. R. (1998). Determinants of research productivity in higher education. *Research in Higher Education, 39*(6), 607–631.

Eagan, K., & Garvey, J. C. (2015). Stressing out: Connecting race, gender, and stress with faculty productivity. *The Journal of Higher Education, 86*(6), 923–951.

Everett, J. E., & Entrekin, L. V. (1994). Changing attitudes of Australian academics. *Higher Education, 27*(2), 203–227.

Fairweather, J. S. (1989). Academic research and instruction: The industrial connection. *The Journal of Higher Education, 60*(4), 388–407.

Fairweather, J. S. (2002). The mythologies of faculty productivity: Implications for institutional policy and decision making. *The Journal of Higher Education, 73*(1), 26–48.

Foote, P. D. (1965). Government-financed research, basic and applied. *Proceedings of the American Philosophical Society, 109*(2), 57–62.

Fox, M. F., & Mohapatra, S. (2007). Social-organizational characteristics of work and publication productivity among academic scientists in doctoral-granting departments. *The Journal of Higher Education, 78*(5), 542–571.

Gappa, J. M., Austin, A., & Trice, A. G. (2007). *Rethinking faculty work: Higher education's strategic imperative.* San Francisco, CA: Jossey-Bass.

Gardner, S. K. (2008). "What's too much and what's too little?": The process of becoming an independent researcher in doctoral education. *The Journal of Higher Education, 79*(3), 326–350.

Giancola, J. K., Grawitch, M. J., & Borchert, D. (2009). Dealing with the stress of college: A model for adult students. *Adult Education Quarterly, 59*(3), 246–263.

Goodwin, T. H., & Sauer, R. D. (1995). Life cycle productivity in academic research: Evidence from cumulative publication. Histories of academic economists. *Southern Economic Journal, 61*(3), 728–743.

Gorman, M. E., & Carlson, W. B. (1990). Interpreting invention as a cognitive process: The case of Alexander Graham Bell, Thomas Edison, and the telephone. *Science, Technology, & Human Values, 15*(2), 131–164.

Grubb, W. N., Worthen, H., Byrd, B., Webb, E., Badway, N., Case, C., & Villenueve, J. C. (1999). *Honored but invisible: An inside look at teaching in community colleges.* New York: Routledge.

Gumport, P. J. (1997). Public universities as academic workplaces. *Daedalus, 126*(4), 113–136.

Gumport, P. J., & Snydman, S. K. (2002). The formal organization of knowledge: An analysis of academic structure. *The Journal of Higher Education, 73*(3), 375–408.

Honan, J. P., & Teferra, D. (2001). The US academic profession: Key policy challenges. *Higher Education, 41*(1/2), 183–203.

Huisman, J., & Currie, J. (2004). Accountability in higher education: Bridge over troubled water? *Higher Education, 48*(4), 529–551.

Jacobs, J. A., & Winslow, S. E. (2004). Overworked faculty: Job stresses and family demands. *Annals of the American Academy of Political and Social Science, 596,* 104–129.

Joyner, L. M. (2003). Applied research in the pursuit of justice: Creating change in the community and the academy. *Social Justice, 30*(4), 5–20.

Kasworm, C. (1990). Adult undergraduates in higher education: A review of past research perspectives. *Review of Educational Research, 60*(3), 345–372.

Kasworm, C. (1993). Adult higher education from an international perspective. *Higher Education, 25*(4), 411–423.

Kasworm, C. (2003). Adult meaning making in the undergraduate classroom. *Adult Education Quarterly, 53*(2), 81–98.

Kasworm, C. (2005). Adult student identity in an intergenerational community college classroom. *Adult Education Quarterly, 56*(1), 3–20.

Kasworm, C. (2010). Adult learners in a research university: Negotiating undergraduate student identity. *Adult Education Quarterly, 60*(2), 143–160.

Kearns, K. P. (1998). Institutional accountability in higher education: A strategic approach. *Public Productivity & Management Review, 22*(2), 140–156.

Kerr, C. (2001). *The gold and the blue: A personal memoir of the University of California, 1949–1967* (vol. 1). Berkeley, CA: University of California Press.

Kincheloe, J. L., & Steinberg, S. R. (1997). *Changing multiculturalism.* Philadelphia, PA: Philadelphia Open University Press.

King, P. M. (2009). Principles of development and developmental change underlying theories of cognitive and moral development. *Journal of College Student Development, 50*(6), 597–620.

Kuhn, T. S. (1977). *The essential tension: Selected studies in scientific tradition and change.* Chicago, IL: University of Chicago Press.

Kuipers, J. L. (2011). PhD and EdD degrees for mid-career professionals: Fielding graduate university. *New Directions for Adults and Continuing Education, 129,* 63–73.

Ladson-Billings, G., & Tate, W. (1995). Toward a critical race theory of education. *Teachers College Record, 97*(1), 47–69.

Lane, J.-E. (1985). Academic profession in academic organization. *Higher Education, 14*(3), 241–268.

Levinson, B. A., & Holland, D. C. (1996). The cultural production of the educated person. In B. A. Levinson, D. E. Foley, & D. C. Holland (Eds.), *The cultural production of the educated person. Critical ethnographies of schooling and local practice* (pp. 1–54). New York: State University of New York Press.

Lipsitz, G. (1995). The possessive investment in whiteness: Racialized social democracy and the "white" problem in American studies. *American Quarterly, 47*(3), 369–387.

Lisi, R. D. (2013). Reflection, reconstruction, and transformation of the EdD: A dean's perspective. *Planning and Changing, 44*(3/4), 127–139.

Lomnitz, L. A., & Chazaro, L. (1999). Basic, applied and technological research: Computer science and applied mathematics at the National Autonomous University of Mexico. *Social Studies of Science, 29*(1), 113–134.

Martin, E. (1999). *Changing academic work.* Ballmoor, Buckingham: The Society for Research into Higher Education and Open University Press.

Massey, W. E. (1997). Uncertainties in the changing academic profession. *Daedalus, 126*(4), 67–94.

McElroy, W. D. (1977). The global age: Roles of basic and applied research. *Science, 196*(4287), 267–270.

Mollis, M., & Marginson, S. (2002). The assessment of universities in Argentina and Australia: Between autonomy and heteronomy. *Higher Education, 43*(3), 311–330.

Montero-Hernandez, V. (2010). *The Construction of professional identity and pathways of participation of full time faculty members in university restructuring in Mexico.* PhD Dissertation, University of California, Riverside. Riverside, California.

Montero-Hernandez, V., & Cerven, C. (2012). Adult student development: The agentic approach and its relationship to the community college context. In J. Levin & S. Kater (Eds.), *Understanding Community Colleges.* New York: Routledge/Taylor Francis.

Nafstad, H. E. (1982). Applied versus basic social research: A question of amplified complexity. *Acta Sociologica, 25*(3), 259–267.

Neave, G. (1980). Accountability and control. *European Journal of Education, 15*(1), 49–60.

Nelson, J. K., & Coorough, C. (1994). Content analysis of the PhD versus EdD dissertation. *The Journal of Experimental Education, 62*(2), 158–168.

Neumann, Y., & Finaly-Neumann, E. (1990). The support-stress paradigm and faculty research publication. *The Journal of Higher Education, 61*(5), 565–580.

Niiniluoto, I. (1993). The aim and structure of applied research. *Erkenntnis, 38*(1), 1–21.

Normore, A., & Cook, L. (2011). The new "proposed" doctoral degree in educational leadership (Ed.D.) at a comprehensive university in southern California. In D. M. Pérez, S. M. Fain, & J. J. Slater (Eds.), *Higher education and human capital: Re/thinking the Doctorate in America* (pp. 103–127). Rotterdam, The Netherlands: Springer Science & Business Media.

Novak, J. D. (1990). Concept maps and Vee diagrams: Two metacognitive tools to facilitate meaningful learning. *Instructional Science, 19*, 29–52.

Nyden, P. (2003). Academic incentives for faculty participation in community-based participatory research. *Jounal of Internal General Medicine, 1*, 576–585.

Olsen, D. (1993). Work satisfaction and stress in the first and third year of academic appointment. *The Journal of Higher Education, 64*(4), 453–471.

Olson, K., & Clark, C. M. (2009). A signature pedagogy in doctoral education: The leader-scholar community. *Educational Researcher, 38*(3), 216–221.

Orfield, G. (2011). *The CSU crisis and California's future*. Retrieved from www.civilrightsproject.ucla.edu

Perlberg, A., & Keinan, G. (1986). Sources of stress in academe: The Israeli case. *Higher Education, 15*(1/2), 73–88.

Pielke, R. (2012). "Basic research" as a political symbol. *Minerva, 50*(3), 339–361.

Ponton, M. K., Derrick, M. G., & Carr, P. B. (2005). The relationship between resourcefulness and persistence in adult autonomous learning. *Adult Education Quarterly, 55*(2), 116–128.

Prins, E., Toso, B. W., & Schafft, K. A. (2009). "It feels like a little family to me." Social interaction and support among women in adult education and family literacy. *Adult Education Quarterly, 59*(4), 335–352.

Reagan, M. D. (1967). Basic and applied research: A meaningful distinction? *Science, 155*(3768), 1383–1386.

Rhoades, G. (2001). Managing productivity in an academic institution: Rethinking the whom, which, what, and whose of productivity. *Research in Higher Education, 42*(5), 619–632.

Rhode, D. L. (2006). *In pursuit of knowledge: Scholars, status, and academic culture*. Stanford, CA: Stanford University Press.

Sawyer, R. D. (2013). Learning to walk the talk: Designing a teacher leadership EdD program as a laboratory of practice. *Planning and Changing, 44*(3/4), 208–220.

Schwebel, D. C., Plumert, J. M., & Pick, H. L. (2000). Integrating basic and applied developmental research: A new model for the twenty first century. *Child Development, 71*(1), 222–230.

Sheckley, B. G., Donaldson, M. L., Mayer, A. P., & Lemons, R. W. (2010). An Ed. D. program based on principles of how adults learn best. In *Educational Leadership Preparation* (pp. 173–202). New York: Palgrave Macmillan.

Schoorman, D. (2014). How should researchers act in the context of social injustice? Reflections on the role of the researcher as a social justice leader. In I. Bogotch & C. M. Shields (Eds.), *International Handbook of Educational Leadership and Social (In)Justice* (vol. 1, pp. 217–232). New York: Springer.

Sissel, P. A., Birdsong, M. A., & Silaski, B. A. (1997). *A room of one's own: A phenomenological investigation of class, age, gender, and politics of institutional change regarding adult students on campus*. Paper presented at the 38th Annual Adult Education Research Conference, Oklahoma State University, Stillwater, OK.

Sissel, P. A., Hansman, C. A., & Kasworm, C. E. (2001). The politics of neglect: Adult learners in higher education. In C. A. H. P. A. Sissel (Ed.), *Understanding and negotiating the political landscape of adult education* (vol. 91, pp. 17–27): San Francisco, CA: Jossey-Bass.

Slaughter, S., & Rhoades, G. (2004). *Academic capitalism and the new economy: Markets, state, and higher education*. Baltimore, MD: The Johns Hopkins University Press.

Spurr, S. H. (1970). *Academic degree structures: Innovative approaches*. San Francisco, CA: McGraw Hill.

Storey, V. A., & Maughan, B. D. (2014). *Beyond a definition: Designing and specifying Dissertation in Practice (DiP) models*: Pittsburgh, PA: The Carnegie Project on the Education Doctorate.

Taylor, P. G. (1999). *Making sense of academic life. Academics, universities and change.* Philadelphia, PA: The Society for Research into Higher Education and Open University Press.

Taylor, S. W., Fender, B. F., & Burke, K. G. (2006). Unraveling the academic productivity of economists: The opportunity costs of teaching and service *Southern Economic Journal, 72*(4), 846–859.

Thompson, C. J., & Dey, E. L. (1998). Pushed to the margins: Sources of stress for African American college and university faculty. *The Journal of Higher Education, 69*(3), 324–345.

Thorsen, E. J. (1996). Stress in academe: What bothers professors? *Higher Education, 31*(4), 471–489.

Tien, F. F., & Blackburn, R. T. (1996). Faculty rank system, research motivation, and faculty research productivity: Measure refinement and theory testing. *The Journal of Higher Education, 67*(1), 2–22.

Tierney, W. G., & Rhoads, R. A. (1995). The culture of assessment In J. Smyth (Ed.), *Academic Work: The changing labour process in higher education* (pp. 99–111). Bristol, PA: Society for Research into Higher Education & Open University Press.

Torres, C. A., & Schugurensky, D. (2002). The political economy of higher education in the era of neoliberal globalization: Latin America in comparative perspective. *Higher Education, 43*, 429–455.

Vaccaro, A., & Lovell, C. D. (2010). Inspiration from home: Understanding family as key to adult women's self-investment. *Adult Education Quarterly, 60*(2), 161–176.

Vaupel, J. W. (1975). Structuring an ethical decision dilemma. *Soundings: An Interdisciplinary Journal, 58*(4), 506–524.

Volkmann, M. J., & Anderson, M. A. (1998). Creating professional Identity: Dilemmas and metaphors of a first-year chemistry teacher. *Science Education, 82*(3), 293–310.

Willinsky, J. (1998). *Learning to divide the world. Education at Empire's ends.* Minneapolis, MN: The University of Minnesota Press.

CHAPTER 5

TRANSFORMING SCHOOLS— FROM THE INSIDE OUT!

Jacqueline Hawkins, Kristi L. Santi, Johanna L. Thorpe,
Janeen R. S. Antonelli, and Elliott J. Witney

A good way to rid one's self of a sense of discomfort is to do something. That uneasy, dissatisfied feeling is actual force vibrating out of order; it may be turned to practical account by giving proper expression to its creative character.

—*William Morris (1909, p. 1454)*

Every day educational institutions feel increasing pressure to educate <u>all</u> students to attain higher educational goals. Expectations are high, resources are limited, and the needs are urgent. On the one hand, society wants its graduates to attain more knowledge, to become better workers, and to be increasingly more tech-savvy; on the other hand, limited resources and more diverse students often stress the current educational systems. Education systems are charged to change the way content is delivered by using evidence-based best practices; to support students to achieve academic success at ever-greater levels of sophistication; and, to ensure that graduates possess the essential skills necessary for future careers.

For some of the larger cities across the United States the pressure to deliver graduates who have attained these higher educational goals is keenly felt. Public

Exploring the Impact of the Dissertation in Practice, pages 73–88.

73

dissatisfaction with student outcomes, large educational enrollments, savvy business leadership, and the economic impact to communities of quality education are some of the drivers of change. In the Houston area, **one of the most diverse cities in the nation, our graduates face the daily challenges of educating students and leading schools in a Gateway city where: the majority of students are African American and Hispanic; the majority qualify for federal FARM; the majority attend community college rather than 4-year institutions (Texas Education Agency, TEA, 2016); and, the business community is focusing its efforts on innovative solutions that show promise.** As the fourth largest city in the nation, with 1.2+ million K–12 students taught within a 75–mile radius of campus, 54+ school districts, and a shifting demographic the demand for different approaches is high, is urgent, and is essential. Business is not as usual in this business city; there is discomfort with the *status quo*, and the charge to create something different resonates.

At the heart of successful changes in educational systems is the need to build leadership capacity at all levels of the education pipeline (Fullan, 2016). Increased expectations in the K–12 educational systems reach back into higher education preparation programs—especially for school leaders. With those changes in K–12 expectations, we see a sea change in the skills necessary for effective leadership preparation. Leaders must acquire the capacity to respond to the needs of an ever-growing and diverse set of learners and do so within the context of changing policies and limited funding. Leaders must develop and activate diverse networks, engage in multiple methods of inquiry, and focus on isolating and responding to challenges that face their communities **(Bryk, Gomez, Grunow, & LeMahieu, 2015)**.

DISSERTATION IN PRACTICE (DiP): URBAN IMPACT

The University of Houston (UH) has engaged with its community as part of the solution for public and public-charter education in the region. **Given Houston's context, it was important to design and implement an educational framework that would not only prepare leaders with both wider and deeper capacity but also prepare leaders in many more fields who could engage with the skills necessary to implement effective systems change.** The re-design of an EdD in Special Education resulted in the UH Education Doctorate (EdD) in Professional Leadership— Special Populations. The degree targets educational leaders at all levels (i.e., classroom, building, division, discipline, or district) and provides instruction, research, and practice that equip leaders to deal with the challenges of the modern education system in relevant, rigorous, and both personally and professionally transformative ways.

The program re-design relied heavily on the work of Shulman (2005). Initially, diversity, urban education, and ensuring access for students who struggle provided the context of our signature pedagogy. That focus has evolved to represent evidence-based best practices that support the success of all students in Early

Literacy, Professional Development for Educators, and Transition through the PK–20 Education Pipeline.

Our program delivery system engages both a cohort model and a critical friends model. Student cohorts are both horizontally and vertically integrated. Horizontal integration occurs when cohorts are taught and network with their cohort members. Vertical integration is achieved when more advanced cohort students partner with initial cohort members to ensure that role models and motivating milestones are witnessed. Cohort groups also are crossed-connected with our Ph.D. cohorts to ensure that the realities of practice (and practicality) can be infused into research. Critical friends protocols (NSRF, 2012) help foster engagement within and across cohorts and provide a format for teamwork and expectations.

As Special Educators, we've focused on learning and improvement science to illustrate how people learn, how instruction and professional development can help people to change, and how to support our EdD students to ask relevant questions of practice that help them change the outcomes in the communities in which they work—and to know when that change occurs. Our graduates focus their efforts on challenges that are relevant to their communities, have the skills to engage in multiple research methods, and design action plans that have the potential to change the field of education. Our doctoral students and graduates are changing their contexts for the better, and we share some of their work in the next section.

Three graduate students present how they have integrated the tenets of Improvement Science into their Dissertation in Practice (DiP) to drive improvement through disciplined inquiry, change their personal mindsets concerning the potential impact of educational innovations, and prepare them to lead systemic reform. Each will describe how their doctoral work has been a transformative experience, both personally and professionally, that results in a capstone project that not only helps them to resolve complex problem of practice but also changes their thought processes, professional identity, and future work agenda.

The three capstone projects have impacted diverse contexts: one studies the mindset (Dweck, 2006) of middle school students who are described as underrepresented minority (URM) students; the second studies self-regulated learning (Pintrich & DeGroot, 1990) for first-generation students in college; the third studies an alternative school—specifically, a mobile school (Partnership for 21st Century Skills, 2008)—where students (the majority of whom are URM) access museums and other community organizations as they engage with the curriculum.

Improvement Science has taught them that education needs to find a better way to support student success; a better way to support social justice in our schools; and a better way to inform leaders. Additionally, Improvement Science dovetails well with both critical leadership and social justice—essential to graduate success in a gateway city.

SCHOLARLY PRACTITIONER EXPERIENCE: *ELLIOTT J. WITNEY*

From the moment I began working in public education in 1997, I prided myself on being an evidence-based field practitioner regardless of the role I held. I have taught, coached, led a school, supervised schools, built PK12 academic strategy, supported charter school growth, led organizational change efforts in a school system serving tens of thousands of kids, trained dozens of school founders, hundreds of school leaders, and thousands of teachers. In every role, I tried to use an evidence base and proof to drive decision-making. I read voraciously, studied data, and looked inside and outside the field of education for insights about how best to do the work.

I have also taken part in numerous improvement efforts at every level of schools and school systems. As a teacher, I visited other classrooms inside and outside my school and at high-performing public and independent schools to learn how to teach more effectively and glean insights about what is possible. As a school leader of a college prep middle school, we studied how our students performed in college prep high schools and used what we learned to inform improvements to our model. When we learned that our exiting middle school students were not competing with writers in elite college-preparatory high schools, for example, I helped found and led a research project focused on improving writing. In addition to writing, we increased our focus on STEM-focused electives like Robotics and Electrical Engineering and changed our approach to math instruction as a reaction to long-term poor performance.

More recently, I have taken district leadership roles in a diverse, traditional school district that had adopted a single, focused goal: to double the number of graduates who ultimately complete a post-secondary credential of some sort—be it a technical certificate, military training, a two-year or four-year degree. A goal like this revealed new challenges to address. This, in turn, has forced the system to study new ways of operating, new approaches to instruction, and innovative solutions. Despite an existing focus on evidence-based decision-making and improvement efforts, the DiP has prepared me to do both far more effectively.

Finding the Fit

The ambitious goal and the complexity of the work required a leader who was better prepared. I looked for a graduate program that would prepare me more effectively to understand and ultimately address an array of complex educational challenges that have not yet been solved. I had been looking for a program that balanced the impossible—depth with breadth, theoretical with practical. I wanted to learn how to learn deeply about a large number of different relevant aspects of public education, and I wanted to understand the theoretical underpinnings of education and reform while also learning how to do something about it. Given the design of the program and the accompanying coursework, I found that balance. Essentially, I had found the program that fit both my needs and my wants exactly.

After a soft start comprising a single course in the EdD program at UH, I committed fully to the program during the fall of 2014.

Something to Talk About

The hardest part of the DiP at first was the topic focus. While some of my fellow cohort members joined the program with a clear picture of their research questions or problems of practice, I joined with less clarity. In part this is because my work touched an entire school system and focused on postsecondary completion as the goal. I had already grown familiar with research suggesting that rigorous academic coursework in high school is a helpful predictor of postsecondary success; and, as a practitioner, I knew that some rising ninth grade students opted out of rigorous, advanced academic coursework. I began wondering what insights could be gleaned from social psychology to inform a holistic, systems strategy to increase postsecondary completion rates. Over time and after numerous productive discussions with my advisor, professors, and colleagues in my cohort, I found my focus—the psychological factors affecting many children as they transition from middle to high school. The program required that I study this literature deeply. Depth gave me the clarity to isolate a single problem of practice and related variables rather than studying everything.

My research ultimately settled on the power and promise of brief mindset interventions that can be integrated into a holistic reform strategy focused not only on students but also teachers. I learned through the literature review that for some students under certain conditions, a growth mindset could be developed. Having a growth mindset positively affects performance outcomes, too, and this is particularly important during key life transitions such as middle school to high school. Also, it seems clear that indirect teacher behaviors—the messages our behaviors send regardless of what we are saying—can influence one's mindset—fixed or growth. If a teacher emphasizes the importance of trying hard or asking for help when work gets difficult (a growth mindset) but always intervenes when a student encounters difficulty, a student might be more willing to give up than demonstrate resilience. Because of this, a plan that would work in practice cannot just focus on mindset interventions; it must also include efforts to address teacher behaviors.

Learning to Walk the Talk

Several elements of the DiP inform my current work, but none more so than the level of research rigor and agility I have developed as a result of exposure to and careful analysis of a multitude of research methodologies. Early in my teaching career, I had the good fortune of being trained by mentors to value evidence-based practices over others. As a result, I have long been drawn to the literature base of a strategy or technique educators attempted to use in the field. As a matter of fact, colleagues have long joked with me that my favorite statement in trainings and conversations was, "Prove it"—prove that something has worked.

Through the coursework and assignments of the DiP, I have developed a stronger ability to evaluate the quality of the myriad of programs and practices that claim to be evidence-based in the field of education. We have been exposed to numerous research methodologies in a variety of educational contexts (some relevant to my research study, but most outside that scope) and been challenged to evaluate the quality and universal capability of research. In addition to reading and analyzing hundreds of research articles, we have also been exposed to case studies of schools and school systems that adopted evidence-based programs and practices that may have worked in the original context but did not transfer; and, we have been challenged to understand why. As a practitioner, this has helped me in my daily work because I ask better, more targeted questions. In having developed the instinct to do so, my ability to make good decisions on behalf of schools and a school system has improved. I am also now able to help others do the same.

The cohort structure of the coursework has fostered learning and development applicable to my work as a practitioner, too. In part, this is because I have joined the members of my cohort on their learning journeys from the beginning—I have watched as their broad interests and what fascinates or perplexes them as practitioners have turned into precise research questions, a comprehensive literature review, an aligned research methodology, and thoughtful analysis. Although I am conducting only one study, pragmatically I have been forced to learn in depth about many others. Through this, I have learned about some of the challenges and trade-offs associated with different research questions and methodologies. This has strengthened my ability to help schools and the school system solve complex educational challenges rigorously because so many of the challenges we face mirror something studied by a cohort member.

The final chapter of our DiP, the action plan component, has required me to consider how to craft an evidenced-based strategic plan that might lead to enduring improvement in classrooms, schools, or school systems. To strengthen our ability to create these plans thoughtfully, we have been exposed to rigorous research focused on areas like adaptive leadership, coaching and consultation, adult learning, and other areas that improve schools. We have been given challenging tasks that are relevant to practitioners and been asked to use a rigorous evidence base to make decisions. Projects I had done in the field for a number of years—creating the budget and professional development plan for a school, for example—were done differently, given I had learned so much about the value of comprehensive needs assessments and shaping decisions with an evidence base.

A New Way to Walk

Many of the headliner challenges we face in education today appear to mirror those of the past, on the surface; in the context of our dynamic world today, though, a surface level understanding of these challenges does not accurately portray the reality. Achievement gaps have persisted across lines of advantage for decades and as such, much has been written about globalization and the need to develop 21ˢᵗ-century skills. However, without holistic changes to the way schooling is delivered these achievement gaps could widen irreparably in some parts of our nation. Addressing challenges like this head-on, at and beneath the surface, requires a level of rigor in research, theory, and practice that programs like the DiP have fostered.

In my work moving forward, we intend to leverage the power of rigorous but agile research to address the large number of different, complex challenges we face. We know that there are some related challenges—e.g., structural, psychological—that must be resolved to ensure our children graduate high school ready for postsecondary success. I am taking what I have learned through this program to scale an organizational strategy for research in practice that aligns those problems with thoughtful research questions and the right methodology. Having been exposed to and analyzed so many different methodologies, I feel more comfortable helping to lead those efforts.

Although we will implement some comprehensive, whole-district strategies to drive systemic improvement and some whole-school strategies to improve whole campuses, we also plan to leverage the power of a multitude of research methodologies simultaneously. We want to learn and scale promising innovative practices as quickly as possible. Rather than designing comprehensive, multi-variable programs that consider a large number of research questions spread across hundreds of students or multiple campuses simultaneously, we are already beginning to pilot "tiny research"—new, rapid-iteration research that starts with a tiny sample size and scales to others at an appropriate rate, driven by learning and organizational capacity. The problems of practice will drive the sample and methodology, and the results will drive the scaling mechanism.

SCHOLARLY PRACTITIONER EXPERIENCE:
JANEEN R. S. ANTONELLI

Over the past four years, I have had the distinct privilege of serving as an adjunct-turned-faculty instructor in the College of Education at UH, and have dedicated myself in that role to educating and empowering a diverse population of incoming and outgoing undergraduate students to develop and achieve personal, academic, and career goals—often on the path to becoming professional educators themselves. I am passionate about my work and find tremendous purpose in collaboratively seeking innovative and effective ways to help all students become self-directed and self-regulated 21ˢᵗ-century learners as a means to achieve success in college and beyond. So, when the opportunity arose to advance my knowledge and skills as a doctoral student in professional leadership for special populations, it was imperative that the added commitment reinforce, not replace, this daily work.

An alternative to the academia-bound Ph.D., the CPED-influenced EdD in Professional Leadership—Special Populations program at UH offers a highly relevant and rigorous "real world" approach to affecting the transformative change our nation's education system needs. The EdD is framed by the tenets of Improvement Science and guided by a distinct set of Shulman (2005) and CPED-informed design concepts that proved to be the perfect fit. The program is action-oriented and cohort-based, culminating in a capstone doctoral thesis aimed at naming, framing, and solving a complex problem of practice embedded in our work as practitioners. While the final EdD product follows the general chapter format of a traditional Ph.D. (i.e., Introduction, Literature Review, Methods, Results, and Discussion sections), it is the distinctive final chapter—the Action Plan—that differentiates this degree from others. Using theory and research as a foundation to understand *what* works, the EdD doctoral thesis is a dynamic document developed as a tool to bridge the *what* with the *how* and *for whom* a practice works in context—equipping each graduate to drive improvement through disciplined inquiry to ensure on-going, evidence-based change in student outcomes for the special populations in our respective professional settings.

From the first day our cohort of nine met in 2014, our doctoral theses were fostered by a repeated invitation to "make this content your own" through critical reflection and analysis, scholarly inquiry, and extensive networking within and across cohorts to develop an authentic learning community. Throughout the program, the faculty coordinated invaluable coursework and activities—blending practical wisdom with professional knowledge and skills—to support our active learning and development as scholarly practitioners. From mindsets and methodologies to Learning Science and legal issues, the breadth and depth of our professional preparation opened me to new perspectives on and a promising approach to educational reform that had an immediate and lasting impact on my work as a scholar, a teacher, and a leader. In fact, while many people still may view the EdD as a sort of *PhD-lite*, I have come to believe that, in many ways, the degree might more aptly be considered a *PhD-Plus*—the highest quality degree for equipping educational practitioners to affect real change in and beyond the classroom.

Reflecting on the growth this educational journey has afforded me, my mind flashes back to my first assignment as a new doctoral student when I was tasked with investigating the global, national, state, local, and institutional contexts and conditions impacting various outcomes for an assigned special population as the foundation for developing a funded project proposal. Do what? I remember the heat rising and the color draining from my face as I read the online instructions before the first day of class. Maybe I had made a mistake. I was clearly in over my head. What made me think I could do doctoral work when I hadn't been a student for over 20 years? It would not be the last time that I asked myself some version of this pernicious question. Each time I felt like an imposter—or heard the word *can't* sneak into my thoughts—something in the course content, a comment from another cohort member, or consultation with my program chair would resonate with my tacit concerns and bolster my confidence. Through this iterative process of challenging my perceptions and gaining new perspectives and successes on my transformative journey to becoming a scholarly practitioner, my assumptions about adult learning and how to improve it—both personally and professionally—have been repeatedly tested and refined. As it turns out, this approach of systematically learning by doing—in which difficulties are desirable and failure is informative—is touted by the authors of *Make It Stick: The Science of Successful Learning* as the optimal way to achieve deeper, more durable learning (Brown, Roediger, & McDaniel, 2014) and is advanced by Improvement Science as a new and necessary paradigm to achieve quality and efficacy reliably at scale (Bryk et al., 2015).

Guided by these cornerstones of the EdD program, my doctoral work concentrated on a complex problem of practice related to the widening performance gaps across lines of advantage that threaten our nation's future. At UH, a rapidly diversifying student population has brought with them unique challenges that contribute to persistence and graduation rates that remain well below the national average. For first generation college students (FGCS) in particular, success has not kept pace with access—with reverberating consequences. The first in their families to attend college, FCGS tend to drop out earlier, finish later and perform more poorly on various academic outcomes than their continuing generation (CGCS) counterparts. Scrutinizing the literature on this problem revealed several overlapping sources of variability in outcomes for this special population. These were associated with their differing class backgrounds and evidence that many struggles students experience can be linked to deficits in self-regulated learning (SRL) processes—a responsive leverage point for academic improvement. In response, my work explores the SRL characteristics of FGCS to inform the design and delivery of effective SRL intervention using a systems perspective to understand what works for whom and under what conditions (Bryk et al., 2015).

Problem-centered and user-specific, the FGCSs and their SRL instructors are active participants in the improvement feedback loop via a semester-length incremental learning project (Plan-Do-Study-Act) based on pre-formative self-assessment scores using the 2nd edition Learning and Study Strategies Inventory, LASSI, (Weinstein & Palmer, 2002). Because we are only able to improve at scale what we can measure, students set a primary S.M.A.R.T. goal to improve an academic issue based on their LASSI scores, then select specific, evidence-based strategies as working theories that they monitor and adapt throughout the implementation phase.

My DiP culminates in a professional development action plan that—through the improvement efforts of a networked improvement community—aims to produce changes in classroom-based instructional practices that can be linked to advances in students' SRL and overall postsecondary achievement (grades, persistence, and degree attainment)—systematically scaling to campus-wide instructors across disciplines and inviting participation of student affairs and other personnel advocating for FGCS success across universities nationwide.

A Journey Shared

As emphasized in Improvement Science, we can accomplish more together through collective problem solving than even the best can achieve alone. Typically a lone learner, I was won over right away by the program's support structure of faculty and cohorts, finding a sense of belonging and passionate purpose alongside like-minded people dedicated to the practical application of scholarship to improve education for all. As a critical friends group, our cohort advanced each other's written work through formal protocols of reflective feedback. In class, collaborative assignments allowed the cross-pollination of ideas and experience. Through phone calls, texts, and meet-ups, we forged friendships and found allies with front row seats to how Improvement Science principles can be applied effectively across different educational settings to address contextualized problems of practice. Sharing articles, resources, training opportunities, and more, we networked together for the benefit of all.

Reflections on Leadership and the Future

Teaching and learning as a scholarly practitioner in the heart of a gateway city where there is no majority population has been an eye-opening experience for me—one that has brought to bear the urgency of finding a better way to resolve issues of social justice and to uphold the national agenda to provide quality education for all students. Through the DiP process of applying the discipline, tools, and structures of Improvement Science, my capacity to lead system reform has expanded on countless fronts. I have emerged from the EdD program with a more pragmatic viewpoint than the one I had nurtured for years in academia. I recognize now that leading quality improvement "to advance efficacy reliably at scale" (Bryk et al., 2015, p. 172) requires a fundamental paradigm shift—a bridging of the legendary gap between research and practice—that values, respects, and translates into action the various voices at the table.

Through laboratories of practice, training in collaborative consultation, and the collection of tools and techniques such as the Concerns-Based Adoption Model (Hall & Hord, 1987)—a system that enables leaders to gauge individuals' experience of change implementation—I have been equipped to cultivate the strong networked relationships necessary for collective problem-solving "to innovate, test, and spread effective practices sooner and faster" (Bryk et al., p. 173) for the special population of first generation college students as a whole and for each individual member of the group. Likewise, I have learned to identify and analyze important interactions occurring within and across organizations and to use several practical tools such as logic models that can aid in managing the scope and sequencing of improvement efforts as well as with communicating clear goals and objectives and the means to achieve them.

Ultimately, the CPED-influenced doctoral program at UH has prepared me as an EdD graduate with the tools and know how to drive problem-specific and user-centered change for the most marginalized groups in higher education through disciplined inquiry framed by the principles and processes of Improvement Science—expanding both my professional identity and the scope of my future work. While my original aim as an EdD graduate was to secure my role as an effective and productive university professor and community advocate for educational improvements, I now look forward to the broader possibilities of contributing to the field as a consultant and coach, extending my professional support to networked educational institutions across the world to meet the unique needs of our diversifying student populations.

Final Thoughts

On my desk sits a small planter of succulent plants that simply reads, "Grow Where You Are Planted." The heartfelt gift contains more than just an end-of-semester gesture of gratitude from a student who struggled and succeeded in one of my courses. For me, it encapsulates the essence of Improvement Science and the nature of today's professional doctorate education. To grow—yourself or others—you must first understand where you have been planted. Context matters. You must know what you want to grow and how to grow it—that is, what will grow for whom and in what environment—attending to the many systemic factors that impact variability, such as spacing, depth, and timing. Then, over time, a collaborative network of soil, air, water, sun, and more is needed to nurture desired growth—with active and attentive pruning and weeding along the way to guide the process—until a remarkable transformation takes place. We grow our students, ourselves, our systems. If we start where we are planted with carefully selected seeds of innovation and we diligently implement principles of improvement science—starting small and learning as we go—we will together harvest quality improvement across the changing landscape of higher education.

SCHOLARLY PRACTITIONER EXPERIENCE: JOHANNA L. THORPE

Do you want to start a revolution? Teach. This powerful slogan has stuck with me throughout my twelve-year teaching career, largely motivating me during the toughest moments in the classroom. Teaching can be the single most impactful gift an adult can bestow on a student's cognitive development. This is as true today as it was thousands of years ago. Yet, with an increasing complexity and diversity of needs surfacing in classrooms nationwide, a multitude of interventions and strategies developed to address those needs, and a desire to personalize instruction in light of environmental, social, emotional, and cognitive factors, teaching has developed into a profession full of multifaceted challenges in need of thoughtful solutions. As an educator who has spent over a decade working with underrepresented minorities, the struggle to meet the individual needs of students in a traditional school setting—often with fewer resources—was a frustrating factor in my languishing desire to continue business as usual. As a teacher, I certainly believed a change was necessary but was less clear what power—if any—I had to help create systemic reform. As large-scale, fundamental questions continued to accumulate, the will to join a networked group of like-minded individuals who were interested in taking action strengthened. More specifically, I yearned to be a part of a professional community who also sought ways to maximize the potential found in underrepresented minorities. Though these sentiments were fairly raw upon reflection, they would eventually serve as a key starting point in my search for a program to support my professional goals and growth.

Finding a Connection

Finding a doctoral program that valued my practical experience as an urban educator while still allowing for the time and space to address central questions was of paramount importance. While my practical experience afforded me an insight into the life of a school, I identified a still missing skill set necessary to engage in transformational leadership. After exploring and connecting with both Ph.D. and EdD programs in the Houston area, I connected with the faculty from the Professional Leadership Education Doctorate (EdD) in Special Populations at UH in large part due to an alignment of philosophies between program and candidate. Heralded as a program designed to develop the specific skill sets necessary to strategically solve a wide set of problems educators encounter in leadership positions, pursuing an EdD at UH appealed to my desire to solve a big problem with targeted solutions that scale. More than a Ph.D. could offer, the EdD program at UH was informed by The Carnegie Project on the Education Doctorate (CPED) and aimed to support my growth as a scholarly practitioner through a specific set of experiences designed to strengthen my ability to test and refine new practices that are socially responsible, evidence-based, collaborative, analytical, and transformational. All tools needed to engage in a *new* revolution.

I began the EdD at UH during the fall of 2014 with a preliminary understanding of my problem of practice. Technology has the power to help us do more with less through the dearth of content available online. Likewise, underrepresented minorities—who more often than not exist in schools with fewer resources—could potentially benefit from the free access of content inherent to the use of technology—if implemented and used responsibly. Throughout my first semester in the EdD program, I worked to shape and reshape my problem of practice through two avenues. First, I developed a collaborative partnership with a personalized, mobile middle school seeking to answer some of the same questions I grappled with during my teaching career. Second, through my coursework, I gained the skills necessary to conduct a national needs assessment to identify the challenges in learning in technology-based schools. Through these two avenues, a thread of evidence began to emerge. It became increasingly clear, through several research findings and among student and teacher reports, that students need to develop certain self-regulatory skills in student-centered, technology-based settings to maximize their depth of learning.

Mapping a Landscape

Preliminary findings in hand and with the help of my advisor and cohort, I began to brainstorm and map the input variables directly associated with a middle school student's ability to self-regulate in a technological setting as well as the output variables which adequately measure a student's success. This map of variables was constructed individually, within the cohort during "knee-to-knee" class interactions, and also during more acute conversations with my advisor. While this step is closely aligned with the type of logical progression a Ph.D. student often steps through, the ultimate goal of my research was not only to ingest the most current research surrounding pertinent variables within my problem of practice but additionally to design actionable steps for my partnered school based on theory, peer reviewed, and original research. Using the principles of Improvement Science, a good working understanding of the personalized, mobile middle school needed to be unearthed. Through my research, a diagram of pertinent components and subcomponents within the teaching-learning system of the school was generated. In the final analysis, it was determined that changing self-regulatory practices of students within the personalized, mobile middle school requires a three-pronged approach. Students must have access to specific strategies that enhance self-regulation, instruction must be developed to support the initial and ongoing use of those strategies, and teachers within the system must be clear about their roles and responsibilities in guiding students towards independence.

Though I may not have realized it at the time, both my variable and teaching-learning system maps served as the light posts to guide my DiP. However, these maps were not sufficient tools to engage in the full extent of my work. Research skills had first to be honed. Throughout my coursework at the UH, I was able to build a repertoire of skills which allowed me to assess the quality and alignment of research being read. During weekly discussions of shared journal articles as a cohort, we identified "goodness of fit" between research methods and research questions. From these same articles, we analyzed key constructs within research like, sample sizes, sample demographics, variables being tested and measured, clear procedures, analysis of results, limitations of each study, just to name a few. By the end of the first year in the program, as a type of summative assessment, each cohort member created a quality indicator rubric for different types of quantitative and qualitative research methods. These rubrics served not only to help evaluate the articles worth consideration for my doctoral thesis but also were immensely helpful in generating a framework for the research design found within my study. Furthermore, and probably most importantly, these rubrics will go on to further support my work as a scholarly practitioner in my ability to select evidence-based practices for program planning.

Rinse and Repeat

The approach used in writing a DiP mimics the way practitioners should engage in their work in schools. Conducting research is a recursive learning process developed with greater sophistication during each phase of the work. Much of my time was spent reading information found within new research articles, rethinking and retooling what I thought I knew about self-regulation in context, and in reflecting and reshaping my work to narrow my scope, gain clarity, and advance thinking. These steps were key to help operationalize and connect major concepts found within my literature review and to select appropriate measurement tools for my study. When Improvement Science principles are enabled in schools they work much in the same way. Implementing a new strategy or intervention requires a recursive process inclusive of constant data analysis against well-defined aims. Through the analysis of appropriate measures, it is the constant reworking of interventions and or programs in schools that allow leaders to grow successfully at scale. This type of disciplined thinking has the power to transform schools.

Critical Friends

The work of schools is never engaged in alone. Likewise, my DiP was supported formally by faculty and informally by my cohort members. The faculty within the program each served to provide an avenue of expertise that helped to strengthen my work. These conversations occurred during scheduled meeting times as well as during workshop sessions in class. Similarly, a collaborative environment was established among cohort members. Students in the program often met outside of class to discuss and share ideas, especially if an alignment between research studies could be established. As the cohort worked to move their dissertation thesis from an outline to a draft stage, critical friends' groups were formed to support the logical progression of thought, while more mundane grammatical or formatting concerns were reserved for appointments with the university's writing center. During each session, cohort members selected protocols that best highlighted the needs of their work to a handful of other cohort members. This discourse and reflective feedback not only served to help each presenter advance his or her thesis but also the work of each critical friend. Though certainly, these collaborative efforts were of great value to my DiP, they will also be an important component of my work as a scholarly practitioner. Improvement Science mandates that change in school cannot occur in isolation. Professional communities must work together to drive networked improvement. This involves communication from all parties to develop and continually evaluate standard processes that work and that keep the integrity of the system in check.

Call to Action

In the near term, as I develop a plan for the personalized, mobile middle school to secure improved self-regulation strategies among their student population, a good working relationship between myself and the adults who work in the school must be established. The greatest degree of impact will occur only if my pre-scribed action steps underscore the complexity of work in schools. To do this, I must take into account how the implementation of my proposed solution will manifest throughout the school's teaching-learning system. However, there is no greater expert on the teaching-learning system than the adults who already work in the personalized, mobile middle school. It is my job, through a consultancy role steeped in the mindset of a scholarly practitioner, not only to gather both teacher and student perspectives of the inner workings of the system but also to bridge the gap between their perceptions and the system's true functionality as described by quantifiable outcomes. These conversations require a great deal of trust and respect among all parties. The relationship skills developed in the program ensure a conducive working relationship to procure both workable and manageable solu-tions.

Ultimately, my life's goal will be to continue to fight for every student's right to gain a quality education regardless of race, income, gender, geography, and or perceived ability. While I believe this revolution will be computerized, I do recog-nize there is still a lot to learn about technology's adequate implementation. The good news is I am well prepared and trained for this lifelong exploration. I envi-sion my next steps, post-doctorate, to involve consultancy work for schools that aim to maximize student learning via technological resources. Specifically, I hope to use a scholarly practitioner's lens to train staff and faculty in gaining strategies which allow students to work independently during student-centered, technology supported instruction. I also hope to be a beacon of light for educational tech companies who seek to create innovative technologies that best maximize student learning as well as for businesses who want to strengthen the self-regulatory prac-tices of employees who use technology. The opportunity is vast. The tools are in place. The pathways are set. The work begins.

DISSERTATION IN PRACTICE: FUTURE WORK

While each DiP has been informed by the CPED doctoral reform process, they exemplify UH's system's approach in Improvement Science. Improvement Sci-ence helps the field of education use evidence-based practices to support student success; to support social justice in our schools; and to inform leaders, which dovetails well with both critical leadership and social justice. Graduates demon-strated how the EdD program helped them to incorporate Improvement Science into the structure of their work to ensure evidence-based outcomes for special populations. They discussed the impact of working as a 'critical friend' in a cohort that engages in networked opportunities and shared experiences; they described a focus on specific problems in their practice and engagement of others from that practice; they discussed researching potential evidence-based solutions that may be effective for the target group as a whole and for each member of that target group; and, they discussed how the program has prepared them for future professional opportunities that include consultancy, professional development, and promotion within the profession. They are scholarly practitioners.

Moving forward, UH will continue the program delivery system that engages students through the cohort and critical friends model. The Dissertation in Practice focus of learning and Improvement Science provides our students with the skill set they need to promote research to practice initiatives. These practices promote the region's economic success through our graduates' focus on early literacy, professional development, and transition—or more recently termed *educonomy*.

REFERENCES

Brown, P. C., Roediger, H. L., & McDaniel, M. A. (2014). *Make it stick: The science of successful learning.* Cambridge, MA: The Belknap Press of Harvard University Press.

Bryk, A. S., Gomez, L. M., Grunow, A., & LeMahieu, P. G. (2015). *Learning to improve: How America's schools can get better at getting better.* Cambridge, MA: Harvard Education.

Dweck, C. S. (2006). *The psychology of success.* New York, NY: Random House.

Fullan, M. (2016). *Indelible leadership.* Newbury Park, CA: Corwin Press.

Hall, G. E., & Hord, S. M. (1987). *Change in schools: Facilitating the process.* New York, NY: State University of New York Press.

Morris, W. (1909). Turning discomfort to account. In *Iron Age* (vol. 84, p. 1454). Chilton, CO. Retrieved from https://babel.hathitrust.org/cgi/pt?id-iau.31858019851363;view-1up;seq-86.

National School Reform Faculty (NSRF, 2012). *Critical friends protocols.* Retrieved from http://www.nsrfharmony.org/

Partnership for 21st Century Skills. (2008). 21st century skills, education, and competitiveness: A resource and policy guide. Retrieved from http://www.p21.org/storage/documents/21st_century_skills_education_and_competitiveness_guide.pdf

Pintrich, P. R., & DeGroot, E. V. (1990). Motivational and self-regulated learning components of classroom performance. *Journal of Educational Psychology, 82*(1), 33–40.

Shulman, L. S . (2005). Signature pedagogies in the professions. *Daedalus, 134*(3), 52–59.

Texas Education Agency (TEA). (2015). *TAPR Report.* Retrieved from: https://rptsvr1.tea.texas.gov/perfreport/tapr/2015/static/region/region04.pdf

Weinstein, C. E., & Palmer, D. R. (2002). *User's manual for those administering the Learning and Study Strategies Inventory.* Clearwater, FL: H & H Publishing.

SECTION TWO

CHAPTER 6

WHY THE DISSERTATION IN PRACTICE APPROACH

Jessie H. E. Holton

INTRODUCTION

When contemplating the decision to continue to a doctoral education, one of the key elements is whether or not there is a return on the investment. Even if the value of the return is not monetary, one could argue that there is always a benefit to higher education within your career. But what if higher education is not considered a significant contribution within your occupation? In the law enforcement culture any advancement in college education is not necessarily deemed a significant attribute. In fact, since the creation of a structured police force in the early 1900s, the push for police officers to have a minimum requirement of a bachelor's degree has been repeatedly defeated by practitioners and administrators in the field of law enforcement (Burns, 2012; Vollmer, 1926). Currently, less than one percent of law enforcement agencies in the United States require some form of college education (Ruberg & Bonn, 2004).

Higher Education in Law Enforcement

Most law enforcement agencies in the country have college education require-ments for middle management and above (Smith & Aamodt, 1997). Although it would seem to be common sense for any organization to at least have managers and administrators with a higher education requirement, this too has been argued by the police practitioners as impractical. Some of the issues discussed with the management requirement are; 1) pre-employment college educated officers pro-mote too fast and lack street experience, 2) many law enforcement agencies are rural or suburban and local officers lack the opportunity to obtain an education, 3) importing college graduates result in getting the leftovers from urban and larger agencies, and 4) there is still no definitive evidence that the education produces a better police officer, manager or administrator in the law enforcement occupation (Burns, 2012; Carlan, 2007; Fincenbauer, 2005; Paoline & Terrill, 2007).

It is this crossroad, which brought me to an enlightenment of my own. I have been in law enforcement for over a decade and previously served in the United States Marine Corps. I come from a family lineage of military Veterans and law enforcement officers,' with both my parents having worn the badge. I have wit-nessed and experienced the positive impact higher education has on officer perfor-mance. From a deeper understanding of diversity, increase in self-efficacy, reduc-tion in negative behavior whether it be use-of-force or off-duty misconduct, to the ability to implement management tactics. Although research studies have yet to produce a statistical significance on job performance, from what I have seen high-er education does produce a more professional officer. What I have also learned from my experience in law enforcement and having obtained a higher education is that the reason behind much of the debate is the inability of researchers to find the proper measurements. For example, previous research studies on performance examined educated verse non-educated officers in areas such as report writing, use-of-force, misconduct, and job retention to name a few (Burns, 2012; Cater & Sapp, 1990; Miller & Fry, 1978). The issue is that many law enforcement officers obtained their education after their employment, as I did, indicating that at one time they were one or the other variable, leading to inconsistent results. What I have found, with evaluating my own agency and several others, is that if you create three variables; 1) non-educated, 2) pre-educated, and 3) post-educated of-ficers, you will find there is a statistical difference in performance in those officers who have obtained their degree after their career as a law enforcement officer has already begun. Also, the lowest performers are those officers who obtained their education prior to becoming a law enforcement officer.

This example is one of many in which I have examined throughout my law en-forcement and academic experiences in which a better understanding of the occu-pation would point research in the right direction. The "Ivory Tower" perception is alive and well in the relationship between the law enforcement practitioners and research academics. Researchers have also been known to conduct flawed studies, consciously or unconsciously, that forces legislative change that burdens law enforcement practices. Especially when examining grant funding opportunities. The police culture has grown to despise researchers as much as politicians, which not only decreases to the advancement in education, but also reduces cooperation, buy-in, and data access that is critical to getting valid and reliable results. This gap is only becoming greater as another round of research is being conducted on law enforcement due to the current events within the United States that have spurred distrust and negative perceptions of police. There is no doubt that proper research and evaluation can provide better law enforcement services and oversight, but this has to be conducted in partnership.

This is where the question of whether or not there is value in the investment when continuing with an advanced education beyond a Master's degree is answered. I will not receive any monetary gain from obtaining a doctorate degree because there is no salary incentive. Nor will I receive any assistance to pay for the tuition or compensation for the time I will put into obtaining the education. The value is whether or not the education will allow me to be an example of how to fill the void between practitioner and researcher in order to create a renewed partnership that provides a significant impact on law enforcement performance. By becoming a hybrid academic, field researcher, law enforcement professional practitioner, or whatever we want to refer to it as, the concept is the same. Bridging the gap between researchers and practitioners creates impact. If I can become an example for others to follow, then the value of investment is multiplied as a new era of law enforcement professionals and researchers work together to develop advanced changes in practice. The law enforcement profession, like many others, is in need of a liaison between research and practice.

Choosing the Right Doctorate

As I began the search for a doctoral program, I found myself reading much of the same processes and requirements from the different institutions. Whether it was an on-line questionable institution or a regionally accredited university, the pathways seem to be identical. As a working student, the demand on having to take core courses, teach as an adjunct, and assist with working on some professor's research project did not fit what I was looking for. Especially since I had no desire to become a professor. As I talked with several graduate students about their programs, the most consistent reply on why they were obtaining a doctorate was so they could be called "Doctor" and have a Ph.D. at the end of their name. It reminded me of those recruits in my platoon who joined the Marine Corps because they wanted to wear the Dress Blue uniform. Many of them did not survive boot camp and it made me wonder how this mentality also affected the academic researcher profession.

One of the main selling points many program directors presented was the ability to work on projects that would help me be published. To be straight forward, I could care less about being published. I know many scholars are probably gasping at that statement, but I am a cop. I do understand the need and point of having peer-reviewed processes, but from my perspective with the number of journals that exist to date, the process has become diluted and the majority of work I have come across makes little impact in the field. It seems academia bases scholarly work of the number of publications one has, not the impact of their work in the real word. I needed a program that would help me make myself and my fellow officers better cops, not having my name appear in a peer-review journal. I then stumbled upon the Doctor of Education at the University of Central Florida. The program advertisement spoke of the program being for professionals outside higher education and would be completed in partnership with the student employer. Additionally, it is a cohort program allowing for a classroom of professionals to discuss similar issues instead of working along graduate students whose life experience only consist of classrooms. This became the selling point for me. Having other professionals in my Master's program created positive discussions and a better understanding of issues. Upon meeting with the director, it was learned that this was a new approach to the doctorate education and would consist of students working within their organizations to create positive impacts. Employers had to agree to allow and mentor students throughout the three-year process with a final project, the Dissertation-in-Practice (DiP), being focused on identifying organizational issues and developing problem-solving concept. This is exactly what I was looking for and, after approaching my administration, they agreed and assigned a command staff member as my mentor. I started in the fall of 2012 and graduated in the summer of 2015.

THE DISSERTATION IN PRACTICE (DiP) PROCESS

My DiP assembled the concept of using therapy dogs as official K–9 teams within criminal investigations involving children into a working program. The program objective was designed to increase communication with victims by reducing anxiety and creating bonds through the use of a therapy dog in order to bridge the gap. Results of the 18–month pilot study indicated that the disclosure rates increased from 36% to 82%, which was significant and supported future research for this change in practice (Holton, 2015). The overall cost to implement and sustain the program was less than $3,500 a year, which was more than acceptable by law enforcement administrators. Seeing how much a child victim benefited from having a therapy dog with them, throughout an extremely frightening and rigorous process, made the work done during this process more than worth it. Yet, knowing that there are thousands of child victims across the country who are not benefiting from this practice is where the DiP provides the most significant impact. The DiP is designed to not just create a program, but evaluate, continue, and replicate changes in practice. Because my DiP contained the details of the pilot program design, evaluations methods, and re-design of the program to allow for sustainable replications, the completion was not necessarily the conclusion of the total impact. But, to understand the complete process of the DiP we have to start from the beginning.

The Beginning

One of the unique aspects of the process, which I figured out near the end, is that from day one you have already started building your DiP. The Ed.D. program format is essentially a model that guides a student through the proper steps for addressing problems of practice. The first year of the program the students begin to learn the basics of how to examine organizational components to determine if a problem exists, what are its causes, and provide plausible solutions. The second year focuses on designing programs and evaluating whether or not the changes are effective. After the first and second year, students must complete a Lab-of-Practice (LoP) and concentration courses. The LoP's are designed to have the students apply the learned methods on a real problem within their organization. The concentration courses are electives that students choose from outside the program for specialization in certain areas. As the students enter the third year to begin formatting their DiP proposal, they have multiple options for conducting the DiP. Students can create a program design model, produce an evaluation, conduct a gap analysis, or a combination of methods that addresses a real problem of practice within their organization. The goal is not only to produce a document that showcases the students' abilities to conduct scholarly work, but also to provide a working product that the students' organization can use to implement a positive change in practice. In the next few sections, I will provide a deeper examination of the processes of the DiP and how it was applied in my work.

First Year—Identifying Problems of Practice

The first semester is learning to create the framework for conducting a Gap Analysis. This process teaches students how to dissect what they believe is a problem, find reliable and valid resources to broaden the understanding of the problem, and begin to analyze the problem through different frames in order to identify main causes. The curriculum provides several models but the methods I focused on examines issues through Clark and Estes, (2008), three organizational components, 1) Knowledge, 2) Motivation, and 3) Structure. By examining issues through these components, the problems are dissected to expose deficiencies. Besides using past and current peer-reviewed research to guide the processes through each component, additional theoretical framing is used to provide a visual understanding. For example, when examining the Knowledge gap for interviewing children, Vygotsky's (1978), *Zone of Proximal Development*, provided the visual concept of how using a therapy dog interaction prior to interviewing a child victim, created the opportunity to examine cognitive development. The engagement allowed the interviewer to observe and adjusted the format of the interview to eliminate confusion and produce better communication.

Once the causal factors are examined, a solution analysis is developed using the same methods. Multiple solutions can be examined by gathering reliable research and applying theoretical framework to discover which constitutes the best option. When examining the gap of increasing communication with child victim's and families, Bandura's (1977), theory of Self-Efficacy assisted in understanding the motivation component. The use of the therapy dog team reduced anxiety for everyone involved in the process, not just the child victim. Parents of child victims who observed the uplifting engagement for their child became more cooperative. As the child's and parents' stress was reduced, so was that of the forensic interviewer who has the difficult job of retrieving valuable information from the child. In a justice system in which only one opportunity exists to interview a child victim, one could only imagine the stress an interviewer must go through. But if a child is calm and engaging, the confidence of the interviewer is not burdened by the anxiety of trying to talk with a child they have never met before. Over time, as the therapy dog program continued, interviewers became more confident, energized, and willing to take on the challenge, as Bandura suggested.

In addition to the framework of the gap analysis the program curriculum, like most doctorates, also focused on ensuring students are understanding the importance of collecting valid and reliable data. When I began skimming through the databases within my organization, it appeared that the datasets would be easy to access and contained the measures I would need. As a homework assignment, we were to utilize the format of checking the reliability of a dataset as provided by Champion, (2002). What I quickly found is that when examining data on a certain crime statistic, the intake software and storage software did not seem to add up. Further exploration found that thirty percent of the statistics I needed were not being coded, and had not for over a decade. Not only would this have significantly skewed my data analysis, but also I would have developed a completely different solution that would have been irrelevant and a waste of resources. The processes of the program and instructors assisted in fixing this flaw and developing reliable data.

Once the gap analysis is complete, the rest of the first year focuses on using organizational theories and reframing methods to construct a method for implementing the solution analysis. The process was instructed in two different modes. The first mode concentrated on the framing of the solutions. This process consisted of using four lenses provided by Bolman and Deal (2003), Structural, Human Resource, Symbolic, and Political. By examining how the proposed solution will filter through each of the lenses, forecasting for known or unknown issues with implementing the solutions can be addressed beforehand. For example, when examining the possibility of deploying a therapy dog canine team within a child abuse investigative group, the lenses exposed that out of the four organizations involved, only law enforcement had the ability to implement the program. Each organization had the organizational structure to support the program, and everyone gained from the Symbolic and Political frame of providing a therapy dog for a child victim. However, when examining the Human Resources frame it was discovered that the cost of insurance was extremely high for all agencies except law enforcement. This was due to the law enforcement agency already having existing insurance because they had patrol K–9 teams. Additionally, because the dog was a nationally registered therapy dog, the insurance company waived the cost, allowing the solution analysis to continue.

The second mode focused more on the delivery and presentation to obtain the necessary buy-in. We examined multiple facets of leadership characteristics, networking, understanding stakeholder needs, and overall effects change will have on both the organization and the outside environment. This process was more of how to get individuals to implement your plan. Much of the perspectives and reasoning for this process I obtained from Hickman (2010). For instance, networking and learning how other experts are getting it done is not only a great opportunity to re-examine your model, but it is a significant networking tool. While preparing to present my proposal for implementing the therapy dog program, I attended multiple law enforcement and academic conferences. This allowed me to acknowledge questions and concerns from experts, which prepared my presentations for administrators. Also, the insight allowed me to adjust the implementation plans, add a few extra variables of measurement, and gave me several contacts for the future. Hickman, (2010), also emphasizes understanding the group, or audience, from whom you will be attempting to obtain buy-in. For my program, I had to cater my presentation to administrators, managers, and field investigators. By understanding what is important to each group you can provide the information in a way so most questions are answered as you present. In presenting the therapy dog program, I began with the expected effectiveness and increase in child disclosures to gain the buy-in from investigators. Next, I focused on the ease of implementation to illustrate to the managers that their duties would not be affected. I then concluded the presentation by discussing the laws, liability, and positive public attention that all supported the program, which sold the concept to the administrators. Without the ability to understand the effectiveness of preparing and delivering the solution, my entire DiP could have stalled in the solution analysis phase.

As the first year concluded, I realized the effectiveness of the curriculum, mostly because I was able to apply the knowledge in a hands-on experience within my organization. Additionally, the cohort began engaging and bouncing ideas off one another, which added to a deeper understanding of the curriculum and provided a more diverse discussion on issues that even changed some students' perceptions on their topics. After discussing my options with my classmates and being able to dabble in several different aspects of my organization, I made the decision to make the therapy dog for child victims program my DiP topic.

Lab of Practice (One)

The Lab of Practice, or (LoP), is probably one of the most important and unique components of the DiP format. The goal of the LoP is to have the students complete the first milestone requirement of the program, which is a Gap Analysis focused within their organization. Upon approval from both the academic and field mentor, the students spend most of the summer semester conducting the project. The process provides the opportunity for the student to showcase what they have learned while also being exposed to the rigors of research such as data collection, coding, survey construction and collection, and institutional review board processes. It also can begin the framework for the DiP if the student decides to continue working on the same problem throughout the program as I did.

As I entered the first LoP the goals that were set included; 1) completing the Gap Analysis, 2) choosing the solution analysis to implement as a pilot study, and 3) apply for a grant to pay for the pilot study. Because throughout the first year I had already completed much of the literature review and developed the causes and plausible solutions, the bulk of the Gap Analysis was constructed. I still had to collect data to determine with which solution analysis I would continue. To assist with the work, I had taken the advice of the program and reached out to an expert in child abuse research. Upon contacting the seminal scholar, she assisted in helping me find reliable variables of measure and constructing the dataset. The method consisted of coding the last three years of child abuse investigations to isolate measures of communication then indicate the rate on which child victims disclosed abuse. Once the data was collected, I compared the results to other reliable research studies. What I found is that not only did the results determine that one of my solution hypotheses was false, but it eliminated several and assisted in narrowing the solution choice. This process proved to be extremely valuable as later work showed that the false hypotheses could have led to significant negative results if I had continued. The hypotheses stated that the forensic interviewers were not obtaining disclosures at the same rate law enforcement investigators could. Therefore, the need for using forensic interviewers was no longer needed if law enforcement investigators could obtain the same, or higher, disclosure rates. The perception among law enforcement investigators at the time was that they were the same, if not better interviewers. This perception had already caused several investigators to no longer utilize the methods of the forensic interviewers, which could have resulted in losing the resource altogether. The results of my LoP analysis showed that the forensic interviewers were twice as likely to obtain a disclosure than law enforcement investigators, which was also supported by other studies. Upon explaining the results to the investigators, I realized that there was also a knowledge gap within the investigative group, which consisted of a lack of education on the practices of forensic interviewing. But, even with fixing the knowledge gap the investigators were still frustrated due to the disclosure rates being 36% (Holton, 2015). Although the forensic interviewers were producing above average disclosure rates for the last three years, everyone in the investigative group agreed that something needed to be done about the additional 64% of children who were not disclosing. The final hypotheses in the solution analysis indicated that if law enforcement investigators provided a therapy dog interaction prior to a forensic interview, the anxiety of the child, child's parent, and forensic interviewer would be reduced, therefore increasing communication and disclosures.

Upon completing the data collecting and choosing the solution analysis, the Gap Analysis was complete. At the same time, I drafted the pilot study concept and applied for a Federal grant. At the end of the LoP, I presented the pilot project concept to my administration, who agreed to move forward with constructing the program. The completion of the LoP was rigorous, but it provided the overall view of everything that is involved with conducting rigorous research method as well as the importance of making sure you examine each process with as much detail as possible.

I also learned a major lesson during this LoP concerning making sure you do not take shortcuts. Having never completed a Federal grant budget, I took it upon myself to draft what I believed the cost would be. In every other section of the grant, I had contacted an expert to review and add suggestions, which was critical. Every time the budget came across my desk I remembered one of my professors insisting, no matter what, have someone with more knowledge than you examine your work. Two days prior to the grant deadline, I happened to run into one of my agency budget managers. After explaining to her the grant proposal, she took it upon herself to review my budget plan. It took her two days to fix my mistakes. I missed the mark by nearly eighty thousand dollars. Not only would this have immediately excluded me from competing for the grant, but if I also presented my budget in front of a group of administrators who already knew what a true budget looked like, they would have lost all confidence in my work and the program would have ceased to exist. I finished the LoP with a renewed understanding of what goes on in the real world of change and the importance of taking in what the DiP process was providing. Although the work was exhausting, I finished the LoP with a rejuvenated mindset for entering the second year.

Second Year—Program Design and Evaluation

The second year of the program began with more in-depth data analysis and organizational concepts. These components assisted in expanding a program concept into an actual program design model. The data analysis focused heavily on reliability and validly of the work. For my therapy dog pilot project, the focus was attempting to locate additional variables for triangulating what the disclosure rate would provide. I utilized a process referred to by Bernhardt, (2004), which involved examining other organizational databases and processes in which critical information could be collected. Basically, if a change is made in one process, there could be multiple effects in other areas and by locating those other changes, one could use that measure to support or oppose the initial findings. In child abuse research, there are often limitations to data collecting methods due to the confidentiality of the cases. This is where the concept of having professional practitioners is critical to research. Because I had the knowledge of what data needed to be collected and the experience and accessibility to child abuse reports, I was able to create an additional intake report within my agency that eliminated all confidential components while providing the information needed to conduct an accurate analysis. It was as simple as creating an Excel spreadsheet that an intake secretary coded. The added work took little time and was not a burden. The information gathered assisted in creating three additional benchmark measures of case closure rates for triangulating the result.

Along with obtaining a more in-depth understanding of data analysis, the beginning of the second year also focused on expanding the understanding of organizational change. This included both leadership characteristics and effects of change. With the first year focusing on the aspects that occur inside the organization, the second year focused on the aspects that occur outside the organization. By understanding that changes from the outside environment can affect organizational process, as well as changes in organizational processes affecting the outside environment, program designs must examine all possible outcomes. This was conducted by utilizing the same tools from the first year just on a broader level. For example, when designing the therapy dog pilot project, I had to determine which organizations would also be affected. This included Children's Advocacy Centers, the State Prosecutor's Office, the Department of Children and Families, the Circuit Court, and other neighboring law enforcement agencies. For each of the organizations, I had to examine the Knowledge, Motivation, and Structural (Clark & Estes, 2008), aspects to locate the needed information that would adjust the therapy dog deployments when entering each phase of the justice system. This also included processing each organization through the four frames of organizational framing: Structure, Human Resources, Symbolic, and Political (Bolman & Deal, 2003). By the end of the process, I had exposed small informational needs and built the procedures for deploying the therapy dog team so that the implementation of the program did not have any negative effects for those involved. For example, the Children's Advocacy Center employs the forensic interviewers who are trained to conduct interviews using empirically backed protocols that can withstand judicial evidentiary scrutiny. If the therapy dog program interfered with these protocols, the evidence obtained to prosecute criminal cases could be thrown out, which would be detrimental to the case and to bringing justice for a child victim. This is why it was highly important to ensure I understood the protocols and worked with the forensic interviewers. I spent a week at the National Children's Advocacy Center where I went through the forensic interviewer training and networked with the leading professionals who assembled the protocols to make sure the processes of the therapy dog program did not hinder the interviewing processes. I then met with Circuit Court Judges, attorneys, civil trial lawyers, therapy dog trainers, and victim's advocates to get as much information as I could in order to cater the therapy dog procedures to fit every aspect of the judicial process. At every level, I had exposed small hidden barriers that could have resulted in problems during implementation. However, because of the processes involved with the DiP framework, I was able to eliminate these barriers prior to implementing the program and create an effective program design.

In addition to learning how to build a program design model, expanding on the leadership and presentation aspect was also important. When having to present the therapy dog concept to so many different groups, investigative practitioners, law practitioners, administrators, and researchers, obtaining buy-in from each is a must. If one presentation was neglected and a group did not wish to participate, the entire project would be placed on hold. What the expanded instruction on leadership provided was additional resources on how to handle different personalities and obtain buy-in from all aspects. During the program construction, I was faced with an administrator who was immediately resistant due to distrust for academic research and wanted no part of the program. As the curriculum suggested, I derived a strategy on understanding others perceptions and how to change those perceptions using methods from Gardner, (2006). According to Gardner, the way to handle this situation is to gather what the person wants to hear, as well as allow the person to insert some of their ideas into the program. I also gathered research that supported the views of the administrator to ease the distrust towards researchers being involved. During the next meeting with the administrator, I deployed the tactics, which even to my surprise was highly effective and the administrator signed on.

The second half of year two centered on the processes of evaluating organizations. After learning how to build programs and implement change, we were now tasked with taking on the role of being the evaluator. Although the scientific methods of data collecting were similar to the research design, the approach to the evaluation is what was different. As the evaluator, we had to learn to look for unconscious biases and make sure we examined the processes of a program and the theoretical framing from all approaches. The process I chose to use that was effective in law enforcement was Bickman's, (1996), model for evaluating social services. The evaluation is conducted using three approaches. First is to examine whether or not the organization implemented the program design properly. Second is the examination of the data to determine what changes occurred and if the changes are effective. The third part provides a suggestive narrative using other research not used in the program to provided reasoning and adjustments. When applying this evaluation plan to the therapy dog pilot project, two evaluations were to take place. The first was an internal-formative evaluation at the 18–month mark. The second was a summative-evaluation conducted by an outside researcher at the 24–month mark. The timing worked out so that the 18 months of the pilot project would occur right as I was entering the dissertation portion of the program, so I figured I would use the second LoP to produce my DiP proposal of conducting an evaluation of the therapy dog pilot project.

Lab of Practice (Two)

At the conclusion of the second year, the second LoP was to be concluded and with the knowledge gain from the second year of the program, I was already starting to see the framework and structure of how my DiP would be completed. I had hoped to spend the second LoP creating the evaluation model for my DiP proposal. However, like with the implementation of the therapy dog pilot program, my field mentor requested I work on creating another program. This unexpected addition would actually work out in my favor in the end. Therefore, besides having the construct an evaluation plan and write my DiP proposal, I also had to build an entire program from scratch. This is when I realized how the DiP process was creating a significant impact.

When I began designing the new program, which consisted of providing forensic medical exams for surviving victims of Domestic Violence strangulation, I went back to the starting point of the DiP process. As I went through step-by-step, it all came together that the DiP was a model. This model allows for a concept to be examined and scrutinized through a process that can eventually result in a change in practice. By the end of the Second LoP, I had assembled a working group of academics and practitioners who were now doing the work to create the new program, as well as completed my evaluation plan and wrote my DiP proposal. What had changed is that I was no longer going to be conducting my DiP on the evaluation alone. My DiP proposal was to design a full Concept-to-Practice model for law enforcement so ideas like the therapy dog pilot program and the Domestic Violence strangulation program can be implemented in researcher-practitioner partnership.

Concentration Courses

Catering the program to the students' professional needs is one of the unique aspects of the DiP process. Concentration Courses allow students to break off from the cohort and focus on subject matter areas more geared towards the profession of the individual students. For me, I chose to select course within the discipline of Sociology, and more specifically, crime and law enforcement organizational effects. Sociology seemed to provide a broad understanding of cause and effects relationships between police and society. This is especially true when it comes to scientific methods of field research. When examining and explaining the reasoning behind the changes in child behavior when introduced to a therapy dog, I used the theoretical tenets of Symbolic Interactionism (Blumer, 1969), which described changing one's perceptions and behavior by providing a meaningful interaction. Understanding that the therapy dog interaction shifts the child's fear of talking to a stranger into a friendship with a social service provider can open the door for additional concepts to provide the same results.

In addition to theoretical frames, Applied Sociology consists of field researchers obtaining information and locating measures by interacting with the groups of study. For example, ethnographic observations have led to some of the more accurate studies on inner-city gangs and organized crime in the U.S. (Levitt, 2004; Venkatesh, 2013; Wilson, 1991). These observations are more than just being a bystander. The practice uses proven techniques for engaging and questioning members of groups in order to eliminate biases and locate micro details that lead to unforeseen variables that explain the uncharted areas research is attempting to locate. The experience as a full-time practitioner combined with the foresight of a research academic produces a type of ethnographic observation that is continuous over years. It is my experience and deep understanding of perceptions, policies, and procedures within law enforcement that allow my research methods to be more precise. Adding the theoretical framework of Sociology analyzes group behaviors and is combined with organizational theoretical concepts to identify problems is just one more lens to add to my Concept-to-Practice Model to ensure the most intimate details are extracted as possible.

Concept to Practice Model

As I entered the DiP, it was very clear to me that the structure of the Ed.D. program was actually a process that taught the students how to create, analyze, evaluate, and sustain changes in practice. It was this process that allowed me to build a therapy dog program from the ground up and watch it grow to become a statewide initiative. During the process, I was tasked to create other programs and evaluate other practices, which I was able to accomplish by reverting back to the process and knowing exactly where to start and what tools to use to complete the task. What I realized is that this process, the DiP model, was something that could be done to address multiple facets within my agency and law enforcement as a whole. This process is exactly what my agency and many other law enforcement agencies across the United States need. By encouraging law enforcement practitioners to participate in solving problems through a specific process that helps identify and understand what the true causes are, then proper implementation and buy-in can occur. Because the process is conducted in partnership with academic researchers, many of the current issues we have been attempting to address for several decades will now have a better chance of creating a positive impact and providing a proper change in practice. In Figure 6.1, I have provided the Concept-to-Practice model I assembled as my DiP. The law enforcement therapy dog program was the first concept I produced through the model. What you will observe is that all of the processes explained thus far in the text are in the same order as the program was presented. As you examine the model, you will see the DiP process unfold from the first year beginning with literature reviews and gap analysis, all the way to the final product in year three.

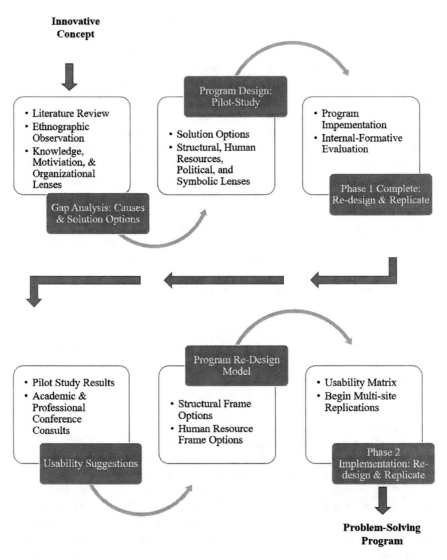

FIGURE 6.1. Concept to Practice Model

IMPACTS FROM THE DISSERTATION IN PRACTICE (DIP)

Creating an Impact

The DiP was not just my final requirement for graduating, but it is now a published manuscript that is being used to deploy additional law enforcement therapy dog teams across the State of Florida and the United States. The process allowed for such detail within the program design that it can be molded easily into other law enforcement organizations at minimal cost. Since the completion of the original pilot study, my agency has added an additional therapy dog team and created an entire training facility for the purpose of replicating our program. We now have a 40–kennel facility that obtains dogs from local humane societies and animal shelters. These dogs are trained and cared for by female jail inmates and screened by a K–9 specialist on their abilities for which adoption route they will take. We not only provide law enforcement therapy dogs and training for other agencies free of charge, but we now have partnered with a local counseling center and produce comfort dogs for children with mental and emotional disabilities. In addition, we have partnered with local colleges, Veteran centers, and victim advocacy groups, to provide comfort dogs to disabled or special needs adults, all at no charge. All funds for the program have been paid for using grants and inmate commissary profits. Plus, the inmates who enter our program receive training certificates in dog grooming and basic obedience training in order to assist with employment opportunities upon re-entry into society. None of this would have been possible without having experienced the DiP process. The DiP is exactly what practitioners like myself who want to create impacts within their fields have been looking for in a doctoral program. Providing this style of education in occupations like law enforcement increases professionalism and produces a much better product by eliminating communication gaps and creating partnerships between practice and academia. It is one thing to show someone how to use a tool in a classroom setting. However, it can make a significant difference when the tool is handed off to the student and there is a requirement to show proficiency. This is a piece of the DiP process that is often missing in the traditional doctoral process. One would argue that traditional doctoral programs have students collecting and examining data and developing a theoretical hypothesis, which is considered a type of hands-on experience. However, as I have attended academic and professional conferences and spoken with many students from different universities around the world it seems that the traditional processes for doctoral students often steer within the confines of ideas and methods of whoever their research advisors are. Many students I spoke with would express their discontent for having to complete a dissertation process that was irrelevant to their future goals. The reoccurring statement that the dissertation is just a manuscript for completing requirements and no one will ever read it, appears to be an industry standard in the realms of academia. Like myself, many students desired to have the hard work they put into the dissertation process to be meaningful and provide the catalyst of what the future will hold. The perception that the gatekeeper for entering academia is referred to as a meaningless document needed to complete a process counters the whole point of obtaining a doctorate. This is where the DiP process is different. The student is not expected to create a significant piece of work that changes practices and adds to scholarly research throughout, but the student is expected to create a significant piece of work that creates an impact on the student's organization. The idea is to start with small impacts and continue on using the tools from the higher education to create large impacts. This is exactly what has occurred in my situation and those within my cohort. The impact I have been able to provide for my organization because of the DiP process is just one of many. I still keep in contact with several members of my cohort and their testimony about the program impact is the same as mine.

Additional Impacts

One of the goals of the DiP process is to provide organizations with graduates who can hit the ground running when it comes to affecting their organizations. Since completing the DiP and graduating, my agency has created the first Research & Development Unit. I was given a full-time position as the Research Coordinator and I now facilitate program evaluations and multiple research projects. I have been able to address our agency retention issues by successfully implementing application screening tools for selecting better candidates, restructured our recruit training processes, and completely overhauled our rank and promotional processes. Multiple law enforcement agencies are now requesting the materials and processes I have developed to address their organizational issues. I also created a research working-group in partnership with the University of Central Florida called the L.E.A.D.E.R.S initiative. The acronym stands for Law Enforcement Academic Direct Engagement Research System. This working group is currently involved in eleven research programs, placed 12 graduate interns within our agency to assist in collecting and creating better datasets, presented work at six academic conferences, and together we have published several peer-review articles. For a person who could have cared less on being published, I have co-authored eight articles that are now either published or pending publication and my dissertation has been cited multiple times in peer-review journals. We are now gaining national attention on our approach to changing law enforcement practices and professionalizing our agency, and it has all been done in the 10 months since I completed the DiP. My impacts will attest that the DiP process works. The knowledge is invaluable and the need for more practitioners armed with this style of education is vital to expanding research and practice.

REFERENCES

Bandura, A. (1977). Self-efficacy: Toward a unifying theory of behavioral change. *Psychological Review, 84*(2), 191–215.

Bernhardt, V. (2004). *Data analysis for continuous school improvement*. Larchmont, NY: Eye on Education.

Blumer, H. (1969). *Symbolic interactionism: Perspective and method*. Englewood Cliffs, NJ: Prentice-Hall, Inc.

Bickman, L. (1996). *Evaluating managed mental health services: The Fort Bragg experiment*. New York, NY: Springer Publishing.

Bolman, L. G., & Deal, T. E. (2003). *Reframing organizations: Artistry, choice, and leadership*. San Francisco, CA: Jossey-Bass.

Burns D. (2012). Reflections from the one-percent of local police departments with mandatory four-year degree requirements for new hires: Are they diamonds in the rough? *Southwest Journal of Criminal Justice, 7*(1), 87–108.

Carlan, P. (2007). The criminal justice degree and policing: Conceptual development occupational primer? *Policing: An International Journal of Police Strategies and Management, 20*(4), 608–619.

Carter, D., & Sapp, A. (1990). The evolution of higher education in law enforcement Preliminary findings from a national study. *Journal of Criminal Justice Education, 7*(1), 59–85.

Champion, R. (2002). Choose the right data for the job. *Journal of Staff Development, 23*(3), 12–16.

Clark R., & Estes, F. (2008). *Turning Research into results: A guide to selecting the right performance solutions*. Charlotte, NC: Information Age Publishing.

Fincenbauer, J. (2005) The quest for quality in criminal justice education. *Justice Quarterly, 22*(4), 413–426.

Gardner, H. (2006). *Changing minds. The art and science of changing our own and other people's minds*. Boston, MA: Harvard Press

Hickman, G. (2010). *Leading organizations, Perspectives for a new era*. Thousand Oaks, CA: SAGE Publications..

Holton, J. H. E. (2015). *Applying problem-of-practice methods from the discipline of higher education within the justice system: Turning the concept of therapy dogs for child victims into a statewide initiative*. Orlando, FL: ETD-FCLA, State University Library Services.

Levitt, S. (2004). *Ted talks: The freakonomics of crack dealing*. Retrieved from http://www.ted.com/talks/steven_levitt_analyzes_crack_economics

Miller, J., & Fry, J. (1978). Some evidence on the impact of higher education for law enforcement personnel. *Police Chief, 45*, 30–33.

Paoline, E. A., III, & Terrill, W. (2007). Police education, experience, and the use of force. *Criminal Justice and Behavior, 34*, 179–196.

Ruberg, R., & Bonn, S. (2004), Higher education and policing. Where are we now? *Policing 27* (4), 469.

Smith, A. B., & Aamodt, M. G. (1997). The relationship between education, experience, and police performance. *Journal of Police and Criminal Psychology 12*, 7–14.

Venkatesh, S. (2013). The reflexive turn: The rise of first-person ethnography, *The Sociological Quarterly, 54* (3–8).

Vollmer, A. (1926). The prevention and detection of crime as viewed by a police officer. *The Annals of the American Academy of Political and Social Science, 125*(1), 125–148.

Vygotsky, L. (1978). Interaction between learning and development. In M. Gauvain & M. Cole (Eds.), *Mind in society* (pp. 79–91). Cambridge, MA: Harvard University Press

Wilson, W. J. (1991). Studying inner-city social dislocations: The challenge of public agenda research: 1990 Presidential address." *American Sociological Review 56*(1), 1–14.

CHAPTER 7

TRANSFORMING EDUCATION LEADERS

Impacts of the Dissertation in Practice on Graduates of a Global Executive Level EdD

Rob Filback, Cathy Krop, Helena Seli, and Tracy Tambascia

This chapter reports on a study of the impacts of a Dissertation in Practice (DiP) in an executive level, professional doctorate program for global education leaders. The Global Executive EdD is situated in the Rossier School of Education at the University of Southern California. The program was launched in 2012 to prepare educational leaders and policymakers to enact change in the international education arena. It enrolls a select cohort of approximately 20 students each year and as of July 2016 the program will have produced its third cohort of graduates. Just over two years in duration, the program design involves nine quarterly one- to two-week intensives—five on campus and four at other sites around the world, currently in Hong Kong, Qatar and the U.A.E. The goal of the program is to strengthen the leadership of its candidates in three areas: utilizing evidence-based problem solving, fostering institutional cultures that promote creative thinking and innovative solutions, and ensuring scalable impact through effective policy development, implementation, and assessment.

Exploring the Impact of the Dissertation in Practice, pages 109–124.

Rossier's Global Executive EdD program has adopted an organizational problem-solving DiP model as part of its "signature pedagogy" (Shulman, 2005, p. 52). Students complete their DiP by using a specific conceptual framework, a gap analytic case study. Gap analysis is a systematic method that helps to clarify organizational goals and identify related performance indicators, followed by an examination or "diagnosis" of the underlying factors needed to achieve the desired performance level (Clark & Estes, 2008). The process culminates with solutions that specifically target the underlying issues or needs. Most often, the issues or needs involve a combination of factors in the areas of stakeholder knowledge, motivation and organizational culture, policies and practices (KMO, in short). This problem-solving process is specifically designed to avoid organizations "jumping into solutions" before understanding the nature of the problems at a deep level. While the organizational goal setting and the KMO conceptual framework are applied by all dissertations, based on their sample size and other considerations such as participant anonymity, students decide to gather either qualitative or quantitative data—or both—about organizational and stakeholder performance. This data enables them to identify the barriers, needs or assets that impact performance, and generate research-based recommendations. Most of the students conduct the DiP in their own professional contexts. The dissertation is embedded throughout the program and supported through coursework and an advisement committee.

The chapter begins with a review of key literature concerning the challenges and issues facing the professional doctorate. This is followed by a description of the methodology used for this study. We then turn to findings concerning the impact of the DiP on graduates of the Global Executive EdD across four areas: impact on their professional practice, personal impacts, impact on career goals and aspiration and impact on their capacity to lead systemic change. The chapter concludes with a discussion, including implications for practice for those involved in administering an EdD or other related programs.

BACKGROUND LITERATURE

Vigorous discussion has taken place over the last decade about the future of the professional education doctorate (EdD), with a specific focus on the type of dissertation that EdD students conduct (Evans, 2007; Shulman, 2005; Zambo, 2011). While the goal of the education PhD has remained relatively stable, to prepare students to create generalizable research by completing a traditional dissertation, the goals and format of the EdD dissertation have been more contested. The production of EdD culminating products similar to the PhD has caused some to call the EdD a "watered-down doctorate" (Levine, 2005, p. 10).

In addressing the issue, Wergin (2011) recommended that the purpose of the EdD be clearly defined as a practice doctorate complete with an appropriate capstone that demonstrates a student's ability to apply existing research to solve specific contemporary educational problems. First and foremost, Wergin recommends that EdD holders "situate their profession in practice" (p. 120). Therefore, he adds, the capstone would ideally be conducted in a student's own professional context, addressing problems that students themselves have identified.

Another means of distinguishing the EdD from the PhD comes from Shulman (2005), who suggested that degree programs adopt a "signature pedagogy" as the "types of teaching that organize the fundamental ways in which future practitioners are educated for their new professions" (p. 52). As an example of a signature pedagogy, Shulman referred to medical students learning to "think like physicians" while conducting clinical rounds; and to law students learning to "think like lawyers" when engaging in Socratic dialogue. Shulman encouraged EdD programs to develop similar unique, practitioner-focused signature pedagogies. Supporting this call to focus on cultivating scholarly practitioners, Wergin (2011) called for the signature pedagogy to "require a demonstration of expertise that showcases the candidate's mastery of inquiry into practice" (p. 130).

Over the last decade, the Carnegie Project on the Education Doctorate (CPED) has focused on the redesign of the EdD. As a result of CPED's convenings, the concept of the Dissertation in Practice (DiP) emerged as the appropriate EdD culminating project. While many different formats exist, the currently accepted definition of the DiP is a "scholarly endeavor that impacts a complex problem of practice" (CPED, 2014 as cited by Storey et al., 2014). Current designs result in a range of final products including policy briefs, journal articles, executive summaries and portfolios of professional practice; with the scope of these products ranging from case studies to program reviews (Storey et al., 2014). The goal of the DiP, irrespective of variations in design, generally encompasses equipping students to conduct "rigorous analysis in a realistic operational context" (Smrekar & McGraner, 2009, p. 52), solve a problem of practice and make a contribution to their profession. CPED has operationalized other specific criteria, such as framing the study in existing research on both theory and practice, integration of practical and research-based knowledge, selecting appropriate methods of inquiry, and creating recommendations that align with data (Storey et al., 2014).

METHODOLOGY

This study used a qualitative case study methodology to gather data on the impacts of the DiP on Global Executive EdD graduates' professional and personal journeys. Data were gathered through both in-depth interviews and surveys. At the time of the study, 29 students had graduated from the program, including 11 students from Cohort 1, 15 students from Cohort 2 and three students, who defended early, from Cohort 3. Through purposive sampling, graduates who are representative of overall student demographics were selected to participate in the interviews. Factors considered for inclusion in the interview were graduation year, country of work and professional field. Based on these criteria, eight of the 29 program graduates were invited to participate in an interview, of which seven agreed. Of the seven interviewees included in the study, two were from Cohort 1, four were from Cohort 2 and one was from Cohort 3. In terms of country of work, the interview participants represent seven countries that include China, Singapore, Brunei, Qatar, United States, Taiwan, and Ghana. These participants held positions spanning K12 and higher education and both private and public sectors. In addition, all graduates of the Global Executive EdD program at the time of the study were asked to participate in an open-ended survey. Of the 29 graduates, 21 completed the survey. On average, those who completed the survey had about 21 years of professional work experience, 13 years in a professional leadership position and had worked at their current organization for about 8 years.

The interviews and surveys were designed to gather data on the impact of the DiP across four specific themes: impact on professional level; impact on personal level; impact on aspirations; and impact on the capacity to lead systemic change. Both the interview and survey instruments included specific questions aligning with these four themes. The interviews were conducted one-on-one with a study team investigator. They were conducted online and audio and/or video recorded and lasted approximately one hour. Following the completion of the interviews, the recordings were transcribed and the data coded for types of impact under each of the four main themes. Two researchers were assigned to each transcribed interview for initial code validation before codes were validated across all interview transcripts and across all four researchers. The anonymous survey, completed using the online Qualtrics utility, included both Likert-style questions and open-ended questions and required approximately 15 minutes to complete. Survey data were similarly coded and validated and used in concert with the interview data to deepen the findings and discussions that follow. Member checking was also conducted with all seven of the interview participants. The first complete draft of the manuscript was shared with each of them to confirm our interpretations of the data and elicit corrections to ensure the most accurate results.

FINDINGS

The following presents the findings that emerged from this study. The first section provides backdrop by reporting common observations of participants concerning the EdD degree, including how the EdD is viewed in their contexts. The remaining sections outline the impacts that the DiP has had on graduates. These sections are organized around the four themes: impacts on a professional level; impacts on personal level; impact on aspirations; and, impacts on capacity to lead systemic change.

Perceptions of the EdD

Since most of the students in the Global Executive EdD live or work in countries outside of the United States, we asked interviewees to share their thoughts on the EdD and on how the degree is perceived in their environment. Nearly all participants said they understood prior to enrolling that the EdD was a more practice-based degree, involving less theory and research than the PhD. In general, participants felt the EdD would be beneficial to their work and for some, earning a doctorate was necessary for professional advancement.

Completing the Global EdD dissertation changed some perceptions, such as the level of research and theory involved. "Well, I think it's definitely more heavily research-focused than I thought it would be...so that was great." Another graduate had not "expected as much theoretical as actually was built into the process." In other cases, expectations were confirmed, such as the applied nature of the degree. For example, a graduate noted that "every course, every assignment that we had, we could apply directly to our work. I think, in that sense, it was exactly what I had hoped for and expected." Overall, completion of the Global Executive EdD is perceived to be an important accomplishment, a "substantial piece of work," in one graduate's words, which provides a "showcase" of what they are capable of.

Several participants commented that their EdD degree was sometimes misunderstood by friends and colleagues who mistakenly referred to it as a PhD. As one participant said, "when I say doctorate, there's an automatic assumption of PhD. I don't think that the EdDs are widely as known." Some participants reported hearing that the EdD has less academic value than a PhD and others know that the EdD was not recognized officially in their international setting. Despite these realities, graduates pursued the EdD because it offered a more applied focus, which they needed professionally. As one graduate stated, "my goal was different than getting a PhD."

Professional Impacts

All of the participants in our study agreed that the DiP had a positive impact on them professionally and a variety of examples were offered to illustrate this. A common refrain was that the dissertation strategies now permeate their work. It is "rare," in the words of one student, to not be "applying or thinking about the skills and knowledge gained, at least once a week." Three main themes emerged in analyzing the types of influences reported: enhanced professional confidence, increased problem-solving abilities, and the acquisition or improvement of other skills pertinent to their professional practice.

Enhanced professional confidence. Graduates emerged from the DiP experience with a greater self-efficacy concerning their professional capacities. This led to new types of actions and thinking. One graduate, for example, felt empowered in a "core job" of a leader: the ability to "turn dilemmas into decisions." Learning how to "break down a dilemma" in order to "come up with a decision" enabled this graduate to feel "more comfortable putting myself into new opportunities" than before the program. Another graduate described how knowledge gained from the program resulted in less reliance on consultants. Working in a context where the use of outside advisement is common, this person talked with pride about having "actually built [a] program with no consultants...based on my experience in writing the DiP." When consultants are used, this person reported asserting greater control: "Actually, we insist on the consultant [doing] the Kirkpatrick evaluation;

for every stage we say, 'Oh, we need for you to actually find out whether you delivered.'" Consequently, this graduate experienced greater self-efficacy: "I am standing on my own feet" and "more significant on [my] own merits."

Increased confidence also allowed graduates to expand their role as mentors or teachers. As a result of the DiP experience, for instance, a graduate who teaches in a college is more able to help students think with clarity: A new teaching objective is to "keep my students focused. Think one thing at a time. If you write, if you speak, keep yourself focused." Another graduate talked about "trying to infect other people" with the gap analytic approach. In working with groups of education leaders, this former student described "sitting with each of the teams" and trying to "become their coach" and "guide them" on "diagnosing" root causes of organizational performance issues. Another graduate told of having developed an organizational model in his DiP and now "teaching the model to help people to be able to redesign the organization and transform their business offices."

Increased problem-solving capacities. A prevalent theme among study participants was the integration of the DiP's problem-solving approach into their own practices. As one graduate put it, once you learn the approach, it becomes "part of your DNA." Another stated they "probably apply this daily" and that it "alters my thinking and response[s]" and another described "constantly applying [it] in my view of the world." The DiP's systematic problem-solving methodology appears to be a provision that graduates carry with them and translate into their work. In reviewing the ways graduates talked about this, four processes emerged as areas where they experienced the most growth: problem identification, determining organizational goals, use of evidence and generating solutions.

Identifying or framing problems is a step that several interviewees mentioned in illustrating how they had been impacted as problem solvers. The survey respondents also all agreed, half strongly, that the "DiP enabled them to identify organizational problems more effectively." One graduate recalled as particularly impactful the process of learning how to "break down problems" and how to "address them by...finding the causes and then questioning those causes and determining, well, are those true or not?" Another remembered "very clearly, how frustrating it was that the problem we thought it was, was really a problem with something else. Narrowing it down to something that was so simple as three or four words was really quite eye opening." Graduates described ways they applied the process of analyzing root causes in their work. One reported "often trying to break down problems to understand their root cause before visiting solutions." Another explained that the "DiP has helped me to be able to delve deeper into problems to determine what are the root causes of the problems in my organization."

Another practice related to organizational problem solving where graduates reflected growth is goal setting. The second highest score among survey questions was agreement that "the DiP influenced how I set professional or organizational goals or objectives." One graduate recollected the process during the DiP of trying to craft "a simple goal statement" that was "specific and measurable." Learning to generate more effective goals allowed one graduate to better assess "our achievement" and "what we need to do." Another graduate talked about the ongoing influence of this new skill: "You can't think without saying, okay, what is my ultimate goal? Where am I now?" In addition, another graduate spoke about now trying to move their organization "away from vague [or] nebulous" goals and toward "some system of measure[ment] to ensure we are meeting them."

Graduates also reported using evidence more due to their DiP experience. As one graduate explained, the "DiP experience has led me to place more weight on research" and on "evidence-based solutions to practical problems identified in my work." Another wrote about being "more mindful" to "execute evidence-based decision-making." For one graduate, in particular, the practice of using "evidence to support everything that I think, everything that I say, everything that I propose, everything that I do" was "probably the most impactful lesson…from the whole DiP." Some of the nuances in the way graduates now use evidence included being more discriminating, such as understanding that there are "different levels of evidence, in terms of credibility," "reliability," and "accuracy." Another example is the use of organizational performance data, such as one graduate's pursuit of more program data "so that we have evidence on how well it went and what are the strengths and what are the areas that we really need to look at to improve." Finally, evidence was reported being used more in communications. One graduate said, "the DiP has assisted me in the experiences of communicating new thinking" and that now their "thinking is associated with new research." An additional outgrowth for this person is that this mindset has "provided a basis for continuous discovery and knowledge sharing."

Finally, participants described ways that the DiP positively impacted their ability to generate solutions. This included having a better ability to identify the criteria for effective solutions. One graduate described being "in a much better position now to dive into the literature" and "look at what other people have done… what research has been produced, what results have arisen out of implementing some of these models." Another felt more able to identify the appropriate course of action, once the root problems are identified, in order to determine "what are we going to do about it as opposed to just pulling [a solution] out of the air." Another former student revealed that engagement with the more deliberative, and more time consuming, process of problem finding and root-cause analysis has produced dividends in better decisions and the ability to move quicker with those decisions. This graduate explained how the process "slows me down in my decision making…but also helps break [down] the issues…so that when I do reach a conclusion, I feel more comfortable with my assessment and then act more quickly." Few graduates offered examples about the process of actual solution implementation and one suggested that this is an area where more work during the dissertation process would have been valuable.

Expanded professional skills. The third area of professional influence that graduates reported experiencing from the DiP coalesced around new or enhanced abilities that they now use and find relevant in their work. Examples that graduates offered fell into three categories: collaboration, research skills, and writing.

The first practice area where graduates in this study experienced growth was collaboration. One aspect of this is graduates' collaboration in their own organizations. One graduate explained that the DiP exercise "increased my bond with my colleagues" and ultimately helped more broadly with the ability to "work with a team to discuss and solve a problem together." Another aspect is collaboration with peers in the program. The general value of the "networking" component was mentioned; something that occurs when "someone knows someone and an opportunity becomes available." More salient to the DiP itself, however, two graduates chose to collaborate on a national initiative due to their alignment around a shared approach. These two graduates are working together on "compressing" the problem-solving model they used in the DiP to apply it in equipping educational leaders in their context.

Another area graduates spoke about was improved research skills. One of these skills, for example, is the ability to review and synthesize research. One student "really valued" learning how to do "a large in-depth review of work" and other abilities associated with this, such as "the ability to be a better researcher, how to read articles quicker…how to find the themes that are coming out and how to assess the quality, that was a huge learning experience for me." Another graduate described benefitting from the ability to meaningfully present data: "I had so much data…it was everywhere. I learned how to present my data…to make it interesting." Another graduate described data analysis as "one area that I lacked" but a competency acquired through the dissertation and one that "I'm now using in my work."

The third skill area where graduates cited improvement in and subsequent increased value in their professions was writing. A graduate who does "a lot of policy writing" reported, "I have to say I write excellent papers now." Specific aspects of the writing process where graduates experienced growth included a greater ability to organize one's thinking and writing. "My thoughts became so organized," one interviewee described, "this goes first, purpose of study, importance of issue, and then research question…this has become second nature." Further, this graduate reported, "when I address an issue…write a…paper, report, email, anything, I try to address one issue at a time instead of three or four…I [tell] myself…'Focus on one issue.'" The ability to structure writing from general to the specific was also something learned through the DiP. For some graduates, these are types of writing moves that they had never done before and for one of these graduates, "it really put my thoughts in place." Another aspect of writing that was mentioned is writing with a particular audience in mind. One former student reported this as one of the more significant realizations about writing, about the need to "write so my readers feel it is easy to follow" and to "keep my audience focused." Finally, a graduate found the "Dissertation Showcase" to be particularly instrumental. The showcase is an event where students present their DiP projects to a public audience in a PechaKucha type format—a presentation with a fixed length where the presenter talks along to slide images that advance automatically. The event helped this graduate reframe writing and research as something to be shared and not just to "put on the shelf for reference." Consequently, this individual created a venue for educational leaders in their organization to share their work with each other. The new practice is enabling developing leaders "to actually learn about what each individual has done" and helping to ensure "that studies are done seriously."

Personal Impacts

Graduates reported that the DiP impacted their personal lives and habits in a number of ways. All of the survey participants agreed or strongly agreed that the knowledge and skills from the DiP had a positive impact on them personally. Fifteen of the survey participants agreed or strongly agreed that "I have made a change in my personal life or behaviors that is directly or indirectly related to my experience completing the Global EdD DiP" and 15 felt the DiP has influenced their ability to address problems outside of work. Though participants spoke more frequently about the impact of the DiP on their professional work, it was evident through this study that the DiP also had an impact on the way they organize their lives, the way they think about challenges, and the way in which they interact with friends or family members.

Organizational skills. The DiP process helped several participants improve in the area of personal organization. One participant noted how in general the skills and knowledge gained through the DiP spilled over into the personal sphere: "Knowledge and experience garnered throughout has grown my personal approach in conducting other activities." This graduate then provided a specific example in the area of personal planning, explaining that now, "before embarking on any activity, goals and objectives have to be clearly stated." Another graduate illustrated the impact of the DiP in the area of self-organization: "The DiP process has helped develop my personal organizational skills. I am more effective in my personal life now than I was prior to beginning the program."

Thinking reflectively and critically. Participants said the DiP process trained them to think more reflectively and critically. One participant responded on the survey, "I have become more focused and deliberate in my personal life." Another wrote, "I set more realistic, short-term goals that are in chunks rather than large umbrella type ones. I find myself being even calmer when addressing problems and quicker to consider and identify assumed causes, which helps me get to a solution." Three interview participants shared that as a result of the DiP process, they now ask many more questions and are more critical of information they read in the news. One participant reported that the DiP had the effect of encouraging her to ask "too many" questions. It is evident that the personal and professional impacts of the DiP experience are intertwined, as illustrated in the words of one participant, who wrote: "I am seeking new challenges in my professional life, which will serve to extend the impact that I personally believe I should have and be able to make upon my community and nationally."

Interactions with others. Some participants found that they approached working with people differently. As previously mentioned, the conceptual framework used in the DiP encourages students to explore the factors in the areas of knowledge, motivation, and organization—or "KMO" for short—which may affect organizational performance. Some graduates reported applying this same framework in their analysis of family members or of personal decisions. One participant said that he applied the KMO approach to parenting, and another participant said "I don't know if students have said this to you, but...a couple of us...we KMO everything." On the survey, another participant wrote, "I am viewing a lot more problems from a knowledge, motivation [and] organization standpoint. That framework has helped put things in perspective for me and others." These statements suggest that the deliberative process of analysis used for the dissertation became ingrained in the thinking of participants and that some graduates found it difficult to consider the actions of others without it.

PROFESSIONAL IMPACT

Graduates also reported impacts from the DiP on their professional practices. These types of impacts fall into two broad categories, which will be discussed next: impacts on their career goals and aspirations and impacts on their capacity to lead systemic change.

Impacts on Career Aspirations

When probed about the impact of completing the DiP on their career goals and aspirations, graduates' responses clustered into three clear themes: career direction, professional autonomy, and contributions to the field.

Career direction. Slightly conflicting findings emerged about the impact of the DiP on the direction of the graduates' careers. Two interviewees pointed out that the process of completing the DiP helped them confirm and focus their career plans. Specifically, one mentioned that her goal is to "just do what I do but do it better" and the other that "it was going through that process really helped me solidify what it is I wanted to be doing in my career and focus and emphasis." On the other hand, one graduate noted that the DiP and EdD program left him with "more questions than answers" about his future career, but added that this was welcomed. Another graduate shared this sentiment, stating "it was very easy for me when I entered the program to say what I wanted to be. It's hard for me to say that now." This graduate also viewed this tension positively, however, and as an indicator of growth, explaining: "That's actually an opportunity in of itself. I'm comfortable with that in a way that I, probably without this experience, would not be." Based on the data, completing the DiP impacted the students in different but welcomed ways with respect to their career direction and goals.

Professional autonomy. A prominent theme that emerged was the graduates' interest to have greater professional autonomy. Three of the seven interviewees made clear references that the DiP process enabled them to see themselves as autonomous professionals, even if embedded in an organization. One, specifically, is planning to start an educational consulting business in addition to his full-time employment. He mentioned, in contrast to past endeavors, "this time I'm at the helm, I'm the one driving. That time I was just one of the people in the car but this time I'm the one driving it." Another graduate mentioned, "I don't actually need to work for an organization to have the visibility." This person elaborated by explaining:

> I've got offers from different organizations from right here and even in Washington, DC. Lately, a lot of organizations have been trying to seek me out to join their teams and help their early grade reading programs to grow and build a portfolio, and I just keep pulling back because I just feel like I just love the flexibility to work with different organizations and to support them and to have the freedom.

A graduate who was an entrepreneur before joining the program stated, "I found that the DiP helped me in terms of working with start-ups, working with business owners that want to be entrepreneurs." The interview data demonstrated that the experience of completing a DiP with an organizational problem-solving focus enabled graduates to perceive themselves as more autonomous and to support a more entrepreneurial mindset.

Contributing to the field. The final theme related to the graduates' career aspirations and goals was their desire and efficacy to contribute to the field of their professional practice. As a result of completing their DiP, graduates saw themselves—and felt being viewed—as "specialists" in their field. This, with the increased confidence in skills like writing and presenting, prompted them to participate in their profession at a level they had not previously, such as by presenting at conferences or publishing their work. At least one graduate had already presented at a professional conference, mentioning that "it boosted my confidence in writing, it gave me more knowledge and it increased my visibility." Another graduate mentioned that "…a door has opened around publishing and research" and, as a result, they are "looking at something in a way that I did not expect going into the program." Completing the DiP, therefore, enabled students to see themselves in a different role with regard to the ability to make contributions to their profession.

Impacts on Capacity to Lead Systemic Change

The fourth theme explored with graduates was the impact of completing the DiP on their capacity to lead systemic reform. Their responses assembled into two main types of impact on leading systemic change. These included their ability to lead systemic change at the organizational level and their ability to lead systemic change at a larger, more macro level. Each of these impacts will be discussed below.

Systemic change at the organizational level. Following completion of the DiP, graduates saw themselves as more capable to address systemic change within their teams or organizations. This was due to factors that included new skills to solve organizational problems as well as an enhanced ability to initiate and proceed with new reform initiatives. The majority of survey respondents, 90 percent, agreed or strongly agreed that the problem-solving skills learned through the DiP increased their ability to solve organizational problems. As one survey respondent stated, "The DiP process enabled me to think holistically about organizational change management and identify the root causes of problems and address them systematically." Similarly, a graduate responded during the interview, "I have kind of introduced the KMO as part of our business operation and model. All our managers...they have to substantiate and support what they are proposing [so] we'll get the best possible result."

While graduates were not always able to incorporate all of the organizational problem-solving steps that were involved in their DiPs, respondents generally expressed that the DiP changed the way they approach change within their organizations and how they interact with their colleagues. One graduate explained: "To be fair, clearly I can't go through KMO with everything to the root cause, but it's always on my mind. I think it changed how I interact with my supervisors and how I interacted with my colleagues and my direct reports." Taking on more complex organizational challenges can add a new level of complexity and, as one graduate expressed, "...I tend to always want really challenging work so I can really get in and solve complicated problems, but the more complex they are the harder it is, so I tend to, I think, take on more than I should at this point."

At the same time, graduates expressed that the DiP enhanced their ability to initiate and proceed with new reform initiatives in their organizations. This included thinking about new organizational initiatives differently, reforming and transforming organizations in a more focused and intense way and supporting initiatives at a more systemic level. One interview participant credited the DiP's gap analytic methodology for helping him come up with recommendations around his company's education initiative. Another graduate described how the DiP inspired a shift in focus toward organizational vision and goals:

> ...now, I ask myself, 'What is the vision of the school?'...That was a major change for me...when I think about the next step, the next five or ten years for the university...What is our vision? Then we design a program in alignment with the mission and vision.

Systemic change at a macro level. Graduates also expressed the impact of the DiP on their ability to engage in systemic change at a larger, more macro level. This was due, for some, to upward mobility within their positions that allowed them to address change at a more macro level. One such interview participant stated, "I meet with everybody in the Ministry of Education…I work at all levels…the goal now…is shifted towards sustainability and I'm really looking at what capacity needs to be built within the education system in order to sustain these programs." In terms of the survey, 80 percent of survey respondents agreed or strongly agreed that completing the DiP has had an impact on their capacity to lead systemic change or large-scale reform efforts. One of the graduates discussed how his company was recently approached by another company that wanted to expand into his part of the world. This graduate attributed the problem-solving skills learned in the DiP to helping him map a plan, the system and the procedures on how to develop this joint venture. As another graduate stated, "I am in a better position to look at macro aspects…it has helped me to think in a much bigger way, and given me a helicopter view of whatever challenge I face." Another graduate related how she is increasingly identified and called on to solve increasingly larger challenges, "I think regardless of whether it's a bigger scale or small scale, the application of knowledge and skill is similar. It's just that you are dealing with more people, bigger organization…I think it's good practice ground for potential leaders."

DISCUSSION

Our interviews with graduates and the survey responses we gathered revealed a range of positive impacts resulting from completion of the DiP in the Global Executive EdD program. Graduates experienced influences on their professional practices, on a personal level and on their career goals and aspirations. We also saw evidence of an enhanced ability to bring about systemic change within their organizations and more broadly. In reflecting on these findings, we wish to address three questions: the degree to which the program has met its stated goals, possible critiques the data has surfaced about the DiP and implications for practice that we can distil from this study.

To assess the effectiveness of the DiP as manifested in the Global Executive EdD, we can return to two key aims noted at the top of this chapter: the goal to offer a dissertation experience that is applied and practice-oriented and the aim of creating a signature pedagogy. First, the experience of graduates indicates that the DiP helped them to focus on their practice and to carry into their work practical yet research-based knowledge. Their reports revealed increased self-reflection about their professional decisions and strategies, the use of theoretical frameworks to justify their actions and an emphasis on deriving solutions that are aligned with evidence. One area where the practice of these graduates may be weaker is in their versatility with a variety of methods of inquiry. A second programmatic aspiration to consider is whether we see evidence that this DiP approaches a true "signature pedagogy." We believe so on the basis that it seems to have provided a vehicle for these graduates to demonstrate expertise first in their dissertation product itself and then in their real world contexts. There is adequate evidence suggesting that the DiP methodology they experienced provided a framework to support their ongoing pursuit of inquiry into practice.

This project has revealed a few critical observations that may be useful in further advancing the Global Executive EdD DiP. First, the data suggest that the graduates are strong on identifying and analyzing problems, but weaker on identifying solutions and even weaker on implementation. To round out the problem-solving abilities of its graduates, this is likely something that the program would need to address. Next, this DiP has achieved impact by equipping its graduates with a well-developed conceptual framework, gap analysis, while maintaining flexibility in its methodological approach to gathering data. Nevertheless, exposure to a wider range of other conceptual models may lead to greater flexibility in problem-solving. Similarly, while graduates provided ample examples of practical and procedural practices and outcomes, less observed in the data is the reflection on rationales for change or alternative change theories or analyses of broader societal forces or systemic inequities. Augmenting graduates' theoretical footing in these areas could enhance their ability to generate the most meaningful solutions. Finally, reviewing the desired curricular outcomes in light of the data suggests that the goal of equipping students to practice evidence-based problem solving was achieved. Reports from graduates clearly reveal a new and consistent focus on looking for both quantitative and qualitative evidence to support their thinking, their decisions and their assessments of organizational performance. The data were more silent, however, concerning the DiP's impact regarding other goals of the program such as producing graduates who promote creative thinking and innovative solutions or who effectively develop and implement policy.

Finally, this study revealed several implications for practice for those involved in administering an EdD or other related programs. While Rossier's Global Executive EdD program is unique in aspects of its design, it provides some broader implications for practice to be considered. These implications include:

- The EdD degree is not widely known or understood in some global contexts. Given the increasing global nature of education and employment, it will be important for EdD programs to leverage learning in different contexts and bring together students from around the world. Additional outreach and education around the role and rigor of an EdD are called for.
- The length of the typical EdD program and the breadth of topics that could reasonably be included mean that there are practical constraints that require choices being made in terms of the curriculum design. These include the types of knowledge and skills to focus on, competencies to include and the relative breadth or depth of themes to cover. In practice, administrators of these programs need to be cognizant of the choices being made and leave room for assessment and continuous rethinking of those choices.
- The Global Executive EdD is grounded in a systematic, well-defined problem solving conceptual framework. This provides students a substantial

context and focused lens by which to define and address problems both in their dissertations in practice and continuing into their work environments. While there are clear benefits to this grounding as reported by students, programs also need to ensure they are equipping graduates to be flexible problem solvers. As the EdD continues to evolve, additional thinking is called for around the extent to which EdD programs adopt a program-wide conceptual framework as one of the signature pedagogies or build in additional flexibilities in efforts to best develop adaptable problem solvers. For example, though a specific framework may be adapted for the DiP, programs can consider increasing the application of a variety of other conceptual frameworks in the different courses.

- The DiP examined in this study proved to have broader influences beyond practical skills and knowledge and touching on areas and benefits that are more intangible. These include influences on collaboration, working in teams, networking and confidence building. In terms of implications for practice, these are substantial outcomes to be recognized and built on by those involved in administering an EdD or related program.

CONCLUSION

The professional doctorate faces continuing challenges and opportunities, which calls for intensified leadership around the project of redesigning the DiP. This chapter has offered direction by describing impacts of the DiP for graduates of the University of Southern California's Global Executive EdD. Influences of this DiP were seen on graduates' professional and personal practice, career goals and aspirations, and on their capacity to lead systemic change. The findings also pointed to areas for further attention. As faculty and graduate program administrators consider changes to curricula and DiPs, they may well keep in mind the challenges related to the recognition of the EdD in a global context. Prioritization of curricular content in intensive professional programs represents another area to consider, given the broad range of skills and knowledge that could be addressed. Lastly, less tangible outcomes also have important implications for graduates, and program designers should be deliberate about fostering growth and understanding in areas such as confidence building, mentoring, collaboration and contributing to one's field.

REFERENCES

Clark, R. E., & Estes, F. (2008). *Turning research into results: A guide to selecting the right performance solutions.* Charlotte, NC: Information Age Publishing, Inc.

Evans, R. (2007). Comments on Shulman, Golde, Bueschel, and Garabedian: Existing practice is not the template. *Educational Researcher, 36*(6), 553–559.

Levine, A. (2005). *Educating school teachers.* The Education Schools Project. Retrieved from http://files.eric.ed.gov/fulltext/ED504135.pdf

Shulman, L. S. (2005). Signature pedagogies in the professions. *Daedalus, 134*(3), 52–59.

Smrekar, C., & McGraner, K. (2009). From curricular alignment to the culminating project: The Peabody College Ed.D. capstone. *Peabody Journal of Education, 84*(1), 48–60.

Storey, V. A., Caskey, M. M., Hesbol, K. A., Marshall, J. E., Maughan, B., & Dolan, A. W. (2014). Examining EdD dissertations in practice: The Carnegie Project on the Education Doctorate. *International HETL Review,* 5(2). Retrieved from https://www.hetl.org/examining-EdD-dissertations-in-practice-the-carnegie-project-on-the-education-doctorate

Wergin, J. F. (2011). Rebooting the EdD. *Harvard Educational Review, 81*(1), 119–139.

Zambo, D. (2011). Action research as signature pedagogy in an education doctorate program: The reality and hope. *Innovative Higher Education, 36*(4), 261–271.

CHAPTER 8

HOW MY EdD PROGRAM TURNED ME INTO A SOCIAL JUSTICE PRACTITIONER-SCHOLAR

Laurie Scolari

At the start of my doctorate program, I sought out a research topic that resonated with me at my core. I started with several self-reflection questions: Why did I pursue a doctorate? What will it mean personally and professionally? What can it mean for my community? These questions led me to consider my own identity. My choice to be a college administrator was connected to my desire to go back to the lettuce fields where I grew up to tell my community that a college degree is the pathway out of the backbreaking work and poverty that plagued us. However, I knew first hand as a first-generation student of color of the challenges that would be encountered.

My mother immigrated to the United States from Mexico and cleaned houses for a living. Though she encouraged me to go to college, she could not tell me the steps I needed to take to successfully transition to post-secondary education. She always taught me, however, to be self-reliant. To that end, I taught myself to build my own social capital in consideration of my transition to college. In my neigh-

Exploring the Impact of the Dissertation in Practice, pages 125–133.

borhood, I knew of only one person who went to college, a young woman two years older than me: Veronica Martin. Whilst on a weekend visit from college, she helped me complete my college application, but the application was only the first phase: I also needed help with subsequent steps of the enrollment process. There was no one else I could ask in my family or neighborhood because I did not have access to adults with college degrees.

Consequently, I sought the help of my teachers and track coach with the final stages of my college application. A key point is that I had to seek out their assistance; they did not explicitly offer their help with college planning. To my surprise, they were all knowledgeable about the college application process because they had all been through it themselves. Experts surrounded me, yet they were not readily imparting their knowledge. There was no plan to distribute college admission information to students. Like most Latina students who are first in their family to pursue college, I struggled to navigate a college application process that was not designed with me in mind.

As a practitioner, I witnessed thousands of students who were first in their family to go to college experience the same difficult transition. But now I could do something about it—I was on the other end, an administrator with the power to address the transitional barriers. This personal and professional reflection confirmed my chosen research topic: First-Generation Students of Color—Easing their Transition to Community College. Armed with a research topic that rang true to my soul, I lived for it—both in my doctoral studies—and in my practice.

BECOMING A DATA ADVOCATE

Throughout my doctorate studies, I was the Dean of Counseling and Student Support Services in the largest Community College in California. Prior to the doctorate program, I did not consider systemic change. I was squarely focused on overwhelming daily tasks and seemingly endless administrators' meetings. Systemic change was neither on my job description nor in the college's strategic plan. However, the EdD program transformed me into a practitioner scholar—suddenly it became clear that systems needing change surrounded me, many of which I controlled. I witnessed the atrocities I was studying. The number of Latino and African American students negatively affected by the equity gap at my college was striking (City College of San Francisco, 2009). Locally, every year approximately 1000 San Francisco Unified School District (SFUSD) high school graduates do not pursue any post-secondary education (John W. Gardner Center for Youth and Their Communities, 2011). On average, 31% of Latino students and 30% of African-American students did not pursue any post- secondary education, despite the fact that City College of San Francisco (CCSF) is accessible to them. Comparatively, only 16% of White and 14% of Chinese high school graduates did not pursue any college (John W. Gardner Center for Youth and Their Communities, 2011).

To tackle the problem, I first needed to understand the data. Knowing how to pull data, how to analyze it and how to dissect it was an invaluable part of the doctorate program. As a practitioner, looking at data was neither commonplace nor encouraged. The college itself was not driven by data. Personally, data was interesting, but I needed to learn how to be a data advocate—for the sake of the students. When I asked for data, I needed to ask the research office to pull it again and again until I could continuously slice it differently and dissect it from a variety of angles. Additionally, my Dissertation in Practice (DiP) was a mixed method sequential design that provided me with a direct understanding of how to take quantitative trends, derive questions from them, and form focus groups to respond to outstanding data questions from a qualitative perspective.

However, understanding the data was only part of it. In addition to seeing the equity gaps in real time, I was enlightened by many theorists who described the foundational issues behind these gaps. For example, the large majority of current admissions policies are based on a system of meritocracy and social stratification (Oakes, Rogers, Lipton, & Morrell, 2000). Students from mainstream cultures and middle-class status are at an advantage because these admissions policies were designed to serve them. Not surprisingly, members of privileged groups embrace the ideology of merit as being morally fair, and therefore, justify its use. This practice also allows them to maintain a competitive advantage in admissions (Oakes & Guiton, 1995; Solórzano & Ornelas, 2004). Additionally, Daniel Solórzano (1997, 1998) identified five tenets of Critical Race Theory (CRT). He states that race and racism are central, endemic, permanent, and a fundamental part of defining and explaining how American society functions. Layers of racialized subordination exist based on gender, class immigration status, surname, phenotype, accent, and sexuality. CRT challenges White privilege and exposes deficit-informed research that silences, ignores, and distorts the funds of knowledge that people of color hold. Additionally, CRT has a commitment to social justice, and therefore, recognizes the experiential knowledge of people of color as legitimate and critical to understanding, analyzing, and teaching about racial subordination (Solórzano 1997, 1998).

Now I understood that the access gap was not happenstance, but rather due to a historic system of racial bias. Most disturbing to me—I was now part of this system. And by not doing anything to change it, I was perpetuating it. Armed with this, I became simultaneously furious and inspired.

DISSERTATION IN PRACTICE (DiP): MY GUIDEBOOK FOR SYSTEMIC CHANGE

In my daily work, I often ask myself: How can this meeting or discussion turn into something that will change lives on a practical level? Given that this is how my mind works, I knew my DiP needed to be practical and useful in order to be inspired to write it. With this in mind, I decided to craft my DiP into a guidebook for establishing change.

My study revealed first generation students were reliant on their high schools to provide support in their transition to college—yet high schools were not equally supporting all students. Findings showed Asians had the highest levels of support from teachers, after-school service providers, and counselors—above Latinos and African-Americans. Additionally, though most seniors were not meeting 4–year university entry requirements, high schools were disproportionally promoting the 4–year university and spending minimal time on the community college admissions process (Scolari, 2012). And of those students that did enroll in our college, most were not matriculating in enough units to be full time nor were they accessing English and math classes due to low registration priority (Carew, Gurantz, & Scolari, 2013).

Based on these findings, my DiP outlined several recommendations that aimed to: a) ensure that school-based social capital, in the area of college planning activities, is distributed equally to all students; b) to increase access to pivotal adults for students of color; and c) to promote the community college equal to four-year institutions in homes and in the schools. Ultimately, these strategies were designed to ease the transition of high school students of color to the community college. My recommendations chapter outlined a 38–page plan of action to combat the issue.

Recommendation 1: Strategic Partnerships Grounded in Data-Driven Decisions

First, given that the transition from high school to college occurs between two distinctly different institutions, a partnership needs to be formed between the two. However, partnerships need to go beyond getting leaders in a room. There is a need to move away from working in silos, as large bureaucratic institutions often do, to a unified approach towards tackling the transition issue. In fact, every high school should have a college access strategy (Tierney, Bailey, Constantine, Finkelstein, & Hurd, 2009), but if the community college were to meet them half way, this would strengthen that strategy further. A high school/community college access strategy would likely be well received by educational leaders. Such partnerships need to be strategic, intentional, and grounded in data-driven decisions. A primary aspect of the partnership includes transparency of data. An honest look at data regarding transitional issues should be presented to top leaders from both institutions (Moore & Shulock, 2010). Ideally, to minimize bias, an outside institution should conduct a comprehensive analysis of transitional issues. Then, based on the results, and with input from practitioners and students, a realistic educational transitions strategic plan should be implemented to tackle the issues at hand (Noeth & Wimberly, 2004). Each institution should assign a practitioner to lead and champion the work at their respective institution.

At the start of my doctorate program, we formed this very kind of partnership in San Francisco. What has been critically important to this partnership is the fact that the Chancellor of the community college, the Superintendent of the school district and the Mayor's office each assigned a critical leader to move the action plan forward. I had the honor to serve as the assigned leader from my community college, and therefore, have had a first-hand perspective as to how these partnerships worked. In San Francisco, once transition data were presented to executive leaders, an annual action plan, grounded in that data, was created and implemented. Critical leaders were assigned to move action items forward at the district and at the college. Having this partnership gave me a platform to move the work forward. Therefore, creating a strategic partnership grounded in data-driven decisions is a foundational first step towards action. Then I could effectively build a coalition of leaders who could work towards minimizing the transitional barriers.

Recommendation 2: Engage Every Student in College Application Process

Transitioning to college can be overwhelming and usually involves tests, applications, orientations, and educational plans. Often students are expected to complete this process on their own. This practice suggests that once a student reaches their high school commencement ceremony, their job is done. However, the word commencement means, "a beginning." In order to earn a living wage in today's economy, that beginning means the start of a college education. It is irresponsible for educational leaders to believe that a high school is an ending point. Instead, intentionally making the college application part of the school day is imperative. This approach allows educational leaders to directly support students who are four-year-bound, community college-bound, and those who do not have a plan with clear direction and options. The second recommendation, therefore, encourages leaders to engage every student in the college application process by taking a universal approach. In order to implement this primary recommendation successfully, three suggested actions are presented including making the college application mandatory, increasing access to pivotal adults, and equally promoting of the community college.

Typically, four-year colleges have orientations that last several days or even weeks while community college students often complete all the matriculation steps in one day, including a 2- to 3-hour placement exam. A majority of incoming community college students do not prepare for placement exams because colleges do not often readily advertise or provide prep courses. A study by Andrea Venezia surveyed matriculation officers at 73 community colleges and found that less than half (44%) indicated they provide practice tests for their students. Even in those cases where test prep was offered, students did not know practice tests existed. The larger problem related to these findings is that study respondents indicated that they did not understand that placement test scores would determine course placement, and further affect how long it would take them to complete community college (Venezia, Bracco, & Nodine, 2010). Students are often surprised by this step in the matriculation process and once they take the exam, there is often no turning back as re-take test policies often require students wait weeks or months to retake the exam. In the end, students take an exam of which they do not grasp the impact until they are stuck in a remedial sequence that will take years to complete (Adams, 2010).

One assured way to increase students' understanding of the college enrollment process is to make the college enrollment process a mandatory high school activity for every student. It is important to bring the community college application process to high school students before they graduate. Obviously while they are in high school, educators still have access to students as a captive audience, minimizing the need to seek them out after high school is over. But this recommendation takes it a step further—to make the college enrollment process a part of the school day, essentially including it as a component of the curriculum and making it mandatory for all students, even for those who did not originally have a plan to pursue post-secondary education. Although students may ultimately decide not to participate in post-secondary education, at least they have the option and hopefully, with the right messaging, have been convinced of its pertinence in today's economy.

As a result of this recommendation, I led the college in a new direction—making the community college application process a part of the high school curriculum. The five required enrollment steps (application, placement exam, counselor meeting, orientation, and registration) now occur for every SFUSD senior as a mandatory part of the high school day. Since most SFUSD students are not meeting California State University/University of California entry requirements with a C grade or better, the largest majority of their student population have the community college as their only option. For steps one and two, CCSF now sends college counselors out to the 18 public high schools to conduct application workshops and orientation sessions for community college-bound students and for those who do not have a plan. To accomplish the third step, the college sends testing proctors out to the high schools to conduct assessment tests among these students or in some cases buses the students to the college. For the fourth step, college counselors return with test results and meet with students via one-on-one counseling sessions to create their first semester educational plan. This step is critically important because students who start college with an academic plan based on advisement from a college counselor increase the likelihood that they will persist (Center for Community College Student Engagement, 2012). The final step, registration, now occurs every April. Additionally, we now give local high school graduates priority registration. In order increase the likelihood that students complete this final step, all SFUSD graduates, approximately 1000 every year, are bussed to the college in April during the school day to actually register for classes, among other activities intended to build social capital among students. This step of visiting the community college campus is important since many first time students do not understand the value of registering early, and late registration decreases student success in the classroom (CCCSE, 2012).

At its inception, there were varying levels of enthusiasm about this initiative to bring the community college enrollment process to the high schools. One high school, for example, is so invested in students engagement with this process that they have not only made it a requirement for graduation, but they have also indicated that they will cancel prom if students do not complete the community college application process. However, this comprehensive approach met some resistance at first for a number of reasons. First, it took me six months to find 18 college counselors, one assigned to each high school, who were willing to go out to the high schools. Creating a mandatory system for every high school graduate was a new concept for many. Despite some initial resistance, after I gave six months of presentations grounded in data, CCSF counselors were up for the challenge. Another caveat to this recommendation is to expect resistance from some high school principals and teachers in that completing the college application during the school day takes students away from classroom-based learning. However, with consistent data presentations and relationship building, now all high schools in the district participate.

Should an educational leader wish to adopt this recommendation, it is important to allow time for the buy-in process to occur. In the end, high school students were connected with pivotal adults that had direct knowledge of the application process, effectively removing this barrier.

Recommendation 3: Equally Promote the Community College

Even once the college application was made mandatory and each student was assigned to an adult to directly assist him or her with the college application, there was hesitation on the part of some students, educators, and even parents because community college is rarely promoted. Community colleges were not being promoted equally to the four-year institutions, and further yet, my study found that there were negative sentiments from parents, peers, and high school staff that discouraged students from pursuing the option. An intentional mind shift among all leaders of the high school needed to occur (Scolari, 2012).

There are a number of ways I attempted to create this shift in the schools. First, I presented school-level data to high school administration and faculty to convince them that not promoting the community college presents a major problem from an economic stability perspective. For example, at the high school where my study was conducted, I found that in 2009, 39 of their students (31%) went nowhere after high school graduation, 46 (28%) did not meet 4–year entry requirements, and 43 dropped out before they could graduate. Added up, that is annually upwards of 128 students for just that high school that had only one option for post- secondary education; however, this option was never promoted. And earning a living wage in one of the most expensive cities in our nation is a persistent challenge. By not connecting our high school graduates with postsecondary opportunities, we can negatively affect their ability to earn a living wage.

Second, it is important to inform high school counselors and teachers of college entrance requirements and programs (McDonough, 2004). Therefore, I implemented an outreach program for faculty. Community college counselors began to present at several high-school site faculty meetings about the local community college offerings. Also, community college counselors offer professional development to the high school counselors. Additionally, we gathered a group of twenty counselors, ten from the community college, and ten from the high school district to discuss ways to better coordinate services on a monthly basis. Through this process of convening counselors across both institutions, high school counselors admitted they do not promote the community college at their high schools. Current professional development activities are now designed to convince the high school counselors that the community college is a viable, and often the only, option for the large majority of their students.

SUSTAINED CHANGE

Though systemic change presents many challenges, our college saw dramatic results. As a result of the aforementioned recommendations, in 2010, the percentage of African-Americans enrolled in our college increased by 18% and Latinos by 24.5%. The number of high school graduates who enrolled in English or math increased at 63% and 270% respectively (Scolari, 2012). Now that the students are receiving priority enrollment, the number of units they were enrolling in on average went from 8 to 12.5. Since twelve units are considered full-time, they were now accessing critical financial aid scholarships, book loan programs and access to a key program, Extended Opportunity Programs and Services (EOPS). By enrolling full time, we are directly impacting their retention rates. In that first year, the retention rate was 89% in year one, a 14% increase from previous years. Six years later, these policy changes remain in place and these increases have been sustained.

My doctorate did that for thousands of students. For that, I am convinced of its implicit value to me personally, as a first-generation student, and professionally, for those that I serve. My newfound strategy values the use of data as an advocacy tool and the application of theories, which fuel my understanding of equity and social justice. This has been my story for how the EdD program turned me from a passionate educator into a practitioner-scholar who is now driven by a fierce social justice agenda.

REFERENCES

Adams, C. (2010, October 14). Students underprepared for community college entrance Tests. *Education Week.* Retrieved from http://blogs.edweek.org/edweek/college_bound/2010/10/_thad_nodine_an_independent.html

Carew, M., Gurantz, O., & Scolari, L. (2013), Cross-agency collaboration and shared data from the community perspective: You can't point fingers at data. In M. McLaughlin & R. A. London (Eds.), *From data to action: Using data and institutions to improve youth outcomes* (Ch. 5, pp. 83–101). John W. Gardner Center for Youth and Their Communities, Stanford University. Cambridge, MA: Harvard Education Press.

Center for Community College Student Engagement. (2012). *A matter of degrees: Promising practices for community college student success (A first look).* Austin, TX: The University of Texas at Austin, Community College Leadership Program.

City College of San Francisco. (2009). *Preliminary report on student achievement gap and social equity resolution.* San Francisco, CA: Office of Research and Planning.

John W. Gardner Center for Youth and Their Communities. (2011). *Supporting transition to postsecondary education.* Stanford, CA: Youth Data Archive at Stanford University.

McDonough, P. M. (2004). *The School-to-College transition: Challenges and prospects.* Washington, DC: American Council on Education.

Moore, C., & Shulock, N. (2010). *Divided we fail: Improving completion and closing racial gaps in California's community colleges.* Sacramento, CA: Institute for Higher Education Leadership and Policy at California State University, Sacramento.

Noeth, R. J,, & Wimberly, G. L. (2004). *College readiness begins in middle school.* Iowa City, IA: ACT Policy Research Center.

Oakes, J., & Guiton, G. (1995). Matchmaking: The dynamics of high school tracking decisions. *American Educational Research Journal, 32*(1), 3–33.

Oakes J., Rogers. J., Lipton M., & Morrell E. (2000). The social construction of college access: Confronting the technical, cultural and political barriers to low-income students of color. In W. Tierney & L. S. Haggedorn (Eds.), *Extending our reach: Strategies for increasing access to college* (pp. 2–25). Albany, NY: SUNY Press.

Scolari, L. A. (2012). *First-generation students of color: Easing their transition to community college.* Retrieved from ProQuest Digital Dissertations. (Accession Order No. 3545586).

Solórzano, D. (1997). Images and words that wound: Critical race theory, racial stereotyping, and teacher education. *Teacher Education Quarterly, 24*, 5–19.

Solórzano, D. (1998). Critical race theory, racial and gender microaggressions, and the experiences of Chicana and Chicano scholars. *International Journal of Qualitative Studies in Education, 11*, 121–136.

Solórzano, D. G., & Ornelas, A. (2004). A Critical race analysis of Latina/o and African American advanced placement enrollment in public high schools. *The High School Journal, 87*(3), 15–26.

Tierney, W. G., Bailey, T., Constantine, J., Finkelstein, N., & Hurd, N. F. (2009). *Helping students navigate the path to college: What high schools can do: A practice guide* (NCEE #2009–4066). Washington, DC: National Center for Education Evaluation and Regional Assistance, Institute of Education Sciences, U.S. Department of Education. Retrieved from: http://ies.ed.gov/ncee/wwc/publications/practiceguides/.

Venezia, A., Bracco, K. R., & Nodine, T. (2010). One-shot deal? Students' perceptions of assessment and course placement in California's community colleges. San Francisco: WestEd.

CHAPTER 9

THE COLLABORATIVE COHORT MODEL

A Group Perspective on the Issues and Impact of Collaborating on a Dissertation in Practice

William E. Collins, Christopher D. Casavant, Erica A. Faginski-Stark,
Jason P. McCandless, and Marilyn A. Tencza

A NEW PROGRAM EMERGES

To understand the impact of the Dissertation in Practice (DiP) upon a Doctorate of Education (EdD) program and its graduate's future work and influence in the field, one must first examine the underlying characteristics of the DiP process, which, by its very design, results in an experience unique from a Doctorate of Philosophy (PhD) and a traditional Doctorate of Education (EdD). The DiP, like its sibling the dissertation, has a profound impact on the individual's scholarly knowledge and results in contributions to contemporary research. Unique to the DiP, that is not found in the dissertation, is the concurrent fieldwork that defines the practical, real world environment based on the applied research of doctoral candidates.

Exploring the Impact of the Dissertation in Practice, pages 135–150.
Copyright © 2017 by Information Age Publishing
135

The EdD came into inception at Harvard University in the early 1920s to address the specific needs of the practicing professional in education (Bengtson, Jones, Lasater, & Murphy-Lee, 2015). Affirmation of the EdD was followed by its acceptance at Columbia University's Teachers College in 1934 (Perry, 2012). Continued validation and evolution of this degree have persisted over time with most recent influence made by the Carnegie Project on the Education Doctorate (CPED). In 2007, spurred on by CPED, a consortium of 25 schools of education came together to transform doctoral education for practitioners (Perry, 2012, p. 44).

It was in the initial consortium of schools from 2007, that these authors engaged in the DiP and Collaborative Cohort Model as our path to earning an EdD. As a result of CPED, the Lynch School of Education at Boston College, in partnership with the Massachusetts Association of School Superintendents (MASS) and Teachers 21, piloted a first of its kind, Collaborative Cohort Model (CCM) approach within the Lynch School of Education's Professional School Administrator Program (PSAP) in 2009. CPED and PSAPs' goal was to "redesign the degree to make it the highest-quality degree for the advanced preparation of school practitioners" (Perry, 2012, p. 42).

The PSAP program had been designed forty years prior as an intensive three-year doctoral program to provide opportunities for full-time school administrators to obtain a Doctorate of Education in educational leadership, satisfy the academic requirements for licensure as a school superintendent, and build a district-level leadership network throughout the Commonwealth of Massachusetts. The adoption of the Collaborative Cohort Model by PSAP was a significant departure from the individualized approach to dissertation experienced by doctoral students in the traditional Apprentice Master Model (AMM) and "was developed in response to concerns about completion rates and the quality of research supervision" (Burnett, 1999, p. 46).

According to the Council of Graduate Students PhD Project, "students in the physical and biological science and technology fields, more than half of those in entering cohorts are earning a doctorate between year six and seven of a program. In the social sciences, year seven sees only a completion rate of just over 40 percent; in the humanities, the figure is 29 percent" Sowell (2008). Azad and Kohun (2006) suggest that a significant influence in high doctoral attrition rates stems from student's feelings of isolation, citing a lack of student-to-student communication as a specific contributing factor. The Collaborative Cohort Model removes boundaries between the competitively diverse systems and isolating educational experiences individual doctoral students face and in its place propagates daily discourse on educational research and practice linking "theory with systemic and systematic inquiry" (Perry, 2012, p. 43).

The Collaborative Cohort Model within a DiP applied transformational leadership that "occurs when one or more persons engage with others in such a way that leaders and followers raise one another to higher levels of motivation and morality" (Burns, 1978, p. 20) encouraging thought, negotiation, and consensus building which are core elements in systemic reform. Actualizing transformational leadership skills, while applying theory to practice, impacts future educational leaders by maximizing their capacity to affect organizational change.

With this vision in mind, a modern and new PSAP at Boston College was born. The redesigned program began with 25 doctoral students losing only 1 student in its first month. The remaining 24 students, organized into 4 groups, of five to seven students would pioneer this significant journey together.

The formation of the groups within the Collaborative Cohort Model was determined solely by the geographic location of the participants. While our formation was based on geography, our development into an effective learning community was based on trust, transparency, teamwork, and exemplary communication skills. "Proponents of cohorts argue that the model is more than a group of students with a common schedule, but rather an adult learning model characterized by affiliation and strong sense of purpose" (Greenlee & Karanxha, 2010, p. 358). The affiliation of the members of our cohort was that we were all from the western part of the state; hence, we became affectionately known as the "Westside."

WESTSIDE'S STORY: A SHARED EXPERIENCE

As members of Boston College's inaugural DiP and Collaborative Cohort Model class of 2009, the authors of this chapter were five practitioners of educational leadership. Our identity is important to understanding how we became known as the Westside. A name we continue to call ourselves and associate with scholarship, honor, and pride.

At the time we first embarked on the DiP Collaborative Cohort Model, each member was simultaneously a doctoral candidate and a full-time public school administrator. The members of the Westside cohort were from various school districts in central and western Massachusetts with duties spanning various grade levels, roles, and influence. Westside cohort members included a superintendent of a small rural school district in Western Massachusetts, two middle school principals from northern and western Massachusetts, an elementary school principal from the Springfield area, and a high school principal from a large regional school district in north central Massachusetts. Prior to being accepted into PSAP at Boston College and forming the Westside cohort, the individual members were unknown to each other.

Each cohort member describes their initial attraction to PSAP's EdD as understanding that the educational doctorate is the highest quality degree for educational practitioners seeking professional preparation and advancement because of the tight coupling of research and application. This perception is consistent with CPED as

> ...CPED members envision EdD graduates as stewards of the practice, scholarly practitioners, capable of blending their practical wisdom with their professional

> knowledge to identify, frame, and solve the problems of practice they face. Unlike students in PhD programs, students in newly designed or redesigned EdD programs are able to work full-time as they pursue their degree; take core courses based on their professional and intellectual needs; receive support through cohort structures; write dissertations focused on problems of practice; and, if on track, graduate in two to four years. (Zambo, Zambo, Buss, Perry, & Williams, 2014, p. 129)

With this understanding, we committed to Boston College, PSAP, and CPED's Collaborative Cohort Model.

As participants in the PSAP, our academic year started in the summer and we began each summer of the three-year program with a two-week *session in residence* at Boston College. The purpose of residency is to assimilate the cohort to the intense programming and the academic rigor but of equal import is the time spent together, developing personal and professional trust, and establishing relationships. The latter would prove to be the most important element to our success. The Westside's story affirms Boston College's primary cornerstone as to *Why Choose PSAP?* which is that "students learn collaboratively to support each other throughout the doctoral process" (*Why Choose PSAP?*, n.d., para. 2).

The Westside cohort began to take shape during the first two-week summer in residence program in 2009. The Westside members lived the farthest west from Boston of all PSAP cohort members. As a result, we remained on campus in the evenings and on weekends when other cohort members could "run" home to check on their work and families. This was our initial opportunity to bond and to get to know one another. During this communal summer session, we were able to share our professional experiences and begin to understand the work each of us was doing in our respective schools or districts and reflected upon who we were as individuals, providing greater insight into one another's character.

It was during this time that we each had multiple opportunities to try out different roles and responsibilities within the group. According to the CPED, Cohort Development: A Guide for Faculty and Program Developers (Brown-Ferrigno & Maughan, 2014) the structure of closed-cohort models, "provides continuity and opportunities for participants to learn and practice skills in group goal setting, community building, conflict resolution, and culture management" (Brown-Ferrigno & Maughan, 2014, p. 2). We developed the ability to "purposefully engage in group learning activities" (Brown-Ferrigno & Maughan, 2014, p. 2). A fundamental characteristic of effective groups is that members can participate in group discussions, consider differing viewpoints, and allow for diverse perspectives that will enrich the decision-making process (Fisher & Ellis, 1990). As we began to form an effective team, each member of the group felt valued and opinions were respected.

During this time there was as a growing sense of comfort with each other fostered by what Maher (2005) suggests as an opportunity to collaborate individual talents in an emerging group dynamic. From the start of the program, the Westside members formed a close-knit group. Thus roles began to take shape, similar to the nucleus of a family, which would define each member throughout our three-year program.

The formation of the Westside cohort was naturally evolving, while our lives were steeped in academic learning. In year one, the Westside completed research projects, immersed ourselves in scholarly literature, wrestled with moral and ethical dilemmas, and presented conclusions using qualitative and quantitative data methods under the instruction and guidance of our professors. Simultaneously, in year one most cohort members completed additional coursework required to meet Commonwealth of Massachusetts superintendent licensure criteria.

It was not until year two, after our research skills were validated, that we were sent forth to blend theoretical scholarship with practice by addressing authentic problems in educational settings. These projects took us into schools and school districts to apply our knowledge and test our theories. A major portion of our studies in year two included the completion of an Equity Audit in a school district in the Berkshires. This project required research, the development of interview questions, site visits, and interviews, qualitative data analysis, and formalized conclusions about findings resulting in an official report to the school district as well as a grade. This real world experience was not only a chance to learn but it was an opportunity for growth allowing us to hone our burgeoning working relationships and share experiences on a professional level.

By the end of year two, the Westside was prepared to establish our dissertation topic. We were arranging for comprehensive exams that would officially determine our readiness for the final stage of the PSAP program. This was the point at which we realized what was at stake and how our ability to work together would sustain us through the defense of our DiP.

The final summer in residence and year three proved to be the most intense. Comprehensive exams were due two weeks after our last summer residency, DiP questions, solidifying a research site and participants, choosing data collection methods, as well as course completion, were all taking place.

By fall, the Westside was fully immersed in research and the writing of our DiP. Weeknights and weekends were spent together focused on any given task that brought us closer to the completion of our DiP. Intertwined with learning to become an effective cohort, there continued to be numerous opportunities to develop strong bonds among the members of the Westside.

In order to complete our DiP research and create a plan for our problem of practice in educational leadership, we began meeting with greater frequency. These meetings initially began by rotating each member's school or home as a meeting place, but ultimately we decided upon selecting those locations most geographically centralized. Our work sessions quickly incorporated a social aspect, typically involving food; the act of "breaking bread" together seemed to reduce stress, increase good-natured banter, and ultimately strengthen our relationships. These meetings taught the group to negotiate, tolerate one another, and appreciate the strengths and weaknesses of each member. We found that relational awareness and comradery that the Westside developed continued to be our strongest asset.

As with all DiPs, numerous iterations were worked through, concepts were added and discarded, and daily communication with each other and our DiP chair were commonplace. If one could go back in time, this is the time that should be captured for all to see! The intensity of the collaborative work that transpired is the most profound element of the DiP and the Collaborative Cohort Model. This is when our relationships, our values, and our professional self, were put through the ultimate test. We knew what our goal was and word-by-word, line-by-line, all five cohort members deliberated the text of our DiP arduously contested the meaning of research, questioned the practical application of proposed solutions, and disagreed with each other. Is this not the true meaning of a scholar? The professional discourse that challenges the boundaries of what is understood resulting in change to a body of research or practice. This is what makes the DiP and the Collaborative Cohort Model most worthy of the doctoral title.

As professionals we not only held the knowledge of our study but we examined and applied every facet of that knowledge in a way that no single research student and doctoral candidate could ever do alone. Not only was there greater substance to our research findings but the depth of knowledge, collaboration, and professional skill gained in the Collaborative Cohort Model process influenced change in our work because we questioned each other's, as well as our own, thinking as scholars and as practicing educational leaders. It was as if each work session was a mini-defense of our DiP.

We suggest that through this intensive, three-year journey the Westside developed what Maher (2005) labels a "family orientation" (p. 208) to our peer interactions. We began to realize that "simply being together over time was beneficial because cohort members shared the same experiences and developed deeper interpersonal ties" (Maher, 2005, p. 202). As the Westside cohort evolved we became a family with a naturally occurring equity in responsibilities where everybody pulled his or her weight in equal measure.

Throughout the three years, an observer could predict the ebb and flow of our work, our behaviors, and our interactions among the group members. Whenever something had to be accomplished, deadlines had to be met, there were always one or two members who would pick up the pace motivating the group to accomplish the task. It seemed to naturally occur that if a member of the cohort began to lag, another cohort member would take up the slack. The result being that the whole group's momentum never faltered, the pace was steady, despite the ongoing fluctuation among individual candidates. In the final analysis, each cohort member carried his or her weight equally, if not always consistently.

The Fifth Discipline (Senge, 1990) describes systemic thinking as the most important of the disciplines that define a learning organization. When the authors reflect on the DiP model, we are reminded of Senge's salient point that "Reality is made up of circles, but we see straight lines. Herein lie the beginnings of our limitations as system thinkers" (Senge, 1990, p. 75). Alone we saw straight lines, but together we were able to think circuitously.

Upon reflection, we are now able to describe with clarity the benefit of being a part of the DiP and the Collaborative Cohort Model process. It transformed a group of "straight line" thinkers and practitioners into scholars and leaders who valued the intradependency and relational trust of the educational community and its influence on the quality of our work. Through collaborative discourse, we were far more effective in our ability to analyze information in a cohort than we could have on our own.

The authors' DiP capitalized on the considerable strengths, and diverse backgrounds, of the individual members to formulate our ideas and findings into a single voice. The path that we carved along our journey that brought us to this point was as difficult as it was professionally enlightening. We learned as much about each other and ourselves and what it takes to work collaboratively as we learned about research and scholarship.

We cannot imagine an academic undertaking that could replicate the level of teamwork and collaboration that this process required. Although writing a DiP, in any form, is a difficult, time-consuming, arduous process demanding a level of scholarship, commitment, and sustained discipline to which few are accustomed. When we factor in that this single document needed to be written with the collective efforts of four other individuals who were accustomed to being the leader, the brightest and, at the very least, the most influential person in the room at any given moment of the work day, the challenge of producing a comprehensive, coherent document that met everyone's standard increased exponentially. Beyond the expected and unexpected pitfalls of what a typical dissertation process can produce, the Collaborative Cohort Model DiP process was also an education in patience, diplomacy, and time-tested lessons in humility.

IMPACT ON PRACTICE

Candidates in EdD programs with a Collaborative Cohort Model, in contrast to candidates in traditional dissertation programs, experience a complex, dynamic environment in the collective negotiation of a DiP. We discovered that an element of vulnerability is present; perhaps it can be best described as intradependency or simply as reliance within a group. Individuals who are independent may feel a sense of vulnerability in establishing relational trust within a group. However, once established the positive rewards of intradependency outweigh the short-term discomfort of vulnerability because the isolation associated with a traditional dissertation is avoided and a strong support system is omnipresent.

> One of the strong features of this new movement is often called the cohort effect, that is, a group of students start together and build up a sense of community, with peer group support and group identity, thus avoiding the social and intellectual isolation that a PhD student might experience. (Guo & Rose, 2015, p. 6)

In a microcosm, our DiP cohort was experiencing the same systemic issues that many organizations face. We attempted to organize our DiP in small isolated sections, with each person solely responsible for her or his own piece. Our initial efforts can be likened to a disjointed sports team, wherein five players are drafted to an all-star team because each player had been the star on her or his former team. The problem was that no one had previously been required to effectively pass the ball or maximize individual efforts away from self and toward supporting the whole team's goals. In short, the Westside consisted of five individuals and our initial teamwork shortcomings illustrated this reality.

Our first submission of our scholarly efforts to our DiP Chair was in a word-terrible. During the 20-minute conversation he never once raised his voice, nor did the smile ever leave his face as he explained in painstaking detail how lacking our first effort was. What will forever resonate with us was his straightforward description of our poorly written and disjointed first submission. It was so painful that it prompted one of the members of our team to beg him to stop. The embarrassment was excruciating and we were crestfallen. What we quickly learned was that the DiP process required a greater level of teamwork than any of us were accustomed. There was a high standard that needed to be met and working cooperatively as individuals we were not going to come close to meeting it. We were learning a hard lesson about the difference between individual cooperation and team collaboration.

At first, we couldn't even identify where our writing went wrong. We wondered how we could have been so mistaken and even questioned where to begin to correct our issues. Upon further reflection, we began to recognize ours as an "organizational/systems issue" directly related to the way we were going about writing the paper as a group. It was at this point we assessed not only *what* we were writing in our DiP but also *how* we organized to write our DiP. It felt like we were trying to change a tire on a moving car.

The inevitable entwining of candidates' fate, which is inherent with involuntary intradependency, was not lost on us. Each candidate willingly signed on to a program that was experimenting for the first time with operating under the Collaborative Cohort Model; however, the resulting intradependency that, ultimately, meant the success or failure of the individual candidate to obtain an EdD resided within the cohort's capacity to work as a team was beyond the sphere of influence of each individual candidate. This knowledge became a strong motivator for individuals to build collective efficacy as a group.

Operating within a model where one was not solely responsible for the results of one's own efforts, each candidate bore the additional burden of responsibility for the success or failure of the entire cohort. Horn (2001) suggests that the "review of literature on cohorts clearly and profoundly centers on the idea of the cohort experience as a social and cultural phenomenon." (p. 323). The cohort model would seem to counterbalance participants' stress related to "a combination of both personal and program and/or institutional factors influenced their decisions to withdraw from doctoral studies" (Janz, 2016, p. 102). The stress in cohort could be a double-edged sword. Recognizing that any candidate dropping out of the Westside could jeopardize the success of the entire cohort caused each of us to become highly invested in the well-being of our fellow cohort members. Bista and Cox (2014) suggest that this mutual bond is a common experience among program participants. Cohort members "report and update incidents of mutual care and encourage individuals to stay in the program" (p. 5).

The strongest influence on our practice to emerge from the collaboration in the cohort model of DiP was that of mutual trust. Coincidentally, findings from our cohort's DiP, which focused on perceptions in school principal performance evaluations, likewise suggested trust as a key component in meaningful evaluation. As trust was built a synergy evolved; the whole became greater than the sum of its parts. We became cognizant of belonging to something bigger than ourselves.

Experiencing group synergy is a well-documented phenomenon among sports teams, elite military units, firefighters, and other small groups of intradependent people facing a common challenging task. When, during a particularly intense period in the dissertation process, one of the cohort members lost a family member, the other four members redistributed writing responsibilities to free that member to attend to family matters. The culture of a traditional doctoral program may not be designed to rally with the same degree of support and encouragement. Greene's research (2015) suggests

> The culture and structure of academia came up as a significant barrier to doctoral student persistence, with participants noting the systemic nature of attrition and lengthy times to completion. The culture of the institution and a lack of 'perceived' support was also seen as an impediment to progress. (p. 508)

Supporting each other through the rigors and challenges, both personal and professional, and sharing the successes of the doctoral process forged lasting bonds among the cohort members.

Senge (1990) encourages administrators to look at problems from a universal perspective and stop trying to divide problems into smaller pieces and then try to solve each individual part. The metaphor Senge (1990) uses is the example of the broken mirror. When all small pieces of a broken mirror are glued back together, the reflection of the mirror will not be the same as the reflection from the originally unbroken mirror.

The issue Senge described is a familiar one. As Burnett (1999), and Ali and Kohun (2006), suggest a significant influence in high doctoral attrition rates stem from student's feelings of isolation, citing a lack of student-to-student communication as a specific contributing factor. The benefit of writing our DiP utilizing the Collaborative Cohort Model was there was never a time (no matter how difficult it was) that any of us felt isolated or couldn't communicate our successes, questions, or concerns with each other.

As time passed and the Westside spent countless hours on evenings and weekends laboring together, we learned how to work together and a synergy began to form. Our cohort slowly evolved into something more than the sum of its parts. We were part of something bigger than ourselves. Subsequent meetings with our DiP chair demonstrated through our work that we were learning how to collaborate with the cohesiveness of a true team.

The PSAP experience continues to influence our lives in many ways. When practicing, the values of social justice and ethical leadership are ever present. As Starratt (2012) wrote ethical leadership "involves educators practicing their profession with an integrity that goes right to the core of their work" (p. 3). The PSAP program and the cohort model offered each of us a lens with which to view our work in education. In the cohort, we learned to be leaders and we learned to be followers. There were natural ebb and flow. This experience directly relates to our work in the field and the need to form strong teams, to negotiate roles and responsibilities, and to create strong professional learning communities in order to improve student achievement. As Maher (2005) found in her research, "The characteristics of shared learning, focused discussion, and increased trust among participants were trademark of the cohort investigated here; and their appearance reinforces the idea that participants of learning communities generally enjoy these benefits" (pp. 207–208). The cohort format positively affected our experience and continues to do so.

IMPACT OF THE COMPLEX PROBLEM OF
PRACTICE UPON THE SCHOOL DISTRICT

The collective action research project, performed in partial fulfillment of the DiP, required examining a real-world complex problem of practice. The authors' cohort responded to the problem of practice in a small urban New England school district. The cohort members were invited into all schools in this district to conduct action research, with a focus on the perceived strengths and weaknesses of criteria and process of the existing principal evaluation system.

The New England School District, the action research subject district of the DiP, comprised twelve individual schools including eight elementary schools, two middle schools, and two high schools. In addition, the system also had under its umbrella an adult education program that served the entire central section of its home county, an alternative education center runs in coordination with the County Sheriff's Office, and several other smaller, specialized programs in partnership with area human service nonprofits. With a team of over 1,100 employees, the New England School District employed twelve principals who served nearly 6,000 students in a small-city setting.

In the action research study of the New England School District and its principal evaluation practices, central office staff described their current process as inconsistent, damaging to relationships among and between principals and central office staff, and well connected to personal growth plans and school improvement plans (Casavant, Collins, Faginski-Stark, McCandless, & Tencza, 2012). In contrast, principals described the process to be consistent, but lacked "explicit feedback" and "disconnected from personal-professional growth and school improvement" (Collins et al., 2012, p. 7). Both central office administration and principals agreed that the evaluation process for principals yielded little in way of personal growth, and that statewide test results weighed heavily in the evaluation of school principals (2012).

In addition to the DiP, upon completion of the research, the cohort members returned to the district to present specific data-driven recommendations to the school district administration team. This cost-free consultancy was the EdD program's gesture of gratitude for the school district welcoming doctoral student research.

The recommendations established in the DiP included the following:

- Recommendation One: Make principal evaluation more of an ongoing process and less of an event;
- Recommendation Two: Schedule time in each building with principals to gather data and discuss their work;
- Recommendation Three: Clearly identify the criteria and supportive evidence used in evaluation of principals;
- Recommendation Four: Use a standardized rubric and evaluation instruments that delineate process, evidence, employs measurable outcomes and defines performance levels;
- Recommendation Five: Use an evaluation instrument and feedback mechanism that better recognizes the expansiveness and complexity of their jobs;
- Recommendation Six: Provide meaningful feedback via principal evaluation to foster personal-professional growth and school renewal; and
- Recommendation Seven: Base summative evaluation on agreed upon goals for annual personal-professional improvement and growth.

Drawing on a host of notions from the professional literature, and leaning heavily on the state's model system for educator evaluation, the New England School District instituted a new set of practices that embraces all seven of the above recommendations, in addition to several other key components missing from their previous evaluation experience.

In the Summer of 2015, the New England School District adopted a comprehensive District Improvement Plan comprised of four key areas that included work in curriculum, social-emotional education and wellness, academic and social-emotional intervention planning, and improving the district's level of cultural competence. These four key work areas are now embedded in every single school improvement plan and form the basis for goal setting for principals and teachers in the context of the educator evaluation system. The connection between district level initiatives and personal-professional improvement plans is clear and present.

This has led to greater collaboration between central office staff and principals, and among principals as colleagues working toward similar goals.

Central office staff, including the superintendent, has made it a priority to be in school buildings observing principals at work in a variety of tasks. This has led to more frequent and informal feedback conversations and modeled the work that principals are expected to complete with their teaching staff. The desire of all parties to treat principal evaluation as an ongoing part of practice, rather than as a drop-everything and "do evaluations" event has led to greater trust among and between parties and has facilitated a spirit of collegiality that will only enhance school renewal work and improvement of instruction.

Were one to visit that same New England School District today, in 2016, one would observe drastic improvements in the principal evaluation system. The implemented changes with a principal evaluation system align closely with the new state educator evaluation regulations. These changes have led a more consistent set of practices being followed year after year, which depend heavily upon professional goals agreed upon mutually by the superintendent and the principals themselves.

Through ongoing efforts to follow the state's guidelines, rubrics and regulations, paired with a dedication to putting the recommendations of the dissertation in practice team to use and embed in everyday practice, the New England School District is living proof that sound, standards-based, fair evaluation practices—when completed as a real and ongoing process in a trusting, student-centered environment work to make individual principals and thus teachers and schools better and help students grow and achieve.

IMPACT OF DISSERTATION IN PRACTICE (DiP) ON FUTURE WORK OF COHORT MEMBERS

Conducting action research, and the associated review of the literature, provided a depth and breadth of understanding about principal evaluation specifically but, more lastingly, the experience prepared us to become discerning consumers of scholarly research. The melding of research and practice employed in conducting action research offered practical applications for us in our professional capacities.

It would be impossible to simply "list" the lessons that we have learned by being part of a Collaborative Cohort Model, but given the experiences and mentoring that we have received, we felt more than ready to take the "next step." In addition to the camaraderie, we learned how to be more thoughtful educational leaders through exposure to, and interactions with, the larger cohort of 24 highly qualified and experienced administrators from across the region. The breadth of knowledge of our fellow EdD candidates, accomplished administrators all, augmented the impressively long list of professors' experiences and added another level of richness to classroom interactions.

As we take on educational leadership roles of increasing responsibility, we realize how well both the criteria and the process of our EdD program prepared us. We have witnessed how both the school district community and the superintendent must be professionally committed to improving the district. This was made clear, during the recent selection process of one of the Westside cohort members to a school superintendent position, both he and the School Board shared a common understanding of what they wanted and needed to accomplish. Our EdD program emphasized that partnerships must have a "good fit" between the Superintendent and the School Board.

The interview process proved an excellent way to determine if his core values and the board's collective goals for the district were compatible. It has been our experience that it is important that there is a "good fit" between the district and the superintendent (Blumer, 2000; King, 1999) to develop the ongoing, transparent communication, relationship building, and consensus building necessary in establishing a cohesive and professional working relationship. These ideals were deeply instilled into our preparation as EdD candidates.

As our Westside cohort members go on to become school superintendents, or move up to lead in larger superintendencies, we better recognize how our EdD preparation has made us more fully aware that core values at their most basic level are simply words. To make values more than mere words, our core values must permeate everything that we do. Hargreaves and Fink (2006) maintain that a "superintendent's responsibility is to lead by example with an unwavering sense of moral purpose" (p. 23). In order for people to truly internalize a vision it must be genuine, Senge's (1990) decades old truism that "people excel and learn not because they are told to, but because they want to" (p. 9), still resonates well into the twenty-first century.

As leaders we have come to realize that we cannot address the issues that affect those we lead through just one lens, in doing so, we risk as Bolman and Deal (2003) suggest, "becoming a victim of one of the most common afflictions of leaders: seeing an incomplete or distorted picture as a result of overlooking or misinterpreting important signals" (p. 4), or what is more commonly referred to as being "lost at sea." Given its four frames: structural, human resource, political, or symbolic, Bolman and Deal's (2008) model provides leaders with an appropriate, conscious approach from which to construct decisions. As we move forward in our new administrative roles we are reminded of the importance of consistently framing issues as they present themselves.

In the same way a patient might find it ludicrous for her medical practitioner to lack the authentic practical experiences required of a doctoral candidate for an MD, as educational leadership practitioners, it is difficult for us to imagine how different our educational leadership preparation had we not selected to pursue an EdD. As we reflect upon how well our action research opportunities, the authentic complex problems of practice, helped to prepare us for the challenges of our current leadership roles, and how often we utilize the learnings from these experiences, we would unhesitantly again choose the EdD and the Collaborative Cohort Model.

CONCLUSION

The DiP and working in a Collaborative Cohort Model has influenced our thought process as well as our mindset. The cohort's experience set the bar high for future collaborative work. Future work teams lacking the same degree of synergy felt, by comparison, ineffectual with less capacity to achieve the desired outcome. Once part of a truly synergistic team, it is conspicuously apparent when settling for less.

The members of the cohort have all taken on new administrative roles since earning their doctorates but years later still consider one another trusted confidants. Bista and Cox (2014) speak to this cohort bond, "In such shared learning communities, students form a bond based on interests, gender, academic knowledge, and social awareness to pursue the goals by sharing personal stories and school related experiences" (p. 5). The bonds established during the DiP continue to endure. The cohort remains in contact four years after graduation.

In 2016, three of the five members are in the role of superintendent; one member is coordinating graduate educational leadership programs at a university, and one member is a Director of Curriculum. We still occasionally meet for social gatherings, which during the three years as a cohort were a very important part of our history. We continue to rely on our colleagues for advice; we interact at conferences, and we depend on one another as sounding boards for honest feedback and continue to put the knowledge and skills of collaboration to good advantage in our jobs.

In conclusion, we find that we are better prepared to work collaboratively with District or University stakeholders when we know that we can draw upon the collective knowledge of our cohort if in need of advice or simply a sympathetic ear. Most importantly, we have never felt alone as we embark on new chapters in our respective professional careers. We feel assured that by sharing a common cohort experience, the Westside has each other's backs. We continue to benefit from each other's experiences as well as the professional relationships we have cultivated. The value of being part of such an academically challenging team endeavor, one that we knew would never be replicated, has created the shared sense of participating in a once in a lifetime experience, a time-bound event bigger than any one of us individually; as such, our collective dissertation in practice left an indelible mark on each of us, and an enduring special bond among us.

REFERENCES

Azad, A., & Kohun, F. (2006). Dealing with isolation feelings in IS doctoral program. *International Journal of Doctoral Studies, 1*, 21–33.

Bengtson, E., Jones, S. J., Lasater, K., & Murphy-Lee, M. (2014). Research courses in the CPED Phase I institutions: What's the difference? (White Paper, pp. 1–30).

Bista, K., & Cox, D. W. (2014). Cohort-based doctoral programs: What we have learned over the last 18 years. *International Journal of Doctoral Studies, 9*(1), 1–20.

Blumer, I., & King M. (2000). TA good start. *Phi Delta Kappan, January*, 356–360.

Bolman, L. G., & Deal, T. E. (2008). *Reframing organizations: Artistry, choice, and leadership* (4th ed.). San Francisco, CA: Jossey-Bass.

Browne-Ferrigno, T., & Maughan, B. D. (2014, September). *Cohort development: A guide for faculty and program developers.* Pittsburgh, PA: Carnegie Project on the Education Doctorate, Duquesne University.

Burnett, P. C. (1999). The supervision of doctoral dissertation using a collaborative cohort model. *Counselor Education and Supervision, 39*(1), 46–52.

Burns, J. M. (1978). *Leadership.* New York, NY: Harper & Row Pub.

Casavant, C., Collins, W. Faginski-Stark, E., McCandless, J., & Tencza, M. (2012). *Perceptions of the principal evaluation process and performance criteria: A qualitative study of the challenge of principal evaluation* (Unpublished Doctoral Dissertation). Boston College, Boston, MA.

Elmore, R. F. (2005). Accountable leadership. *The Educational Forum, 69*(2), 134–142.

Fisher, B. A., & Ellis, D. G. (1990). *Small group decision making: Communication and the group process* (3rd ed.). New York: McGraw-Hill.

Four ways cohort models benefit graduate students. (2015, June 4) Retrieved from http://education.gsu.edu/4-ways-cohorts-models-benefit-graduate-students/

Gay, G. (2000). *Culturally responsive teaching: Theory, research, and practice.* New York, NY: Teachers New College Press.

Greene, M. (2015). Come hell or high water: Doctoral students' perceptions on support services and persistence. *International Journal of Doctoral Studies, 10*, 501–518.

Greenlee, B. J., & Karanxha, Z. (2010) A study of group dynamics in education leadership cohort and non-cohort groups. *Journal of Research on Leadership Education, 5*(11).

Guo, X. E., & Rose, S. (2015). Challenges navigated by 11 doctoral students in ensemble style group collaboration for the Ed. D. nontraditional Dissertation in Practice (DiP) at Lynn University. *International Journal of Educational Policy Research and Review, 2*(3), 41–46.

Hargreaves, A., & Fink, D. (2006). *Sustainable leadership.* San Francisco, CA: Jossey-Bass.

Horn, R. A., Jr. (2001). Promoting social justice and caring in schools and communities: The unrealized potential of the cohort model. *Journal of School Leadership, 11*(4), 313–334.

Janz, L. M. (2016). *The decision to leave a Doctor of Education program: An explanatory sequential mixed methods design study* (Doctoral dissertation). University of Calgary, Canada.

King, M. (Ed.). (1999). Partners in progress: Strengthening the superintendent-board relationship. In *New directions for school leadership.* San Francisco, CA: Jossey-Bass.

Maher, M. A. (2005). The evolving meaning and influence of cohort membership. *Innovative Higher Education, 30*(3), 195–211.

Perry, J. A. (2012). To EdD or not to EdD? *Kappan Magazine, 94*(1), 41–44

Senge, P. M. (1990). *The fifth discipline. The art and practice of the learning organization.* New York: Bantam Doubleday Dell Publishing Group.

Sowell, R. (2008). *Completion and attrition: Analysis of baseline data* [PowerPoint slides]. PhD Dissertation. Retrieved from http://www.phdcompletion.org/resources/CG-SNSF2008.stowell.pdf.

Starratt, R. J. (2012). *Cultivating an ethical school.* New York: Routledge

Storey, V. A., & Maughan, B. D. (2014). *Beyond a definition: Designing and specifying dissertation in practice (DiP) models.* Pittsburgh, PA: The Carnegie Project on the Education Doctorate.

Why Choose PSAP? (n.d.). Retrieved June 30, 2016, from http://www.bc.edu/schools/lsoe/academics/departments/eahe/graduate/PSAP/whychoosepsap.html

CHAPTER 10

CHANGE IN ACTION

The Education Doctorate and Dissertation in Practice

Katy Farber and Sara Ewell

INTRODUCTION

This chapter explores a doctoral journey, as a teacher moves from a practitioner to scholar practitioner and the impacts this process has on my professional, personal, and scholarly work. It will provide personal exploration of the doctoral and Dissertation in Practice (DiP) process during my Doctor of Education (EdD) program and how this work is impacting the educational field. A shift is happening— moving from separate practitioners and academic roles, toward a connected, collaborative field that fosters teacher voice, growth, and emerging leadership (ASCD, 2014).

I specifically reflect on writing the DiP, a unique entity to the professional doctorate, and its influence on my work as an educator. As the landscape of EdD programs is changing it is critical that practitioners, academics, and scholar practitioners have a clear understanding of the DiP and the impact it is having in the field (Carnegie Project on the Education Doctorate, 2015).

Description of Doctoral Program

My doctoral journey took place in Northeastern University's Scholar Practitioner (Labaree, 2003; Nganga, 2011; Short & Shindell, 2009) Doctor of Education program. The NEU program is online with an on ground summer residency requirement. As scholar practitioners, NEU students' academic program is grounded in their professional work and bridges theory and practice in every aspect of the program. "Students develop a plan of study that applies to their own experience. While they come from different backgrounds and locations, our doctoral students are all striving to enact change in society—actively working to solve today's most demanding educational challenges (Doctor of Education Program, 2015).

Jenlink (2005) states, "The scholar-practitioner's work is that of the intellectual whose efforts are guided by an epistemology of social inquiry as critical practice and a concern for the 'others' who populate the school—'others' reflective of ethnic, racial, cultural, linguistic, political diversity; 'others' that are situated within and shaped by the 'social'" (p. 6). It is within this framework that students identify and research a problem of practice within their organization.

Students take a common series of foundation and research courses and select one of the program's three concentrations to focus their work. The concentrations offered are: Organizational Leadership; Curriculum, Teaching, Learning and Leadership and Higher Education Administration. I completed the Curriculum, Teaching, Learning and Leadership concentration.

EdD students are required to complete two one-week summer residencies on the Boston, Massachusetts campus. The residencies provide an opportunity for students to take an 8-week hybrid course with one week of the course taking place in an intensive on ground face-to-face meeting. During the residencies, students also participate in afternoon workshops aimed at developing their skills as independent scholar practitioners and further building community among faculty and students.

The culminating requirement of the doctoral program is to write a DiP that includes conducting an original, empirical study addressing a problem of practice in the student's professional environment. The study is presented in a five-chapter structure with similarities to a traditional dissertation. However, the DiP generates local and particular knowledge rather than fill a gap in the literature. The fifth chapter of the DiP also includes a section that speaks to the implications for practice. Doctoral students complete their DiP under the guidance of their advisors in mediums such as Google Hangout, Go to Meeting, phone calls, emails, and Skype. Due to our locations I did not meet my advisor in person until graduation day even though we had been in close touch throughout the DiP process. I did have the opportunity to take several online courses with her.

MY STORY

Beginning. Like many, I came into teaching from an alternative pathway. In my undergraduate studies at Colorado State University, learning came alive for me, because for the first time in my education, I had choices, a voice, and a big stake in my own success. There, I learned to love learning, and particularly the hands-on work and applications of the Natural Resources, Recreation, and Tourism department. As part of that program, I surveyed and studied a beaver population at a local nature center, I trained to become a sea kayak guide and naturalist as my internship and traveled to Belize to study the governments' focus on preserving their natural resources. This constructivist coursework gave me an opportunity to engage with the work on a higher level than ever before. I graduated from CSU with high honors and began work as an environmental educator in southern New York State.

While teaching at a residential outdoor education center, I began to love the process of planning curriculum, working with teachers, and teaching lessons to students from New York City. Students in grades 4–8 would stay at the outdoor center for 3 days, and the environmental educators would deliver curriculum tailored to their school needs and goals. The students who would visit had often never been in a forest, an unlocked cabin at night, or gone on a night hike. Sharing these experiences with them was extremely rewarding. Many of these students came from high poverty communities and at the time, the AIDS epidemic was harming families. I connected with these students and they wrote to me after their experiences at the center. I remember thinking clearly that I wanted to be with students for more than these 3 days. I wanted to become a teacher and bring a constructivist and compassionate philosophy into public school teaching.

I applied to a Master's program in Education, with a focus on science at the middle level, at the State University of New York at Plattsburgh. After two years of intense coursework, student teaching at both the third and eighth-grade levels, I graduated and began searching for my first teaching job. I found it in neighboring Vermont, in a rural K–12 school. In those first two years of teaching, I tried to expand the offerings in fifth grade by fundraising to take students to a local outdoor education center for team building and environmental education in all three seasons, culminating with an overnight experience. We built birdhouses, with students analyzing the cost of the materials, finding the best plans for creating them, and learning how to price them to earn a profit. One Saturday students, parents, and I worked all day creating kits and building birdhouses. We raised enough money for the students to go in the fall and spring to the outdoor education center.

As a classroom teacher, I wanted to provide hands-on, relevant work that motivated my students. We put on plays with original scenes written by students, we wrote letters to the editor, and we studied the forest where our school was located. The constructivist lens remained, as did the focus on project and service learning, before I knew that was what it was called. I also began to learn about advocating for families, students, and teachers. When there were teaching reassignments without consulting the teachers, I knew it was time to find another position.

Veteran Teacher. I was fortunate to find another teaching position at a progressive, small and community minded elementary school. Within my first year there, I was working with two community members to create and lead service learning projects with 60 fifth and sixth graders. I quickly learned how this kind of work motivated students who were disadvantaged, or learned differently. I watched as students who did not like school loved to be in charge of their own learning, to work as a group, and do authentic work that mattered to our community. This became a cornerstone of my teaching, and a passionate focus of my professional development.

I also began leadership work, in the form of mentoring new teachers, leading professional development, and working on district committees. When our staff struggled with climate, we turned toward literature and worked through it together. We came through stronger and in that process, I learned about the kind of leadership and colleagueship that supports professional learning communities. It is one that is open, supportive, compassionate and empowering to teachers.

When my mentee decided that after two years of teaching, she was going to quit, I needed to look for reasons and answers. I began an independent study of teacher attrition, reading and collecting educational literature on the topic, and interviewing colleagues that had left the profession. I set up a blog to collect comments as well. I gathered wisdom, tips, and resources from master teachers in the field, wrote a book proposal and had it accepted by Corwin Press. *Why Great Teachers Quit and How We Might Stop the Exodus* was published in 2010. I made presentations at state and national conferences in support of this work. People asked me, was this your PhD work? This thought had never occurred to me. It was a passion project and came from the experience—but the seed had been planted.

Why EdD? After 12 years of teaching experience, publishing two education books, many articles, and becoming a teacher leader in the district, I found myself thinking about doctoral work. I had always considered this a goal but wasn't ready to move my whole family to pursue this opportunity.

I began exploring options. One issue that was very important to me was the idea that I wanted to be an agent for change in education. I wanted to continue the work of helping teachers provide authentic, hands-on, relevant and meaningful projects for students in compassionate, inclusive learning environments. A program for me had to value my teaching experience, give me depth and understanding of research and its applications, and be applicable to my school context and beyond.

I found several blended learning programs across the country where I could earn my doctorate. I wanted a combination of both in-person and online learning. As a motivated, independent adult learner, I thought I could be successful with this model. I did worry about the lack of time for studies with full-time teaching, parenting, and coursework. I applied to Northeastern and was accepted. What appealed to me was the flexible nature of the coursework, the credentials of the professors, and the focus on becoming a scholar practitioner and a change agent in the field of education.

Coursework Journey. The coursework was all encompassing for me. I taught during the day, would take care of my family in the evening, and write, read, and do course projects late at night and on weekends. During this time, I let expectations and goals for freelance writing, social obligations, exercise, and recreation take a back seat.

The coursework started to cause me to see my teaching and current events differently. It was as if I had a new reflective lens with which to view my world. It was one that was more informed by studies of leadership, equity, human development, and educational systems. I noticed myself engaging in conversations with colleagues and administration citing something I had read from my coursework, or sharing a different perspective on a school problem or issue.

At times, I wasn't sure I could keep up the pace with coursework, teaching, and parenting anymore. My family, friends, cohort of fellow students, professors, and husband gave me the support I needed to continue. This was powerful. I knew that hard things take time, work, and a great deal of perseverance. Knowing that the professors had all experienced this, that my fellow students struggled and were succeeding, all helped me see I that could too.

Dissertation in Practice (DiP) Topic. When I started the EdD program, I knew what I wanted to study. It was clear to me before I began the first class. I was passionate about the authentic, community-based learning that I had seen transform my students as part of service learning for the last 12 years. I wanted to create more than my own subjective view of the impacts of service learning, and to design a research study that documented the impacts (if any) of service learning on early adolescent students. My idea was to study a service learning program I had created with colleagues at my school for sixth-grade students. It was called the Sixth Grade Leadership Institute and involved every sixth grader having a leadership position within the school or community for the entire school year. This program had quickly become a pillar of the school, with all students labeling it as the thing they were looking most forward to in sixth grade. The school community began to count on the students' leadership and it guided the culture and focus of the school year.

During my EdD coursework, two articles and researchers particularly intrigued me. This research and article exemplified what I had known as a teacher for years—that middle school students have unique and often unmet developmental needs (Blackwell et al., 1993). These needs are critical for the academic, social, and personal success of these students. I began to think of my research differently, as in, is service learning a better pedagogical approach for early adolescent students? This provided a frame and focus. Other research that pointed out the importance of middle school in getting students ready for the all-important ninth grade year made clear to me how high the stakes were. If students are not engaged and successful in ninth grade, they are more likely to drop out or not finish high school on time. Yet another study showed a link between sixth-grade females benefitting the most from service learning, including in academic, personal, and social ways. This was exciting. Researchers had been working on the issues I cared about and had been studying the very concepts and ideas that I was considering for my research. This research gave me more confidence in my interactions with parents, fellow teachers, and the administration about teaching middle-level students, planning curriculum, and school policy.

In another article that changed my thinking about the possibilities of my research as a classroom teacher and researcher, Michelle Fine (Ravitch & Riggan, 2011) wrote about the possibilities, benefits and potential limitations of conducting research as an insider. Her tone, of a passionate practitioner, positioned to share the stories of participants more truly because of her embedded position of belonging, struck a chord with me. It demonstrated that research can be dynamic, personal, storytelling, and change making. Giving voice to participants, authentically, in environments where they feel comfortable to be exactly who they are, became most important to me. Early adolescents, like many other groups, have been the victims of repeated (and in many cases, misinformed) educational reforms, often without any consideration of their stories, opinions, and needs. Telling their stories, from the classroom teacher's perspective, seemed not only possible but also full of potential as high-quality qualitative research (Cochran-Smith & Lytle, 1992).

Proposal. It is in this vein that I created the proposal to study the Sixth Grade Leadership program at my school. I developed a research plan that protected the identity of my students, helped to reduce the limitations and potential biases, and applied for IRB approval. I sent permission forms to my administrators and was hopeful to begin in the fall. My goal was to study my students throughout their sixth-grade year, before, during and after participation in this yearlong leadership and service learning program.

Roadblock. I gained approval quickly from my building principal and fellow teachers. I waited several weeks to meet with the superintendent. When I finally did, my progress was halted. Even after multiple assurances that the research would not name the school, or even the state of the research, and that I would pull out any mention of myself as the classroom teacher, my request was put on hold. Weeks later, the superintendent's administrative assistant sent me a letter stating a list of limitations that would need to be in place if I was to begin this research. I would not be allowed to write articles or books about the work, and the publication of the DiP was to be delayed by two years. Publishing my dissertation was required by Northeastern. This made the research virtually impossible to complete. This was disappointing, not only because of the impacts on the project but because of a lack of support for teacher research and voice in leadership. I had to switch gears.

I quickly contacted teachers and community leaders who put me in touch with teachers across the northeast who were doing similar service learning work. After extensive searching, phone calls and emails, I found a research site and began attempting to secure permissions. This time I had no trouble, only words of encouragement and support. I had to edit my whole proposal to reflect this change. Ultimately, the roadblock turned into an opportunity to research service learning at another site. While not what I had planned, this likely worked out for the best and gave me new research experience and learning. The dissertation in practice will have roadblocks for sure, and these can hopefully yield opportunities that you did not expect.

After securing the site, I altered the research question to reflect a new population. The purpose of the research was to gain insight and understanding of fifth-grade students' perspectives of their experiences in a service learning class in a middle school (grades 5–8). The research question was: How did fifth-grade students' participation in a service learning program influence their personal development, including their engagement and self-efficacy? I settled on this question after several revisions, working with my fellow students, advisor, and professors.

Study. Through document reviews, interviews, observations, a questionnaire, photographs, and conversations, I worked to describe the student experience in this course and the personal development of participants during the 5–month study period. I developed a case study with thick descriptions of the town, school, classroom, students, and teachers. I observed at the school 10 times over the course of two 5–week sessions. I completed 20 interviews of students and 3 school staff interviews. During the research period, I kept careful notes and observations and wrote regular field memos about emerging themes and ideas. I also collected written and online documentation and photos to analyze with the body of data.

Writing. During data collection and analysis, and intensely afterward, I wrote chapters 4 and 5 of the DiP. This was an exhausting experience, but powerful as the ideas and themes emerged from the research just as I had read that they would. The students and the teachers told the story of this program, and what emerged was clear—that service learning was a developmentally appropriate pedagogy for early adolescents and led to increased self-efficacy, engagement and personal growth in these students. Writing about the findings, themes, and recommendations solidified all of my years of teaching experience. It was as if all of my practice and studies had led me to this moment, where I was about to present original research to my DiP committee.

My doctoral journey gave me the confidence to pursue research in any topic I was passionate about. Personally, reading research, interacting with motivated peers, and completing coursework gave me a new lens on my work and leadership. I felt as though I had burst through a silo. No matter what decisions were being made in my district, I was part of research, a wider academic community, and a conversation about improving education. This gave me purpose and focus and showed me that even if my voice is unheard in certain contexts, it is invited, encouraged and fostered in others. This provided a change in a daily voice of the self— and showed a wider world of possibility.

Doctor of Education: Reflecting Beyond Myself

The doctoral program can have powerful impacts on educators' practice at the personal level. This is different for each teacher and his or her own context, but the personal is where educational leadership starts for many. Teachers, in large part, are personally connected to their practice and profession. The doctoral process can lead to many levels of personal transformation in the daily practice of educators. This was certainly true for my journey.

Lack of Teacher Leadership Opportunities. Unfortunately, many times, teachers are used to being silenced. They often work in silos and isolation (Dana, 1995). In many educational policy decisions, teacher voices are absent. While great progress has been made with professional learning communities, more avenues for teacher leadership and voice, there is still much work to be done to foster the development of teacher leaders and scholar practitioners who develop, share and advocate for their students, profession and fellow teachers.

Mid and late career teachers have a wealth of experience under their belts. They have a deep knowledge of students, communities, school culture, and curriculum. They want to use their expertise and voice to improve education. Often times, teachers are too busy with the practice of teaching to join leadership opportunities and are underutilized in terms of decision and policymaking. Yet, a lack of free agency, or self-determination, is a reason teachers leave the profession (Farber, 2010). In fact, according to Barnett Barry of the Center for Teaching Quality (2010, para. 1), "Teachers who report more control over the policies in their schools and greater degrees of autonomy in their jobs are more likely to remain in teaching and to feel invested in their careers and schools." In other words, teachers need feel their voices and experience are part of improving school systems and educational opportunities for students in order to be satisfied with the work and stay in the field of teaching.

The DiP process and doctoral journey can give teachers an avenue for this voice. It provides a platform for research, study, collaboration, and role modeling for teacher leadership and scholarship. Teachers in flexible, blended doctoral programs can feel isolated or powerless by day, and finding their passion, outlet, and voice by night in their studies. Then, taking this new experience and learning, teachers can try to push change in their own contexts, when and how they can. By participating in doctoral studies, the teacher can feel a part of the larger educational research community and this can empower and inspire teachers in their school settings.

This is not without a struggle. Many in leadership are used to and encourage teachers to follow their directions without question. There can be a "father knows best" mentality of administrators, which harkens back to the 1950s model of gendered employment. Male and female school employees have had separate and distinct roles for decades in the field of education (Chase & Bell, 1990), "The message women teach and men manage still remains," (McGovern-Robinett & Ovando, 2002, p. 2). While significant progress has been made in terms of increased females in administration, and increased males in teaching, the pattern largely remains. This hampers teacher voice, because issues of gender and power can play out in terms of leadership, decision-making, and collaboration.

Another issue that hampers teacher voice in leadership is systems designed to exclude teachers from participating in decision-making. These are many, ranging from a lack of time (because of teaching responsibilities) (Barnett et al., 2011) to strict protocols that can limit true dialogue, to a lack of vulnerability and inclusiveness on the part of administrators and sometimes school boards.

With these limitations in place, encouraging teacher voice, advocacy, and leadership becomes critical. Just like Dewey said that education is real life, so is the DiP process. It is practice. It is a guidepost. Most importantly, though, it is empowerment in a society where many blame and demonize teachers. It is using my voice to push education in the direction I feel it should go after almost two decades in the field. While administrators have different levels of comfort with involving teachers in decision making and leadership, teachers can forge their own path by pursuing their interest based research and study. Just as we know that students are more engaged, more motivated, and work harder when they are in charge of their own learning, the same idea applies to teachers. They need to feel like they are the captains of their own professional ships, reflecting on their practice, applying what they learn, and making valuable contributions to the field.

Influence on Practitioner. My DiP examined a hands-on service learning program at a middle school that provided rich data about the benefits of this type of work with early adolescents and how it provides a developmentally appropriate approach for the challenges of adolescence, which include decreasing levels of engagement and parental communication (Eccles et al., 1993). In addition, service learning engages learners, reduces bias and stereotyping, and this can, in turn, lead to greater personal development in middle-level students (Fair, Davis, & Fischer, 2011). My research demonstrated that students who participate in a high-quality service learning experience in the middle-grade years could increase their engagement and feelings of self-efficacy (Farber, 2016). Schools can use service learning, or a related hands-on, community tied, authentic project-based learning experience, to promote engagement and equity in their students.

This research was a focused study on deep practice. By being immersed in the research site, I constantly reflected on my own practice. The process was cyclical. Because the research occurred while I was still classroom teaching, each research session was not only rich data gathering but also a reflexive, reflective learning space. It allowed for me to apply my learning directly on a daily basis. Each evening for me was about study, reflection, writing and reading. Each school day was about practice. How to see a problem through a difference lens? How to view a "gap" not as an achievement gap but as an educational gap (Ladson-Billings, 2006) instead. The cyclical nature of study, reflection, and practice continued throughout the program, providing contexts and meaning and growth where study alone could not. This is a benefit of a scholar-practitioner model, because the practitioner and academic worlds are not silos, but iterative, connected, growing. Learning in this way as a professional educator makes sense.

In addition, providing teachers opportunities to get outside of their own schools, and into other classrooms for observation, action or academic research provides valuable opportunities for professional growth (Cochran-Smith & Lytle, 1992). Showing teachers the wider world brings them possibility beyond their contexts. It broadens their perspectives and widens the lens. Working with educators from across the country in this doctoral program provided that opportunity for me.

Also impacted in practice by the DiP process was my teacher voice in staff meetings and professional learning communities. Based on my research and experience, I spoke to the unique developmental needs of early adolescents. In my daily work as a teacher, this meant co-creating with students and building curriculum that featured authentic, hands-on learning, even with increased pressure for the opposite. In practice, it was as if a new voice was informing my daily decisions, one based on research, study, and reflection.

At the district level, the DiP gave me a lens through which view other school systems and my own. To see what innovations were driving other districts, to hear about changes that were successful and schools that were struggling, gave me a new lens to view district work. It is one of opportunity and possibility. The trouble is, there was a limited venue for sharing this growth. In meetings, the roles were very scripted and the opportunities for open dialogue were somewhat limited. So while the view was wider, the opportunity to act, to be an agent for change, was limited in this particular context.

Influence on Scholarly Work. The influence of the DiP on scholarly work is significant. For the first time, teachers in the doctoral program are submitting a significant piece of original research to their chosen fields. The feeling of authoring and sharing the DiP transforms a teacher's thinking about themselves as solely a teacher into a researcher, scholar-practitioner, officially for the first time. Teachers can gain confidence to stretch into other scholarly work based on this success. This can be applying to present at conferences, authoring articles and books, or reviewing the research of others.

For me, the impact on scholarly work is ongoing. I have applied to present my original research at a national conference and will be working at the university level to help teachers develop innovative, personalized learning programs with their students. My DiP provided me with experience discussing early adolescent development, pedagogy, research and leadership at high levels during the interview process. This gave me the confidence to engage in these discussions and see how I might be helpful in leading change in public schools. I also plan to turn my DiP into a book with my previous publisher, and/or write articles for educational publications and journals.

In addition, I am eager to participate in new media in scholarly and professional learning communities. These might be weekly chats on Twitter about educational technology, innovation, or new ideas, or it might be publishing original articles about education on Medium. Being part of the national conversation about improving education with teachers, scholars, researchers, and innovators makes me feel less isolated, more connected, and part of a national movement. This busts through silos. Researching service learning gave me the opportunity to discuss my program and others like it with real data behind me, not just my subjective feelings as a teacher.

Moving Ahead as a Leader and Agent of Change

I was in a unique position as my dissertation was defended and I was graduating. I had been teaching at the same K–6 school for 15 years. The school was making some policy decisions I felt were not in the best interest of early adolescent students. This had happened other times in my tenure there, along with many points of progress, innovation, improvement, and collaboration. Some teachers, including myself, struggled to find a way to voice our opinions and to feel heard in the decision-making process.

At this point, I was faced with my own decision. I applied for a position at a university to work directly with teachers to help them innovate, personalize, and transform their teaching to engage middle-level learners. I had decided that to become a change agent I needed to impact more than my class of students and my school community. I wanted to take what I had learned from my doctoral studies and research and apply it to helping to improve and transform teaching in my state. I was offered the position and took it. While I will miss my students and colleagues greatly, I know that I can be more of a catalyst for change by working directly with teachers across the state, researching, and writing about education. This is the direct result of my DiP.

In the end, the school made the decision to keep the service learning program that was beloved by many students and families. They saw its worth in terms of providing opportunities for all students and felt the pressure from students, teachers, and parents who saw the benefits and wanted it to continue. I am gratified to know that students will continue to have a personalized, hands-on service learning and leadership experience at their school and will continue to work for other students to have similar opportunities in my new role. As a professional development coordinator, I will continue to help teachers develop service learning experiences that can transform student learning, and to support teacher voice and leadership in school decision making and planning.

CONCLUSION

The doctoral journey and the influence of the DiP will inevitably look very different across individuals and institutions. However, it is my belief that the experience provides all with the opportunity to deeply engage as agents of change and provide meaningful voice in their professional settings and beyond. The professional doctorate is one that honors the work of the practitioner and the scholar and melds the power of these two worlds to bring new, prominent voices into the field.

As I reflect back on my own doctoral journey, I think about challenges, triumphs and the ways in which I am forever changed as an educator and person. I feel empowered to share my work in professional and academic settings and know that I will make a difference for students by providing the resources, rationale, and training for teachers to create meaningful service learning opportunities. I see earning my doctorate as the beginning of the next chapter of my work as an educator and advocate.

REFERENCES

Association for Supervision and Curriculum Development (ASCD). (2014). *Teacher leadership: The what, the why, and the how of teacher leaders.* Retrieved from http://www.ascd.org/ASCD/pdf/siteASCD/wholechild/fall2014wcsreport.pdf

Berry, B., & The TeacherSolutions 2030 Team (Barnett, J., Betlach, K., C'de Baca, S., Highley, S., Holland, J., Kamm, C., Moore, R., Rigsbee, C., Sacks, A., Vickery, E., Vilson, J., & Wasserman, L.). (2011). *Teaching 2030: What we must do for our students and our public schools... Now and in the future.* New York, NY: Teachers College Press.

Blackwell, M., Eccles J., Midgley, C., Wigfield, A., Buchanan, C. M., Reuman, D., Flanagan C., & Iver D.M. (1993). Development during adolescence. The impact of stage-environment fit on young adolescents' experiences in schools and in families. *American Psychology, 48*(2), 90–101.

Carnegie Project on the Education Doctorate. (2015). *General format.* Retrieved from http:\\cpedinitiative.org

Chase, S. E., & Bell, C. S. (1990). Ideology, discourse, and gender: How gatekeepers talk about women school superintendents. *Social Problems, 37*(2), 163–177.

Cochran-Smith, M., & Lytle, S. (1992). *Inside/outside: Teacher research and knowledge.* New York, NY: Teachers College Press.

Dana, N. F. (1995). Action research, school change, and the silencing of teacher voice. *Action in Teacher Education, 16*(4), 59–70.

Eccles J., Midgley C., Wigfield A., Buchanan C. M., Reuman D., Flanagan C., & Iver, D. M. (1993). Development during adolescence. The impact of stage-environment fit on young adolescents' experiences in schools and in families. *American Psychology, 48*(2), 90–101.

Fair, C. D., Davis, A., & Fischer, V. (2011). It makes them so happy: 4th–Graders' reflections on intergenerational service learning. *Childhood Education, 87*(3), 177–178.

Farber, K. (2010). *Why great teachers quit and how we might stop the exodus.* Thousand Oaks, CA: Corwin Press.

Farber, K. (2016). *The doing revolution: Service learning, early adolescents, and personal growth* (Doctoral dissertation, Northeastern University). Retrieved from http://search.proquest.com/openview/6143455fcc17f9e0ce7f86ad30dfcfae/1?pq-origsite=gscholar&cbl=18750&diss=y

Jenlink, P. M. (2005). Editorial: On bricolage and the intellectual work of the scholar-practitioner. *Scholar-Practitioner Quarterly, 3*(1), 3–12.

Labaree, D. F. (2003). The peculiar problems of preparing educational researchers. *Educational Researcher, 32*(4), 3–12.

Ladson-Billings, G. (2006). From the achievement gap to the education debt: Understanding achievement in US schools. *Educational researcher, 35*(7), 3–12.

McGovern-Robinett, D. E., & Ovando, M. N. (2002). Standing side by side with 'The 91 Brethren' lessons from the leadership perspectives of female high school principals. Paper presented at the annual meeting of The University Council of Educational Administration, Pittsburgh, Pennsylvania.

Nganga, C. W. (2011). Emerging as scholar practitioner: A reflective essay review. *Mentoring and Tutoring: Partnership in Learning, 19*(2), 239–251.

Northeastern University Doctor of Education. (2015). *General format.* Retrieved from http://www.cps.neu.edu/degree-programs/graduate/doctoral/education/

Ravitch, S. M., & Riggan, M. (2011). *Reason & rigor: How conceptual frameworks guide research.* Thousand Oaks, CA: Sage Publications.

Schnabel Kattula, H. (2011). *Women and the high school principalship: Metropolitan Detroit principals' and superintendents' perceptions regarding barriers and facilitators for job attainment.* Wayne State University Dissertations. 395. Retrieved from http://digitalcommons.wayne.edu/oa_dissertations/395

Short, D. C., & Shindell, T. J. (2009). Defining HRD scholar-practitioners. *Advances in Developing Human Resources, 11*(7), 472–485.

CHAPTER 11

TEAM-BUILDING PROFESSIONAL DEVELOPMENT

Denise Goodhue

INTRODUCTION

Earning my doctorate had been a goal of mine since completing my Master's degree, but I did not see it as a realistic objective because I did not want to leave my teaching position to pursue doctoral studies full time in a PhD program. In addition to my academic goals, I also had personal and professional goals that I did not want to discount. I wanted to start a family as well as continue to gain experience as a classroom teacher. I did not want to remove myself from my professional environment to study educational issues from an abstract standpoint, but instead, wanted to remain immersed in the day to day nuances of public education. I decided that doctoral studies would need to be put on the backburner, something I would potentially explore several years down the road.

As I resigned myself to the fact that a doctorate may be an impractical goal, something I may never have the opportunity to accomplish, a friend of mine became a member of the first cohort in a newly structured EdD program at a major research university. After completing their first semester in the program, he encouraged me to attend an information session and consider applying. I wor-

Exploring the Impact of the Dissertation in Practice, pages 165–176.
165

ried that if I began pursuing my doctorate, I would not be able to find a balance between work, home, and my studies. My reservations were quickly eased when I learned that the program was designed for working professionals. In the information session I also realized that pursuing an EdD would allow me to focus on issues of practical importance. The focus would have a direct connection to my work as a teacher, which was not something I felt I would have if I pursued a PhD. I was drawn to the fact that I would not only focus on identifying problems that exist in both my school context and the field of education at large, but I would also focus on potential interventions that could have a positive impact on those problems of practice. I did not want my doctoral studies to be purely theoretical in nature; I wanted to study problems of practice that I have experienced first-hand. When studying the problems of practice practitioners encounter, I did not want to just focus on the "why," but also on the "how."

My EdD program utilized a cohort model, with a structured schedule for coursework completion and dissertation studies. Summer sessions consisted of three courses, which took place four evenings a week, for three-week sessions. Fall and spring semester classes consisted of one course taken with your cohort and one class taken with students in your program concentration, which in my case was Teacher Leadership. In addition to required coursework, we also took elective courses meant to provide us with additional opportunities to interact with content relating to our area of interest for our dissertation study. After passing qualifying exams and completing the requisite number of program credits, we were assigned to Dissertation in Practice (DiP) groups composed of students with topics that related to one another in some capacity. Groups met together with their chairs on a regular basis both in person and online through systems such as Skype.

Throughout my coursework, I was able to identify the problems of practice about which I was most passionate. Completing coursework with a cohort meant that we all became familiar with each other's interests and passions, which led to more in-depth discussions and collaboration. Rather than continuously describing problems of practice in our workplace to fellow students at the start of each semester, we were able to start from a more productive place and analyze each other's problems of practice from a new perspective as soon as our classes began. Our experiences together were ongoing and our collaboration evolved with each new course. We did not have to start from the beginning because we had already developed a deep understanding of each other as professionals.

I felt a level of support participating in a cohort model that I would not have experienced otherwise. When my DiP defense was announced I received emails of congratulation from fellow cohort members. Some cohort members that had not yet completed their DiP still attended convocation ceremonies to show support for their classmates. I received pictures of myself getting hooded at my convocation from a classmate who had not yet completed the program. The climate in my program of study was not one of competition but of solidarity. I feel like this level of camaraderie and support is only possible in a cohort model EdD program.

There was always a climate of respect in our studies because no matter what our profession or area of interest, we all connected on an important level, which is our dedication to the ongoing work of providing a quality education to students of all ages and backgrounds.

The discussions, reflections, collaboration, and assignments that were a part of our coursework challenged us to not only define and describe the problem of practice but also challenged us to analyze these problems of practice from the perspective of a change agent. This EdD program allowed me to interact with problems of practice in an intimate way and allowed me to focus on bringing about tangible, relevant changes. In my experience, an EdD program provides students with the opportunity to contribute in a practical and relevant manner that can have an immediate positive impact on practitioners.

DISSERTATION IN PRACTICE (DiP) PROCESS AND OUTCOMES

Problem of Practice

The action research that was embedded in my coursework provided me with multiple opportunities to identify problems of practice in my workplace and explore the problems of practice I felt were the most relevant to me professionally. Throughout my coursework, my professors tied the content of the course to practitioner research and the problems of practice in our school context. Course material never existed in isolation and always made us ask ourselves, "How does the content of this course relate to my context?" and "How can I take what I am learning in my classes and utilize it in practitioner research?" Rather than just studying a problem, my coursework helped me to focus on how interventions can be implemented to provide solutions to problems, which I feel helped to prepare me for my DiP study.

Co-teaching in secondary schools was the topic I was most interested in exploring. Implementing co-teaching effectively can be particularly challenging for middle and high school teachers due to the emphasis on content area knowledge, the importance of student study skills, rapid pacing, and pressures associated with high stakes testing (Keefe, Moore, & Duff, 2004). From experience I had found that both general and special education teachers can lack the preparation needed to co-teach successfully with special education teachers needing deeper content area knowledge and general education teachers needing more knowledge of disabilities and modifications (Keefe & Moore, 2004). Secondary special education co-teachers can be even more unprepared to co-teach than their general education counterparts because they may be entering into co-teaching placements without the content area knowledge and training they need to take on an active role in their co-teaching assignments (Rice, Drame, Owens, & Frattura, 2007). General education teachers tend to have ownership of co-taught classes because the majority of students in their co-taught classes are general education students, and they tend to have more content area knowledge than their special education counterpart

(Scruggs, Mastropieri, & McDuffie, 2007). However, general education teachers may also be unprepared for co-teaching in secondary inclusion classrooms because they may lack the training needed to accommodate the special education students in their classes and can rely on traditional methods of instruction in their inclusion classrooms (Scruggs et al., 2007). Secondary general education teachers may prefer instructional strategies that can be applied to the whole class and these instructional methods can be a source of stress for special education co-teachers because they do not account for the unique needs of the special education students in the class (Scruggs et al., 2007).

Special education students are placed into co-taught inclusion classrooms so they may gain access to the general education curriculum but issues may also arise if general and special education teachers do not define "access" in the same way. General educators may feel that special education students are given access by exposing them to the same curriculum and materials, in the same setting, as non-disabled students with the support of a special education teacher in the classroom (Dymond, Renzaglia, Gilson, & Slagor, 2007). Special education teachers, however, often define access as providing special education students with an adapted curriculum in a general education classroom that is modified to meet their unique needs (Dymond et al., 2007).

General education teachers tend to take on the dominant role in secondary co-teaching relationships. If common planning time is not included in co-teachers' schedules, the general education teacher may plan lessons without the involvement of their special education counterpart (Bouck, 2007). If common planning times are not included, the special education teacher may take on a less active role in the classroom, which can result in them being viewed by their co-teacher and the students in the class as a glorified classroom aide (Bouck, 2007). Special education co-teachers may find that they are generally responsible for assisting students while the general education teacher may have the role of primary instructor (Magiera, Smith, Zigmond, & Gebauer, 2005).

Successful co-teaching at the secondary level is not a lost cause, but changes in the way it is implemented need to be made. The nature of relationships between co-teachers in high school is an important determinant of success which makes teacher input imperative (Keefe & Moore, 2004). When teachers volunteer to co-teach together based on similarities in their philosophies of learning and behavior management, a beneficial co-teaching dynamic can be created (Bouck, 2007). Co-teaching pairs must be comfortable with difficult conversations regarding grading, student participation, classroom management, and accommodations (Bouck, 2007). Establishing appropriate roles, dividing classroom responsibilities equally, and mutual respect between co-teachers is also important (Keefe & Moore, 2004). Teachers also need administrators to make a commitment to a school-wide focus on inclusive education by providing time for planning and encouraging collaboration (Keefe & Moore, 2004).

The inspiration for my study came from the challenges I encountered as a special education co-teacher in my own school. The challenges I faced on a daily basis mirrored what research said regarding the obstacles to co-teaching effectiveness in secondary schools. I craved professional development that could help me learn to co-teach with a role that I felt content with, but I did not know where to begin. I believed that the lack of professional development for co-teachers was a contributing factor to the negative experiences I and some of my colleagues had co-teaching.

Purpose of the Study

Prior to my doctoral studies, I believed that a lack of parity between co-teachers was a problem of practice that was in need of practical solutions. Despite my desire to make the co-teaching dynamics at my school more collaborative, I did not have a clear idea of how to remediate the issue. Asking administrators to overhaul the scheduling procedures utilized for co-teachers was unrealistic and there was no antidote for a lack of pre-service preparation for co-teaching; however, professional development was a realistic intervention. Two courses that I feel had the greatest impact on my experiences in my EdD program were a class on adult learning theories and models of professional development. These classes gave me the opportunity to design professional development and take on the role of facilitator. It was through my experiences in these courses that I realized my interest and enjoyment in planning and conducting professional development. Once I decided to utilize a professional development intervention in my DiP study, I was able to work on designing a program that could have a positive and relevant impact on the co-teachers in my school. This practical approach to studying problems of practice is not something I feel I could have fully engaged in if I had pursued a PhD.

When creating my DiP proposal I worked under the assumption that teachers needed to function as a team to truly co-teach. Through my DiP study, I wanted to first develop a deeper understanding of my colleague's co-teaching experiences, and provide them with a forum to share their stories. I also wanted to explore the impact team-building professional development had on co-teachers' relationships in both the professional development and back in the classroom. I decided to conduct a team-building professional development program for my DiP study because I wanted to provide my colleagues with a professional development program that could support them in implementing this challenging model of instruction successfully.

The activities in this professional development were designed to help participants build the skills associated with effective teamwork and the design was informed by research on teamwork in the workplace. Research has found communication to be an essential element of effective teams (Buljac-Samardzic, 2011; McCaffrey, Hayes, Cassell, Miller-Reyes, Donaldson, & Ferrell, 2012; Mickan & Rodger, 2005; Sargeant, Loney, & Murphy, 2008). Cooperation and communication have been found to be essential for team effectiveness and providing feedback to colleagues has also been identified as necessary to continually improve team performance (Buljac-Samardzic, 2011). In addition to communication, respect for team member's roles and recognizing that teamwork requires work have been found to be key characteristics of effective teams (Sargeant et al., 2008). A shared vision has also been identified in research as vital to team effectiveness in the workplace (Ahles & Bosworth, 2004; Bittner & Leimesiter, 2014; Mickan & Rodger, 2005; Sargeant et al., 2008). Understanding and respecting team member's roles are main characteristics of effective teams (Sargeant et al., 2008). Research has also found trust to be an important factor in team effectiveness (Chiocchio, Forgues, David, & Iordanova, 2011; DeOrtentiis, Summers, Ammeter, Douglas, & Ferris, 2013; Jones & Jones, 2011; Kuo & Yu, 2009; Tseng, Heng, Wang, & Sun, 2009). Collegial trust is essential for good teamwork, and trust can be enhanced with increased meeting time for team members (Jones & Jones, 2011). After reviewing research on workplace teams, activities to build communication, a shared vision, and trust became the foundation of my professional development design.

Team-building Professional Development

I decided to conduct a case study for my DiP to illuminate the experiences of high school co-teaching pairs in team-building activities. The cognitive goal of this professional development was to build participants' understanding of the importance of teamwork in co-teaching relationships. The affective goal of this professional development plan was to enhance co-teachers feelings of camaraderie in their relationship with their co-teacher and assist co-teachers in developing a trusting relationship. Finally, the behavioral goal of this professional development plan was to change co-teachers' relationships to improve their communication skills and enhance the quality of their collaboration.

I also chose to conduct a multi-session professional development program, that would ebb and flow based on the feedback of participants, because I wanted to provide participants with an engaging, worthwhile, and personal professional development experience. With this in mind, I decided to include games and problem-solving activities to provide participants with the opportunity to play in their workplace. The play activities in this professional development were meant to provide co-teachers with enjoyable experiences together outside of the classroom to boost their productivity together in the classroom.

Study Findings

The findings from the DiP study that I believe were most significant related to how experiences in the professional development provided co-teachers with opportunities to take on different roles, which helped them to change the assumptions they made about their partner. All group members reported positive experiences in the professional development and the most common adjective used to describe each session was "fun." Participants appreciated having the time to "play" and be silly at work because there is often not enough time in the day to laugh with your co-workers and get to know each other in new ways. Group members felt that their experiences in the team-building professional development were uplifting and motivating, and this was something they rarely experienced in past professional development. Every session had an upbeat energy and all participants were observed having fun, laughing, and communicating respectfully. At no point was any tension observed. Group members reported enjoying the opportunity to bond with their co-teacher, and their colleagues, in a relaxed atmosphere and appreciated the opportunity to be reflective of themselves and their co-teaching relationship.

The nature of the professional development activities provided co-teachers with the opportunity to take on new roles, with the special education teacher taking the lead role in some activities and the general education teachers taking on a supporting role. This helped the special education teacher feel more confident in their interactions with their co-teacher, and helped the general education teachers to see their partner as a whole person that is capable of more than just the role of "helper." Participants' who perceived themselves as "all business" in the classroom let their guard down in the activities, which helped them to make connections. It also helped participants who work with a dominating partner to feel more comfortable collaborating.

Group members that already felt they had a strong relationship prior to the professional development still found the experience worthwhile because they had the opportunity to strengthen their bonds and have fun together, which they rarely have time to do with hectic schedules and commitments outside of work. Even though some pairs believed they had a happy and healthy relationship prior to the start of the professional development they still believed that good co-teaching relationships require ongoing work. These pairs believe it is important to take time to bond and refresh their relationship to keep things "on track" so they can continue to work effectively as a team.

Participants in newer co-teaching relationships were not friends outside of school so their only interactions happen during the school day. The professional development provided these pairs with time to work on building their relationship in diverse activities to strengthen their bond. Rather than relying on developing years of experience in a consistent partnership, team-building professional development has the potential to expedite relationship development for co-teachers, which helped them to develop a shared history. These experiences created a foundation for their relationship that can support their ability to work as a team in the classroom.

Not only did the participants of this study have the opportunity to bond, I too had experiences during data collection that allowed me to bond with my colleagues in new ways. Since interviews were one-on-one and took place at the convenience of the participants, the teachers I interviewed were very relaxed and forthcoming. Having my colleagues share their stories with me was a very powerful experience. I was able to get to know them on a deeper level and this is something I would not have had the opportunity to do otherwise. One participant, who I did not know beyond saying 'hello' to in passing before my study, lost their mother during the course of my data collection. Prior to conducting my study, I would have sent a sympathy card and expressed my condolences upon their return to work, but from our time together in interviews and team-building workshops, I developed a rapport and relationship with this colleague that I would most likely not have developed otherwise. I attended the wake because we had developed a more personal relationship throughout my study and upon my arrival, we hugged and they shared with me some of what they were experiencing. I wanted to attend the wake so they knew they could count on my support because they were now my friend; not just my coworker.

Providing participants with low-stakes activities created a "safe space" for newer pairs to practice communicating. Group members with less established relationships expressed that by communicating and compromising in problem-solving activities, they developed confidence in their ability to communicate with their co-teacher. They did not feel afraid to contribute in activities because they knew they would be able to communicate respectfully. The data I collected that focused on participants' communication with their partner before, during, and after the professional development also resulted in some self-awareness on my part. I realized that I am not comfortable having difficult conversations with co-teachers and prefer to avoid conflict. Because of this, I do not share my needs with my co-teacher so they may be unaware of the fact that I am not satisfied or would like to change aspects of our relationship dynamic. I realized through my study that I need to work on my communication with my co-teachers and should not expect changes to occur if I do not share my needs. As a result, I now have discussions with my co-teachers regarding our roles and responsibilities and understand the importance of feeling comfortable communicating.

In addition to bonding and building communication skills, the unfamiliar nature of the activities built trust for some pairs. Some participants felt that they were able to develop more trust because being "playful" helped them to lower their inhibitions. Other partnerships reported feeling more trust in their relationship because they relied on each other to complete the task. My interviews with participants also provided my colleagues the opportunity to build trust with me. In our interviews, participants spoke freely and were very open and honest in their responses. Participants were relaxed and took the time to give reflective and thoughtful responses. I did not observe any participants exhibiting tense body language in our interviews and none of the participants rushed through the interview. The data I collected in my interviews allowed me to realize the level of trust my colleagues had in me, even those that I did not know very well. Recognizing this level of trust made me feel more connected to my colleagues because I felt the mutual respect we have for each other.

Many participants described experiencing equitable interactions during the completion of the professional development activities. The nature of the professional development activities created an environment where both special and general education co-teachers could contribute from an equal position. Experiencing this equality allowed the special education teacher to take more of a leading role, which helped to build their confidence. General education teachers described taking more of a "backseat" at times because their special education co-teacher seemed more adept at leading the team through the completion of the activity. These experiences resulted in general education teachers becoming more aware of their partner dynamics, which helped them to relinquish some control in their interactions with their special education co-teacher. The interactions of co-teachers in the team-building activities provided some participants with the opportunity to interact with their partner and make reflections that challenged the assumptions they had previously made about their co-teaching dynamic. Some general education participants viewed their co-teacher as inferior because they did not trust their content knowledge. Some special education participants assumed they had to maintain an inferior role to minimize conflict, and they felt their co-teacher would not be receptive to their input. The differences in how they interacted in the team-building helped to challenge these assumptions and led to progress in their relationships.

After participating in the professional development all group members reported that team-building should be conducted on an ongoing basis and should be provided to new co-teaching pairs before the school year starts because they found their experiences in team-building had a positive impact on relationship development. Participants also expressed their desire to complete department and school-wide team-building because they feel it helps build relationships that result in positive professional interactions. Team-building has the potential to not only improve relationships between co-teaching partners but also create a more team-oriented climate systemically.

The professional development program I conducted in my DiP study was able to facilitate positive changes in the relationship dynamics of co-teachers in my study setting. By focusing on the "how" I was able to impact my study sample in a way I do not feel would have been possible if I were to have pursued a PhD. When my study was complete and my DiP defended, I did not feel as though I had merely written a document that would sit on my bookshelf never to be revisited. I felt as though I was at the starting line of new endeavors in my career as an educator. I became increasingly more passionate about the importance of professional development to support co-teachers and my study findings only inspired me to want to continue to study the impact of team-building professional development. Participants provided me with positive feedback regarding the design of my professional development and my role as a facilitator of professional development.

I felt as though I had found a niche facilitating professional development and the accolades of my participants resulted in me thinking, "Hey, I'm pretty good at this." I did not feel like completing my DiP was the ending; instead, I felt like it was the start of a new beginning.

My experiences in my doctoral studies changed my perception of myself. My experiences in my doctoral studies allowed me to see myself as more than just a student. I began to see myself as a researcher, someone who enjoys conducting qualitative research and the writing to communicate findings to their audience. I began to see myself as a successful professional development facilitator, someone who is able to provide valuable learning experiences for their colleagues. Finally, the positive experiences my participants shared with me allowed me to see myself as a change agent. Conducting practitioner research provided me with the opportunity to participate in bringing about tangible and practical changes in my environment. My experiences in my EdD program inspired me to continue to focus on imparting positive changes in co-teaching relationships.

IMPLICATIONS FOR MY PROFESSIONAL GOALS

I do not want my role as a researcher to end now that my doctoral studies are complete. The process instilled in me a passion for scholarly research and I crave more opportunities to conduct research that is relevant to my professional practice. The findings from my study demonstrate that professional development is a viable intervention to support co-teachers, which instilled in me the desire to conduct more research. Team-building helped to facilitate relationship development and provided participants with the opportunity to develop characteristics of effective teams. Team-building for co-teachers is an area of research that has yet to be fully explored; therefore, I hope to conduct more research to determine if this professional development intervention is applicable in diverse instructional settings. Participants of this study expressed their desire to participate in department and school-wide team-building to build their relationship with all of their colleagues, not just their co-teacher, therefore, I would also like to conduct research that focuses on the impact of team-building on school climate and culture.

Many participants shared that they felt like team-building was "step one." They were inspired by the progress they made in the professional development and expressed their desire to participate in more professional development for co-teachers. Participants wanted to continue their journey as a co-teacher and develop additional skills that could support them in implementing this challenging model of instruction in a more innovative and collaborative manner to truly make the most of having two teachers in the classroom. My DiP study created a momentum for participants and produced an environment where members became excited to keep evolving in their co-teaching relationship. Because of this, I now am interested in designing a professional development program that can provide co-teachers with opportunities to collaborate and learn from their peers to brainstorm ways to implement co-teaching in a more dynamic manner.

   Changing the way co-teaching is implemented can occur in small ways in individual classrooms, but if administrators make it a priority, and provide relevant professional development, the potential exists to change the culture of a school, which can result in a more equitable and collaborative climate across a school campus. Garnering administrative support can help to facilitate systemic changes but focusing on improving relationships one at a time also can result in systemic changes because participants can carry with them what they learned about the importance of teamwork in co-teaching relationships to their future co-teaching assignments. Currently I am focusing on changing co-teaching one classroom at a time but am always on the lookout for ways to generate more administrative "buy-in" to the power of team-building.

REFLECTIONS

I felt a sense of accomplishment after my DiP defense, not only because I had achieved a goal, but also because I felt like I brought about positive changes for my colleagues. My experiences conducting practitioner research in my DiP study helped me develop more professional respect for myself. I plan to continue to work as a special education co-teacher for the time being to implement the lessons I learned from my DiP study in my own co-teaching relationships, but I now feel that I have far more options professionally. As a result of my experiences in my DiP study, I believe that I can bring about positive changes in educational settings that can result in systemic changes for co-teachers. I have developed a new goal for myself, to become a professional development facilitator and co-teaching consultant. I view myself as a capable and empowered change agent because of experiences in my EdD program and am looking forward to continuing my journey.

REFERENCES

Ahles, C. B., & Bosworth, C. C. (2004). The perception and reality of student and workplace teams. *Journalism and Mass Communication Educator, 59*(1), 42–59.

Bittner, E. A. C., & Leimesiter, J. M. (2014). Creating shared understanding in heterogeneous work groups: Why it matters and how to achieve it. *Journal of Management Information Systems, 13*(1), 111–143.

Bouck, E. C. (2007). Co-teaching...Not just a textbook term: Implications for practice. *Preventing School Failure, 51*(2), 46–50.

Buljac-Samardzic, M. (2011). Perceptions of team workers in youth care of what makes teamwork effective. *Health and Social Care in the Community, 19*(3), 307–316.

Chiocchio, F., Forgues, D., David, C., & Iordanova, I. (2011). Teamwork in integrated design projects: Understanding the effects of trust, conflict, and collaboration on performance. *Project Management Journal, 42*(6), 78–91.

DeOrtentiis, P. S., Summers, J. K., Ammeter, A. P., Douglas, C., & Ferris, G. R. (2013). Cohesion and satisfaction as mediators of the team-trust-team effectiveness relationship: An interdependence theory perspective. *Career Development International, 18*(5), 521–543.

Dymond, S. K., Renzaglia, A., Gilson, C. L., & Slagor, M. T. (2007). Defining access to the general education curriculum for high school students with significant cognitive disabilities. *Research & Practice for Persons with Severe Disabilities, 32*(1), 1–15.

Jones, A., & Jones, D. (2011). Improving teamwork, trust and safety: An ethnographic study of an interprofessional initiative. *Journal of Interprofessional Care, 25,* 175–181.

Keefe, E. B., & Moore, V. (2004). The challenge of co-teaching in inclusive classrooms at the high school level: What the teachers told us. *American Secondary Education, 32*(3), 77–88.

Keefe, E. B., Moore, V., & Duff, F. (2004). The four "knows" of collaborative teaching. *TEACHING Exceptional Children, 36*(5), 36–41.

Kuo, F., & Yu, C. (2009). An exploratory study of trust dynamics in work related virtual teams. *Journal of Computer-Mediated Communication, 14,* 823–854.

Magiera, K., Smith, C., Zigmond, N., & Gebauer, K. (2005). Benefits of co-teaching in secondary mathematics classes. *TEACHING Exceptional Children, 37*(3), 20–24.

McCaffrey, R., Hayes, R., Cassell, A., Miller-Reyes, S., Donaldson, A., & Ferrell, C. (2012). The effect of an educational programme on attitudes of nurses and medical residents towards the benefits of positive communication and collaboration. *Journal of Advanced Nursing, 68*(2), 293–301.

Mickan, S. M., & Rodger, S. A. (2005). Effective health care teams: A model of six characteristics developed from shared perceptions. *Journal of Interprofessional Care, 19*(4), 358–370.

Rice, N., Drame, E., Owens, L., & Frattura, E. M. (2007). Co-instructing at the secondary level: Strategies for success. *TEACHING Exceptional Children, 39(6), 12–18.*

Sargeant, J., Loney, E., & Murphy, G. (2008). Effective interprofessional teams: "Contact is not enough" to build teams. *Journal of Continuing Education in the Health Professions, 28*(4), 228–234.

Scruggs, T. E., Mastropieri, M. A., & McDuffie, K. A. (2007). Co-teaching in inclusive classrooms: A metasynthesis of qualitative research. *Exceptional Children, 73*(4), 392–416.

Tseng, H., Heng, Y. K., Wang, C., & Sun, L. (2009). Key factors in online collaboration and their relationships to teamwork satisfaction. *The Quarterly Review of Distance Education, 10*(2), 195–206.

CHAPTER 12

DISSERTATION IN PRACTICE (DiP) AS OPPORTUNITY

Acting as a Mentor and Leader in a Doctoral Program

Sheri K. Rodriguez

A student's time commitment to a doctoral program can vary based on his or her professional, personal, and familial obligations (Ivankova & Stick, 2007). While research does not point to one specific factor that contributes to persistence, dissertation defense, and completion in a graduate program, institutional support, and personal motivation play a part in graduate student success (Ivankova & Stick, 2007). At the same time, the literature suggests if students are presented with opportunities for program engagement and opt to actively immerse themselves in their programs, particularly within their dissertation experiences, their involvement can yield powerful, long-lasting results beyond the dissertation defense and degree completion (Burnett, 1999; de Valero, 2001; Ivankova & Stick, 2007). This involvement is also contingent upon the institution and academic departments providing participatory opportunities for doctoral students (Burnett, 1999; de Valero, 2001; Ivankova & Stick, 2007).

Exploring the Impact of the Dissertation in Practice, pages 177–191.
Copyright © 2017 by Information Age Publishing
All rights of reproduction in any form reserved.

In terms of my own graduate experience, I chose to pursue a Doctor of Educational Leadership (EdD) program due to my passion for and skills pertaining to higher education, school administration, and organizational leadership. My interest in these areas was peaked during my MA in Higher Education Administration program and had grown throughout my career in higher education. During my EdD program, particularly in the Dissertation in Practice (DiP) phase, I discovered opportunities to become involved with not only my DiP committee, but also with my colleagues who had the same DiP chair and operated as a cohort. Some activities were structured and originated from the program itself initiated by faculty, while others I sought out on my own. Nevertheless, as I progressed with my DiP research, I found myself increasingly and actively engaged with my cohort colleagues as we met periodically, worked through similar DiP-related issues, made presentations on various topics, and offered guidance, support, and tips to each other. Serving in this role provided leadership opportunities, acting in a function that I have come to call a "DiP leader." Interwoven in these interactions were also various opportunities for involvement outside of my program, including national conference presentations, student panels, and participation in faculty searches. Furthermore, reflecting back on my experiences, I also engaged in similar behaviors with my colleagues upon completing the coursework phase of the program prior to embarking on the DiP. During this period, I found myself incidentally providing guidance and mentorship to those students who were behind me in coursework and did not yet enter the DiP phase, operating in a capacity I have labeled "course mentor."

Based on my experiences, I offer that student involvement in a doctoral program as a DiP leader and/or course mentor yields opportunities beyond completing the DiP itself. This takes the DiP beyond the typical research endeavor, making it a dynamic vehicle for learning, collegial interaction, and participation in the broader research community. This engaging environment is best achieved through collaborative communities designed and encouraged by institutional academic departments who oversee doctoral programs (Burnett, 1999; Hampton, 2015). In such cases, the institutions offer opportunities for students to serve in this interactive capacity, however, it is up to the student to take advantage of them (Burnett, 1999; Hampton, 2015).

Throughout this chapter, I explore the concepts and functions of course mentors and DiP leaders who participate in a doctoral program, and the DiP process, in depth. However, to provide contextualization for this discussion, I begin by highlighting factors that may impact DiP and doctoral degree completion and various institutional factors that contribute to students completing their dissertations (Burnett, 1999; de Valero, 2001). I then provide my own definitions of a course mentor and DiP leader situated within a doctoral program based on my own experiences and perspective, acknowledging the murkiness between the two functions while integrating literature related to these areas. I weave accounts of my own mentorship/leadership practices during my doctoral program, addressing positive and negative experiences I encountered while serving in both functions. I also outline the types of involvement students can participate in, based on my personal experiences, if they choose to serve as a mentor or leader: peer to peer, departmental, community, and post-program.

Next, I move into the leadership literature to discuss how mentors and leaders contribute to collaboration and support, taking the position that there is a need for the aforementioned types of leaders and mentors during and beyond completing a doctoral program. I then specify how being a mentor and/or leader impacts the sustainability of a doctoral program in terms of program vibrancy, equity, collaboration, and diversity of students and their research, circling back to the literature on degree completion. Lastly, I close with a discussion of how programmatic success can be measured based on the implementation of course mentor and DiP relations, providing a brief reflection on my own experiences.

The primary focus of this chapter will be my own experiences and perspectives within the context of an EdD Program. While I do consider myself a practitioner first and foremost given my managerial role at my institution, I also have a strong interest in research that developed over the course of my EdD, since my program did include some research-based courses, specifically qualitative and mixed methods research. However, I will not be focusing on myself as a researcher as a result of my program in this chapter. My focus will be how I have advanced personally and professionally because of my work as a course mentor and DiP leader, in addition to suggesting how institutions can provide these types of opportunities for doctoral students.

LEADERSHIP: IMPACT ON COMPLETION

The EdD was created in response to what was perceived as a demonstrated need for practitioners to be able to earn a doctorate in lieu of earning a degree that specialized in a specific area (Nelson & Coorough, 1994). This degree differs from a Doctor of Philosophy, or PhD, which is more research focused and content-area specific, although these differences are not always apparent between these degrees (Basu, 2012; Nelson & Coorough, 1994). The EdD typically has a concentration on organizational theory and change, leadership, and strives to apply theory to practice in a student's workplace (Nelson & Coorough, 1994). There continues to be some debate surrounding the perceived value of an EdD versus a PhD, with some institutions opting to eliminate their long-standing EdD programs for what are considered to be more research rigorous PhD programs (Basu, 2012).

Half of all students who begin graduate programs every year, including EdD programs, do not finish due to being disconnected from their institutions during the DiP phase (Burnett, 1999; Hampton, 2015). The data reveal that students who persist in a doctoral program complete their degree in six years or less in the fields of agricultural and in engineering (National Academic Press, 2010). In the social sciences, however, only 37 percent of students complete in six years or less, with the same percentage of students in humanities fields completing within eight years (National Academic Press, 2010). While these specific statistics focus on PhD programs, they do suggest that programs at the doctoral level overall have low completion rates (National Academic Press, 2010).

It is assumed that doctoral program completion rates remain low because the attainment of a doctoral degree, with all of its rigor, is reserved for those who have the academic ability to persevere (Burnett, 1999; Hampton, 2015; National Academic Press, 2010). However, the continued need to graduate and hire college professors and administrators, especially those from historically underrepresented backgrounds, as will be discussed in a later section, remains (National Academic Press, 2010). Not enough students are completing their doctoral programs and defending their dissertations to fill this void (National Academic Press, 2010). Moreover, these low completion rates call into question what happens to students who pay high tuition rates and do not ever complete the doctoral degree, but could have, with some form of a support system (de Valero, 2001; Hampton, 2015). I posit that support systems within the context of a doctoral program can take the form of faculty-led discussions, workshops, additional office hours, cohort meetings, or putting students in touch with former graduates or others who can provide guidance during the dissertation process (de Valero, 2001). As I mentioned earlier, it is then the decision of the student as to whether or not they want to take part in these interactions. In this chapter, I will focus on student-led efforts that are simply presented as opportunities by the faculty.

As I reflect on my own experiences, I believe that I would not have persisted in my own EdD program had it not been for the opportunities to give and share information with colleagues through such support systems of open communications embedded in mentorship and leadership. Therefore, I offer that fostering mentorship and leadership opportunities can increase degree completion, and even make a doctoral program and the dissertation phase a meaningful, practical experience through cultivating connections among doctoral students (Hampton, 2015). Furthermore, I suggest that being a leader or mentor within a doctoral program creates a cyclical sustainability of leadership, opportunity, and student progress that can benefit students even after degree completion.

MENTORS AND LEADERS: DEFINITIONS

Before discussing my own crafted definitions of course mentor and DiP leader, I would like to point out that there could be repetitive or overlapping terminology given how these terms are interpreted. The concepts of leaders and mentors are not neatly or clear cut. In this section, I provide a context of mentorship and leadership, outlining general characteristics that drove my definitions of course mentors and DiP leaders. I also provide my categorization of ideas within the functions of a course mentor and DiP leader based on the leadership literature. Acknowledging and examining the murkiness of mentors and leaders suggests that further research in doctoral student experiences may provide clarity and contribute to efforts regarding persistence and success for this population.

While there is no agreed-upon definition for mentoring, much of the literature consistently characterizes it as a one-on-one relationship that can occur in a professional or academic setting (Berk, Berg, Mortimer, Walton-Moss, & Yeo, 2005). In either setting, the mentor provides resources for materials relevant to the field, constructive feedback and encouragement to the mentee in expressing ideas, along with challenging him or her to improve professionally or academically (Berk et al., 2005). While I have not used a specific definition of mentoring for this chapter, the aforementioned characteristics seemed to surface in the course mentor relationships I participated in or witnessed, driving my conceptualization of the course mentor role.

Leadership is also a term that does not have a set definition based on the literature, but there are common characteristics that encompass this concept, specifically within the context of what is considered effective and exceptional leadership. For instance, Northouse (2011) defines leadership as "a process whereby an individual influences a group of individuals to achieve a common good" (p. 6). In the context of a doctoral program, "a common good" (Northouse, 2011, p. 6) can be considered not only successful completion of a DiP, but personally and/or professionally changing as a result of the process. Fullan (2001) discusses leadership in terms of "reculturing," or changing an organization's cultural based on effective leadership characteristics such as relationship building, knowledge sharing and creation, coherence making, and serving a moral purpose. Such characteristics became a part of the DiP leader's role, for students can experience their own period of academic reculturing, along with their peers, as they make the shift from coursework to DiP research, leaving the classroom and entering the field.

Generally, I define course mentors as doctoral candidates in the DiP phase who provide support to students who are in coursework and in the DiP pipeline. Based on my experiences, this support can be in the form of student discussion panels for particular courses, meet-and-greets, professor-recommended connections, or just general collegial meetings or conversations outside of class. The idea is that the academic departments and/or professors who work with the doctoral program informally set the foundation for the mentorship by recruiting students who would be interested in engaging in these types of activities, then the students still in coursework take advantage of these opportunities and set up the communication moving forward. This also gives the course mentors experiences with working with students as they themselves navigate the DiP process.

A DiP leader provides active leadership in the DiP phase by conducting timely research, presenting best practices to their peers, and returning post-DiP to discuss their experiences with those in the final phases of their own DiPs. Unlike the one on one coursework-focused relationship that serves as the foundation for the course mentor role, the DiP leader typically provides support to a group of students in a particular cohort and hones in on a very specific research or DiP-related topic. With that said, while the primary function of the DiP leader is group-oriented, he or she can break off from the group and assist students going through the DiP process as needed.

I selected the terms "mentors" and "leaders" to describe the roles that these students play in doctoral programs and DiP experiences for multiple reasons. First, and as alluded to earlier, these definitions are in line with the leadership literature that describes positive, dynamic, and strong leadership based on organizational theory. I assert that these individuals take on these leadership-type roles in their doctoral programs, either incidentally or in facilitation with faculty members. Second, I wanted to use terms that delineated the functions of each role. In line with my experiences, the course mentors assume a one on one role with students, shepherding them through the remainder of their coursework as they developed their DiP topics. A DiP leader on the other hand, collaborates and works with a group of students in a cohort who is moving through the DiP process, providing support and suggestions through perhaps presentations or small group meetings to guide them up through the defense process (although, as needed, he or she can provide individual support as well). Once again, I will point out that there is even murkiness between the terms mentor and leader, and there can certainly be overlap between the course mentor and DiP leader roles, but I argue that it is more important to distinguish at what phase in the program students can assume these roles

Tied to these definitions, and perhaps contributing further to the blurring of these roles, students can act as course mentors or DiP leaders, or both. Sometimes there is overlap in the roles, and they are not as clear cut as defined. Students can engage in one or both of these functions depending on their own interests, abilities, and progress in their doctoral programs. For example, a student in the DiP phase could be mentoring a student who has just completed coursework, working with them on their DiP proposal, and then making a presentation to that student's cohort about moving through the proposal defense. However, there would most likely be a point, once that student defended his or her proposal that the mentor would simply shift into being a DiP leader altogether. Moreover, the longer a student is in the DiP phase, the less likely they would be to serve in the course mentor role since they would be far removed from the coursework phase of the program and entrenched in the DiP experience.

While it is important to discuss the parameters and characteristics that drive course mentors and DiP leaders, it is also helpful to determine what is not encompassed in these roles. Course mentors and DiP leaders are not simply students who "take the lead" on an assigned group project, raise their hand often in class, complete their work first, or are the "go to" student for information and clarity on coursework for other students. These roles may or may not be deliberately assigned based on the design of the doctoral program, but emerge when a student fosters and supports another with the goal of degree completion in mind. This fostering is encouragement-driven, based on feedback and guidance, not assignment-driven, or based on what is listed on the syllabus or the logistics of a course.

MENTORS AND LEADERS: A LOOK AT THE LITERATURE

Behaviors and actions of mentors and leaders are evident in the leadership literature. For instance, collaboration, compassion, and support are inherent qualities in servant leaders, which students who take on the role, either voluntarily or unknowingly, have natural qualities embodied in this leadership style (Fullan, 2001; Greenleaf, 2002). Mentors and leaders both have some level of emotional intelligence, and in alignment with Goleman, Boyatzis, and McKee (2002), set the tone, or vision, for the students they work with, and coach them through either the DiP proposal phase or DiP process itself.

Furthermore, in the spirit of Argyris (1990), the process of seeking, receiving, and working through feedback, on the end of the mentor and leader, and the student, is indicative of single and double loop learning, likely further reinforcing feedback from the student's DiP advisor, challenging him or her, and helping him or her become a better writer, researcher, and practitioner. For example, during my DiP phase, my advisor would pose questions about my writing and research. I would then work through these questions during multiple revisions. Then, as I assisted other students in my role as a DiP leader, I was able to notice similar issues in another student's writing, pose to them similar questions, and then provide them suggestions on how to strengthen their writing, explaining the interconnections between their writing and research. It would be my hope that the student would then serve as a DiP leader for another student or group, pose similar questions, and build on the feedback I provided to them. This demonstrates growth from simply making revisions to one's own writing (single loop learning), and then translating it to practice, but taking it a step further by providing suggestions and deeper critiques through exploring connections between writing and research based on practice and conversation (double loop learning).

As suggested by Goleman et al. (2002), these leadership behaviors contribute to the climate and mood of the DiP and, overall, the doctoral program. For example, in my incidental course mentor role, I had a "mentee" whom I had met during my coursework. I had moved through the proposal stage before she did, however, because I had knowledge of the proposal process, I was able to guide her through a success proposal defense, although she had encountered some personal circumstances that she felt would prevent her from moving forward. Therefore, instead of telling her that she should stop the program and continue at some other point, with course mentor support (and from faculty, who model these behaviors for the mentors and leaders), she only had a minor delay and then moved onto the next phase. In turn, she shared her experiences with another student completing coursework, continuing the cycle of being a course mentor. Without the mentoring relationship, the student would have not likely defended her proposal or ever mentored another student. This example demonstrates that course mentors and DiP leaders are not perfect, and, consistent with the leadership literature (Fullan, 2001; Goleman et al., 2002) should not be perceived as such. They suffer from setbacks that humanize them and make them stronger as individuals and as doctoral students, perhaps with the help from their own mentors and leaders.

In my own doctoral work, and as mentioned earlier, mentor and leader roles occurred incidentally and organically, either by requests of faculty or simply through students who sought support and assistance. Despite these informal relationships, unfortunately, I did not have a course mentor, within the context of the parameters I provided. Similar to the challenges I had mentioned earlier that my mentee experienced, I experienced personal challenges of my own during my doctoral coursework. My father was diagnosed with advanced cancer and I switched positions at my university. Because I needed to take the time off due to these life changes, I fell out of sequence during my coursework, creating a sense of disjointedness as I rotated in and out of courses with established cohorts in which relationships were already formed. I was not able to develop consistent relationships with any of my colleagues until the last two courses of my program, prior to entering the DiP phase. This "bouncing around" certainly creates a challenge with developing course mentor relationships (of course, many times, at no fault of the student, faculty, or program overall), which is something I will address in an upcoming section of this chapter.

MENTORS AND LEADERS: TYPES OF INVOLVEMENT

Taking our definitions of course mentor and DiP leader into account, below I outline the four primary types of involvement for doctoral students that can occur in doctoral programs: peer to peer, departmental, community, and post-program. These involvement types can take place either during coursework or the DiP phase. Course mentors and DiP leaders can engage in a combination of these types of involvement or hone in one type based on their preference and professional goals.

Peer to peer involvement. Peer to peer involvement in a doctoral program at the DiP phase can be the most organic. As in most programs or instructional environments, it happens incidentally, when students are assigned together for group projects, meet during icebreaker activities, or share common academic interests. While, unfortunately, sometimes the peer to peer involvement can have negative consequences, such as a group project meeting that turns into simply complaining about the assignment, other forged relationships can be very positive. Peer to peer involvement can include one on one or group interactions, the idea being that the engagement is scholarly amongst the peers. From my personal experience, I've used these type of relationships to exchange ideas with peers, and later on in my program, my DiP chapters for critical feedback. During these exchanges, I learn as much about myself when reading the work of others through giving constructive, yet critical feedback to my peers.

Peer to peer involvement is demonstrative and, based on my experiences, in the strongest relationships, typically occurs during coursework and persists during the DiP phase. Out of these relationships, course mentors and DiP leaders emerge, as they develop confidence in their own writing, research, and ability to coach and support others who are in the DiP pipeline. Similar to what I alluded to earlier, these relationships are based on more than just students working together on a group assignment, or students seeking out others who are labeled academically superior for some reason by classmates. These relationships involve students who actively seek out others with similar interests, motivational levels, and can be critical, yet collegial, to each other.

Departmental involvement. Student involvement in an academic department can take the form of participation in a student panel for faculty searches or attending job talks, attending faculty-led presentations, or serving as a graduate or teaching assistant. While serving as a graduate or teaching assistant may not be feasible for every student, or an available option at the institution, (my institution did not have teaching assistants, and graduate assistantships were very competitive) seeking out and making time for departmental involvement, especially during the DiP phase, can help students make connections with potential DiP committee members while expanding their knowledge about the field of leadership beyond the classroom.

There are simple activities that can signify departmental involvement. For example, a student may consider doing some research on all of the faculty members in their program's department to find out their backgrounds and research interests. The student can then perhaps have lunch or coffee with a faculty member who may have similar research interests and have the potential to be a student's DiP committee member. This also requires the effort and cooperation of the faculty members as well, for they are opening themselves up to other students and may or may not be willing to put themselves out there in such a capacity.

Community involvement. This type of involvement is a little more nebulous, but I suggest that community involvement encompasses activities outside of the DiP and doctoral program altogether but still have an academic tie to the student's doctoral program experiences. This can include presentations at national conferences, membership to a professional association, reading academic articles of interest that are non-DiP related, gleaning from previous coursework, and applying theory to practice. For instance, during my own DiP experience, I joined two professional associations and gave a poster presentation at a national conference. I was inspired to seek out these experiences from a former doctoral student who gave a presentation to my DiP chair's cohort about presenting research at a professional conference. This instance demonstrates the DiP leader relationship and the cycle of passing along practitioner-oriented advice.

If students do not wish to engage scholarly, or academically, with their communities, they may consider a broader form of civic engagement. For instance, a colleague in my cohort implemented some practices based on her DiP research with a K–12 after-school program she developed. In these cases, it would then be up to the student to let his or her doctoral colleagues and faculty know that they were putting such ideas into practice and participating in community involvement, translating into rich conversation with the cohort.

Post-program involvement. Post-program involvement can be considered the most critical, yet least practiced, form of involvement for a doctoral student. Post-program involvement can take the form of presenting finished DiP products at national conferences, crafting articles based on a DiP, returning to speak to classes and cohort groups about experiences, staying in touch with your DiP committee, and helping doctoral candidates with the DiP process. I offer that this type of involvement can be beneficial in planning a career trajectory, as staying in touch with faculty and peers helps a graduate remain aware of employment opportunities.

I am reminded of my experiences with my DiP chair when thinking about post-program involvement, and its contribution to the DiP. My relationship with my DiP chair began when I had her as a professor for a policy course I had taken when re-entering the program after my short hiatus I referenced earlier. Her research on community colleges and underrepresented students, educational background, and way of teaching peaked my interest, so when I approached the time to begin fleshing out ideas for a DiP topic, I contacted her since she is a leading expert in her field on my research interests. She thoughtfully challenged the relevance, impact, and most importantly, thinking and perspective on my proposed DiP topic. As we worked through honing in on my research topic, she eventually became my DiP chair, and I then asked another professor who was very talented in the area of qualitative research to be my methodologist, as well as an administrator to be my subject specialist given her knowledge of the current transfer student landscape.

Even after defending my DiP, I am still working with my chair, and keep in close touch with my methodologist and subject specialist. My chair and I have collaborated on a few projects, she has co-authored two articles with me, and we frequently discuss research opportunities and career paths. We continue to collaborate and communicate often, and most importantly, she was my inspiration for writing this book chapter. I wanted to express the importance of being immersed in a DiP experience, along with the benefits of engaging with the DiP process specifically, and the doctoral program, in general.

STUDENT DISENGAGEMENT AND RESISTANCE

As I've detailed above, while I chose to immerse myself in my doctoral program and DiP experience, other students may not have the same desire for scholarly program engagement. Common in the leadership literature is the idea of "the resisters," or those who do not agree or "buy in" to a certain philosophy or organizational culture (Fullan, 2001; Kezar, 2001; Lewin, 1947). Of course, during my time as a course mentor and DiP leader, I encountered such individuals in the form of students who felt they could complete the work autonomously, were just "there to get the degree" to advance their careers, or did not embrace the programmatic content as being practical. For example, my program was rooted in leadership theory, and at times, students in this program from the "hard" sciences or STEM backgrounds did not see the value of viewing situations through a theoretical lens. Attempts to engage this group of colleagues in scholarly conversations relevant to the leadership topics being discussed were unsuccessful. My perception was that these disinterested responses were a combination of age and gender prejudice. Despite these reactions, I did continue to serve in mentor and leader roles.

These students, who could be labeled as "resisters," chose to operate independently, and had a very specific pathway and plan to complete their DiPs. These students faired just fine during the coursework (or I believe they did since they moved through the coursework at the same pace I did), although I cannot speak to their DiP progress since some of them chose a different chair or continued to work autonomously during the DiP phase. In fact, I have not heard any news about their doctoral program progress.

While I would take the position that there is not a single or specific solution to this issue, I question if resistance is actually an issue dependent upon how the student operates. If a student is successful in completing his or her DiP, and consciously decides to not embrace mentorship or leadership opportunities, on either the giving or receiving end, then that may be the student's choice. I made the choice to engage with my peers during the DiP process as much as possible, since, as the literature indicates, the DiP can be a lonely endeavor (Burnett, 1999; Ivankova & Stick, 2007)., and I see myself as a social individual. However, if a student exhibits this behavior initially and then later on notices the benefits of mentorship and leadership amongst his or her peers, that student has likely lost the opportunity to engage in this process. Therefore, these relationships need to be emphasized early on, to ensure that students who truly want to be involved with one another can seize the opportunity. It then needs to be made clear to students who choose not to engage in mentoring or leadership that there is a chance that these opportunities may be permanently lost. If these students are unable or do not wish to connect with another student, perhaps a faculty member with a similar interest or background can connect with that student to provide some form of support, especially during the DiP process.

CULTIVATING VIBRANCY THROUGH MENTORS AND LEADERS: RECOMMENDATIONS

Developing mentors and leaders contributes to a doctoral program's cultural vibrancy, or the program's outreach, diversity, and growth (Demers, 2009; Kezar, 2001), given that students' use their skills to drive the program, coming from different sociocultural and professional backgrounds as they serve in either or both roles. (National Academic Press, 2010). Such connections can inadvertently result in unexpected professional opportunities and can be accomplished through faculty suggesting that students connect with one or another, or having students actively discuss their topics in meetings. For example, one of my colleagues that I connected with during the DiP phase was researching recruitment of Hispanic students into the field of nursing. While my research focused on community college transfer students, I was intrigued by her research and her by mine. We then started discussing our topics informally and found that we were using similar literature in the areas of retention and engagement of students of color. We continued to keep in touch, exchanging additional literature we found for our topics, and I was able to connect her with individuals who then hired her for a teaching position within my institution's nursing program where she worked to implement some practical strategies developed during her DiP research.

While we never labeled our relationship (and many times, the mentor/leader relationship isn't labeled if it's not within the structure of the doctoral program to do so), I considered this colleague to be a version of a DiP leader for me, since she not only defended her DiP before me, but helped me see my topic through a different lens, based on her research on Hispanic students, and her diversity-focused presentations in class. She not only added that sought after "vibrancy" to my research and our cohort, but more importantly, a richness to my experience with the DiP overall. In this case, our interests lead to connections, our connections to similarities, similarities to opportunities, and finally, opportunities to apply research to practice. Of course, there are several examples in which I was intrigued with another student's DiP topic, but this example was truly powerful, given there was a clear, and unexpected connection of the DiP, rooted in the program's diversity of research.

My position is that the growth aspect of a doctoral program will be inherent through its vibrancy. The students, especially those that served as mentors and leaders, will promote the program by sharing their experiences with others who are interested in pursuing doctoral studies. This creates a shared vision among the graduates, students, and faculty, as they begin promoting the program most likely using the same language and through similar values (Kezar, 2001). Furthermore, if this model becomes ingrained in the culture of the program, it will become the norm and a role that students who enter the program will be expected to fulfill (Fullan, 2001; Kezar, 2001; Northouse, 2011).

IMPLEMENTATION AND MEASUREMENT OF MENTOR AND LEADER SUCCESS

I strongly feel that course mentors and DiP leaders, in any form, can serve a critical purpose in a doctoral program. While I believe both functions to be important to a doctoral program, if a program had to focus on one or the other, I would recommend making the DiP leader a formalized effort while simply encouraging the course mentor relationships. However, much like an organization measures successful change and effective leadership (Cawsey, Deszca, & Ingols, 2012; Fullan, 2001; Kezar, 2001; Northouse, 2011), there are innovative ways for institutions, academic departments, and doctoral programs to use both leaders and mentors to measure student success and DiP progress.

First, I would suggest that EdD faculty actively seek out students who have the potential to serve as course mentors or DiP leaderships. This can be accomplished by thoroughly interviewing applicants, monitoring student progress toward the DiP proposal phase, having conversations with students potentially interested in serving in these roles, gauging student interest in coursework or the research process, or approaching students who submit high-quality coursework about these opportunities. Once these students are sought out and serving in these roles, ways to measure their success can be implemented. For example, academic departments should consider monitoring and staying in touch with students who present at conferences, and track these numbers to see how they change based on the entering DiP cohorts. Another technique would be to monitor DiP completion rates of DiP leaders, uncovering if DiP leaders complete their DiPs in a timelier manner than non-DiP leaders. Perhaps such measurements and tracking can be incorporated into an institution's accreditation reports as well, further solidifying the strength of its doctoral program.

Despite a program's best efforts, however, the issue remains of the aforementioned "bouncing around" during a doctoral program, when students fall out of sequence with courses, or step out of the program due to outside issues with the intent of returning at some other point. Some programs are a little more lock-step than others, with structured sequences for students to follow. This is particularly common in EdD programs, which tend to have a prescribed, often accelerated, program sequence prior to the DiP phase. Based on my shared experience earlier, I would make the recommendation that if a student is at-risk for dropping out of coursework, or needs to put coursework on hiatus, that he or she be assigned a course mentor. This will at least keep the presence of the program in the student's mind, and these students can stay in touch so they feel a program connection. This is not intended to replace a program advisor, but may provide the student with the support they need if and when they return to the program.

Also, there are opportunities for course mentors and DiP leaders to use the practitioner-related skills they have acquired during their program. Because, as mentioned early, an EdD is known for being more practitioner- focused (although this can also become ambiguous when compared to a PhD program, depending upon the program's design and how much emphasis is placed on scholarly research), truly putting these skills into practice in a place of employment should be the ultimate goal of this model. Perhaps future research could be conducted longitudinally to investigate how doctoral graduates implemented their mentorship/leadership skills in their work environments. Tracking these graduates would provide solid evidence as to whether or not formally implementing mentor/leadership programs are a worthy endeavor.

The DiP, as part of an EdD Program, is a dynamic tool that can be used to set students on a path to become strong practitioners, scholars, and researchers. One way to ensure that the DiP is a positive learning experience would be to implement formal, or informal, course mentor or DiP leader programs, giving interested students an opportunity to use the DiP as a tool for engagement. Such initiatives could improve doctoral degree completion, allowing more practitioners to enter higher education and other fields where the doctoral degree is necessary, specifically for students from underrepresented backgrounds.

CONCLUSION

I began this chapter with discussing the relevance of incorporating opportunities for engagement in a doctoral program, through the application of course mentors and DiP leaders, to aid in facilitating DiP defense and ultimately degree completion. I wove my own personal accounts with my program to show examples of these roles and how they served students in a positive manner, using the leadership literature to support these roles. I also outlined the various types of involvement, discussed how "resisters" to engagement can be addressed, and provided recommendations to facilitate program vibrancy through diversity.

In terms of my own experiences during my doctoral program, as mentioned earlier, I have had articles published, participated in several doctoral faculty searches via student panels, presented at various national conferences, and worked with my DiP chair to apply for a grant to conduct a study on the population that was the topic of my DiP. I would not have thought to take advantage of these opportunities had it not been for working with others in a mentor/leadership capacity. It was not until I had completed my program that I realized that first, I had actually served in these types of roles, and second, that they were a contributing factor to my own progress, degree completion, and success as a practitioner.

At this time, I am surveying the landscape of higher education to determine my future career trajectory. While I enjoy writing and research, I am also passionate about serving students and have administrative skills and experience, so I am pondering what that means for me and my path in higher education. Regardless of my next career choice, I am confident that my doctoral program, and serving in the roles of course mentor and DiP leader, has provided me with the skill sets, confidence, and perspective to be successful and contribute to the broader academic community.

REFERENCES

Argyris, C. (1990). *Overcoming organization defenses: Facilitating organizational learning.* Upper Saddle River, NJ: Prentice Hall.

Basu, K. (2012). Ending the first EdD program. *Inside Higher Ed.* Retrieved from https://www.insidehighered.com/news/2012/03/29/country%E2%80%99s-oldest-edd-program-will-close-down

Berk, R. A., Berg, J., Mortimer, R., Walton-Moss, B., & Yeo, T. (2005). Measuring the effectiveness of faculty mentoring relationships. *Academic Medicine, 80*(1), 66–71.

Burnett, P. C. (1999). The supervision of doctoral dissertations using a collaborative cohort model. *Counselor Education and Supervision, 39*(1), 46–52.

Cawsey, T. F., Deszca, G., & Ingols, C. (2012). *Organizational change: An action-oriented toolkit.* Thousand Oaks, CA: Sage.

Demers, C. (2009). *Organizational change theories: A synthesis.* Thousand Oaks, CA: Sage.

de Valero, Y. F. (2001). Departmental factors affecting time-to-degree and completion rates of doctoral students at one land grant institution. *The Journal of Higher Education, 72*(3), 341–367.

Fullan (2001). *Leading in a culture of change.* San Francisco, CA: Jossey-Bass.

Greenleaf, R. K. (2002). *Servant leadership: A journey into the legitimate nature of power and greatness.* Mahwah, NJ: Paulist Press.

Hampton, N. (2015). New program supports students finishing their dissertations. *The Graduate School News.* North Carolina State University. Retrieved from https://grad.ncsu.edu/news/2015/new-program-supports-students-finishing-their-dissertations/

Ivankova, N. V., & Stick, S. L. (2007). Students' persistence in a distributed doctoral program in educational leadership in higher education: A mixed methods study. *Research in Higher Education, 48*(1), 93–135. doi: 10.1007/s11162-006-9025-4

Kezar, A. J. (2001). *Understanding and facilitating organizational change in the 21st century: Recent research and conceptualizations.* San Francisco, CA: Jossey-Bass.

Lewin, K. (1947). Frontiers in group dynamics. *Human Relations, 1*(2), 143–153. doi: 10.1177/001872674700100201

National Academic Press. (2010). A data-based assessment of research: Doctorate programs in the United States. *Report in Brief.* Retrieved from https://grants.nih.gov/training/research_doctorates.pdf

Nelson, J., & Coorough, C. (1994). Content analysis of the Ph.D. versus EdD dissertation. *Journal of Experimental Education, 62*(2), 1–11.

Northouse, P. G. (2011). *Introduction to leadership: Concepts and practice* (2nd ed.). Thousand Oaks, CA: Sage Publications.

CHAPTER 13

TEACHER LEADERSHIP

A Journey from Classroom
Teacher to Scholarly Practitioner

Cathleen Benedict

Question: What was a veteran teacher supposed to do once she had determined after much introspection that it was time to seek other opportunities outside of the classroom, still within the field of education, yet without entering the main office as an administrator? As an elementary teacher with twenty years of experience in public education in grades 3, 4, 5, and a short stint in the resource room, many before me in similar situations had earned a Master's Degree in Educational Administration. Of course, this would have offered more opportunities for me. However, I felt, it would put me into an office-based position, and, for whatever reason, I viewed this as a problem-solving position rather than one that would enable me to continue to have as much an impact on students as I had been in the classroom. What became clear to me is the fact that I wanted to work with teachers, too. I thought this over and decided that I needed to search for a graduate program with the anticipated result of working with pre-service teachers. This seemed quite satisfying and, while I would be teaching at the university level, I would also keep my foot in the field once I began supervising student teachers. That was my plan.

Exploring the Impact of the Dissertation in Practice, pages 193–206.

Having done a bit of research with regard to the differences between a PhD and an EdD, I thought I would be better suited for a PhD since higher education was the path I had chosen. I studied and took the GRE, applied and interviewed at a private university, and was accepted. However, during my interview the professor spoke with me about my involvement in varied aspects within the context of my current position as an elementary school teacher. I told her that I was very interested in creating change in my current school and had many times been involved in doing just that. She mentioned that she had heard of a new program at Rutgers, The State University of New Jersey. She explained it was cohort-based, had a number of concentrations, and offered an EdD. I knew of two other schools in the area that offered a Doctor of Education, including the one at which I was interviewing, but both were grounded in Educational Administration. The outcome: I applied to the Carnegie Program for the Educational Doctorate influenced program at Rutgers and was accepted into its first cohort with a chosen concentration of Teacher Leadership.

DISSERTATION IN PRACTICE AND AN OPPORTUNITY TO BE HEARD

Recently, there has been a rise of interest in making teaching public, one example being the idea of many schools working as professional learning communities (PLC). Ideally, one of the components of a PLC being teachers talking about what happens in their classrooms with the benefit of learning both from and with each other (Huffman & Hipp, 2003; Reeves, 2008). The idea of further studying PLCs peaked my interest. The more I researched the concept, the more I realized it could be an opportunity to work with and learn from my colleagues. Seemingly, isolation had become a menacing part of our educational system. There is an assumption that individual teachers will automatically and consistently employ effective instruction; yet, there is an attitude within the profession that educational theory and research are "irrelevant, if not useless" (Lieberman & Miller, 2008, p. 20). However, the more classes I completed in my concentration at Rutgers as well as core courses within the EdD program, the more I realized there was a place for further research as I continued to work through my coursework. "What are you passionate about?" was the question presented to us by many professors at Rutgers each time we spoke about our Dissertation in Practice (DiP).

The more I studied, the more I realized there was a large gap between what I was learning and what actually filtered into classrooms or as I sometimes referred to as 'the trenches.' According to research on teacher improvement, instructional practices are not typically refined on the job and within the parameters of collaborative, empirical processes. Typical school culture can work against teachers collaboratively and continuously improving their instructional practices. Yet, this was what a PLC, when structured among its research-based principles, had the ability to accomplish. I began to notice a contradiction in what the research was saying about PLCs and what was actually taking place in our schools. I had re-

✓ **Higher Education: Empirical studies related to teaching and learning**
(Results of studies in higher education remain mainly shelved here
with little filtering through to classrooms)

✓ **Programs, Textbook Companies, Test-Taking Materials**
(Large influx of programs imposed on teachers and students
in relation to state mandated test scores most of which are
advertised as "aligned to CCSS")

✓ **Elementary, Junior High, and High School**

FIGURE 13.1.   Overall Education Framework Depiction.

peatedly been witness to a drive for administrators to find a program to fix needs within the curriculum or to improve test scores. I imagined our educational framework as working against what the program I was working through at Rutgers was defining as a new way to view the dynamics of our system.

As a classroom teacher, the number of new programs that were imposed each year was problematic for many reasons. As a teacher I felt as though I was never quite able to master the components of a new idea, philosophy, or program without something new being imposed. From entry into the EdD program, the cohort had been encouraged to study what we were passionate about in education especially in relation to our current context. We were encouraged to reflect upon where we might make an impact. We knew that our DiP would be practitioner based with most of us deciding to conduct our studies within on our current contexts. I was constantly comparing what I was learning with my own experiences in the profession. Never one to be idle within the realm of professional development, I was used to seeking opportunities for improvement, just as many teachers attend graduate classes and seminars, often with the objective of improving classroom practices. However, through my coursework and as I gained greater understanding of PLCs, I realized a problem lying with the percentage of new knowledge implemented in classrooms as a result of teachers' learning. I had been taking classes in isolation with no real connection to going back to my classroom and school to implement what I had learned. I attended professional development sessions without follow-up. While teacher learning is imperative, what I had been attending contributed to the idea of teaching being an isolated profession.

The coursework leading to the DiP process encouraged me to continually reflect in relation to the implementation of PLCs across our district. The implementation had been in place for about four years before I began studying at Rutgers. The more I learned and reflected the more I realized the potential for growth if

I were to complete my DiP at my elementary school. As a fourth grade teacher and member of that grade level's PLC, what I was learning was not aligning to what was taking place in my school. Our PLC was used to an administrator and the team leader creating an agenda for each meeting, which typically was not data driven or oriented around instructional issues. We were working within a PLC in name only. The DiP process had encouraged me to have the confidence and knowledge, which I believe were equally important, to lead my colleagues through a systemic change to what had become a norm. Did I have my work cut out for me? Of course! However, I had become well versed in professional learning communities and the DiP would provide the opportunity to utilize my new skills and newfound capacity to lead this systemic reform.

AGENT OF CHANGE

Leading the reinitiation of our PLC for our fourth-grade team began with the proposal of my DiP. Coursework at Rutgers provided ample research-based information. As a student in the Teacher Leadership concentration, I was grateful at this point that coursework had been presented in a 'hands on' format. Within my learning, I became part of the process. Yes, there was a tremendous amount of reading and writing. Yet, I did everything with my final goal in mind and that was to reinitiate the PLC for the fourth-grade team. It seemed best to utilize a similar approach within my DiP study; I needed to teach my colleagues, from the literature. The professional development piece had been missing from its original implementation thus allowing many meetings to sway off of the agenda and become sessions of conversation unrelated to teaching and learning.

My intention in reviewing research-based dimensions of PLCs was to give the participants a glimpse of the fact that the restructuring of the team meeting would not simply be a new way of organizing the agenda. Rather, I attempted to present the perspective that we would be using our grade level meetings for teacher learning. I wanted to make substantive changes that would fundamentally alter the work of the group. This would result in a shift in focus from administrative tasks, or typical agenda topics, to improving student outcomes through changes to instructional practices. This was not a common practice in our school, or something we ordinarily would think of as a result of a PLC meeting. I also felt it was important for the participants to recognize that the meetings would not take place as individual events; rather there would be continuity from one agenda to the next, allowing for continuous and systematic discussions about teaching and student learning.

Since my goal was to change the knowledge base of my colleagues about PLCs, I had to figure a methodical means for doing so. There was a need for teachers to recognize the differences in what had become common in our school with the results of empirical studies on PLCs. The result had to be recognition on the part of the participants of the effects a well-structured PLC could have within

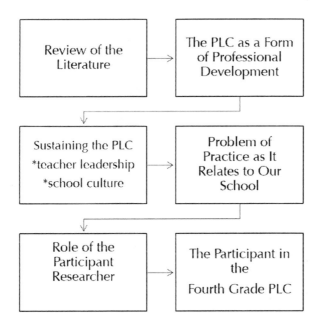

FIGURE 13.2.   Outline of Professional Development Presentation to Participants.

our grade level. Through my coursework I had seen the potential, now my task was to share this with my colleagues.

For example, a lack of routine meant to structure the discourse and analysis that takes place during the meetings had festered into what Little (2007) referred to as the telling of "war stories" (p. 221). When this occurred, external factors took the place of reflection on teaching practices and many times responsibility for slow or ineffective learning was blamed on students, parents, and/or socioeconomic conditions. When this form of dialogue transpired, there was little to no potential for these types of conversations to help teachers make positive changes to teaching and learning. Before the study could take place my task was to enable my colleagues to understand that members of PLCs recognize that once teachers begin to attribute student gains to their own efforts, and inquiry and continuous improvement is recognized as useful and worth the changes to traditional routines, positive changes can be achieved (Gersten, Dimino, Jayanthi, Kim, & Santoro, 2010; Schmoker, 2006;). I remember thinking this is where I want to lead my colleagues, but ineffective norms could be difficult to challenge. Additionally, one major roadblock I needed to keep in mind was that these changes might challenge current teaching practices, which traditionally teachers kept to themselves yet prided on tried and true teaching methods. However, talking about what goes on in your classroom had the potential to become a positive and necessary part of school culture and worthy of a teacher's time and effort (Gallimore, Emeling, Saunders, & Goldenburg, 2009; Hipp & Huffman, 2010; Hord & Sommers, 2008; Lieberman & Miller, 2008). As seen in Figure 13.1, I presented the reform through a systematic means of teacher learning. It was key, and it made sense. I was not imposing a new way to hold our PLC meetings. What actually happened was my enactment of a Teacher Leader engaging my colleagues in the realization of our own potential as a well-structured and fine oiled PLC.

I was clearly working with effective teachers although the notion of "there is always room for improvement" was still applicable. Interestingly aligned with this thought, Schmoker (2006) asserted that the majority of teachers are "potentially quite competent" (p. 28), stressing the idea that the teaching profession denies educators opportunities to study and learn from actions and results. Whether effective or not, many teachers do not have the opportunity to engage in professional discourse that could lead to the sharing of worthwhile strategies or the scrutiny of practices in order to foster improvements leading to effective instruction. A professional learning community can be the venue for teachers to take advantage of such opportunities.

WHAT DIRECTION DO I CHOOSE? HORD VS. DUFOUR

With the professional development completed during our regular team meetings that were embedded once a week into each grade 4 teacher's schedule, it was important to be sure that I had the knowledge base to lead the change. The knowledge gained from my coursework leading up to the DiP played an important role. With the number of books written on PLCs, I had learned that many were not based on research. In fact, most books told of the positive outcomes a PLC could have with the context of a school, yet none had actually followed through on implementing one successfully. As DiP students we learned to be sure that the literature we were reading could be applied to our context. For example, my study was to take place in a small suburban school district with our school's population being about 400 students. Therefore, delving into studies that took place in the heart of Chicago would not provide results to help sustain a PLC in my current context.

The DiP process guided me in sifting through research and the results of studies and determining which of the leading researchers made sense and provided the empirical research needed to steer my thinking and my study. It came down to two: Richard DuFour, EdD, and Shirley Hord, PhD. Since PLCs had been introduced at our school, my colleagues may have been familiar with Richard DuFour and his "big ideas" (DuFour, 2004) since team leaders had been given one of his books early in the implementation. DuFour's big ideas guided the dialogue of a PLC meeting so teachers articulate what they want the students to learn, how they want the students to learn, and what they would do if a student is not learning properly, or not moving forward successfully. While definitions of PLCs vary within the educational arena, Hord and Sommers (2008) asserted that when there is consistent and intentional staff learning within a PLC, an increase in student learning would result. For example, Hord (1997) identified the following characteristics of PLCs: shared and supportive leadership, shared values and vision, collective learning, supportive conditions, and shared personal practice.

I faced a dilemma since I had to incorporate the ideas of one, both, or a compilation of others who had written about PLCs. I decided to delve more deeply into the work of Shirley Hord even though it seemed that the work of Richard DuFour was quoted more commonly within education with my school being one example. With further investigation, I became aware of the longitudinal research conducted by Hord (1997). I believe her efforts give more credence to the use of a framework for the work of a PLC. The DiP brought my skills in determining the best means for my study beyond the notion of who is most talked about in the field to who is more research based on ideas suited to carrying out a DiP in my school along with my fourth-grade colleagues. To sum, because of my work in the EdD program at Rutgers, I was challenged to guide my PLC colleagues in identifying an instructional challenge, establishing a goal, identifying research-based instructional practices to meet it, and then evaluating and revising the design based on learning outcomes.

The DiP creates experts in a profession that is tremendously diverse from any angle in which one looks. In reflecting on my years in public education and the number of programs that teachers have had to implement, the DiP treated teachers as professionals who had knowledge of what is best for their practice. While the collaborative piece, at times, would challenge this notion, the fact that every participant had a voice mattered. Participants challenged each other's ideas, practices, and management. It was uncomfortable, but as we moved forward we began to see the effects that can happen when teachers work with each other and learn from one another. Without the process structured coursework, practice, learning, and independent research before I began the DiP, I would not have been able to carry out such an effective study. The sense of collaboration that was established within our PLC mimicked the cohort model of the EdD program. It led to the "real-life" DiP study in which I was able to share a wealth of teacher learning. Where did the teacher learning lead our PLC? Or, what effect did the teacher learning have? A non-negotiable increase in student learning, of course.

TEACHER LEADERSHIP AND SELF-ADVOCACY

Great things were about to happen, or were they? Before graduation and while writing my DiP I was privileged to be asked to present my findings at a convening of the Carnegie Program for the Education Doctorate (CPED) held at Rutgers University. Additionally, I found myself on the cover of a local teacher magazine with an article titled, "*Doctor in the Classroom*." I successfully defended my DiP, graduated with the rest of my cohort, yet found myself in the same teaching position that I was in when I first entered the doctoral program at Rutgers. The level of enthusiasm and number of professional actions I had been involved with seemed to dwindle a bit. Of course, our fourth grade PLC continued. The exciting part was that the group wanted it to continue where we had left off at the end of the previous school year. I had wondered whether it would be looked upon as a graduate school project. Instead, the teachers wanted it to continue according to the same norms that had taken place, the structure of our meetings, and the discourse that anchored our work and improved our practice. In fact, word has spread and there were other teachers interested in what we had accomplished and how we had re-initiated our fourth grade PLC.

On a personal side, I had been speaking with the principal and vice principal of my elementary school about the work I was doing at Rutgers and what I would like to do once I graduated. I hoped there would be opportunities to utilize my new found and practiced skills in order to make a larger impact on PLCs at our school. However, I also advocated for using skills that involved working with teachers and students. The area most appealing to me was helping all students to learn by working with teachers to differentiate lessons and activities. Over the course of two years, I spoke to these administrators about what I thought I could bring to our school once I graduated. I had explained to them about the DiP, in fact the vice principal was one of the study's participants. The principal had been invited on more than one occasion to come and observe a PLC meeting. Other administrators in the district, including the Director of Curriculum had been invited, too. While each came to at least one meeting and told me that the work we were doing was exactly how they wanted all PLCs within the district to be run, when it came time to plan for the following school year, there did not seem to be an effort made to utilize my work. However, I did not back down easily!

Having the vice principal as a DiP participant was definitely to my advantage. I liked thinking of her as an "academic administrator" with the opposite being one with more of a mindset in the managerial end of administration. She understood what good teaching entailed and continuously advocated for teachers' best efforts. She worked alongside us whenever possible. I felt as though she heard what I was saying when I advocated for myself. I was a scholarly practitioner and although I was still working with fourth-grade colleagues and continuing to make differences, I wanted to expand these experiences to other grade levels. As a graduate of a doctoral program with a DiP at its core, I felt that I was adept at seeking and interpreting research. These two skills being difficult for a classroom teacher to engage in typically due to time and responsibilities.

Because of the hands-on approach to the coursework that comprised the core and Teacher Leadership concentration courses at Rutgers, I graduated with experiences that became a part of my new skillset. There was no need to keep them within the DiP. Again, I found myself advocating for improving teacher learning always with the result of increasing student achievement. I knew I could enact what I was promoting since I had already facilitated these actions within my coursework and DiP study. There were two administrators who heard my call. The vice principal that had been a participant was given a principalship within one year of my graduation. The Director of Curriculum began to engage me in discussions about what I might like to do within the district. The reality seemed to be that I was not sure if the administrators knew what to do with me. There were two people in our district with doctorates, the Director of Curriculum and me. The difference between the two of us and our career aspirations was that I had no yearning to be an administrator. I wanted to work with teachers not evaluate them.

GETTING THE BALL ROLLING

My experience earning an EdD seemed as though it should grant me the opportunities I yearned for outside of the traditional elementary classroom. Throughout the program, I had gained insights into how research-based practices can positively influence teaching and learning, and through successfully completing coursework leading to the DiP I embraced the role of scholarly practitioner. These experiences led to the DiP and afforded me opportunities to work with my colleagues along the way. It seemed most logical when my position as a scholarly practitioner did not present itself that I continue on the path of working with colleagues anyway, so I began to plan for and present opportunities for professional development.

DATA ANALYSIS

Of course, like any other school district teachers were being encouraged to collect and analyze student data. Collecting the data was the easy part. The data was placed on computer documents, large posters, and even the walls in the faculty room. I wondered what its purpose was. Such displays caused angst amongst the faculty. With little to no meaningful articulation concerning the data, staff members often waited out the period of the display of scores. I wondered how many teachers knew what to do with the data and what analyzing these scores meant. I also wondered if the administrative team knew how to analyze the data in order to make it a useful tool for teaching. I knew what to do with the data. I knew that analysis meant working with teachers and using the 'what the data was telling us' to drive teaching. It meant learning how to lead a protocol in order to analyze the data. My experience came from my coursework within the Teacher Leadership concentration at Rutgers.

With firsthand experience through coursework and further application in the DiP, I knew that the use of protocols can encourage meaningful and substantive professional discourse and allow for the "inside perspectives" (McDonald, Mohr, Dichter, & McDonald, 2007, p. 1) that can be crucial to understanding students. Collaboration is key in regard to the degree of professional learning that can occur when teachers talk about student achievement. It can be implied that teachers talking to each other is integral to the process. Protocols consist of agreed upon guidelines for conversation. In general, protocols recommended for use by PLCs are designed to encourage participants to push thinking on a given issue and to structure a discussion around a text (National School Reform Faculty, 2008) such as student work. A protocol can promote focused dialogue while looking at student data, assessment data, or teacher work, and facilitates giving and receiving feedback, solving dilemmas, or working through problems of practice.

Recognizing the power of a protocol as well as both knowledge and the confidence necessary for facilitation was due to my experiences during the DiP process. I made the decision to apply this strategy to a series of after school sessions I lead related to the analysis of student work. Through collective inquiry, and protocol implementation my colleagues' knowledge of data analysis was strengthened, and also their capacity to solve problems of practice leading to more effective teaching practices and greater student achievement (McDonald et al., 2007). Data analysis finally made sense.

A NEW POSITION COMES ALONG

After my graduation along with about two years of talking about how I felt I could add to student and teacher success at my elementary school, I was finally granted a position outside of the general education classroom. I was asked to take over as the Basic Skills Instructor (BSI) while the transition to a Response to Intervention (RIT) program took place. I found myself now working with small groups of children and doing my best to research best practices when it came to working on a newly formed committee of colleagues interested in RTI. I was excited to learn all I could about RTI. Although I worked at one elementary school, the committee was considered district-wide and encompassed colleagues from both of our district's elementary schools. When we first met, some of the members had already done some research and thought it would be a beneficial 'program' for our district. I sat and listened, yet I felt that some of the information committee members were sharing was contradictory to my research and thoughts on how to make RTI successful. Afterward, I spoke to members on the committee who worked in the same school as me. I mentioned that through my research I had discovered that Response to Intervention was not a program. It was a philosophy. Building a RTI program meant making it fit the needs of our students. I was feeling as though I was speaking as Dr. Benedict. I continued and told them it was not something we could simply implement. Yes, there were guidelines and interventions that were necessary components. But as a district set in the suburbs, we needed to look for studies that had been done in a similar context. At the committee meeting, members had shared how the program worked even mentioning how successful it was with students who resided in urban communities. While this was great to hear, it was not applicable to our district. We have an extremely low percentage of students considered to be English Language Learners. Therefore, the interventions that comprised RTI in an inner city context would not be appropriate for our district. In fact, what needed to occur was an outline of what we wanted the program to look like? That is, operation of the program, interventions, the teaching specialists who would be involved, contact people, etc. Additionally, what was needed was a pilot. This way we would be able to survey, reflect, and then be able to put a more definitive program in place. I was speaking from the point of view of an educator who had already designed a study that brought growth to our elementary school in the form of advancement of teaching and student outcomes. I was speaking from the point of view of someone who had successfully completed a DiP.

PROFESSIONAL DEVELOPMENT

Doing 'things' within our profession that I often left to presenters was becoming the norm; however, it also took me out of my comfort zone. Professional development presentations related to the outcome of the DiP as well as presentations that required me to research and then present the topic became a challenge I was willing to take upon myself. The first presentation was entitled "A New Way to Look at Vocabulary" and it took every bit of courage within me to present to my kindergarten through fifth-grade colleagues across my school district. This was most likely due to the number of professional development sessions I had sat through over the years most of which I could not wait to be over. However, I looked at this, my first presentation as a Doctor of Education, through the lens of someone who had completed coursework on professional development. It had been an integral part at the beginning of my study. And the idea of "know your audience" had stuck with me after a professor had referred to this as rule number one in professional development.

Speaking of knowing your audience, I gave an evening presentation for the Parent Academy for Student Success (PASS), part of a series informative talks for parents, entitled "Supporting Student Learning: Connecting Home and School" which was met with success also. I covered the Common Core State Standards, but with a spin on the fact that there might be some value to them. Parents want their students to be challenged, but I also explained that the way information is taught and the expectations for our students are higher today, yet attainable. Parents left that night with an array of materials and tools to help them help their children. The feedback was positive. Here I was speaking to colleagues and parents, both I would never have thought of doing, without the experiences and knowledge gained through the DiP process. I was asked to do both of these presentations (someone in the administration thought I had the ability) and I did.

PROFESSIONAL MENTORING COMMUNITY

The Professional Mentoring Community was instituted by me and still continues as a means of acclimating new teachers to our district. Teachers included in this group range from those needing to be formally mentored as well as those who are new hires with experience. The members teach on either the elementary or middle school level. The timing of instituting this and the implementation of a new teacher evaluation program across out district blended well. The group meets either once or twice a month over the course of the school year. My title as the Professional Mentoring Coordinator made me responsible for the facilitation of all meetings.

The first meetings are devoted to the framework for evaluation. Although it is designed to work within four domains, I further broke it down with deeper and more action based explanations and examples. With this new position, I felt like a Teacher Leader where I could use my new skill base, take charge of making the meetings meaningful and informative, and become familiar with a group of new colleagues on an even playing field. Yes, I was the coordinator, but I was not an administrator. This led to meetings being confidential especially with questions related to evaluations, Student Growth Objective, and more aspects of teaching in the 21st century that many times are not taught on a college campus.

The meetings were run using the same structure I used for the DiP. I began with a session of professional development on PLCs. Then we moved onto creating norms for the meetings and we were off and running! In my professional development session with the group, which was really meeting number one, I explained that we would be working within a research-based framework of PLC. I further explained that my goal by the end of the school year was for the members to have felt that they were part of a unique group that was not a committee, not led from a top-down perspective, and one where all had equal voices. In fact, when I facilitated a new discussion having to do with the evaluation there were a few teachers who asked questions about the results of observations. These questions at first were directed to me, however, the more teachers who spoke about something typically considered confidential, the more other members became comfortable. Group discussions were valuable! How do I know this? I know this because of the end of the year survey the Professional Mentoring Community members completed. This was also something that had been a part of my coursework and been an integral part of the analysis section of my DiP. The data from the survey showed that most members recognized the fact that the meetings and members were treated and acted as if they were part of a professional mentoring community. It also provided information about what I might consider changing and/or doing again moving forward. To reflect means to grow.

MAKING A MARK IN HIGHER EDUCATION

The idea of me as a scholarly practitioner has meant working to make differences in my elementary school, working with colleagues, becoming more involved in district-wide committees, initiating the Professional Mentoring Community and more, I have also kept connections with Rutgers University. Since graduation, I have been a member of the EdD Curriculum Committee at the Graduate School of Education. The committee meets about once a month and works to be sure the Doctor of Education program is growing and continuing as a most advantageous program for educators. In fact, I could not be more thankful to be a graduate and what this had meant for me and the work I have completed as a scholarly practitioner. Most recently, I have been working with a small group of EdD graduates and a professor to create the curriculum for an Endorsement in Teacher Leadership through Rutgers. Legislation passed recently in New Jersey for this special endorsement and I was asked to be a part of creating the program. In addition, I will be teaching one of the required courses. I am delighted to report that in January of 2017, I accepted a full-time tenure track position as an Assistant Professor of Special Education at Centenary University in Hackettstown, New Jersey. I am now where I need to be.

CONCLUSION

I have a skill set that I did not have before completing my Doctor of Education at Rutgers University. I have always had common sense when it came to educational decisions affecting my students, classroom, school, etc. However, the skill set I have attained through the program and specifically through completing a DiP is indescribable. I have great confidence in my abilities to teach, whether it be the elementary students that came through my classroom, my colleagues that work with me on committees or take part in professional development sessions I offer, or even at the university level through the curriculum work and teaching I do to promote teacher leadership. In fact, I had the recent opportunity to travel to Ireland. Before leaving I asked for an appointment with the Head of Teacher Education at the University of Ireland in Galway, Dr. Mary Fleming. We met and it was a great experience. I left my Curriculum Vitae with the possibility of creating a connection in the future. Further research opportunities, teacher leadership opportunities, the possibilities are endless! I have become passionate and confident about working with colleagues, implementing new ideas, leading teams of teachers, educational research, and the many forms Teacher Leadership can take. I am Cathleen M. Benedict, EdD, a scholarly practitioner.

> It is…advisable that the teacher should understand, and even be able to criticize, the general principles upon which the whole educational system is formed and administered. He is not like a private soldier in an army, expected merely to obey, or like a cog in a wheel, expected merely to respond and transmit external energy; he must be an intelligent medium of action.
> —*John Dewey, 1895*

REFERENCES

DuFour, R. (2004). What is a professional learning community? *Educational Leadership, 61*(8), 6–11.

Gallimore, R., Ermeling, B. A., Saunders, W. M., & Goldenberg, C. (2009). Moving the learning of teaching closer to practice: Teacher education implications of school-based inquiry teams. *Elementary School Journal, 109*(5), 537–553.

Gersten, R., Dimino, J., Jayanthi, M., Kim, & Santoro, J. (2010, April). Teacher study group: Impact of the professional development model on reading instruction and student outcomes in first grade classrooms. *American Education Research Journal, 47*(3), 694–739.

Hipp, K., & Huffman, J. (2010). *Demystifying professional learning communities: School leadership at its best*. Baltimore, MD: Rowman & Littlefield Education.

Hord, S. M. (1997). *Professional learning communities: Communities of continuous inquiry and improvement*. Austin, TX: Southwest Educational Development Laboratory.

Hord, S., & Sommers, W. (2008). *Leading professional learning communities: Voices from research and practice*. Thousand Oaks, CA: Corwin Press.

Huffman, J., & Hipp, K. (2003). *Reculturing schools as professional learning communities*. Baltimore, MD: Scarecrow Education.

Lieberman, A., & Miller, L. (2008). *Teachers in professional communities: Improving teaching and learning*. New York, NY: Teachers College Press.

Little, J. W., (2007). *Professional community and professional development in the learning-centered school*. Washington, DC: National Education Association.

McDonald, J., Mohr, N., Dichter, A., & McDonald, E. (2007). *The power of protocols: An educator's guide to better practice*. New York, NY: Teachers College Press.

Reeves, D. (2008). *Reframing teacher leadership to improve your school*. Alexandria, VA: Association for Supervision and Curriculum Development.

National School Reform Faculty. (2008). Retrieved from www.nsrfharmony.org

Schmoker, M. (2006). *Results now: How we can achieve unprecedented improvements in teaching and learning*. Alexandria, VA: Association for Supervision and Curriculum Development.

CHAPTER 14

"I WILL MAKE A DIFFERENCE"

Using the Professional Doctorate to Influence Audiological Care for People with Learning Disabilities

Lynzee McShea

INTRODUCTION

People with learning disabilities are at high risk of hearing loss. Though the most commonly used prevalence estimate is 40%, the actual figure may be higher (Bent, McShea, & Brennan, 2015). Regardless of the exact prevalence, there are many individuals who would benefit from Audiology input. Despite this, the majority are unknown to services and are living with the consequences of an undetected and unmanaged hearing loss.

Several years ago I designed a model to reduce the barriers to better hearing for people with complex needs. It was an award-winning concept and has been published (McShea, Corkish, & McAnelly, 2014). The model recognizes that involvement of key groups, such as caregivers, is vital. However, caregivers often over-estimate the communication abilities of people they support and under-estimate the consequences of undetected hearing loss (Lavis, Cullen, &

Exploring the Impact of the Dissertation in Practice, pages 207–221.
Copyright © 2017 by Information Age Publishing
207

Roy, 1997). Training in audiological issues seems an obvious solution; though caregivers often report that interventions are imposed on them, by people who do not understand their role (Department of Health, DH, 2007).

This chapter explores the steps taken to address this through Professional Doctorate study. I explore my reasons for choosing a Professional Doctorate over the more well-known PhD, and the unique opportunity provided by the Professional Doctorate, to cross practice boundaries and work with a group traditionally viewed as non-professional and low skilled.

Using collaboration via action research methodology, change and improvement occurred.

I conclude by reflecting on my personal experience of Professional Doctorate study and life after the Doctorate, exploring its impact on me professionally and personally.

THE ISSUE AT HAND

To have a learning disability broadly means a reduced ability to learn new skills or understand new/complex information; however, the spectrum of disabilities is varied, ranging from mild to profound (DH, 2001). Learning disability is the preferred term in the UK, (superseding historic terms such as mental handicap or mental retardation). However, the terms "intellectual disability," "developmental disability," and "learning difficulty" are also used. "Learning disabilities" will be the term used throughout this chapter.

People with learning disabilities are much more likely to have a hearing loss than the general population. The exact prevalence of hearing loss in people with learning disabilities is unknown. The most commonly used estimate is 40% (Emerson, Baines, Allerton, & Welch, 2012), though this is likely to be an underestimate, as many of the studies that have published estimates of prevalence have arrived at these figures by review of medical records or interview alone (Bent et al., 2015). Audiology services are of vital importance to this group. Despite this need, the majority of this population have never even had their hearing tested (Hardy, Woodward, Woolard, & Tait, 2011).

When I began my career in Sunderland, the number of people with learning disabilities attending Audiology was negligible. This was in direct contrast to the numbers expected due to high prevalence of hearing loss in this group. It became clear that there was a range of barriers preventing attendance and successful outcomes, and I felt a responsibility to investigate them. Once fully qualified, I began to develop and improve our service. This involved creation of a model to appraise the service and facilitate improvement (the 3As model). This has been well received by colleagues at national meetings and via publication (McShea et al., 2014). The 3As are Access, Assessment, and Aftercare and are relevant to any health discipline, not just Audiology:

- Access—Individuals with learning disabilities and their advocates must have an awareness of the prevalence of hearing loss, must be able to identify hearing loss and be able to access appropriate referral to specialist services, via a GP.
- Assessment—Once known to specialist services (e.g. Audiology), attendance should be facilitated, and accurate, successful diagnostic testing should be achievable.
- Aftercare—Following a diagnosis of hearing loss, management and rehabilitation should be appropriate and adhered to. This may include use of hearing aids, assistive listening devices, and adherence to any follow-up appointments.

People with learning disabilities may not have the communication skills to seek a referral for their own health needs, if indeed they are even aware of a need themselves. Therefore, the onus is on another relevant individual close to that person, usually the "caregiver," to recognize the problem and access appropriate services on their behalf. Clearly, this relies on the individual and their caregiver communicating effectively (Kyle, Melville, & Jones, 2009) and the caregiver having the skills to detect hearing loss. However, caregivers often misjudge the communication abilities of people with learning disabilities (Banat, Summers, & Pring, 2002; Kevan, 2003). The situation is compounded by the fact that the health need in question is hearing loss, which can affect communication in its own right. Although the clues of hearing loss are usually present, they are often attributed to the known learning disability ("diagnostic overshadowing," Carvill, 2001). There is plentiful evidence in the literature (e.g., Kerr et al., 2003) and even in my own experience, to suggest that most caregivers cannot recognize hearing loss in those they support.

Even if a hearing loss is suspected, its effect is often underestimated (Pryce, 2011) or not seen as a priority compared to other health needs (Newsam, Walley, & McKie, 2010). This is disappointing as undiagnosed hearing loss can affect the lives of individuals, their personalities, and their behavior (Hoghton, 2010). It can lead to a poorer quality of life, isolation, and depression (Twitchen, 2014). Although no direct threat to life, the consequences of undiagnosed hearing loss can be profound (McShea et al., 2014).

Though Audiology professionals have a duty to cascade information to patients and their caregivers, they are relatively powerless outside of the clinic as to what happens. In the home environment, this responsibility shifts to the individual or their caregiver. However, paid caregivers have difficulties understanding the use and maintenance of hearing aids (Miller & Kiani, 2008). Training is recommended around the purpose of hearing aids, their function and correct maintenance (Meuwese-Jongejeugd, Verschuure, & Evenhuis, 2007). In most cases, people with learning disabilities rely on others to make choices for them:

- Does this person have a hearing problem?

- Should something be done about it?
- What should be done about it?
- Do they need a hearing test?
- Will they be able to comply with the assessment?
- Will they wear hearing aids?
- Will hearing aids provide any benefit?

There were only two studies in the literature specifically investigating attitudes and training surrounding hearing loss and people with learning disabilities prior to this research. Newsam et al. (2010) conducted semi-structured interviews with 17 paid caregivers, to assess their knowledge and beliefs in sensory loss and people with learning disabilities. They found that though caregivers were aware of the increased risk, they felt other health care needs were more important. A lack of accountability and clarity was also relevant. McMillan, Bunning, K., and Pring (2000) completed hearing loss awareness training for 14 caregivers in England. They found that prior knowledge of hearing loss was poor, meaning minimal knowledge is acquired through work experience alone. They provided training in hearing loss and hearing aid management and seem to be the only equivalent study to this research in terms of hearing loss and people with learning disabilities. Though a gain in knowledge was shown by questionnaire, the authors' caution in assuming knowledge translated to real life situations. They advocated further research in this area, which appears to be lacking 15 years on. Miller & Kiani (2008) also advocate for deaf awareness training for caregivers, but provide no guidance on the content or method of delivery. Hithersay, Strydom, Moulster, and Buszewicz (2014) attempted to provide a literature review on carer-led health interventions in the learning disability population, but were unable to draw any conclusions due to a lack of research. They state there is a need to learn more about the best way to engage caregivers, in order to improve health outcomes.

Caregivers are gatekeepers to accessing services (Pryce & Gooberman-Hill, 2013) and are best placed to identify and manage hearing loss in the home environment (Newsam et al., 2010). The literature suggests caregivers are aware it is their responsibility to do this (ibid), with 88% acknowledging it is part of their role. Despite this need and acknowledged responsibility, people with learning disabilities still face significant barriers to detection and management of hearing loss. Kerr et al. (2003) believe caregivers aim to obtain the necessary knowledge/ skills, but they can only do this if they are aware of the gaps in their knowledge. Literature suggests this may not be the case for hearing issues, where Dalton and Sweeney (2011) found that 45% of residential caregivers were lacking in knowledge and communication skills.

There is clear consensus in the literature that audiological care for people with learning disabilities, continues to rely on caregivers (McCracken, Lumm, & Laoide-Kemp, 2011). The transition of people with learning disabilities to the community has increased pressure on caregivers, by raising their responsibility around detection of health problems such as hearing loss. It would be expected then, that there would be clear guidelines for caregivers to follow regarding audiological issues, though this is not the case. Often, when individuals are accused of neglectful practice, wider issues such as resource availability and explicit standards are not considered (Price, 2013). This suggests that caregivers cannot be deemed incompetent in issues around hearing loss if they have not been made aware of such responsibilities and how to fulfill them.

HOW COULD THESE ISSUES BE ADDRESSED?

I identified gaps in the literature, which I hoped to research through Doctorate study. The research questions I formulated were:

> Is it possible to engage with paid caregivers (of people with learning disabilities and hearing loss) to improve their awareness of audiological issues and to influence their working practice? What are the key elements in achieving this?

I had a decision to make; did I choose a traditional PhD or a Professional Doctorate? I am a Clinical Scientist; though the proportion of "clinician" versus "scientist" I have felt has often changed throughout my career. During my early training, I felt most like a scientist. I had obtained a First Class Honours degree in a scientific subject and felt comforted by quantitative data; numbers, facts. However, during the course of my training, I began to see things from a clinical perspective; where the evidence base would say one thing, patient preference said another. I found this baffling but intriguing in equal measure. In day to day practice, a successful clinician didn't need to be aware of the latest cutting-edge research, they needed to listen to and engage their patients. An excellent academic would struggle in a clinical environment if their knowledge could not be translated into tangible outcomes. Around the time that I was looking for a Doctorate program to suit me, I felt that I identified equally as a clinician and a scientist.

In his metaphor of professional landscapes, Schön described the differences between practitioners (clinical) and researchers (scientists) (Schön, 1983). He suggested that practitioners could produce the most useful and beneficial knowledge due to their direct patient involvement and that knowledge produced by researchers could become elitist and irrelevant to daily practice. This suggests a continuum between research and practice, between clinical and scientist, where the two may not be able to coexist due to such different values and priorities. Viewed more positively, as long as clinical scientists possess both skill sets, they may be important in encouraging scientific principles into daily practice and transforming Schön's professional landscape. This was one reason why the Professional Doctorate was so appealing to me; it allowed me to use my dual role most effectively. Rather than see my clinical experience as unnecessary, or superfluous, it was actually a positive in Professional Doctorate study and previous experiences could be harnessed through submission of a portfolio of evidence.

I also liked that a Professional Doctorate had direct relevance to my work. I saw it as not just a qualification for me, but work that would enhance my professional and clinical practice and that of others. I thought it important that the Professional Doctorate addressed real-life issues in a real-world setting, finding solutions to messy, complex problems. I am a pragmatic person and this appealed to me. I didn't want my thesis collecting dust on a shelf—I wanted it to be useful and contemporary.

Reflecting on this "real-world setting" was important to me, to consider the effect of values, beliefs, and experience, not only my own but also those of other key groups such as caregivers. I felt there was a unique opportunity provided by the Professional Doctorate, to cross practice boundaries and work with caregivers, a group who are traditionally viewed as non-professional and low skilled.

THE EARLY STAGES OF THE PROFESSIONAL DOCTORATE PROGRAM

The first year of the Professional Doctorate in Sunderland comprises of three taught modules. These modules are delivered via monthly study days; an opportunity to spend time with the rest of the cohort in a group learning situation. Individual assignments were also set throughout the year and all components had to be passed before a student could progress into the research-phase of the Doctorate. I felt that I benefitted significantly from this taught year for two reasons:

1. The Interaction With a Peer Group

The monthly study days were an opportunity to meet with others at a similar stage in their Professional Doctorate journey, though not necessarily at a similar stage in their career. There were around 12 people in my cohort, and I estimated that I was the youngest by a considerable margin (I was 28 years old when I first enrolled). The other students came from a range of backgrounds including nursing, IT and teaching. It became clear at the very first session that despite our differences, there were significant benefits to this group interaction.

Group sessions lent themselves to the presentation of ideas and discussion. The heterogeneity of the group meant such interaction was rich and varied and brought perspectives to each of our work that we had not considered prior. It also surprised me that, although our professions were different, the issues we encountered throughout these early stages were similar, and that even when others were presenting their ideas, there was personal benefit to be taken away from hearing their stories. In my opinion, this social, supportive network is one of the key advantages of a Professional Doctorate over a more traditional PhD.

2. The Opportunity to Focus my Ideas, Values, and Beliefs

As well as benefitting from a peer group of support, I also felt the taught year itself provided a supportive framework to shape my ideas. Rather than having to commence the first year with a firm idea of what I wanted to achieve, it was OK (in fact, preferable), to have a more general vision, which was shaped over the first year.

In Sunderland, the taught year consists of three modules: Research Methods, Reflective Practice, and Contextualisation and Planning. I feel this provided a solid foundation for the research phase. It allowed me to refresh my knowledge of research methods, acquired through previous Masters level study. It became clear that the research I was planning to carry out should be qualitative in nature, and I was particularly drawn to Action Research as a methodology. Action research stems from a critical theory paradigm; which is not only concerned with examining practice but also wider influencing factors (Fulton, Kuit, Sanders, & Smith, 2013). Critical theory does share some commonalities with interpretivism, such as information gathering involving an appreciation of values and experience. Though interpretivists use qualitative information, the researcher remains objective and impartial (Koshy, Koshy, & Waterman, 2011). In critical theory, the researcher takes a conscious and active role and believes value can be obtained from this (McNiff & Whitehead, 2011). I felt this approach was preferable as it helped to demonstrate the collaborative nature of hearing loss between caregivers and Audiology.

Researcher reflections are an essential component of action research and can be considered as one of the research methods (Fulton et al., 2013). I therefore found the taught module on Reflective Practice particularly valuable. It gave me the opportunity to explore my values and beliefs prior to commencing the research phase. This helped to guide my ontological stance in the final submission of work, and to ensure that this stance aligned well with the epistemological perspective of the research. My ontological perspective is critical realist: I believe that a reality exists independent of our perception and that "truth" is dependent on context (Patton, 2015). I believe that patients and the people in their lives are not subjects without influence or opinion. Their experiences and attitudes can shape outcomes. Their choices and preferences can have more impact than protocols, as they can decide not to use hearing aids, or to not attend Audiology in the first place. For this reason, I believe research into outcomes or pathways in Audiology should be inclusive of this group and their opinions. Critical realists retain that although there is a "real world" which exists independently of our thoughts or opinions about it, our knowledge of the world is shaped by our experiences and perspectives (Maxwell, 2012) and that in order to increase understanding, it is important to appreciate social factors that may not be directly observable (Bryman, 2016).

The final module, Contextualisation and Planning, culminated in the submission of a detailed research proposal, using all of the learning and experiences of the taught year to produce a detailed and realistic plan. This plan was then "examined" by a viva panel, a component that had to be successfully passed before the research could commence. A viva (*viva voce*) is an oral examination, where questions are posed by a small group of examiners, to ensure the candidate's submission and performance is at the necessary standard to proceed. A final viva would take place after submission of the full body of work for the Professional Doctorate. Even at such an early stage I felt supported, with the final viva clearly in focus with opportunities such as this arranged to simulate the experience and process. Personally, I valued the first year and all it entailed. At no point did I feel impatient to start the research, or that the taught year was wasting time. On the contrary, I do not think I could have produced such an informed and considered plan without this experience. This allowed me to move into the research phase with sound preparation and a clear idea of what I was undertaking.

THE RESEARCH PHASE

Using the action research methodology I had planned, I completed four novel cycles of research, which have all been published in the literature (See McShea, 2015a; McShea, 2015b; McShea, Fulton, & Hayes 2015, for detail), highlighting my novel contribution to theory and practice. The cyclical and reflective nature of action research is important. It ensures that action is timely and relevant and provides a robust framework for understanding complex situations (Reason & Bradbury, 2008). Three of the cycles in this research were planned; one occurred due to an identified need, demonstrating the reactive nature of this methodology.

Cycle 1

I shadowed and interviewed 20 paid caregivers in my local area. All caregivers supported people with severe-profound learning disabilities (who were unable to live independently and required support in all aspects of their lives, such as feeding and personal care). The caregivers knew that they had a responsibility in ensuring the health needs of these individuals were met, and engaged with training that they felt was necessary. However, this did not including training on hearing loss. Most caregivers generally underestimated the expected prevalence of hearing loss (carer estimate 25%; compared to literature guidance of 40%). More worrying than this, was that at the time of the interviews, the prevalence of known hearing loss in the individuals supported by this group of caregivers was only 7%, suggested there was a significant level of undetected hearing loss. The caregivers interviewed had little confidence in their own ability to detect hearing loss, in the ability of Audiologists to be able to complete a successful hearing assessment for someone with learning disabilities, and also little confidence in hearing aids as being a beneficial management option for people with learning disabilities and hearing loss.

This first cycle was important, as it gave me the opportunity to experience a different workplace culture, to understand issues from another perspective. I used the theory of symbolic interactionism (Denzin, 1992) to account for the caregivers' perspectives. This theory suggests that opinions and beliefs are shaped by environment and experience. Work experience of caregivers was not sufficient to inform them about hearing loss. However, the theory suggests that changing their experience could change their perspectives.

Cycle 2

I worked with 45 caregivers in this cycle (including some who had partici-pated in Cycle 1), to design and pilot a hearing training program (called "Hear-ing Champion Training"). Caregivers made suggestions regarding the format and content of the training. There was a clear preference for face-to-face, hands-on training. This was conducted in their "workplaces" (the homes of people with learning disabilities), to increase the relevance and applicability of the training to daily practice. The training was underpinned by Kolb's theory of experiential learning (Kolb, 1984). Interest in experiential learning began in the 1970s in the USA as people became disillusioned with more traditional forms of learning, and it spread to Britain during the same decade (Evans, 1994). It was appreciated that adults in particular bring their previous experiences and beliefs to learning, and that no adult learner "arrives as a blank slate" (Burnard, 1989). Three key aims were built into this training: to increase knowledge, changes attitudes and pro-mote long-term change to practice.

Six group training sessions were completed, with pre and post-training ques-tionnaires showing an increase in knowledge and confidence as a result of the training. Caregivers pledged to "make a difference" and suggested follow-up vis-its between 3–6 months post training to assess their continued progress.

Cycle 3

Evaluation of the training occurred in this cycle, with a re-visit of all groups trained in Cycle 2. Within six months, 96% of the pledges made had been com-pleted, with several examples of how individuals with learning disabilities had benefitted directly (for example being referred to Audiology, diagnosed with hear-ing loss and now being successful hearing aid users). In focus groups in this cycle, caregivers reported feeling more confident and empowered, and many described this as "a new chapter" in their working lives. However, there were several reports of caregivers now suspecting hearing loss in individuals they supported, making appointments with primary care professionals to discuss referral to Audiology, and the request for referral refused. Though unplanned, these reports warranted investigation in a final research cycle.

Cycle 4

This cycle occurred in a similar manner to Cycle 1, but involved General Prac-titioners and Practice Nurses in primary care settings, rather than paid caregivers. Here the estimate prevalence of hearing loss was also low (only 20%) and the known prevalence of hearing loss ranged between 0–14%. Even in this environ-ment, there were misconceptions about hearing loss, Audiology, and people with learning disabilities. Negative value judgments were made about the benefit of treating hearing loss and the capabilities of Audiology in assessing this group.

Completing this research led to tangible changes in my own practice, the practice of caregivers and the wider Audiology profession, through the dissemination of this work. One of the outputs of the research involved enhancement of my original model (3As model) into an improvement framework (5As model). This reflected the need for multidisciplinary engagement and action through awareness and assembly, which became apparent through the course of the research. Though it could be seen as tempting to "blame" individual groups, such as caregivers or primary care professionals, I also began to recognize the responsibility of Audiology as a profession to engage with others and raise awareness.

PREPARING FOR THE VIVA

It was this change of focus from questioning other groups, to questioning my own profession that was shaped during the research phase, and in the meetings I had with my supervisors. I met with my lead (and co-supervisor) on at least a monthly basis. I used these frequent meetings to pace my work, ensuring I always had new draft chapters or concepts to discuss. As well as writing the research report, it was also necessary to submit a portfolio of evidence alongside this. I liked this approach, as it was an opportunity to submit evidence (such as audits, reflections, and experiences) that occurred during, or even before the research phase. This helped to give context to the research being completed, and reiterated the feel of the Professional Doctorate compared to PhD; that this was a submission of a career of relevant work, or contemporary research embedded in professional practice, and not simply a project that existed in isolation.

I began the research phase of the Professional Doctorate in October 2013, and successfully defended my work at a viva in February 2016, to three examiners (an internal and external academic, and an external practitioner). I particularly valued the inclusion of a practitioner on the viva panel, rather than the purely academic focus of a PhD. It was important, as this encouraged examination of contribution to practice, as well as theory.

PERSONAL AND PROFESSIONAL IMPACT

Professional Impact

I believe this research has made an important contribution to both theory and practice. Through the use of action research methodology, it can be viewed as a successful educational intervention. I have established that it is possible to increase the audiological knowledge of paid caregivers and facilitate translation of that knowledge to changes in practice. This has not been demonstrated in the literature previously.

Such translation resulted in significant benefits, not only for the caregivers themselves, but also for the individuals they support. The lives of some individuals have been transformed as a result. It highlights the need for greater importance to be placed on audiological issues for people with complex needs and a greater awareness of their supporters, advocates, and healthcare providers. This research has highlighted the role of the wider team and other stakeholders through the development of a conceptual model (the 5As model) to facilitate multidisciplinary engagement for Audiology.

The findings from this research are being used to contribute to national best practice guidelines for people with learning disabilities in Audiology, regarding training and service delivery. They are also being used as evidence of healthcare science transformation in the National Health Service (NHS), which further highlights the contribution of this work across disciplines. The training package designed is one of the most important contributions to practice in this research and, since its design, has been used to train over 200 individuals, with numbers continuing to rise. The training in its current format had been commissioned by Sense (a UK charity for those with dual sensory loss).

As well as contributing theoretically to the evidence base through publications of the findings, I have aimed to change practice of those in the action research group, the local services and wider professionals in my community of practice and even across other elements of healthcare. With this in mind, the research has been disseminated in a variety of formats, regionally and nationally. We now have a truly multidisciplinary team, with shared goals and visions. The service for people with complex needs in Sunderland has won several awards, which serve as a useful mechanism to publicize the work that has been achieved.

Personal Impact

When I reflect back on the person I was when I started the Professional Doctorate journey, I feel a little embarrassed by my early naivety. I approached the taught year with a clear idea of the results I would find and how the research would develop. In such a short time, I can see how much I and my thinking have changed as a result of the Professional Doctorate. My early experiences were rooted firmly within my professional silo, and, as a consequence, I viewed everything through an Audiology lens. In Audiology, hearing loss is important to address and it is easy to detect. In Audiology, we believe that hearing aids are effective. I mistakenly believed that these principles could be applied in the outside world, with caregivers. Simply transfer the knowledge, and the results will follow. I was surprised no one had attempted this before! I quickly realized that I was wrong. Even other professionals within Audiology were not sharing my lens and were yet to address the hearing needs of people with learning disabilities. Until the profession as a whole were doing this, how could we judge anyone else?

By reading and reflecting during the course of my studies, I realized that my beliefs were constructed by my own experiences and that these would be different to those of caregivers. I also realized I had no idea what experiences and beliefs caregivers would have and that the first thing I needed to do was find out.

I reached an uncomfortable stage where the whole project felt like a mess, a huge tangled web in my mind that I felt I would never be able to unravel and organize. There were so many factors to consider; social policy, education, historical context. In fact, very little of the project was actually about Audiology and this made me feel uneasy. Audiology was my comfort zone. Though I still feel like a novice in these other areas, I understand more about them and have learned to apply them to my work. My thinking has broadened and my perspective widened. Though I have always wanted to help people and improve situations through equality and communication, I have realized that the real world is complicated and that there is no easy answer.

My perspective has changed significantly during the course of my studies. Initially I placed the responsibility of the issue with caregivers. However, I realize this was naïve and simplistic. There is a range of other factors to take into account and if responsibility must be shared out, some lay with primary care, but the majority rests with Audiology. Rather than sitting in the hospital casting judgment on the community for not receiving our message, we needed to look at ourselves and the way we deliver this message. Instead of a piece of research around educating caregivers, it transformed into a body of work to develop the role of Audiology and consider its place within a multidisciplinary team.

The Professional Doctorate has challenged me academically and personally. It has reinforced my belief that I am a determined and resilient person. It has allowed me to experience life outside of my community of practice, which is essential for professionals in the modern NHS.

We often say we engage in "multidisciplinary practice"; I myself said this before I started the doctorate, because I thought I did. However, I came to realize that simply being aware that different groups exist is not the same as forging links and working to maintain them. The links we now have help to increase our sense of empathy, respect, and mutual understanding.

Not only has this research made a significant contribution to theory and practice within and beyond my profession, it has made a significant contribution to me. As a professional and a person, I have changed substantially over the last four years. I am much more reflective, and feel I now appreciate the "bigger picture." I enjoyed stepping out of my "scientific" comfort zone, using qualitative methods. I was always a person who appreciated communication and discussion, though I am now even more passionate about these and truly see their value.

Like many others who work in the NHS, I first joined to make a difference and I am even more determined to do so, with an enhanced perspective. More than anything the Professional Doctorate has reinforced my passion for my work, and those I support. Gaining this qualification will not be the end of my journey, but a new chapter in my career. I feel that the skills I have acquired and the experiences I have had will prepare me well for more senior leadership positions within the NHS.

At the time of writing, I have officially been able to use the title "Dr" for four months. Over this time, many people have said, "you must be so relieved it's all over!" and "now you can relax and get back to the day job." Although there is no doubt that I have more free time at weekends now, I don't actually feel that my work is over. And I consider this to be a positive, as it proves the research I completed was relevant and an integral part of my professional practice. If anything, it has led on to further opportunities and further cycles of development, which I have approached with enthusiasm

REFERENCES

Banat, D., Summers, S., & Pring, T. (2002). An investigation into carers' perceptions of the verbal comprehension ability of adults with severe learning disabilities. *British Journal of Learning Disabilities 30*, 78–81.

Bent, S., McShea, L., & Brennan, S. (2015). The importance of hearing: A review of the literature on hearing loss for older people with learning disabilities. *British Journal of Learning Disabilities 43*, 277–284.

Bryman, A. (2016). *Social research methods* (5th ed). Oxford, UK: University Press.

Burnard, P. (1989). *Teaching interpersonal skills. A handbook of experiential learning for health professionals.* London, UK: Chapman and Hall.

Carvill, S. (2001). Sensory impairments, intellectual disability and psychiatry. *Journal of Intellectual Disability Research, 45*(6), 467–483.

Dalton, C., & Sweeney, J. (2011). Communication supports in residential services for people with an intellectual disability. *British Journal of Learning Disabilities, 41*, 22–30.

Denzin, N. K. (1992). *Symbolic interactionism and cultural studies. The politics of interpretation.* Oxford, UK: Blackwell.

Department of Health. (2001). *Valuing people—A new strategy for learning disability for the 21st Century.* London, UK: Department of Health.

Department of Health. (2007). *Promoting equality: Response from the Department of Health to the Disability Rights Commission Report, "Equal treatment: Closing the gap."* London, UK: Department of Health.

Emerson, E., Baines, S., Allerton, L., & Welch, V. (2012). *Health inequalities & people with learning disabilities in the UK: 2012.* London, UK: Public Health England.

Evans, N. (1994). *Experiential learning for all.* London, UK: Cassell.

Fulton, J., Kuit, J., Sanders, G., & Smith, P. (2013). *The professional doctorate.* Basingstoke, UK: Palgrave McMillan.

Hardy, S., Woodward, P., Woolard, P., & Tait, T. (2011). *Meeting the health needs of people with learning disabilities* (2nd ed). London, UK: Royal College of Nursing.

Hithersay, R., Strydom, A., Moulster, G., & Buszewicz, M. (2014). Carer-led health interventions to monitor promote and improve the health of adults with intellectual disabilities in the community: A systematic review. *Research in Developmental Disabilities, 35*, 887–907.

Hoghton, M. (2010). *A step by step guide for GP practices: Annual health checks for people with a learning disability.* London, UK: Royal College of General Practitioners.

Kerr. A. M., McCulloch, D., Oliver, K., McLean, B., Coleman, E., Law, T., Beaton, P., Wallace, S., Newell, E., Eccles, T., & Prescott, R. J. (2003). Medical needs of people with intellectual disability require regular reassessment, and the provision of client- and carer-held reports. *Journal of Intellectual Disability Research, 47*(2), 134–145.

Kevan, F. (2003). Challenging behaviour and communication difficulties. *British Journal of Learning Disabilities, 31*, 71–80.

Kolb, D. A. (1984) *Experiential learning. Experience as the source of learning and development.* Upper Saddle River, NJ: Prentice Hall.

Koshy, E., Koshy, V., & Waterman, H. (2011). *Action research in healthcare.* London, UK: Sage.

Kyle, S., Melville, C. A., & Jones, A. (2009). Effective communication training interventions for paid carers supporting adults with learning disabilities. *British Journal of Learning Disabilities, 38*, 210–216.

Lavis, D., Cullen, C., & Roy, A. (1997). Identification of hearing impairment in people with a learning disability: From questioning to testing. *British Journal of Learning Disabilities, 25*, 100–105.

Maxwell, J. A. (2012). *A realist approach for qualitative research.* London: Sage

McCracken, W., Lumm, J., & Laoide-Kemp, S., (2011). Hearing in athletes with intellectual disabilities: The need for improved ear care. *Journal of Applied Research in Intellectual Disabilities, 24*(1), 86–93.

McMillan, L., Bunning, K., & Pring, T. (2000). The development and evaluation of a deaf awareness training course for support staff. *Journal of Applied Research in Intellectual Disabilities, 13*, 283–291.

McNiff, J., & Whitehead, J. (2011). *All you need to know about action research* (2nd ed.) London, UK: SAGE.

McShea, L. (2015a). "I will make a difference"—Training caregivers to improve the hearing of adults with learning disabilities. *British Journal of Healthcare Assistants, 9*(3), 124–127.

McShea, L. (2015b). Managing hearing loss in primary care. *Learning Disability Practice, 18*(10), 18–23.

McShea, L., Corkish, C., & McAnelly, S., (2014). Audiology services: Access, assessment and aftercare. *Learning Disability Practice, 17*(2), 20–25.

McShea, L., Fulton, J., & Hayes, C. (2015). Paid support workers for adults with intellectual disabilities; their current knowledge of hearing loss and future training needs. *Journal of Applied Research in Intellectual Disabilities, 29*(5), 422–32. doi 10.1111/jar.12201

Meuwese-Jongejeugd, A., Verschuure, H., & Evenhuis, H. M. (2007). Hearing aids: Expectations and satisfaction of people with an intellectual disability, a descriptive pilot study. *Journal of Intellectual Disability Research, 51*(11), 913–922.

Miller, H., & Kiani, R. (2008). Inter-relationships between hearing impairment, learning disability services and mental health: Are learning disability services "deaf" to hearing impairments? *Advances in Mental Health and Learning Disabilities, 2*(2), 25–30.

Newsam, H., Walley, R. M., & McKie, K. (2010). Sensory impairment in adults with intellectual disabilities—An exploration of the awareness and practices of social care providers. *Journal of Policy and Practice in Intellectual Disabilities, 7*(3), 211–220.

Patton, M. Q. (2015). *Qualitative research & evaluation methods* (4th ed). London, UK: Sage.

Price, B. (2013). Using narratives and discourses in neglect-prevention training. *Nursing Management, 20*(3), 28–35.

Pryce, H. (2011). How can you help older people to hear? *Nursing & Residential Care, 13*(9), 423–425.

Pryce, H., & Gooberman-Hill, R. (2013). Foundations of an intervention package to improve communication in residential care settings: A mixed methods study. *Hearing, Balance & Communication, 11*(1), 30–38. doi 10.3109/21695717.2012.756224.

Reason, P., & Bradbury, H. (Eds.) (2008). *The SAGE handbook of action research: Participative inquiry and practice.* London, UK: Sage.

Schön, D. A. (1983). *The reflective practitioner: How professionals think in action.* Hampshire, UK: Arena Ashgate.

Twitchen, G. (2014). To screen or not to screen? *British Academy of Audiology Magazine, 30,* 16–17.

CHAPTER 15

STORIES OF NATIVE EDUCATORS IN HAWAI'I NAVIGATING THEIR EDD JOURNEYS

Makalapua Alencastre, Jocelyn Romero Demirbag, Mary Perez Hattori, Cathy Kanoelani Ikeda, and Walter Kahumoku III

Native perspectives of epistemology emerge from and are sustained by lived and oral traditions. Within oral societies, recitation and storytelling are a valued means of transmitting cultural and historical wisdom, histories, values, and beliefs. Recitation of the 2,102 lines of the cosmological genealogy known as the Kumulipo narrates the creation and evolution of the earth, its flora and fauna, including the deities of the Hawaiian pantheon and Hawaiian people. Ancient Polynesian and Micronesian migration chants relate epic stories of navigation spanning the Pacific Ocean. Ancestral experiences are brought to life within families; a Marshallese wave pilot remembers lying in his father's arms listening to his father's stories and feeling that he was in the canoe with him. Recent brain research reveals the abilities to navigate are directly tied to our ability to imagine, make decisions, learn from our past, and plan for the future. Furthermore, navigation is directly tied to our mental processes that enable storytelling (Tingley, 2016). "If storytell-

Exploring the Impact of the Dissertation in Practice, pages 223–237.

ing, the way we structure and make meaning from the events of our lives, arose from navigating, so too, is the practice of navigation inherently bound up with storytelling, in all its subjectivity" (Tingley, 2016, p. 14).

As Native educators, we use our subjective stories to navigate our personal journeys. We create individual maps that represent our reality through symbols of landmarks and milestones in our lives, and significant places in relationship to our experiences (Tingley, 2016). The five stories here reflect non-traditional experiences of five members of the pioneering EdD cohort of the University of Hawai'i at Mānoa. The authors are Native Hawaiian, Filipina, and Chamoru educators including a faculty member and four graduates who are associated with private and public domains of elementary through higher education. The diversity of the authors' backgrounds and areas of expertise authentically represent Hawai'i's multi-cultural community and educational landscapes. As such, the perspectives offered provide multiple lenses to address the critical, unique spaces created through this new doctoral pathway and illustrate how the EdD is expanding the confines of traditional academia.

Presented as a collection of short essays, the authors take this opportunity to share our stories by highlighting experiences of significant learning that occurred as we navigated through our doctoral journeys. This EdD journey was unique not only because it brought together very diverse educators from Hawai'i's independent schools, public schools, university system, and the Kamehameha Schools, but it also required two capstone projects: a group consultancy project and an individual action research based Dissertation in Practice (DiP). Each author sought to find our places as members of a large cohort, to set the rhythms that would see us through coursework, the consultancy project, and the formation, research, writing, and presentation of the DiP. As Native educators responsive to social justice issues affecting Native and community-based contexts, pursuing the doctoral journey was a critical means to benefit Native Hawaiian education, to promote understandings of culturally responsive conflict, and to call for the courageous articulation and implementation of our true missions.

CATHY: NAMING OURSELVES

As an educator who continues to battle social justice issues in education, pursuing my doctoral degree was about responding to the "politics of distraction." Smith (2003) defines the politics of distraction as the colonizing process of being kept busy by the colonizer, of always needing to respond, account, follow, or explain one's Indigenous lens. As the only Native Hawaiian director of a National Writing Project site, I wanted to create an Indigenous summer writing experience for the teachers that taught our minority students. Two obstacles stood in the way. First, with just my master's degree, I could not teach the 600-level university summer course without a professor "co-teaching," which basically meant that I ran the program and the professor got paid. Second, although the professor of record let me design and run the course, I was tasked with continuing to translate, codify, and define the experience through a western lens so that this professor could try to publish the experience of "our" program in a journal. The "distraction" of translating my Indigenous lens led me to seek out a doctoral program where my voice and my lens was enough.

I spent one year in the PhD program in educational curriculum studies before I found out about the first cohort of an EdD in Educational Professional Practice. What attracted me to this EdD program was that within the PhD program in the same College of Education, one of my professors was openly hostile toward this new program, feeling that this was a "less than" program—less than worthy, less than rigorous, and less than the already established PhD programs already offered. This EdD program brought together professors who were willing to battle their own institution in order to offer a different kind of doctoral experience. They weren't sure how to forge a new path, but they were willing to choose applicants who might define what that different kind of doctoral experience could look like. This was exactly what I was looking for. A program built out of the fire and hostility of the university system was ripe for creation, wayfinding, and naming. It was ripe for the social conditions necessary for Indigenous scholars to speak and most importantly, to be heard (Waitere & Johnston, 2009).

This is the story of our being heard, and our transformation in this program through our ability to, early on in the program, name ourselves in order to purposefully confront the institutional practices of the colonizer as well as confront ourselves in our collective journey to first "free ourselves before we can free others" (Freire, 1970). The turning point came with our first semester. Through a difficulty in timing, what was supposed to be a nine-credit-hour load in the summer was moved to the fall even though all of us worked full-time jobs, and three of us traveled from the neighbor islands for twice monthly Friday-Saturday courses. Out of "survivance" (Vizenor, 1998), a group of women, like magnets, formed a group to hold on to each other, eat, laugh, and cry together, and fuse our stories together as Mana Wahine. The power of naming ourselves, of choosing Mana Wahine and the implications of that self-naming, was our way of navigating through uncharted waters. It was a way to raise our collective voices to be heard, and not just to be present.

The term Mana Wahine, for Waitere and Johnston (2009) is a shield against the structures and processes that constrain our very ways of knowing and engaging with the world as Wahine Māori (17). Like these Wahine Māori, as Indigenous women, we also used the name Mana Wahine for the same type of shielding so that our own ways of knowing and engaging with the world might be brought forward. Broken down into its two parts, wahine in Māori and in Hawaiian is woman or women. Mana is authority, power, divinity, and empowerment. Mana is an integral component in the relationships that link cosmological, spiritual, human and physical elements. Choosing our name, Mana Wahine, was about recognizing our dignity and authority, of empowering ourselves as indigenous scholars, and therefore engaging in political work to ensure that others recognized the same dignity.

For each of us, our political work is individual, but I firmly believe that the audacity to do our own work was only made possible by naming ourselves as Mana Wahine. For me, owning the name, Mana Wahine, gave me the courage to create an authentic dissertation framework. At the point of frustration with the traditional five-chapter frame, I was able to tap into the expertise of my kūpuna, my elders, as well as the women around me to create my metaphor and flesh out the bones and sinew of my moʻo, a dissertation frame that used the Hawaiian moʻo, commonly known as a large lizard, as the root word to create the succession of my dissertation story. For example, my fourth chapter was the moʻolelo, a series of stories told by my participants. The last chapter was the moʻopuna, grandchildren. This chapter was an acknowledgment of who the action research was for, and how the work does not stop, but continues forward. That empowerment was made possible because the DiP created time and space for these relationships to form. The program marked our attendance, thus removing us from the list of absentees by allowing us to say our names, imagine its significance, its history, and its connectedness to wider events and circumstances. It allowed us to turn up and navigate toward the realization of our identity as Mana Wahine in institutions that have historically shut us out.

JOCELYN: FOLLOWING THE THREAD

My father emigrated to Hawaiʻi from the Philippines and my mother came from a white pioneering family in the state of Florida. Dad served all of the Filipino plantation workers on Maui as the first Filipino doctor to establish a regular practice on the island, freely speaking Ilocano or Tagalog with them and with our neighbors who slaughtered animals in their backyard. As we grew up, my sisters and I trained in the Indigenous dances of the Philippines—Igorot and Kalinga, as well as Moro, the minority Muslim group in the country. We also spoke Hawaiian Creole English, studied hula, and felt somewhat like minorities within an Oʻahu-centric state (Demirbag, 2015). All of these experiences left me identifying with a Native perspective, though it was not always clear which one or why.

The Native perspective drew me to the women of Mana Wahine within our doctoral cohort. These women were grounded in their values and persistently sought to include them in their research. They inspired me to speak my own truth, an esoteric aspect of my research that I had been hesitant to reveal to others. Authentically following my interests, intuition, and observations led to an unfolding development of ideas on a path that now feels like my destiny. Looking back at the journey I understand that what I was doing came to me in a dream: "following the thread."

Upon completing my DiP, I carried the thread I was following with me and soon realized that it was actively shaping my leadership. I was applying the ideas presented in my research and conference workshops to my new school's direction, the kuleana of its mission, and the presentation of its curriculum. As a school we explored the history of the land beneath the buildings and asked questions:

who had owned it and lived here, and what did the family that gave the land to the school stand for? What values did they support that allowed them to make this gift, and what kuleana did we accept when we accepted this land fifty-five years ago? Today my living educational theory of practice (McNiff & Whitehead, 2010) is that understanding what is imprinted or ensouled in the land beneath the school, along with the intentions of the school's founding families, will reveal the school's kuleana and serve as the foundation of a living mission (Kornberger, 2016). It will form the backbone of Honolulu Waldorf School's unique form of social justice that is the purpose of Waldorf education (Neil Boland, personal communication, February 13, 2016). In addition, the school will flourish once we can articulate this unique kuleana and mission, attracting those families who resonate with it.

Following the thread parallels closely with the experience of the Marshallese. The Marshallese ri-meto is a master of wave piloting—a process of navigation between the islands where they move forward by feel. In order to be accepted as a wave pilot, the pilot must be able to navigate the canoe from one island to another while wearing a blindfold (Tingley, 2016). The pilots are trained to feel for "dilep," a road that runs between atolls.

When I stand at the front gate of my school, greeting students and shaking their hands as they enter, it is as if I am blindfolded in that canoe, literally sensing what the school's path is. I look to the mountains where the family that gave us our land still lives; I look to the massive monkey pod trees that serve as school guardians, and I see the manuokū birds swirling, perhaps leading us to our right path as they lead fishermen to fish. I stand at the water fronting our ocean-side high school campus and watch a wide range of fishermen actively pursuing their craft, throwing net, walking the reef, or waiting alongside their poles as the waves roll in. Their success depends on using their senses, on their patience, and on the bounty of the land itself.

The ability to stand and sense is referred to by Senge, Scharmer, Jaworski, and Flowers (2004) as "presencing"—"seeing from the deepest source and becoming a vehicle for that source" (p. 89). The seed for their theory emerged from one of their research participants describing a "different sort of knowing." "You don't act out of deduction, you act out of an inner feel, making sense as you go. You're not even thinking. You're at one with the situation" (Senge et al., 2004, pp. 84–85).

Through presencing and connecting with the spirit of our place, we connect with spirituality and the universe. "The universe is the context for creation. That is the akua (gods). That is the wellspring of mana. And as soon as you realize that, then you realize you are just a part of all that; you can relax" (personal communication, Kiope Raymond, February 10, 2015). Through presencing and the connection to nature we are open to a different kind of knowing. This knowing serves as a basis for following your thread, sharing your story, and ultimately navigating your journey.

MARY: A PATH WITH HEART

The decision to enter a doctoral program was a weighty one. I was keenly aware that it would affect many aspects of life for me and those close to me. When pondering this commitment, I was led to this Castaneda (1968) quote:

> Does this path have a heart? All paths are the same: they lead nowhere. They are paths going through the bush, or into the bush. In my own life I could say I have traversed long, long paths, but I am not anywhere. Does this path have a heart? If it does, the path is good; if it doesn't, it is of no use. Both paths lead nowhere; but one has a heart, the other doesn't....One makes you strong; the other weakens you. (p. 76)

Four years hence, this passage is even more apt. This program was indeed a path with heart, an arduous, enriching, and joyful journey that made me stronger. Its positive impacts continue to resonate in my life and the lives of others.

I am a Chamoru of Guåhan (Guam), born to Fermina Leon Guerrero Perez (familian Titang) of Chalan Pago and Paul Mitsuo Hattori. I moved to Oʻahu to attend the University of Hawaiʻi- Mānoa (UHM) where I completed a baccalaureate degree and Professional Diploma in Secondary Social Studies, a Master's degree in Educational Technology, and an Educational Doctorate degree in Professional Educational Practice.

The EdD degree was a logical next step in my development. I enrolled with a career that included over a decade of teaching and leadership experience in the position of director of technology services at the largest community college in the state and lecturer for UHM's Learning Design & Technology program. I taught educational technology courses on my campus and delivered technology-focused professional development programs for higher education faculty. Having an awareness of problems of practice at all levels of an educational system, this program offered me a holistic and experiential approach to resolving such problems, grounded in an ethos of empowering its students to make positive contributions to society and improve education in our region. The program provides two key research experiences to its students–a group consultancy project and an individual Dissertation in Practice (DiP). Much of this work is done in, with, and for communities such as Native Hawaiians and recent migrants from the islands of Micronesia–communities not often included in educational decision-making processes and whose members face numerous barriers to academic achievement. This curriculum resonates with my Chamoru heritage because it promotes learning that can be applied toward helping others, a cultural imperative often expressed in the term, inafaʻ maolek (making right for others, striving for harmony).

As an Indigenous person using educational technologies as both a student and professor, and as a teacher of pre-service educators and in-service college faculty, I experienced what McNiff and Whitehead (2011) label "a living contradiction when one's values are denied in one's practice" (p. 44). I engaged in teaching educators to integrate technology into the curriculum following Euro-American principles and values while ignoring any way that those practices may contradict my own and other Indigenous peoples' beliefs and values. My DiP was a way to resolve the contradiction; it enabled me to work toward culturally responsive educational technology praxis and help others do the same.

My DiP was also an exercise in culturally responsive research. Navigating mainstream research processes and expectations to craft a path and DiP that honored me and my participants' cultures was complicated. The EdD community supported the development of an Indigenous research inquiry framework, a holistic approach that recognizes the relationship between ways of being and ways of knowing, our ontology and epistemology, and recognizes that these are grounded in cultural values. Relationships with people, places, and ideas were also an important aspect. Participants were recruited from a personal network, permitting me to conduct the research as a member of the community of indigenous academics, engaging in a collaborative knowledge-generating, meaning-making, transformative enterprise.

During the study, I was involved in professional activities that while not germane to the study, were inspired by it. These activities illustrate McNiff and Whitehead's (2010) statement that action research "becomes the grounds for other social and professional practices; professional development is understood as grounded in the capacity to offer explanation for our work" (p. 19). Curricula for courses in Educational Technology and Multicultural Education were enhanced to include culturally responsive education and culturally responsive educational technology. Professional development workshops for P–20 educators have since been delivered across the state. Learning orientations, axiologies, epistemologies, and ontologies of Pacific Islanders are now becoming part of conversations among researchers, educators, and policy-makers. The DiP itself has informed subsequent research by and about Pacific islanders. Voices underrepresented in discussions of educational policy and practices are thus being amplified. Chamoru scholar Lee (Cecelia) Perez (1997) writes, "There is power in the articulation of thought and sense. Dialogue can only begin when you find your voice" (p. xi). For some in our cohort, this program was a path to finding our voices; for some, a journey to using our voices in more powerful ways; and for many, a vehicle for giving voice to underprivileged and underrepresented groups. It is a path with heart.

MAKALAPUA: AS A KOA

E ola koa, (Pukui, 1983, #365, p. 44) to live as a koa tree, is a traditional Hawaiian metaphor symbolizing my stance as a Native Hawaiian educator who values traditional Hawaiian cultural wisdom as an essential source of inspiration and well-being. It is an honor to be described by family and colleagues as a koa, an activist committed to the Hawaiian language revitalization movement as I embrace the "Hawaiian immersion way of life" as an educator, a mother, and Tūtūmā to my 14 grandchildren.

As the koa tree is endemic to Hawai'i,

a symbol of being forever connected to this land.

As the roots of the koa provide the foundation for growth and sustenance,

mana and spirit are nourished through genealogical lineages.

As the koa hardwood grows strong as a valuable resource,

courageous and purposeful living is fortified.

As the koa plays a vital role in the vibrancy of the upland forest ecosystem,

the well-being of family and community is nurtured.

As koa stands are reforested,

Hawaiian education for present and future generations is cultivated.

As the last generation of native speaker kūpuna departs, a real sense of urgency is felt within the Native Hawaiian community with efforts to revitalize the Hawaiian language from the brink of extinction being a constant race against time. Hawaiian cultural revitalization through education is community driven social activism; it is a direct response to over a century of colonization of Native Hawaiian society. Re-culturing Hawai'i's educational landscape has become a definitive pathway for Native Hawaiians to self-determine educational intentions and processes. It has produced dynamic linguistic domains and registers aimed at naturalizing the use of the Hawaiian language and culture, fostering positive cultural attitudes, and providing the means for intergenerational transmission. It is movement away from compliance to oppressive educational policies as we rebuild foundational connections to traditional, spiritual, familial, and environmental sources of knowledge. Advocating for parity of cultural and academic opportunities requires maintaining a vigilant stand to promote the recognition and valuing of Hawaiian cultural knowledge as an essential component of re-culturing Hawai'i's school systems. As such, as Native educators we frequently find ourselves having to battle against the pervasive intrusion of American assimilation policies, laws, and attitudes that impede Hawaiian language and culture educational initiatives.

While embarking on a doctoral journey was a quest for personal and professional renewal, the real impetus was to engage in scholarship as a meaningful contribution to provision the current leg of an ongoing journey of cultural restoration: a rebuilding of Hawaiian nationalism. I enrolled in this doctoral program intent upon deepening my learning and expanding my understandings beyond the borders of my personal and professional existence as a Hawaiian educator. I challenged myself to be open, to listen deeply, and respectively engage as a member of a learning community with divergent perspectives. In hindsight, those interactions were opportunities of enlightenment broadening my own thinking while actualizing the growth and potential of this EdD program. I was conscious to assert a Hawaiian presence, hoping to expand the paradigms of educational leadership and our role as researchers. All the while, I sought out slivers of relevance to my own worldviews and work by building internal pathways to stay emotionally and cognitively connected. Fortunately, being a member of the EdD's initial cohort allowed for a great deal of flexibility to navigate through the coursework and research both as collective and individual quests. Overall, a spirit of collaboration was cultivated between cohort and faculty to be responsive to and supportive of Native ontologies in helping to shape the depth and breadth of this new doctoral program's identity.

Both the group consultancy project (Akiu-Wilcox, Alencastre, Hattori, Lucas, & Seto, 2012) and my Dissertation in Practice (DiP) (Alencastre, 2015) were invaluable opportunities to engage as a practitioner researcher. These studies were designed to critically explore issues and challenges, document distinctive practices, and affirm achievements within the contexts of P–12 Hawaiian language immersion education and the preparation of its teachers. The development of culturally grounded research practices along with the potential of the consultancy project and dissertation's key findings were specific to advancing Hawaiian language education.

Visualizing, internalizing, and designing appropriate research processes was a vigorous undertaking requiring extensive dialogue with peers and mentors and coupled with researching compatible theories and methodologies. Principles of indigeneity found within Indigenous research (Brayboy, 2005; Dei, 2011; Kawai'ae'a, 2012; Kovach, 2009; Smith, 2012; Vaioleti, 2006) resonated well with contemporary Native Hawaiian education and provided the foundation for developing appropriate research frameworks. As such, cultural concepts and processes emanating from Hawaiian philosophies and values were intentionally incorporated into the design, implementation, and analysis—including the predominant use of the Hawaiian language—throughout all research activities. Distinctive research practices purposefully situated the two studies within their particular contexts by incorporating Native concepts, philosophies, and protocols; addressing relevant community issues; and valuing community expertise.

In concert with the dynamics of Indigenous research, the inclusive nature of both studies was an acknowledgment honoring the lived experiences of Native Hawaiian students and educators. The numerous opportunities to gather and dialogue were instrumental in stimulating community building by rekindling and extending relationships. As participants generously shared their wisdom, experiences, and perspectives, their expertise provided a rich knowledge base leading to deeper understandings that were distinctive to these particular Hawaiian language educational contexts. Emergent themes defined essential characteristics and qualities of cultural identity, collaboration, culture-based educational programming, and achievement and success. In the short time since completion, the key findings of both the consultancy project and the DiP have been valuable in generating possibilities that are further advancing cultural and professional learning by stimulating authentic and sustainable initiatives.

'Ike i ke au nui me ke au iki (Pukui, 1983, #1209, p. 131) refers to the depth of knowledge needed to face the large and small ocean currents and ensure forward momentum of one's journey. As these field-based research studies were conducted as practitioner inquiries, learning the skillful arts of a Native researcher were experiences in honing a reflective praxis to transform practices at both programmatic and systemic levels. The capacity to successfully navigate the intricacies encountered was increased by being mindful of infusing my work with mauli ola—the well-being of spirit—into its essential intentions, processes, and outcomes. I found that identifying and relying on sources of inspiration and sustenance were essential practices to holistically provision each day.

Interactions with brilliant, dedicated, and visionary educators who served as doctoral faculty as well as fellow members of the EdD cohort were especially powerful. I relied heavily on the group of women educators in our cohort who as Mana Wahine inspired each other to elevate our personal and professional selves. The genuine aloha and collective wisdom of this group truly enhanced our endeavors as we chartered this journey together. As Mana Wahine, we met frequently on our own-journeying throughout Hawai'i's island communities and to distant shores-deepening our learning through collaborative inquiry and reflection. All in all, I am appreciative of the opportunities afforded during this doctoral journey as a contribution to Native Hawaiian self-determination. The attributes of E Ola Koa sustained my journey and are now providing the sustenance for me to serve as one of the mentors and advisors to the second EdD cohort; provisioning a new leg of the journey.

WALTER: KAULIKE—SEARCHING FOR BALANCE

I often pause at moments in my lifespan pondering purpose, performance, and provision. Why I exist, how appropriate are my actions, and what contributions I make on behalf of my family, ancestors, and the greater lāhui. As a father, an adjunct professor, husband, department director, son, scholar, and at times introverted socialite, I struggle to balance a malevolent yearning to be unseen with the visible requires of boss-hood, activist, and educator.

My role as a co-teacher to this cohort and community mentor to three of its participants has provided a moment to admire from afar the growth of people who in their own right are far more experienced and exceptional as leaders, more erudite and estimable as mentors and coaches, and more efficient and effective as writers, thinkers, practitioners, and advocates of education than me. Who was I to guide, mentor, and teach them?

Although involved in the design of this cohort program, my first introduction to its members arrived when teaching a seminar on the "Social and Cultural Contexts of Education." As my co-teacher, Dr. Ideta, and I dived into class, we were struck by a disgruntled disquietude rumbling among the group. Though the cohort had completed their first full year together, rather than the solidarity and general harmony we experienced with other cohorts, there seemed to be tension that appeared in their vernacular and behavior toward one another. Even as they described their experiences in the program up until this point, my colleague and I heard a general disdain for the coursework and the lack of time taken to build community. Not quite understanding the discord among them, we unfolded the course as we always do: we stated that this class was a safe, nurturing learning space. Class session by session, we began reveling in moments of 'ah-ha-ness' when these amazing human beings found their various voices and personal mo'olelo mirrored in the theories and contexts we explored. We were moved by instances of soul-enriching discovery, contested within higher education—the bastion of Western thought—that prides its existence to a selective elitism that has long discriminated against women and minorities. By the class' end, we sensed a determined, resoluteness bounded in a strengthened, connected cohort.

While we conducted class, our students were executing the first of two capstone assignments—a consultancy project. Although I and a number of other community mentors were not directly involved in this capstone, we were invited to support the DiP process. I was blessed with three brilliant Hawaiian women to mentor, all of whom intended to research various forms of Hawaiian education. But as the cohort attempted to complete their consultancy projects and start their individual dissertations, the program's professors realized that executing both capstones in the three semesters remaining would require each student to become highly resilient, dedicated, and single-minded. In the case of these three women, they were trying to finish their consultancy while simultaneously constructing a research question, writing an introduction, and submitting their Institutional Review Board (IRB) application. From my perspective, the confluence between both capstone projects created a tug-of-war of energies and time. Lesson learned: mentors and advisors who are working with the second cohort have guided their teams to finish the consultancy project and initiate the DiP process by the third semester.

As a mentor and someone committed to supporting other kanaka Hawai'i to puka (attain, graduate) through one of the most difficult rites of passage devised by Western minds, I struggled with balance. Eager to lele (leap, move forward) on this DiP journey yet cognizant of their responsibilities to the first project, I languished between moments of pause and push, never clearly attaining equilibrium between either. I would distribute articles and books or suggest topics of exploration for their literature review knowing all the while that these incredibly intelligent researchers were trying to balance two projects, work, home, family as well as personal needs. Even more alarming, these amazing women were reaching exhaustion and as such, the readings added to fodder in the file of "will get to's."

My own sense of urgency exacerbated when other faculty advisers, many of whom did not have the research background to support Indigenous and culture based DiP, hesitated at taking the lead in this process. Unquestionably, I understood their pause; had I not the expertise, I probably would not have committed to working with someone whose research area I had not studied myself. But because of the disinclination, I began questioning my own abilities. Pricked by requisite work demands and pressed by a self-imposed urgency to support Hawaiians, I often wondered whether I was helping or hindering. Were my suggestions for readings truly what they needed, my advice about methodology accurate, my formatting requirements counterproductive to what they were constructing? I was in a constant state of teetering between subsuming the advisor role and reclining back to the place of mentor.

Once the consultancy project was completed, I mistakenly believed that all three women would then capitalize with singular force on completing the DiP. What I discovered was that the switch from a group-learning environment to an individual one posed significant hurdles for all three. From my vantage, it seemed that each questioned her inadequacy, lack of brilliance, inexperience, and little ability. I became counselor, advisor, mediator as well as friend, always wondering whether my comments lifted these beautiful souls out of dark, foreboding spaces. What dawned on me was that for these three native women, I stood as a lama kū (beacon)—someone who "got through" the DiP process and at the same time, may have intensified these feelings of "less than." I pray that each knows...I am involved because I believe in them.

These questions of kaulike intensified with the requirements for graduation. Though all three had gathered most of their data and had done some analysis, only one had written her introduction and methodology chapters. For example, I wondered whether each went into the final DiP presentations with a solid understanding of the theoretical lens that framed their work. I sat pensively, saying pule (prayers) for their success while admonishing myself for not preparing these wonderful, powerful females for the gauntlet of queries that normally would be hurled during a DiP "defense."

Mahalo ke Akua (Thank God), the standard intense interrogation never materialized. In fact, the momentousness of graduation arrived and departed in short order. Three years later, only one of the three has completed. I was proud and humbled—such poor lyrics to describe the song that sings in me—when this incredible researcher won the Carnegie Project on the Education Doctorate (CPED) dissertation of the year award. Though I was not allowed to experience her award ceremony, I thanked ke Akua for such a rare opportunity to support this brilliant scholar.

Yet as true with the concept of balance, I pray that the other two incredibly gifted wahine (women) finish soon. I acknowledge the pointedness of me saying, "you do not do this alone...you must complete this process because you are a role model for other Hawaiians and for the members of your family" to motivate each to complete their study. But as I point out to each, "you do this work on behalf of the lāhui" and "when you finish, you will need to support other Hawaiians through this process," I question whether my guidance is more a reflection of my own need for these ladies to finish than their desire to not become another statistic of Hawaiian failure. I ponder thoughts of frustration and shame that lie beneath my inability to support these women to complete their study and stand proudly in the light of their degree attainment. I hope that they know…as I promised at the start of this journey…I will stand behind each one, ready to feed and provide rest for a moment...before they rise again to continue their journey. This process has been and continues to be one of balance.

CONCLUSION

These stories represent our journeys as Native students and faculty members of a doctoral cohort that navigated through an EdD program. Throughout our journeys, we persevered in navigating through each of the experiences while staying true to the integrity of our core values. We engaged in scholarship to articulate and implement our collective mission of positively transforming Hawai'i's education. We have emerged as Native educators who are courageous and humble enough to *be* enough through the wisdom of our Native cultures. One of the most powerful stories of navigation is seen in the crew of the Hawaiian voyaging canoe Hōkūle'a. Their determination to make the inaugural journey from Hawai'i to Tahiti took them 2,700 miles across open ocean without any navigational instruments. As ancestral cultural knowledge transmitted through stories and chants serve as inspirational accounts of skillful adventures, our experiences are humbly shared to provision the success of future journeys. Bill McDonough, an American architect, asked, "What will it take for us to become indigenous once again?" (Senge et al., 2004). There are some who would reply, "We have never stopped being Indigenous," some who would say, "I have reclaimed who I am," and some who would say "I am still searching." But regardless of where we are on this journey, we know that "the ultimate aim of the servant leader, the quest, is to find the resources of character to meet your destiny, and to find the wisdom and power to serve life that way" (Senge et al., 2004, pp. 221–222). Name yourself, follow your thread, live as a koa tree, and search for balance. In this way you will navigate a path with heart.

APPENDIX A

Hawaiian Glossary

Aloha: Love, compassion, tolerance, kindness.
Akua: God, spirit.
Holomua: Progress.
Kanaka: Human being, Hawaiian.
Kaulike: Balance.
Koa: Brave, bold, fearless, large native tree.
Kuleana: Right, privilege, concern, responsibility
Kūpuna: Grandparents, ancestors

Lāhui: Nation, people, race.
Lamakū: Torch.
Lele: Jump, leap.
Mana: Authority, power, divinity, empowerment.
Mauli ola: Breath of life, healing life force.
Moʻo: Succession, series, especially a genealogical line, lineage.
Moʻolelo: Story, history, tradition, record, article.
Ola: Life.
Puka: Graduate.
Pule: Pray, bless.
Wahine: Female.

Retrieved from wehewehe.org

REFERENCES

Akiu-Wilcox, K., Alencastre, M. Hattori, M., Lucas, K., & Seto, L. (2012). *Defining student success in a Hawaiian language immersion charter school.* Unpublished manuscript.

Alencastre, M. (2015). *E hoʻoulu ʻia nā kumu mauli ola Hawaiʻi, Preparing Hawaiian cultural identity teachers.* (Unpublished doctoral dissertation). University of Hawaiʻi at Mānoa, Honolulu, HI.

Brayboy, B. (2005). Toward a tribal critical race theory in education. *The Urban Review, 37*(5), 425–446.

Castaneda, C. (1968). *The teachings of Don Juan: A Yaqui way of knowledge.* Los Angeles: University of California Press.

Dei, G. (2011). *Indigenous philosophies and critical education.* New York: Peter Lang Publishing.

Demirbag, J. (2015). 'Giving voice' through the practitioner based EdD. In V. Stead (Ed.), *The education doctorate: Perspectives on EdD access, diversity, social justice, and community leadership* (pp. 237–246). New York: Peter Lang Publishing.

Freire, P. (1970). *Pedagogy of the oppressed* (MB Ramos, Trans.). New York: Continuum.

Kawaiʻaeʻa, K. (2012). *Kūkohu: ka nānaina kaiaola o nā kaiaaʻo ʻōlelo Hawaiʻi (*A study on the cultural ecology of Hawaiian medium and Hawaiian immersion learning environments*).* (Unpublished doctoral dissertation). Union Institute & University, Cincinnati, OH.

Kornberger, H. (2016). Geoliteracy: Reading the Script of Place. *Pacifica Journal, 49*(1), 1–4.

Kovach, M. (2009). *Indigenous methodologies: Characteristics, conversations, and contexts.* Toronto, Canada: University of Toronto Press.

McNiff, J., & Whitehead, J. (2010). *You and your action research project* (3rd ed.). New York: Routledge.

McNiff, J., & Whitehead, J. (2011). *All you need to know about action research* (2nd ed.). London: Sage Publications.

Perez, C. (1997). *Signs of being—A Chamoru spiritual journey.* (Unpublished Master's thesis). University of Hawaiʻi at Mānoa, Honolulu, HI.

Pukui, M. (1983). *'Ōlelo noʻeau, Hawaiian proverbs & poetical sayings*. Honolulu, HI: Bishop Museum Press.

Senge, P., Scharmer, C. O., Jaworski, J., & Flowers, B. S. (2004). *Presence: Human purpose and the field of the future*. New York: Crown Business.

Smith, G. H. (2003, October). *Indigenous struggle for the transformation of education and schooling*. Keynote presented to the Alaskan Federation of Natives Convention, Anchorage, AK.

Smith, L. (2012). *Decolonizing methodologies: Research and indigenous peoples* (2nd ed.). Dunedin, New Zealand: University of Otago Press.

Tingley, K. (2016, March 17). The secrets of the wave pilots. *The New York Times Magazine*. Retrieved from www.nytimes.com.

Vaioleti, T. (2006). Talanoa research methodology: A developing position on Pacific research. *Waikato Journal of Education, 12*, 21–34.

Vizenor, G. (1998). *Fugitive poses: Native American Indian scenes of absence and presence*. Lincoln, NE: University of Nebraska Press.

Waitere, H., & Johnston, P. (2009). Echoed silences. In abstentia: Mana Wahine in institutional contexts. *Women's Studies Journal, 23*(2), 14–31.

CHAPTER 16

DISSERTATION IN PRACTICE (DiP)

Influences to Guide Professional Development Reform

Michelle Rosen

I was teaching first grade in 1997 when I enrolled in a graduate program for my Master's in Reading as well as my Reading Specialist Certification. I *taught* during the day and *was taught* at night. One year later, I became pregnant and decided I would not return to the first grade classroom. Luckily for me, I connected with a professor who was looking for someone to help her with a professional development conference. I immediately jumped at the chance, working from home with a newborn. My operational responsibilities included venue liaison, correspondence, daily schedules, audio visual and budgetary issues. I developed a holistic view of the professional development process. Here, I was in an administrative role, looking at aspects I never considered as an attendee: What is the budget? How many attendees do we need to break even? Can we afford a car service for speakers to get them or do we need to send a student to pick them up? How much food should we order? How many vendors can we fit, etc.? Two years prior, as a first grade teacher, my professional development experiences were the polar opposite: What

Exploring the Impact of the Dissertation in Practice, pages 239–251.
Copyright © 2017 by Information Age Publishing

workshop do I attend? Is my district paying for it or am I? Will I be able to use what I learn in my classroom? Will the topic fit within my district professional development plan? Interesting how quickly the tides turned.

Working on that professional development conference part-time turned into a full-time position as a Director of the University Professional Development Center (UPDC), which provided varied workshops for teachers, supervisors, and administrators. Though a division of the Graduate School of Education the UPDC was not funded by the school, as a self-supporting organization, a leading goal was to make enough money to cover the center's running costs.

Eventually, the center was impacted by reduced school districts professional development budgets. By 2005, local teachers were not allowed to leave school to continue their learning. As a professional development director, it was time to rethink the model. It was clear, from the research, that professional development in many schools and districts had been undergoing a transformation: changing from the traditional emphasis on one-day workshops (often provided out of district, or by outside consultants that come in) to a more innovative and increasingly common, in-district, teacher-led, and consistently sustained professional learning (Darling-Hammond, Andree, Richardson, Wei, & Orphanos, 2009; DuFour, DuFour, Eaker, & Many, 2006; Harwell, 2003; Katzenmeyer & Moller, 2001). This was occurring for a few reasons. Paid professional development days commonly written into teachers' contracts had become a rarity. School budgets, in most local districts, had been cut significantly over the past few years. Therefore, teachers were less frequently granted permission to attend costly, out of district workshops. Many schools had cut costs by refusing to pay workshop registration fees as well as substitute teachers' pay to cover teachers' absences while attending professional development, thus eliminating teachers' ability to attend out of district professional development. With budgetary restrictions, districts frequently did not have the funds to bring in expensive presenters and programs. Ironically, this economic reality was perhaps a blessing in disguise, given that the old one-day workshop approach to professional development has been found to be generally ineffective; whereas, the new shift towards professional development that is sustained and embedded in teachers' professional contexts has been found to be more effective (Darling-Hammond, 2009; Harwell, 2003; DuFour, DuFour, Eaker, & Many, 2006; Katzenmeyer & Moller, 2001). Teachers who participated in one-day workshops were likely neither to retain information they were taught, nor to share it with colleagues (Pancucci, 2007).

Learning that the way professional development would now be offered had changed along with knowing that we would have to financially support a center, we created a model that we thought would achieve our goals. Due to the fact that I had a background in literacy as a certified Reading Specialist, we created a professional development center focused on literacy teachers, leaders, and administrators. In 2007, we created a Center for Literacy Development (CLD) where we would host a series of five workshops that addressed various literacy topics and would encourage districts to "join" as members and attend as a group. Our goal was to have the same group attend all meetings in an effort to create a community of practice, both at the meetings and back at the participants' districts. This model was an attempt to meet in the middle between raising enough revenue to the support the center and creating a meaningful professional development initiative for its members. The CLD became a popular enterprise for area districts. Attendance was high at all meetings, the speakers were excellent, and the participant feedback was overwhelmingly positive. At the same time, the CLD was thriving financially. With over one hundred teachers at each meeting, we were generating ample revenue to pay all of our bills, with a little extra to save.

During this time, I had heard about a new Doctorate in Education program being developed at our university. It would be different than the previous program in the way that all EdD students would work in a cohort model, functioning together as a group. For me, this addressed the issues of loneliness and isolation, which had been my greatest concern when considering the doctoral process. Having the opportunity to work with others was enticing. I took the chance and in the summer of 2010 I applied (and was accepted) to the first cohort of the university's newly revised Doctorate in Education program, which was influenced by the Carnegie Project in the Education Doctorate (CPED).

From the very first meeting of our 2010 cohort, it was stressed that we would study a "problem in practice." This course of study had to be real and meaningful and attempt to make a difference in actual classrooms. As I sat there, I thought about the CLD and its impact it had on its members. I pondered the following questions: Was it successful in helping members' turnkey the information back to their colleagues? How did this professional development model provide meaningful experiences for those who attend? What would be an important problem to consider for my Dissertation in Practice (DiP) study? After careful thinking and collaboration with my advisor and cohort, I decided to examine the factors that affect teacher leaders who attend the CLD's series of workshops.

The purpose of the study was to examine the factors influencing professional development that teacher leaders provide. It was intended to highlight the supports and challenges that accompany these educational experiences. For the purposes of my study, teacher leadership referred to the process by which teachers, individually or collectively influence their colleagues, principals, and other members of their school community in order to improve teaching and learning practices. Teacher leaders are facilitators of teacher learning within the school and can be seen as an important element in strengthening and sustaining school improvement efforts (Durant & Frost, 2003). Teacher leaders are uniquely positioned to work with teachers as a constant support within the school. Wasley (1991) identified teacher leaders as those who possess "the ability to encourage colleagues to change, to do things they wouldn't ordinarily consider without the influence of the leader" (p. 64). This concept is strikingly different from the off-site consultant offering a one-day workshop with no follow-up. On-site teacher leaders, who are a part of the school's culture, are well positioned to facilitate the learning process, which leads to teacher change and improvement.

The research in the study supported the idea that such an understanding may offer a more plausible insight into the work that teacher leaders assume as professional development providers. This understanding could be beneficial to leaders, at all levels, schools, and institutions of higher education that are focused on teacher leadership, as well as educational policy makers. Research questions included: What do teacher leaders who receive professional development through the CLD do as professional development providers once they return to their schools? What influences their activities? What are the supports and obstacles they face in doing so? The research design (case study) was selected to generate data that would inform educators about the practice of teacher leaders, who take part in a university-run literacy center, as they provide professional development to their colleagues. The questions were aimed at understanding supports and challenges that teacher leaders faced through this process. Examining this data provided information about how to better develop and support teacher leaders in their roles as on-site professional development providers.

A case study (Creswell, 1998) was used to describe what influences the professional development that teacher leaders have provided within their schools. More specifically, a case study was used so that units of analysis in the "bounded system" were studied over a five-month period (Creswell, 1998). In order to examine the factors affecting the professional development teacher leaders provide, an inductive investigative strategy (Patton, 2008) was used. Interviews with teacher leaders, building principals, and observations of professional development sessions were conducted. The main sources of data collection were observations of professional development sessions as well as teacher leader and principal interviews. In addition, I kept a research journal to record information about factors affecting professional development that teacher leaders provide.

A purposeful sample was used in my study. To choose the participants, I began by selecting a district that was a member of a CLD and also had a formal, designated teacher leader role in their schools whose primary role was to work as a professional development provider within their assigned building. There were eight teachers with the teacher leader role in the selected district, the only district in the literacy center with a formal teacher leader role. From within this group, I selected three varying participants to achieve diversity with my results. I picked one participant who had more than fifteen years of experience as a teacher leader, one who had more than seven years as a teacher leader and a third participant who had less than five years as a teacher leader. Additionally, these three participants all took part in the CLD as well as being formally designated teacher leaders in their schools. The principals interviewed were chosen by default, as they were the principals in the schools where each of the selected teacher leaders worked.

While the study showed that, a majority of the time, these teacher leaders were given professional development topics that were mandated by either state testing regulations, curricular changes, or district initiatives, there were often times they used what they had learned at the CLD. Had I not been a part of the Educational Doctorate program, I wouldn't have uncovered the information that follows. Without taking part in a program that required us to look at a "problem in practice," my approach to professional development programs would have stayed stagnant and facilitated in a way that is not based on sound research and evidence. The EdD program challenged me to reevaluate my work in an effort to improve it for those involved in developing professional development opportunities. For these purposes, the most critical finding was the implications for the CLD and my work as a professional development provider. Additionally, the research is helpful to other universities and organizations that provide professional development.

UNIVERSITY LITERACY CENTER

All three teacher leaders reported that the professional development sessions they attended as a result of their district's affiliation with CLD was a source of ideas for professional development offerings at their schools that complemented, but was not planned to be directly responsive to district or state mandates and initiatives. During the year in which the data was collected and the previous year, each teacher leader attended eight professional development sessions provided by the CLD. Topics, resources, and information from three of the sessions were used in the observed teacher leaders' professional development offerings at their schools, while interview data showed more was used but not observed.

The sessions focused on ways to help students take compositional risks by including more thoughts, feelings, actions and dialogue. According to one principal, Mr. Walton, the teachers were excited to try these new strategies in their classrooms and communicated their appreciation of the commitment both the principal and teacher leader had in creating learning opportunities for them. One of the teacher leaders continued to work on this issue with teachers by grade level, in small groups and individually. She visited classrooms, talked with teachers, and modeled lessons for those who requested it.

The teacher leaders used resources from the CLD to help plan professional development sessions that were the result of numerous directives from the district to align the current curriculum to new standards. For example, Donald Bear, co-author of the book, *Words Their Way: Word Study for Phonics, Vocabulary and Spelling,* presented a full-day session at CLD on strategies to improve phonics, vocabulary and spelling instruction in the elementary classroom. Coincidentally, the teacher leaders' district used the *Words Their Way* book as a guideline for administering, scoring, and analyzing word study assessments in order to determine appropriate word study group placement and instructional foci for students. The teacher leaders reported that this meeting was an important resource for them; each used the PowerPoint and instructional videos from the session to take information back to their colleagues. These ready-to-use materials provided research-based strategies, which could be used to easily communicate to teachers.

Teacher leaders provided turnkey training on the information they attained at CLD meetings in various venues, some for large group meetings and other times for individually targeted instruction. The teacher leaders reported that the topics of the CLD meetings sometimes influenced their choice of topic for professional development sessions they provided; at other times information they gathered from these sessions were used to add research-based support to a session topic they would have offered anyway. The resources from the CLD they used most often were the materials provided by the presenters; including their PowerPoint slides, sample videos, and speaker's publications. Teacher leaders drew on CLD topics for the professional development they planned either because it fit with their schools' goals, addressed an observed need, felt it would benefit the teachers' practice, or was aligned with a district mandate. It is evident that teacher leaders participating in the CLD benefited from obtaining access to highly effective research-based professional development topics, content, and strategies.

Although the study set out to uncover factors that affected teachers leaders and their professional development experiences at their schools, a most critical finding was how a university professional development center can be more effective and meaningful for its members. Even though it is clear the CLD played an important role in the work of the teacher leaders, it may not have always hit its mark in terms of immediate application. The teacher leaders did not always have permission or time to turnkey the information they gained from meetings. Analysis of the data suggests that the teacher leaders who were positioned as professional development providers and took part in their own learning experiences through CLD were not always able to use what they learned when working with their colleagues. The information they delivered was most often dictated by district and state mandates. A smaller fraction of the time they spend with teachers is a result of teacher leader or teacher generated topics.

Although the findings illustrated most professional development sessions the teacher leaders provided were both collegial and congenial, they were seldom collaborative. The literature points to how a more constructivist approach helps teachers learn and change, but these teacher leaders spent more time disseminating "knowledge for practice" (Cochran-Smyth & Lytle, 1999), the formal knowledge generated by research and passed on by external consultants, trainers, and publishers representatives to other educators in order to improve practice. *It is* imperative to impart this type of knowledge established and selected by others seemed to overtake any other type of knowledge building experiences.

Using teacher leaders as expert educators to transmit knowledge to other teachers is one way to provide professional development, but researchers are suggesting a more constructivist and reflective learning approach would help the teachers truly learn, change, and improve instructional practice (Harwell, 2003; Fullan, 2006). Using an approach in this manner allows for the teacher leader to be more of a facilitator by guiding the teachers in an effort to bring about change in instructional practice. This has implications for the CLD and other professional development organizations by the way in which it addresses their professional development needs.

The findings of this study suggest that the teacher leaders used topics, information, and materials from the CLD when planning and providing professional development to their colleagues. However, they did not automatically use everything they learned about at meetings. They did so when meeting topics, information, and materials were aligned with already established professional development goals, or added to sessions teacher leaders would have presented for their colleagues anyway. They sometimes used information that seemed like it would be relevant to teachers, even if it did not fit with an established professional development topic, but they did not always have the latitude to do this. The teacher leaders participating in this study illustrated that the CLD served as a viable and crucial resource for the schools with which the teacher leaders are affiliated. The teacher leaders showed that, given the increased levels of responsibilities for teacher leaders without an increase in time available, they were happy to have and use their connection to the CLD. They perceived that it provided high-quality, evidence-based professional development and materials that they can turn around and easily use in their everyday practice. This was helpful for them in their roles as teacher leaders because it helped maximize the efficiency and effectiveness of their training design; they found the resource extremely helpful because it provided them with topics, information, and materials without having to hunt them down. By providing resources and models, the CLD offered resources for teacher leaders who were then able to turnkey what they learned for their colleagues. Additionally, university-based literacy centers financially benefit school districts because they provide training for a single delegate, the teacher leader, to attend off-site professional learning opportunities and then bring that knowledge back to the staff of the individual schools. The advantage to school districts is that they do not have to pay for an outside trainer to train an entire staff. This proved to be a cost-effective option.

While there were numerous benefits to the teacher leaders who attended the CLD, the research proves that there can be an improved approach to designing and implementing professional development initiatives for teachers. The study revealed that although teacher leaders do convey the content knowledge they gain from participating in professional development if it fits with local priorities, they did not necessarily help their colleagues improve their practice using effective professional development approaches. This may be because they do not have the knowledge or tools to do so. The CLD focused on giving the teacher leaders professional development content, but teacher leaders also need to develop skills related to facilitating teacher learning that is designed around research-based professional development practices. Therefore, in addition to focusing on information and instructional strategies in the target content area, professional development for teacher leaders should include opportunities to learn about a range of topics related to being professional development providers including: effective strategies for overcoming teacher resistance to change, how to build trust, gain buy-in, and establish a culture of collaboration and cooperation. They also need to understand that an effective professional development model is typically school-wide and long-term with many opportunities for follow-up and processes that encourage collegiality (for example through learning communities and extended dialogue). In order to strengthen learning about professional development best practices, the learning experiences that teacher leaders participate in should model effective approaches and explicit activities should be built in to help develop skills in this area.

Overall, this study uncovered critical information for both district supervisors as well as professional development center providers. Factors that affected teacher leaders' abilities to provide professional development were often out of their hands. When the topics are mandated by district and state policies and priorities and curricular changes, there is little decision-making power teacher leaders can exercise pertaining to the content. Yet, outside providers can support their work by providing activities aligned with local and state initiatives and by modeling and explicitly working to develop skills for facilitating professional development using research-based best practices that have the potential to help teachers change and improve their practice with the support of teacher leaders.

Completing the doctoral program gave me an opportunity to become a full-time tenured track faculty member at another university. Within the first year of my appointment, I, along with two of my colleagues, received a grant from our State Department of Education. The purpose of the grant was for universities to partner with school districts to help teachers understand the Common Core State Standards shifts, as a result of its implementation, through a professional development initiative and be able to have a broad impact on schools as a whole. Having just completed my doctoral work in this area, I took the lead in conceptualizing what our model would look like. Based on the results of my research, I was certain of a few things: the professional development had to be meaningful, it should be the same group at each meeting, it had to encourage collaboration, teachers had to have time to reflect and debrief with each other, and we had to incorporate opportunities for teacher leaders to practice turnkey skills, in addition to gaining content knowledge. These factors would help teacher leaders become effective professional developers back at their schools. In other words, focusing on the "process" was equally important to the "product."

The EdD program helped me shape a more successful professional development initiative. As a result of the grant, the Common Core Academy (CCA) was created in 2013. CCA was a partnership between my university and three neighborhood urban school districts. There was a total of 50 participants. Each of the three schools had a team of teacher who principals identified as "teacher leaders." Additionally, principals were required to attend the meetings with their teachers. This team was a direct result of my research knowing that the relationship between principal and teacher leaders may become the key to lasting school improvement. How the principal supports and promotes teacher leaders and what role they play will, often times, determine the success of teacher leaders. The research literature clearly illustrates that the principal can influence, and be influenced by, the success of teacher leaders. Without them, a principal working alone is unlikely to be able to respond successfully to the increasing levels of responsibilities necessary to be an effective leader (Darling-Hammond, 1996; Fullan, 2001; Spillane & Louis, 2002).

In addition to having the same group attend all of the meetings during the year, in this new iteration of a professional development initiative, the focus was one topic. While there are numerous educational shifts associated with the Common Core State Standards, our year was dedicated to *regular practice with complex texts and their academic language.* Providing professional development in the same topic over the course of the year allowed the teachers to gain much deeper understandings of the focus, in an effort to ingrain the information in a more helpful way. This approach was two-fold; meaning, as participants they were able to learn over time and most likely able to have a broader understanding for when they turnkey information to other teachers in their schools. In sharp contrast to the CLD, this newly created professional development center's goal was to delve deeper into one topic in hopes of cultivating teacher leaders who can make an impact back in their schools.

Another change, as a result of my research, was the way in which each of the days was structured. In my previous work at the CLD, the speaker worked with the group for the entire day. A typical meeting was passive; meaning, delete blue meaning teachers usually sat, listened, and took some notes. It was seldom interactive and rarely did participants work with other teachers. In this new model, the speaker worked with the teachers and principals during a morning session. In contrast the older model, CCA devoted the afternoon session to debrief and reflection of the morning session with the speaker. Divided into school groups, everyone was given a planning sheet (see Table 16.1 on the next page).

Working with their colleagues encouraged discussions that allowed everyone to reflect on what they had just learned (while fresh in their minds). They were given ample time to confer on how they would be able to create goals based on the morning meeting's information. For example, when a speaker discussed the strategy of close reading, participants now had the time to reflect on how they can implement close reading with their students. Creating this time for them allowed the important discourse pertaining to how they will accomplish this goal, whose help do they need, what resources are necessary, how will they assess it and what evidence will they identify to show academic growth. What was critical to this opportunity was the fact that the principals were included in these conversations. Working as a team of teachers and principals promotes a more authentic form of collaboration and hopefully creates a more open line of communication for when professional development is implemented back at the schools. Additionally,

TABLE 16.1.   Think Aloud: Getting Starting With Aligning the Common Core State Standards to my Instructional Practice

Goal	How will I accomplish this goal?	Who will help in reaching this goal?	Necessary resources (time and materials)	How will I assess my progress?	What evidence will indicate growth?	Notes

working together fosters a more positive culture in the workplace and places a value on everyone's role in the professional development process.

Another change from the old model to the new, as a result of my DiP work, was the inclusion of two components to enhance collaboration amongst the group as well as time to reflect and enhance what was already learned. First, on-site coaching, and second, an online learning platform. Both proved to be successful for the teachers in their efforts to turnkey the professional development to colleagues.

Onsite coaching was provided to each of the three schools on a weekly basis. A university professor was assigned to each school and worked with the group during a mutually arranged planning period. Since the school days are filled with a plethora of teacher commitments and differing schedules, most meetings took place before the school day started. It worked best at a time when teachers were contractually obligated to be there but students had not yet arrived. The onsite coaching sessions were an opportunity for teachers to talk about how they would convey the information from the meetings to their colleagues. The principals were not present at these sessions. Time was spent on discourse addressing implementation challenges and ways to overcome them. Teachers seemed to really enjoy this informal, unstructured, and safe atmosphere where questions could be answered and plans could be thought out. Often times, the university professor brought supplemental materials to address items of interest. The materials ranged from articles focused on the Common Core shifts, additional research by the speakers who presented or information regarding effective processes to turn key information to colleagues or what successful professional development looks like. In addition, the fact that the university professor was not associated with the school, in any way, created a safe haven for teachers if they wanted to vent and/or ask for judgment-free advice.

The online platform was the second add-on that promoted communication and collaboration amongst the teachers and principals. Incorporating online learning communities and effective use of technology into this professional development initiative served multiple purposes. First, online professional learning communities provided a virtual environment for teachers, principals, and university professors to engage in an ongoing professional learning without time and space barriers. Participation in the online learning community provided everyone not only the opportunity to engage in a continued professional learning that was essential to perfecting their craft, but also an opportunity to experience effective instructional strategies that they can transfer to their teaching practices and in their work as professional development providers (Dede, 2006). Second, through participation in the online professional learning community, teachers learned valuable technology skills such as effective use of learning management systems and web-conferencing solutions to facilitate learning communities within their own schools.

The final major change that the CCA incorporated was the inclusion of a culminating one-week summer institute. The goal was to have all participants leave with a concrete professional development plan to implement in their schools the following fall. As a result of the CCA, 47 teachers and 3 principals attended 30 hours of professional development workshops, over 15 hours of onsite coaching with a university professor, and over 50 hours of engaging in an online professional learning community, all focused on learning about how to tackle the Common Core State Standards shift which addresses *regular practice with complex texts and their academic language.* With that amount of work under each of their belts, they now had to create a plan to turnkey this information.

The first day of the institute was focused mostly on process. A large portion of the day was spent engaged in dialogue regarding professional development experiences in which each of the participants had participated. The outcome of the discussion was a list of concrete ideas as to what they wanted their professional development to look like (and what it should not look like). From there, school groups worked with their plethora of materials they had gained throughout the school year. Each group had the freedom to produce professional development materials that would meet the needs of their individual schools. It was authentic and organic, each different in its own way.

Everyone was engaged and on task for the week. The conversation was meaningful and important. While everyone did not agree 100% of the time, fair and trusting dialogue led them to acceptable compromises. School groups worked endlessly to create professional development experiences for their colleagues back at their schools. The final products were shared on the last day with the entire group. Learning was still occurring at this point as teachers were strengthening their own work with what they were hearing from other school groups.

The CCA feedback was overwhelmingly positive. A majority of the members felt the workshop sessions were where they gained a lot of content knowledge for their work as professional development providers. They felt having the same group attend over the course of the entire series was also beneficial as they created bonds with their school teams. Equally important was the fact that each of the school had their principals in attendance as well. We often heard about experiences where teachers attended other professional development workshops but nothing came out of them due to the fact that they did not have principal support. Furthermore, they found themselves talking about the work back at their schools, whether in the faculty lounge or passing in the hallway. Participants were engaged in this work in and out of the time they spent with us.

The teachers also reported the onsite coaching was invaluable for various reasons. First, the opportunity to reflect and debrief the professional development workshops in an effort to gain a deeper understanding was reposted to be instrumental in their work. Secondly, with the creation of a safe and judgment-free atmosphere, they were able to work through issues and concerns. Thirdly, the timing of the sessions occurring before the school day began was favorable for most. The educators liked the quiet time before the kids came in as well as the fact they were not rushing to drop off and/or pick up during a prep time. Finally, since the group's roles varied by grade level, this was a guaranteed opportunity for everyone to see each other once a week.

The online platform continued the professional conversation. It also kept a permanent record of ideas, questions, and conversations, which can be more difficult during face-to-face meetings. To this day, teachers and principals have access to the platform should they wish to retrieve any information or refresh themselves with the materials. This component allowed for deeper conversation as well. Working online sanctioned more honest conversation, at times. It encouraged significant and critical dialogue that may not necessarily happen in a face-to-face meeting.

In the end, the work was meaningful, relevant and set up in a way that it could be implemented and sustained. The feedback we have heard since the year ended has been that professional development experiences have been occurring at participating schools as a result of the work from this model. The CCA has been successful in initiating a design where teachers and principals are able to learn relevant educational information in an environment that is set up to foster critical thinking, communication, and collaboration within its participants. The most significant impetus for this model came directly from my Doctorate in Education program that guided me to examine a problem in practice. Moving forward, my goal is to continue to inquire into complex problems in our professional practice and work toward using evidence to improve the practices that surround us as educators.

REFERENCES

Cochran-Smith, M., Lytle, S. L. (1999). Relationships of knowledge and practice: Teacher learning in communities. *Review of Research in Education, 24*, 249–305.

Creswell, J. W. (1998). *Qualitative inquiry and research design: Choosing among five traditions.* Thousand Oaks, CA: Sage.

Darling-Hammond, L. (1996). The quiet revolution, rethinking teacher development. *Educational Leadership, 44*(3), 26–41.

Darling-Hammond, L., Andree, A., Richardson, N., Wei, R. C., & Orphanos, S. (2009). *Professional learning in the learning profession: A status report on teacher development in the U.S. and Abroad.* Dallas, TX: National Staff Development Council.

Dede, C. (Ed.). (2006). *Online professional development for teachers: Emerging models and methods.* Cambridge, MA: Harvard Education Press.

DuFour, R., DuFour R., Eaker, R., & Many, T. (2006). *Learning by doing: A handbook for professional learning communities at work* (2nd ed.). Bloomington, IN: Solution Tree Press.

Durant, J., & Frost, D. (2003). Teacher leadership: rationale, strategy, and impact. *School Leadership and Management, 23*(2), 173–186.

Fullan, M. (2001). *Leading in a culture of change.* San Francisco: Jossey Bass.

Fullan, M. (2006). *The new meaning of educational change* (4th ed). New York: Teachers College.

Harwell, S. H. (2003, July). *Teacher professional development: It's not an event, it's a process.* CORD Communications, Inc.

Katzenmeyer, M., & Moller, G. (2001). *Awakening the sleeping giant: Helping teachers develop as leaders.* Thousand Oaks, CA: Corwin Press.

Pancucci. (2007). *Train the trainer: The bricks in the learning scaffold of professional development* (Manuscript submitted for publication). Ontario, Canada: Brock University St. Catherines.

Patton, M. Q. (2008). *Utilized focused evaluation: The new century text* (4th ed.). Thousand Oaks, CA: Sage Publications Inc.

Spillane, J. P., & Louis, K. S. (2002). School improvement processes and practices: Professional learning for building instructional capacity. *Yearbook of the National Society for the Study of Education, 101*, 83–104.

Wasley, P. (1991). *Teachers who lead: The rhetoric of reform and the realities of Practice.* New York: Teachers College Press.

CHAPTER 17

REFLECTIONS OF DISSERTATION IN PRACTICE (DiP) RESEARCH

The Reacculturation Experiences of First-Generation College Students with Undecided Majors

Tracey Glaessgen and Cynthia MacGregor

Reflecting upon the transformative orientation in May 2013 for the University of Missouri's educational leadership doctoral program, I can vividly recall feelings of excitement, anxiety, and wonder. I soon learned from my advisor, Dr. Cynthia MacGregor, that my cohort would be the first to fully implement a Dissertation in Practice (DiP) model, a model that broke from the traditional dissertation model (MacGregor & Fellabaum, 2016). Honestly, at the time, I did not fully comprehend the impact this model would have on my personal and professional life.

The purpose of this chapter is to explore the impact of the newly implemented University of Missouri Statewide Cooperative Program in Educational Leadership model. The chapter begins with the significance of the Education Doctorate, both from my personal and professional perspective. The bilingual intentionality of the program, which includes bridging the PK–12 and higher education arenas of practice along with the scholarly-practitioner role, is discussed. Then, I provide

Exploring the Impact of the Dissertation in Practice, pages 253–268.

an overview of my DiP, which includes setting, problem of practice, conceptual framework, research questions, methodology, and findings. The influence of the DiP on my roles as an educational leader and scholar, as well as on the organization, is presented next. The chapter concludes with future implications for my continued work as a scholarly-practitioner.

SIGNIFICANCE OF THE EDUCATION DOCTORATE

Working at a university has afforded me an opportunity to constantly surround myself with endless learning opportunities. Whether it is attending faculty members' book readings or watching a theatrical play performed by students, I am constantly learning. Because these experiences put me in the role of a passive learner, I wanted to recapture the role of an active learner. The following section recounts my desire, once again, to become an active learner as I detail the significance of the education doctorate from a personal and professional perspective.

Personal

As a graduate teaching assistant in the English department, I taught composition courses, served as a writing consultant in a writing center, and assisted the Director of Composition while I studied Rhetoric and Composition. During that time, I had contemplated pursuing a PhD in Rhetoric and Composition; however, upon facing the harsh reality of the lack of tenure-track positions, I opted instead to explore advising and instructional non-tenure track jobs at the university and local community college. After one year of teaching various composition courses as a per course instructor at both the university and local community college, I received a full-time position as an academic advisor working with students who were undecided with their academic major selection. At times, though, I regretted my decision not to pursue a PhD, not because of the possibility of perhaps someday landing a tenure-track teaching position but because I missed being a part of the academic conversation. While I could listen to faculty members speak of their research projects, I did not have much to contribute; I yearned to join the conversation of scholars (Bartholomae, 1985), but I did not view myself as a theoretical researcher. The prospect of studying theory without actually having a practical use for it did not meet my pragmatic nature. Several years later, a colleague told me about the Cooperative Doctorate Program with the University of Missouri (MU) in Educational Leadership and Policy Analysis. I was intrigued.

Learning more, I realized that the program was designed "to integrate theory and practice in a real world context to enhance the professional preparation of educational leaders" (MacGregor & Fellabaum, 2016, p. 55). The thought of attending doctoral classes while working full time was simultaneously relieving and stressful. Due to the program's mission, students were encouraged to work in an educational setting, which would serve as their laboratory of practice (MacGregor & Fellabaum, 2016), thus allowing for an intertwined nature of theory and practice. As I listened to phrases such as "inquiry as practice" and "problem of practice" I did not quite grasp the concept of performing research within my job in order to make data-driven decisions. While I was grateful that I could still keep my job, I knew it would not be an easy feat to work full time while undergoing the rigor of this doctoral program. However, an opportunity not only to gain research skills that could readily be applied to my job and inform my practice, but also one that would allow me to join the academic conversation, solidified my decision to apply. Unknowingly, I had embraced the program's bilingual intentionality (Mac-Gregor & Smith, 2015).

Daunting. That is the word I would use to describe how I felt when I looked at the Summer One syllabus, which was kicked off with Pre-July homework. I took a deep breath and calmed myself as I held onto the words my advisor used to describe the program's intensity: "complicate thinking to simplify understanding." For someone who is more comfortable being in charge of a situation instead of not, I instantly knew, for myself, I would need to trust the people, the process, and the program.

Professional

The MU educational doctorate is a statewide cohort model, which means each of the five partnering institutions' regional sites has its students taking the same courses taught by the regional site coordinator and/or other faculty members during the two years for the fall and spring semesters. During July, all students in a statewide cohort convene at the home campus in Columbia, Missouri. Cohort students say "Summer One" or "Fall Two" as a means of referring to the six semesters of coursework. The two-year curriculum is designed by the statewide instructional team and incorporates four crucial themes: leadership theory and practice, organizational analysis, educational policy, and content and context of learning. These curriculum topics were purposely selected to heighten students' understanding of educational leadership with assignments designed to help students transfer coursework learning to their actual practice (MacGregor & Fellabaum, 2016).

The collaborative and individual assignments were purposely developed to build upon students' growing areas of knowledge, leading to the culminating individual project: the DiP. Each semester, students benefitted from both individual and collaborative assignments as they progressed through the curriculum (Lei, Gorelick, Short, Smallwood, & Wright-Porter, 2011). The majority of the individual assignments were intended to assist students to look at their organization through the lens of a scholar-practitioner, that is, to conduct research that informs practice. This sense of bilingual intentionality was at the crux of assignments because "scholars and practitioners need to become bilingual, learning to communicate in the language of the other. The research of scholarly practitioners needs to be disseminated in publications read by other practitioners AND in publications read by scholars" (MacGregor & Smith, 2015, p. 303).

From The Carnegie Project on the Education Doctorate (CPED), the University of Missouri has incorporated its conceptual design (CPED Initiative, 2016) and allows students not only to improve their practice but also to contribute to scholarship by becoming scholarly practitioners (MacGregor & Fellabaum, 2016). As a result, my DiP is not the traditional five-chapter dissertation, which typically includes Introduction, Literature Review, Methodology, Findings, and Discussion. Instead, this DiP model includes six components (i. e., Introduction, Practitioner Setting, Scholarly Review, Contribution to Practice, Contribution to Scholarship, and Scholarly-Practitioner Reflection). Unlike the traditional five-chapter dissertation, this DiP model has no Methodology chapter; rather, the methods are summarized in three other places, which include the Introduction, Contribution to Practice, and Contribution to Scholarship. The Findings chapter is no longer separate; the findings are presented in the dissemination-ready pieces, i. e., Contribution to Practice and Contribution to Scholarship. The Scholarly Review (Literature Review) is one of two "context" chapters; the second of which is the Practitioner Setting. Thus, the DiP model at the University of Missouri has two contexts, scholarly and practitioner; it has two output ready pieces designed to return to the two contexts.

For individual assignments, I seized the opportunity to look at problems of practice within my department. Notably, each semester, as expectations increased for greater data collection and problem-solving abilities, I noticed that my own abilities to deliver also increased. I was no longer grappling, as my advisor forecasted, to complicate my thinking to simplify my understanding; I was internalizing the ability to look at situations through different frames to achieve a greater awareness and understanding (Bolman & Deal, 2008). With each passing semester of coursework, I was becoming more prepared for the DiP .

Yet another intentional decision of this cohort model is the student composition. Unlike some cohort models that only admit students from either PK–12 or higher education, MU comprises a mix of both students. I had never worked in PK–12, nor ever had any desire to, so how could this cohort mix possibly be helpful, I wondered. By the end of Summer One, I could definitely see the benefit of the PK–20 cohort model because it "allows students to gain a broader understanding of educational systems across the lifespan" (MacGregor & Fellabaum, 2016, p. 58). As a higher education professional, I have been guilty of thinking high schools should do more to prepare students for college. Listening to my cohort members, some of whom worked in PK–12, I was impressed with their level of competence, knowledge, and passion for student success. It was then I realized one of the great strengths of this program was the PK–20 cohort design because it built a bridge between PK–12 and higher education with its bilingual intentionality. As someone who works mostly with first-year college students, I have found learning more about the PK–12 educational system, particularly the nuances of high school administration, to be especially beneficial to understanding my students' needs.

Personally and professionally, I felt prepared from the coursework and cohort design to tackle the culminating assignment: the DiP. After having written numerous papers, I felt that my writing skills had sharpened, and I was back in the familiar and comfortable role as a student. Analyzing articles for their research and data collection merit along with examining for bias and pre-drawn conclusions prepared me for writing a well-developed and well-supported DiP. I had learned to embrace the bilingual intentionality of this program's design by learning with, and from, PK–20 practitioners as I began to conduct my own scholarly research with a problem of practice.

MY DISSERTATION IN PRACTICE (DiP)

Summer One kicked off with what the instructional team called a Wicked Problem. This wicked problem (Grint, 2005) was essentially a very complicated problem of educational practice, and as part of the collaborative learning setting, each small team, comprised of PK–20 students, would have the same wicked problem to solve and, subsequently, present their solution to classmates. It became obvious that wicked problems are just that: wicked. Keeping that thought in mind as I reviewed possible problems of practice within my university and department, I knew I wanted to eventually select a dissertation topic I felt strongly about, mainly because there would be no easy solution to this problem of practice. For this reason, when the decision time arrived, I selected first-generation students who were undecided with their academic major. This topic served as a confluence for several interest areas: my own first-generation status, my former position as an academic advisor for undecided students, and the university's focus upon trying to improve the retention rate of first-generation students. The following sections include an overview of the setting, the problem of practice, conceptual framework, research questions, methodology, and findings.

Setting

Originally founded as a college in the midwest to prepare students to become teachers, the university is a public, comprehensive, residential, selective admissions institution with over 20,000 students who attend its seven colleges and graduate college. The university has approximately 4,000 employees with a similar amount of students living in residential housing. In addition, there are smaller campuses located regionally in close proximity and an overseas campus. The university provides additional educational opportunities, such as distance learning and study away, based on community needs. With a university mission "to develop educated persons," it received a designation in public affairs, which includes the three pillars of ethical leadership, cultural competence, and community engagement.

Problem of Practice

The university has a required first-year seminar course, a course that is taken by all students who have fewer than 24 hours post-high school and/or are not in the Honors College. This two-credit hour course has three goals, which include academic skill development, an understanding of the university's Public Affairs mission, and awareness of campus resources, to assist students with their transition to university life; all course goals were derived with the singular purpose to improve retention, as first-year retention is particularly important (Tinto, 1999). Within the last two years, the university has focused on first-generation students' retention rates because they are lower than continuing-generation students. The university defines first-generation student as having neither parent graduated from a four-year institution. One support option created by the university was to offer specialized sections of the first-year seminar course for first-generation students based upon the college of their declared or undecided major status. For fall 2015, 35% of first-time undergraduate students self-identified as first generation.

Prior to my current position, I worked as an academic advisor for undecided students, so I knew the various processes they go through to select their academic majors, ranging from extremes of thoroughly conducting career exploration, to wishing for an epiphany to strike, to leaving the university due to an unclear direction. I could not help but wonder what additional complications first-generation students must have as they attempt to navigate their way through an unknown environment combined with the lack of family knowledge of how the academic major selection works. As part of a course assignment, I conducted a literature review, which revealed very limited research focused upon the first-generation, undecided student. From the lessons learned in this doctoral program, I began to review enrollment reports, so I knew institutional retention data revealed undecided students have lower retention rates than declared students as well as first-generation students have lower retention rates than continuing-generation students. Similar to the literature review results, the university did not have a report already created to track the retention rate of first-generation, undecided students. To me, it just made sense if students were uncertain about the academic environment, coupled with a lack of academic direction, they would be less likely to remain at the university. Working with one of my DiP committee members who had access to generating new enrollment management reports, I confirmed my suspicion: Over a three-year period, first-generation, undecided students had the lowest retention rate in comparison to first-generation, declared students, to continuing-generation, declared students, and to continuing-generation, undecided students. I had identified my problem of practice.

Conceptual Framework

With my problem of practice identified, I needed to select a framework for my research study. During Spring Two, I became reacquainted with a favorite book,

Collaborative Learning: Higher Education, Interdependence, and the Authority of Knowledge by Kenneth Bruffee (1999). As a former master's student studying Rhetoric and Composition and working in a university writing center, I immediately became a fan of Bruffee because much of writing center theory is based upon his notion of collaborative learning and the social construction of knowledge. I had previously observed parallels between writing center consultants and academic advisors; both writing center consultants and academic advisors make suggestions, but the students make the decisions. Rereading the assigned pages of Bruffee, I thought about how my first-year students had to reacculturate to the university's expectations. With probable framework selected, I met with my own DiP advisor for feedback and mutually agreed my DiP would be framework driven, which would then influence the research questions and data analysis.

The purpose, then, of my DiP was to understand better the reacculturation experiences of first-generation students who are undecided about their academic major as they transition to being a part of a university and how universities may better support them in this transition. Applying Bruffee's reacculturation (1999) concept allowed me to understand students' experiences as they attempted to gain access to a culture that is new and unfamiliar to them. Prior to entering college, many first-generation students had access to family members (who most likely had some familiarity with the PK–12 educational system) to assist in the transition from different levels of school. Upon entering the unfamiliar territory of higher education, many first-generation students had to reacculturate to this unknown academic environment alone. Embracing the scholar-practitioner bilingual intentionality (MacGregor & Smith, 2015), I took a framework that is scholarly driven not only so practitioners may better understand students' reacculturation (Bruffee, 1999) experiences but also so I can contribute to the scholarly conversation by producing work that is read by scholars.

Research Questions and Methodology

The research questions that guided the study were (with italicized words derived from Bruffee's framework):

1. How do first-generation, undecided students:
    a. *Reacculturate* to the unknown academic environment of a university?
    b. Gain access to a university's *culture*?
    c. Select *translators* within a university?
    d. Form *transition communities* within a university?
    e. Use academic advisors as *translators*?

2. What support should universities offer to assist first-generation, undecided students as they *reacculturate* to their academic environment?

Data collection included observations from 9 advising appointments, writings and questionnaires from 21 former first-year seminar students in the specialized first-generation section for undecided majors, interviews from 14 former first-year seminar students in the specialized first-generation section for undecided majors, and one focus group with five students. From my classroom observations, workshops, and other first-generation student related meetings, I maintained a practitioner's log to jot field notes (Emerson, Fretz, & Shaw, 2011).

Summary of Findings

Though Spring One included a course on qualitative research and subsequent group assignment, I had to independently gather my own research for my DiP. Thankfully, coursework included writing interview questions, conducting an interview/focus group, observing meetings, taking field notes, coding, and transcribing. With this experience, I felt prepared to conduct my own qualitative data collection, analyze the data, and articulate the findings (Drake & Heath, 2011).

Most first-generation, undecided students reported very stressful transition experiences; these included a high level of stress initiated by college applications and financial aid applications. Stress also resulted from repeatedly being asked what their major is and uncertainty of university language. Becoming comfortable both within and beyond the residence halls was extremely important, which included decorating their rooms with reminders of the life they left as well as finding their classrooms. A smaller number of students joined organizations or other university-sanctioned activities, such as band or athletics.

Acclimating, or reacculturating, to the university with the help from continuing-generation and/or sophomore roommates provided easy and convenient access to information for some students. The majority of students found the specialized first-generation, undecided section of the required first-year seminar course to be a reassuring and supportive environment, an environment that also provided a key to unlock some of the mystical surroundings. Students did not view their academic advisors as helpful in their integration to the university, mainly because of uncertainty in advisors' roles. Finally, this repeated pattern of uncertainty was continued in students' thoughts on additional campus support.

Ironically, while I suspected that first-generation, undecided students felt some level of stress during their first semester, I have to admit I was surprised as to the frequency the word *stressed* appeared in my data collection. Though I worked as an advisor for undecided students, some of whom were first-generation, I never thought to inquire into my advisees' overall understanding of the college culture. Fortunately, in the last two years, students who self-identify as first-generation or continuing-generation have an indicator on the university's advising notes system, so advisors now have the information, without having to ask.

DISSERTATION IN PRACTICE (DiP) INFLUENCE ON ROLE AS AN EDUCATIONAL LEADER

As I was writing my dissertation proposal, I had to contemplate what information would be the most relevant for my organization to know. Additionally, I began to consider what format would be the most useful to my organization when I wrote section two, Practitioner Setting. This section included two important overviews: organizational setting and leadership analysis. The information I included in these two sections led to my selected audience and purpose as well as dissemination plan. Since part of my DiP topic involved academic advising, I selected the top university-wide advising committee, a committee that included advisors and administrators. My purpose was to garner their support for ways to improve first-generation student retention. Consulting with my advisor, I decided upon a complete practitioner's report as my contribution to practice. This report would include problem of practice, conceptual framework, research questions, methodology, findings, and recommendations. Pragmatically speaking, since I also knew that many people do not have time to review a full report, I decided to create a two-page executive summary.

After my DiP proposal hearing, I discussed ad nauseam with my advisor my data collection process in preparation for the Institutional Review Board application process. I planned to conduct interviews and focus groups with my former first-year seminar students and with students with whom I had no prior relationship. Once I received Institutional Review Board approval, I became particularly diligent in following ethical practices and procedures so my student participants would trust the research process (Wurtz, 2011). Further, I was even more committed to honoring my students' experiences by encapsulating their voices throughout the DiP because I realized my students trusted me when I said their experiences would help improve the experiences of future students. Northouse (2013) purported that authentic leaders form a relationship based upon trust with others. I trusted my students to share true stories and experiences with me; in turn, my students trusted me. For the students who were not in my first-year seminar course, I did not have the opportunity to forge an authentic relationship. Though I did try to clearly explain my research purpose and their important role in it, I am not confident the students whom I observed and conducted a focus group with would say they trusted me. The conversations did not yield as rich (Merriam, 2009) of data as with the students whom I already knew.

From my coursework and DiP research and writing, I have learned it is essential to review decision-making processes and related data that could be used to make those decisions because if the selected data is not relevant or current, using it as a basis for the decision will likely provide erroneous results (Davenport, 2009/2013). Additionally, Hammond, Keeney, and Raiffa (2006/2013) encouraged leaders to maintain self-awareness so as not to anchor their decisions with premature judgments and decisions. Accordingly, Lasley (2009) argued that the most effective decision-making interweaves a balanced approach between data and content; therefore, data that has been collected, analyzed, and processed, should lead to a data-driven decision, and consequently, a continuation of evidence-based practice (Kowalski, 2009). I have heightened my ability not only to ground decisions in practice or theory but also to articulate the reasoning for my decisions. During my data collection research and subsequent analysis, I learned that first-generation, undecided students were not likely to attend university-sanctioned events without the encouragement of their friends, particularly sophomores or continuing-generation students.

As I was writing the Contribution to Practice section, I realized a previous chapter on organizational setting and the key constituents played a pivotal role in the recommendations that I made. Further, by situating this DiP within my own organization, I had the opportunity to analyze my surroundings with more of a critical eye and to spot elements of adaptive leadership, which was the selected leadership framework that I used for my chapter on organizational setting. With new mandates passed down from the federal and state government not to mention from the organization's leadership, it has been extremely useful to embrace adaptive leadership (Northouse, 2016) by asking the questions that most people do not *want* to address but questions that *need* to be asked. Because the organizational structure within the university overlaps, the importance of knowing the influential players (Bolman & Deal, 2008)), may help to bring the recommendations through to fruition. To keep the recommendations as grounded and compelling as possible, I based them upon both my findings and framework. While I had been aware of the importance of ethical decision making and cultural inclusiveness, this DiP process, along with the selected subject matter of first-generation, undecided students, has certainly heightened my appreciation and respect for those aspects. Fostering an environment in which questions are welcome as well as exploring varying viewpoints has become even more important to me, mostly because I find enjoyment in the process of critical thinking and problem solving.

Under my advisor's guidance, I spent an exorbitant amount of time selecting the executive summary content. I needed to demonstrate my ability as a scholar but also present the information in a clear and succinct form that practitioners would understand. When I shared my DiP with my committee, their comments also centered upon the importance of making the executive summary an independent document yet one that would meet the bilingual intentionality of both scholars and practitioners on the committee.

Audience awareness. Such a simple phrase but I would be remiss if I did not discuss the importance of knowing one's audience since the Contribution to Practice section is disseminated back to the organization from where the problem of practice originated. A paradox exists for students with the Contribution to Practice: for students who have a good relationship with their organization's leadership, then their findings and recommendations, regardless of content, may be better received, and students who have a questionable relationship with their organization's leadership may have to put extra thought into their information delivery. For me, in the ten years I have worked at my institution, I have developed strong relationships with faculty and staff members across campus, so I hope my research and subsequent recommendations will be well received.

My practitioner's report and executive summary were written with the university-wide advising committee in mind, a committee that I am also a member. At the next designated meeting, I plan to distribute my executive summary and provide an overview of my research. Considering the committee is comprised of academic advisors and administrators, I anticipate that my findings will be of direct interest as much of it is relatable and beneficial for all advisors to know. Should any committee member have an interest in reading the report in entirety, I will send it to him/her. Further, one of my recommendations pertaining to advising student awareness can be achieved through the subcommittee that I chair.

DISSERTATION IN PRACTICE (DiP) INFLUENCE ON ROLE AS A SCHOLAR

Bruffee (1999) posited, "Good talk begets good thought" (p. 134); these conversations with classmates, instructors, and committee members helped me to continually reflect on my own learning and my role in other people's learning. Interestingly, I knew before I even started this program I viewed learning as a socially constructed activity (Merriam & Bierema, 2014), one in which knowledge is socially constructed, in part, by the conversations, whether with other people, self-dialogue, or the text, that I engage. Throughout this DiP process, I have had conversations with my advisor, my supervisor, my colleagues whose interests are also focused upon first-generation initiatives, and the students with whom I conducted research. These conversations have, as Bruffee (1999) theorized, raised my level of thinking and knowledge construction. By engaging in conversations focused upon a mutual topic of interest with other individuals, my DiP is a tangible view of socially constructed knowledge that may not have been produced otherwise. I am mindful of Hannah Arendt's (2003) telling quote: "For excellence, by definition, the presence of others is always required" (p. 198).

For someone who had never written a journal article, I found the process to be quite time-consuming, with multiple revisions, yet also enjoyable. Due to the program's structure, I had been thinking about the submission-ready journal article for quite some time. As part of the proposal hearing, I had to write a Plan for Contribution to Scholarship, in which I selected a target, refereed journal, and then provided rationale for the target journal, outline of contents, and plan for submission. Because I knew the selected organization, I had determined my research study should be of direct interest to their audience of advisors and advising administrators, plus, as an unpublished author, I liked the fact that the review board provides constructive comments for any journal submissions. Unlike some journals that have a standard outline of contents required for submission, this selected journal did not, so I reviewed a handful of articles with similar methodology and research focus to ascertain a better idea of what content to include.

In a way, the actual writing process was yet another round of "complicating my thinking to simplify my understanding," but this time, I had to juggle the ability to explain the nuances of my research focus but simplify my writing to make it accessible to any advising audience. To adhere to the journal submission process, I had to write an abstract, provide authors' notes, and references used; all of these journal requirements were included in my DiP to make it as disseminated-ready as possible. I even created an author account, so following my DiP defense I could easily submit.

Notably, the first book that provided me with a basic understanding of the differences between a scholar and practitioner is Stephen North's (1987) *The Making of Knowledge in Composition: Portrait of an Emerging Field.* North (1987) described the similarities and differences among theoretical approaches, including the scholar, researcher, and practitioner to rhetoric and composition, and I readily identified with the following practitioner description: "Practitioners reflect, they talk, they read" (p. 45). Further, practitioners viewed it as permissible to accept an "informed intuition and trial and error" (North, 1987, p. 45) as reason enough to do something. While I still believe a practitioner is an extension of a social constructionist point of view, I have learned through the DiP process that simply having a feeling that something is right is not enough. Within a university environment and surrounded by researchers and scholars who can actually support their positions with theory and research, practitioners need to perform their own research to support their intuitions. Thus, the scholarly practitioner approach allows practitioners, such as myself, to gain the ability to make data-driven decisions (Petrides, 2003) to improve their practice and defend those decisions from a foundation of scholarship.

As such, I have had the learning opportunity to identify a problem of practice, in this case, the higher attrition rate of first-generation, undecided students. I must admit that I, initially, made the assumption that first-generation, undecided students had a higher attrition rate than first-generation, declared majors or continuing generation, undecided majors and continuing generation, declared majors, but I did not have the evidence to make a valid statement. I was simply, as North (1987) would propose, operating on an informed intuition because it just seemed to make sense. With the assistance of my DiP committee, I can now state with accuracy that first-generation, undecided students had a higher attrition rate for the past three years.

Conducting a literature review not only provided a comprehensive understanding of my targeted population but also allowed my findings to be anchored. The selection of a framework served as a foundation for my data collection process; from the qualitative approach to the semi-structured interview questions (Merriam, 2009) to the a priori coding (Creswell, 2013; Saldaña, 2016) and in vivo coding (Saldaña, 2016), my DiP is framework driven and methodologically sound. Writing a separate and detailed findings section, though now an optional component of the MU model, ensured that I thoroughly analyzed my data collection.

My understanding of the qualitative research approach allowed me to apply the methods to an educational problem of practice in order to fill a research gap. Learning to combine theory, framework, and practice-oriented knowledge (MacGregor & Fellabaum, 2016) to a problem of practice and then creating a submission-ready article provided an opportunity for me to contribute to existing research. Ultimately, the DiP has taught me how to make meaningful, research-based contributions to my organization and to disseminate the knowledge to different audiences, including practitioners and scholars.

DISSERTATION IN PRACTICE (DIP) IMPACT ON THE ORGANIZATION

For chapter four of the DiP, I had to select an audience for my contribution to practice. Giving it careful thought, I decided to share my findings with the Provost's Academic Advising Council in the form of an executive summary, to allow for brevity, and a full report to allow for the inclusion of detailed information. I selected the Provost's Academic Advising Council because there is university-wide membership of faculty, staff, and administrators who are all directly involved with advising. Since I have served on and previously chaired this committee, I determined that this audience would be the most appropriate and the most interested to learn the results from my research. Ultimately, I wanted an audience that would be invested in improving support for first-generation students with undecided majors in the hopes the council would support actions that were derived from the study's findings. For the practitioner's report, my advisor and I decided to include an Introduction, Purpose of Study, Conceptual Framework, Research Questions, Design of the Research Study, Findings, and Recommendations. Because my advisor and I felt that the executive summary would be more widely read than the practitioner's report, I limited it to a two-page, front and back, handout.

An exciting aspect of this DiP model is seeing the direct and immediate contribution to my institution in the form of implemented recommendations. For instance, during my scholarly review and data collection, I learned families could benefit from extra-institutional support. Upon discussing an idea with the new student orientation program leaders, I volunteered to provide a family and student breakout session focusing on first-generation students and support families could provide. This recommendation has been implemented, and I am providing first-generation students and their families with an overview of the college culture and highlighting particularly useful campus resources. After I share the full report and recommendations, hopefully more improvements can be made.

FUTURE IMPLICATIONS

Since I successfully, and very recently, defended my DiP, I am extremely thrilled to have a seat at the planning table (Cervero & Wilson, 2006) with five university key players; all of whom will be attending a summer institute to focus upon increased institutional support for first-generation students. While I do not know the exact level of implementation of my recommendations from my dissemination-ready practitioner piece, I plan to share my research with the summer institute group. Upon being, as Donald Schon (1983) described, a reflective practitioner, I will create an assignment to have my students attend several university-sanctioned events early in the fall semester since I learned first-generation, undecided students tend not to participate in student organizations and campus events. Pertaining to the dissemination-ready journal article, my status as a published scholar is pending, based on the peer-review of my journal article submission. Since I did not harvest all of my findings within my journal article, I may even work on another article for a different scholarly audience.

As a result of the professional relationships made during this program, I plan to collaborate with a high school principal to focus on the transition students face from high school to college. This collaboration will be particularly insightful because the research will be from two different perspectives: high school principal and first-year seminar administrator. This partnership with high school leadership in order to better understand students' transition and reacculturation processes is an example of the continued bilingual intentionality of this cohort model as we will continue to bridge the gap between PK–12 and higher education while simultaneously bridging the gap between scholars and practitioners. Even better, as we complicate our thinking to simplify our understanding of students' reacculturation experiences, we can make recommendations and improvements to our current practices and then share positive results through scholarship.

From a broader and overarching perspective, the MU cohort model will continue to benefit students, including me, beyond DiP completion through the newly-formed alumni association (MacGregor & Fellabaum, 2016). This alumni association provides an opportunity to network with students throughout PK–20. In addition, to celebrate the twentieth year of the MU cohort model, Summer 2017 will serve as the inaugural statewide research alumni conference. This planned annual conference will provide opportunities to foster conversations with current and former students while embracing the bilingual intentionality of PK–12 and higher education as well as scholars and practitioners; further, this conference will provide educational leaders across PK–20 by "improving practice, informing policy, and developing more effective programs. To this end, the conference would ideally focus on disseminating scholarly practitioner research and offering networking opportunities for EdD students and graduates of CPED-affiliated programs" (MacGregor & Fellabaum, 2016, p. 15). I have eagerly volunteered to serve on the conference planning committee.

As I look ahead, it is hard to know where else the knowledge, experience, and confidence gained from the DiP will lead. Perhaps in part due to the dissemination-ready pieces and this new DiP model, my DiP committee has not dissolved upon the completion of my defense. My committee members are still invested in my success. Recommendations are already being implemented. I have made an impact, albeit small at this point, but I am confident the impact will continue to grow. I am now an educational leader who can "speak" multiple languages, including the "language" of not only scholars and practitioners but also across the persistent divide between PK–12 and higher education arenas of practice. My thinking is very complicated while my understanding of wicked educational problems has been greatly simplified.

REFERENCES

Arendt, H. (2003). *The portable Hannah Arendt* (Edited by P. Baehr). New York, NY: Penguin.

Bartholomae, D. (1985). Inventing the university. In M. Rose (Ed.), *When a writer can't write* (pp. 134–165). New York, NY: Guilford Press.

Bolman, L. G., & Deal, T. E. (2008). *Reframing organizations: Artistry, choice, and leadership* (4th ed.). San Francisco, CA: Jossey-Bass.

Bruffee, K. A. (1999). *Collaborative learning: Higher education, interdependence, and the authority of knowledge.* Baltimore, MD: Johns Hopkins University Press.

Cervero, R. M., & Wilson, A. L. (2006). *Working the planning table: Negotiating democratically for adult, continuing, and workplace education.* San Francisco, CA: Jossey-Bass.

CPED Initiative. (2016, June 26). *Design concept definitions.* Retrieved from http://www.cpedinitiative.org/design-concept-definitions

Creswell, J. W. (2013). *Qualitative inquiry and research design: Choosing among five approaches.* Thousand Oaks, CA: Sage.

Drake, P., & Heath, L. (2011). *Practitioner research at doctoral level: Developing coherent research methodologies.* New York, NY: Routledge.

Davenport, T. H. (2013). Making better decisions. In *HBR's 10 must reads on making smart decisions* (pp. 133–143). Boston, MA: Harvard Business Review Press. (Reprint RO911L, Originally published in November 2009)

Emerson, R. M., Fretz, R. I., & Shaw, L. L. (2011). *Writing ethnographic fieldnotes* (2nd ed.). Chicago, IL: University of Chicago Press.

Grint, K. (2005). Problems, problems, problems: The social construction of 'leadership.' *Human Relations, 58,* 1467–1494. doi:10.1177/0018726705061314

Hammond, J. S., Keeney, R. L., & Raiffa, H. (2013). The hidden traps in decision making. In *HBR's 10 must reads on making smart decisions* (pp. 1–19). Boston, MA: Harvard Business Review Press. (Reprint R0601K, Originally published in January 2006)

Kowalski, T. J. (2009). Evidence and decision making in professions. In T. J. Kowalski & T. J. Lasley (Eds.), *Handbook of data-based decision making in education* (pp. 3–19). New York, NY: Routledge.

Lasley, T. J. (2009). Using data to make critical choices. In T. J. Kowalski & T. J. Lasley (Eds.), *Handbook of data-based decision making in education* (pp. 244–258). New York, NY: Routledge.

Lei, S., Gorelick, D., Short, K., Smallwood, L., & Wright-Porter, K. (2011). Academic cohorts: Benefits and drawbacks of being a member of a community of learners. *Education, 131*(3), 497–504.

MacGregor, C., & Fellabaum, J. (2016). Dissertation redesign for scholarly practitioners in educational leadership: Increasing impact through dissemination-ready components. In V. A. Storey & K. A. Hesbol (Eds.), *Contemporary approaches to dissertation development and research methods* (pp. 53–69). Hershey, PA: IGI Global.

MacGregor, C., & Smith, M. (2015). Bridge-building: Can EdD redesign connect scholars and practitioners for social justice? In V. Stead (Ed.), *The education doctorate (EdD): Issues of access, diversity, social justice, and community leadership* (pp. 293–305). New York, NY: Peter Lang Publishing.

Merriam, S. B. (2009). *Qualitative research: A guide to design and implementation* (2nd ed.). San Francisco, CA: Jossey-Bass.

Merriam, S. B., & Bierema, L. L. (2014). *Adult learning: Linking theory and practice.* San Francisco, CA: Jossey-Bass.

North, S. M. (1987). *The making of knowledge composition: Portrait of an emerging field.* Portsmouth, NH: Boynton/Cook Publishers.

Northouse, P. G. (2013). *Leadership: Theory and practice* (6th ed.). Los Angeles, CA: Sage.

Northouse, P. G. (2016). *Leadership: Theory and practice* (7th ed.). Los Angeles, CA: Sage.

Petrides, L. A. (2003). Turning data into decisions. *Business Officer, 37*(5), 25–28.

Saldaña, J. (2016). *The coding manual for qualitative researchers.* Los Angeles, CA: Sage.

Schon, D. A. (1983). *The reflective practitioner: How professionals think in action.* New York, NY: Basic Books.

Tinto, V. (1999). Taking retention seriously: Rethinking the first year of college. *NACADA Journal, 19*(2), 5–9.

Wurtz, K. (2011). Ethical issues affecting human participants in community college research. *Community College Journal of Research and Practice, 35*(4), 301–311.

CHAPTER 18

THE INTENTIONAL GARDENER

Catherine E. Zeisner

Of course there must be lots of Magic in the world, he said wisely one day, but people don't know what it is like or how to make it. Perhaps the beginning is just to say nice things are going to happen until you make them happen. I am going to try and experiment.

—Frances Hodgson Burnett (1911)

In 2013 when sharing my commitment to enroll in Western University's Doctor of Education (EdD) program, superintendents and colleagues expressed their shock. They shifted in their chairs or long pauses were sensed over the phone. They were interested to know why I would attempt a rigorous three-year, expensive, on-line program while just having recovered from cancer, working full time as an elementary school principal, and maintaining a full family life. I explained that I didn't want to sit around anymore while other people told me what to do and how to think. I shared that I wanted to investigate how school principals manage their leadership adversity with resiliency strategies. I wanted to create a legacy of encouraging, supporting, and inspiring the next generation of school leader to cultivate their belief in education and improve student learning.

This chapter will discuss how my EdD and Dissertation in Practice (DiP) have influenced me as a school principal, scholar, and my organization. Also, it describes what capacity I have developed to provide future support for education

Exploring the Impact of the Dissertation in Practice, pages 269–282.
Copyright © 2017 by Information Age Publishing

on a grander, hopefully, more global scale. Written from the perspective of a gardener, I am avoiding the popular "journey" reference when describing learning because *journey* indicates there are a beginning, middle, and end. I explore how the EdD and subsequent DiP provides continual growth opportunities like a garden; hence I have used F. H. Burnett's *The Secret Garden* as an inspirational lens for the chapter. Cycling through seasons, waiting and watching, trying and failing, weeding and harvesting, the EdD and DiP learning experiences allow me to reap what I sow. Just as Burnett's main character was transformed once inside a secret garden, the EdD and DiP has allowed me to unlock knowledge to enhance my organization and develop my leadership capacity.

I am not embarrassed to share that completing a doctoral degree was once located at the top of my "bucket list" in order to prove to my parents that all their hard work and support through the years was worth their struggle. In fact, completing this EdD has been the greatest educational experience for me personally and professional because of the sense of pride I feel in the accomplishment of completion, the knowledge I have acquired and share with fellow leaders, and the hope I have gained for educational systems throughout the world.

INFLUENCING AS A SCHOOL PRACTITIONER

Where you tend a rose, my lad, a thistle cannot grow.
—*Frances Hodgson Burnett (1911)*

Kouzes and Posner (2002) exposed that knowledge is the new economic resource and intellectual capital is no longer supreme. Leaders who get extraordinary things done are those who are right in the middle of human networks developing social capital and building relationships. Similarly, Tennant (2004) wrote about the need for "knowledge workers" to enhance the required new "knowledge economy" (p. 431). Tennant's knowledge worker is described as innovative, flexible, multi-skilled, has the capacity to adapt to change, creative, and a life-long learner. Participation and completion of a DiP allowed me to model Kouzes and Posner's definition of *leadership* and demonstrate Tennant's *worker* in which ordinary people bring forth the best from themselves and others. In particular, Tennant recommended the professional doctorate as the vehicle for "doctoring" the knowledge worker because the programs produce different types of researchers and different types of knowledge (p. 435). Not only would I grow through this experience but my DiP would influence the success of students and leaders across a multitude of school communities, districts, and potentially, Canadian provinces.

Prior to entering the EdD I was frustrated with education and the role of principal, which did not allow me to be a productive or positive school leader due to the numerous constraints of the job. Senge (2006) described these feelings as the lack of understanding regarding one's *purpose* and that I saw myself in a system over which I had little or no influence. I was doing my job, putting in my time, and trying to cope with forces outside of my control. Senge claimed that "small, well-focused actions can sometimes produce significant, enduring improvements" (p. 63). I wanted to tackle the challenge of transforming the role of school principal and Senge reassured that it can be done if you identify where the highest leverage rests. Leverage is defined as "a change which—with a minimum of effort—would lead to lasting, significant improvement" (p. 63). In my professional practice, and through reading and writing about research during the EdD and DiP, Senge's *leverage* would have me learn to see underlying structures rather than events and expand to think in terms of processes of change. Seeking the opportunity to participate in an EdD and complete a DiP allowed me to investigate fresh thinking about increasing the effectiveness in my work and consider the most efficient ways for increasing my influence on student and adult learning (Sparks, 2007).

Favorably, this need for balance between knowledge and action is also captured by Shulman, Golde, Bueschel, and Garabedian (2006) who explained the importance of doctoral students striking equilibrium between the practice of education and the research of education. This balance was modeled while I worked and studied full time allowing me to surround others and myself with my constant learning from coursework and DiP research. Rich dialogue, sharing of resources, and reflection from learning experiences allowed me to document my journey for my school's teachers and staff for over three years. The sharing of my learning didn't wait till I was finished the whole program, I tended and shared my garden's riches season after season.

Firstly, I modeled Shulman et al.'s (2006) explanations through the completion of a DiP that brought forth the best in others by allowing school district employees to participate in doctoral research. Being a participant in my DiP allowed principals, and a superintendent of education, the opportunity to discuss the difficulties associated with the role of school principal. Research participants also had the chance to help create meaning in their professional and personal lives by reflecting on challenging events and resiliency strategies they use to manage adversity in school leadership. Secondly, the DiP 'recommendations' allowed for school districts to reflect on their current practices to support the development of their administrators and aspiring leaders and most importantly, to begin deeper conversations about supportive relationships available to school leaders to manage adversity and develop effective resiliency strategies. Finally, the DiP allowed me the opportunity to turn information into knowledge and improve the role of school principal by providing direction and support during complex educational times based on data from principal colleagues.

Throughout my three years, the conditions to grow and flourish ebbed and flowed because of both personal and professional circumstances. Trying to balance numerous complex needs in my role of principal, unstable political climates, my declining health, and program kinks (due in part to being the university's first cohort of Faculty of Education doctoral students) provided dilemmas to overcome. But, by seeking and receiving the encouragement of key professionals at the university and recognizing my role to provide a voice of my study's partici-pants, led to a spring awakening that reinvigorated my efforts to finish strong.

INFLUENCING AS A SCHOLAR

> Much more surprising things can happen to anyone who, when a disagree-able or discouraged thought comes into his mind, just has the sense to re-member in time and push it out by putting in an agreeable, determinedly courageous one. Two things cannot be in one place.
> —*Frances Hodgson Burnett (1911)*

I experienced great impact personally and professionally through my participa-tion in the full-time EdD program using a cohort model that included 20 fellow students. The cohort structure provided ongoing professor and colleague student support during course work, development of a province-wide professional learn-ing community, and extensive conversations surrounding our thesis research top-ics and capstone projects. Educational leadership literature, conversations, and assignments exposed the cohort during coursework to relevant research and appli-cation of theory into practice. The research and theoretical knowledge progressed into my role as school principal and expanded to other participants' workplaces because of real world application requirements during coursework projects.

Shulman et al. (2006) categorized the EdD as a preparation for managerial and administrative leadership in education that focuses on preparing practitioners who can use existing knowledge to solve educational problems. While I don't anticipate completing another DiP during my career, the knowledge, skills, and values I developed while producing the research will remain invaluable to me as a lead learner. Shulman et al. used the phrase "stewards of the discipline" (p. 27) to describe EdD scholars because Schulman et al. believed they are the future lead-ers who will generate new knowledge, critically protect valuable and useful ideas, and responsibly transform understanding through writing, teaching, and applica-tion. I embody Shulman's et al. label with pride because they asked me to think about education and how to preserve the best of the past, consider how to prepare the next generation, and reminded me that it is my professional responsibility to transcend accomplishment and skills.

My greatest learning transpired during a required ethics course. Understanding the ethical implications of conducting research on human subjects in Canada was an area of education and research I had not experienced. Exploring the Tri-Coun-cil Policy Statement: Ethical Conduct for Research Involving Humans (TCPS 2) was a critical learning piece. In order to speak with principals in an Ontario school board, I was required to obtain ethics approval twice, from the university with whom I was studying and, from the school board in which I was conducting my research. Since my Master's degree was an examination of a program, it did not require these extensive applications to pursue a qualitative study in a school district. In order to gain perspective and experience, I immediately volunteered to be a participant in numerous research projects across Ontario in order to be exposed to letters of consent, letters of information, and the process by which other researchers were maintaining an ethical study. Learning about anonymity, demographic information, collection of additional documents, recording and transcribing data opened my eyes to the serious aspects of ethics in research. I wanted to bring my participants' stories to life and the DiP allowed me to model safe, effective, and ethical research while proving my integrity.

COHORT AS FELLOW GARDENERS

As she came closer to him she noticed that there was a clean fresh scent of heather and grass and leaves about him, almost as if he were made of them. She liked it very much and when she looked into his funny face with the red cheeks and round blue eyes she forgot that she had felt shy.
—Frances Hodgson Burnett (1911)

A very insightful aspect of the doctoral experience occurred when my group project partners no longer came from those working in elementary or secondary educational settings. I stretched out of my comfort zone to choose to work with cohort members from the nursing, police, or non-for-profit sectors. Collaborative group project experiences with these cohort members allowed everyone to offer deep reflection regarding leadership in their organization while providing for fresh perspectives on other's shared challenges. Mezirow (2000) explained that the cohort aspect of a program provides students the opportunities to engage in reflective dialogue about their organizational knowledge and vocation. Also, during the third year, the cohort and small group model allowed for collaborative work between faculty and practitioners to study contemporary problems in leadership on a monthly basis with topics posed by students or timely topics delivered by the faculty. For example, during mock defense experiences, students presented their DiP findings to a small group from their cohort who posed questions for practice and debriefing opportunities. Again, seeking and receiving feedback from a multitude of students provided rich dialogue and feedback from their diverse working and leading perspectives while being supervised by expert university staff and faculty.

Once I had experienced the power of these collaborative opportunities with non-public school educators, I only sought those experiences for the remainder of the program. Listening and learning from cohort colleagues that have further experiences and knowledge of other forms of leadership and learning gave me a revitalized unbiased perspective on my own organization. Sparks (2007) reminds us that "high quality connections with others are a fundamental source of direction and energy for your work and your life. Conversations rich in candor, purposefulness, committed listening, and dialogue can have a profound effect on individuals" (p. 204–205). Because our conversations were so insightful, these members of my cohort were those who I approached through the writing and defending of my DiP because their support and learning were so greatly valued.

In the early 80s, Andersen (1983) was able to differentiate between a PhD, which he described as a scholarly degree, and concluded that it orients toward the conduct of research while an EdD is a professional degree that orients toward practice. Most importantly, the EdD supports the notion of "development of practitioner competencies...candidates can substitute a practical field problem for a research study for the dissertation" (p. 57). Further examination by Bourner and Simpson (2014) in the United Kingdom investigated the fit of action research learning and the learning goals of professional doctorates. Writing a conceptual paper, the authors concluded that action learning can support the learning of students enrolled in professional doctorates by helping them realize three key learnings outcomes: "the capacity to contribute to the advancement of knowledge that is relevant to professional practice; their own personal and professional capabilities as practitioners; and their capacity to bring about change that directly enhances professional practice" (p. 122). My experiences align with their outcomes and have transformed my decision-making abilities, thought processes during planning, and a maturation that was needed in my leadership.

Possibly causing concern is Deering (1998) who wrote about the need to eliminate the Doctor of Education degree. Deering tried to make his case by comparing the EdD to the PhD and framed the later as a superior program because it developed scholars who were skilled in research and teaching while the EdD improved the skills and added to the knowledge of the field-based educator. I can attest to the fact that my experience in Western's EdD program and completion of my DiP allowed for all those skills to be acquired. I am very confident in my research skills because of the rigor of the assignments in my course work, have excellent teaching abilities thanks to face-to-face projects and symposium presentations, and developed deep knowledge from collegial discussions and candor.

HAVING AN ONLINE PRESENCE

I'm lonely," she said. She had not known before that this was one of the things which made her feel sour and cross.
—*Frances Hodgson Burnett (1911)*

While I mostly distinguished my fellow cohort members by their online course discussion postings, the use of Skype, FaceTime, and synchronous sessions through various platforms, brought my colleagues presence into my office and living room on a weekly basis. Tennant (2004) investigated contemporary doctoral education and recognized new versions of learning expanding on the traditional "autonomy" and making way for "self-work" (self-examination, self-reflection, and self-regulation) (p. 437). These structural changes are associated with engaging the "working knowledge" in doctoral education and importantly, the emergence of more diversified and flexible doctoral education experiences. I enjoyed participating in this kind of online method and had chosen to complete my Master's degree in the same fashion. I liked reading and responding to discussion boards on my own timelines due to my busy work schedule and valued the flexibility of the program structure.

In a mixed methods study conducted by Kumar (2014) in Florida, the author measured the impact of a professional doctorate in education. The author described online learning in doctoral programs and the ability for students to have a "social presence" which is the method by which online learners portray themselves online. Kumar stated that "professional doctorates that enable students to study at a distance while embedded in practice can contribute to students' professional growth and bring about change in their local environments" (p. 179). Kumar found that the cohort model allows learners to move through a program and have multiple forms of interactions and opportunities for reflection that could facilitate community building among students. In comparison, a weekly in-class requirement would have contributed great stress to my life knowing that my job of elementary school principal is unpredictable and I might not be able to attend a class due to a crisis at work that would not allow me to leave at a regular time. Luckily, face-to-face contact was made often with several weekend seminars which focused on methodologies, writing techniques, and research. It was a great opportunity to share successes, challenges, distribute group work tasks, and sometimes it allowed for commiseration about workload or an instructor.

My participation and completion of my DiP is one of the most profound things I could have done for myself, but more importantly, for the students and community I serve as school principal. Having deeper knowledge about leadership, knowing I am a more capable leader, and using my learning and results to bring about change for the role of school principal is the greatest gift I could give a school community and district. I have proven my commitment to students' success and get to model the value of being a life-long learner for my colleagues.

MY DISSERTATION IN PRACTICE (DiP)

> Hang in there. It is astonishing how short a time it can take for very wonderful things to happen.
> —*Frances Hodgson Burnett (1911)*

Three years of course work consisting of ten courses, nine textbooks, hundreds of professional readings, videos, on-line discussion postings, forty-four assignments, and work on the DiP culminated all my new learning, habits of mind, and collaborative cohort experiences. As a pinnacle of the EdD, my DiP; *How elementary school principals in an Ontario school board use resiliency strategies to manage adversity in their leadership,* investigated how school principals face multiple adversity challenges in their role requiring resiliency strategies to manage and what supports, professional learning and/or programs exists to help them develop further skills. Importantly, I was able to provide school boards and principal organizations in Ontario, Canada recommendations to support leaders during times of crisis, conflict, and chronic challenges.

Supportively, the structure of the EdD program embeds DiP work almost from the onset of the first course. Purposeful steps and actions were taken by course instructors to align literature, assignments, and readings to begin the development of ideas for students' research projects. Taking full advantage of these opportunities, I began to hone in on my problem of practice and establish a personal library of literature on the topics of resiliency and adversity while submitting assignments using those themes for feedback and further research direction. By the end of the required three years of course work, I had accumulated three of the six chapters towards my DiP allowing for deeper focus on the findings, discussion, and conclusion sections, therefore allowing for a shorter timeline reaching completion.

I often get asked why I chose the topics of adversity and resiliency for my DiP. Interestingly, in a quantitative study by Isaac, Koenigsknecht, Malaney, and Karras (1989), in which they used a survey questionnaire with all doctoral graduates from a major university in the United States, the authors determined that a number of factors influence the selection of a dissertation topic. They explored the student-advisor relationship, differences among fields, and if the dissertation could be viewed as a contribution to the general body of knowledge. Importantly, Isaac et al. wanted to explore these factors in order to help evaluate graduate programs and the contribution of dissertation level research to the general body of research. They concluded that advisor preference, likelihood of publication, effect on job prospects, and trends in the field as central in the selection of the dissertation topic. I can assure you those factors played a minimal role in my topic choice. Kaomea (2001) reminded students to choose a topic that will sustain one's interest over time, one that is not highly political or controversial, and isn't something that you are emotionally invested in because those topics may require expending a lot of emotional energy which may get in the way or impede progress. However, Kumar (2014) shared that research projects often originate from problems of practice that are identified by students or from their professional goals and interests. I agree and specifically chose to complete a DiP on a problem I was facing in my professional practice and that numerous colleagues identified as affecting their leadership abilities. I wanted to provide answers to questions I had, that were affecting learning in my school board, and sought to understand what is contributing to the complexity of the role of school principal.

In my role of principal, the themes of adversity and resiliency are common discussions with aspiring leaders, community members, and fellow administrators because of the misconceptions and complications associated with the role. I wanted to investigate if the challenges and feelings I were experiencing as principal were common to other administrators and to establish some methods for myself and others to handle the trials and tribulations of the role more success-fully. More importantly, I wanted to ensure future administrators were prepared for a job perhaps tougher than they imagined or have been told and provide a list of strategies for them to develop prior to entering the world of administration. My supervisory team, career aspirations, or education trends did not play a part in my topic choice but I now feel confident to explore other career avenues and publica-tion opportunities due to my completion of the EdD and DiP.

The Carnegie Project on the Education Doctorate (CPED, Perry, 2015, p. 277) encouraged the notion of *inquiry in practice,* defined as "the process of posing significate questions about complex problems of practice and utilizing research, theories, and professional wisdom to design innovative solutions" (p. 60). I was able to model this purpose of an EdD student who attempts to transform their field of professional practice and become an advanced educational practitioner who ad-dressed a complex problem of practice. Specifically, the role of school principal is now so multifaceted that fewer teachers want to become a formal leader. With the idea that the workplace is a site of knowledge production (Tennant, 2004), I was able to flush out specific challenges to the role that fellow principals deem as leadership adversity, sources, and how they use (or don't use) strategies to man-age their challenges. The data collected allowed me to understand and evaluate the effects of an action and in particular, the findings provided for understanding information using a just-in-time approach that is transferable to other administra-tors (CPED, Perry, 2015).

Wanting to produce a DiP that made a "contribution to knowledge" (Yates, 2004) required critical analysis of a system, organization, and problem. Far too of-ten organizations move too quickly to implement a solution to a problem without clearly defining the problem and understanding its roots. As a result, symptoms are addressed rather than underlying causal factors which frequently allows for the problem to recur in similar or different forms (Sparks, 2007). Completing a DiP allowed me, other practitioners, and organizations time to collect suffi-cient data and ask relevant questions regarding deep beliefs and values to uncover symptoms, factors, and root causes contributing to an identified problem. Then, thinking and acting strategically based on the findings of a study can help create work environments and building learning organizations that produce results and awareness (Senge, 2006). Hopefully contributing to this knowledge was a prod-uct of our "good" research. Yates (2004) described what work is defined as *good research*. The author claimed that research that is "good" demonstrates an original voice, perspective, and is creative (p. 65). Thanks to a supportive and experienced supervision team, the research project modeled Yates (2004) perspectives.

EXAMINING AND DEFENDING MY GARDEN PLOT

If you look the right way, you can see that the whole world is a garden
—*Frances Hodgson Burnett (1911)*

Any good gardener knows that while they may appreciate their work for its colors, beauty, and rewards, others may harshly judge their choices or decisions requiring deep conversation and reflection. Similarly, the DiP required defending. Luckily, I had a team of professionals who had been with me throughout my entire involvement in the program. Being assigned a supervisor and subsequent committee team members allowed for feelings of safety, support through my challenges, and their professional experiences which could not be replicated. I do not think that I will again experience so many committed people who are enthusiastically helping me develop as a scholar. Perry (2015) acknowledged that the traditional mentor-mentee relationship is no longer the norm in EdD programs. Rather the faculty member brings their set of research and theoretical knowledge and skills while the practitioner-student brings their experience and practitioner knowledge. This type of relationship provided for me the respect I was looking for from other professionals and demonstrated the university's commitment and care to their students.

Judgement of my scholarly work was welcomed in order to demonstrate the highest level of achievement to appear most robust and therefore, I understood was subject to scrutiny. In particular, Yates (2004) expressed that research that is judged as "good" by the student, supervisors, and examiners demonstrates that you know your professional community and appreciate what kind of contribution you are making to it and importantly, the research is judged relative to a particular, already existing research community. Being judged also comes with the territory of being a school leader. I was prepared with a thick skin, honest and clear understanding of the value of defending my choices, and welcomed any and all feedback to reflect on my work.

IMPACT ON MY ORGANIZATION

She made herself stronger by fighting with the wind.
—*Frances Hodgson Burnett (1911)*

Kumar (2014) found that doctoral programs help students "to think outside the box and that their involvement with like-minded peers has increased their morale and motivated them" (p. 179). Four themes emerge from Kumar's participants regarding the impact of the doctoral program on their professional practice. They obtained increased confidence, appreciation and usage of research, credibility in their practice, and change in their professional roles. I agree with all four of Kumar's findings and feel very confident in my ability to research and communicate in a more academic way. Having a school principal who has completed their doctorate is a sense of pride to my school board. My superintendent constantly shares her admiration of me completing my DiP in the required timelines while working full time and persevering through difficult political and personal crisis. I receive full support to participate in conferences or speaking engagements in which I present my research and share with fellow graduate students and administrator colleagues.

Importantly, my EdD completion and DiP has allowed me sustained service to my organization due to my renewed energy. Demands of my principal role, school, and school systems can often take a toll on a leader's personal health, emotional well-being, and relationships. Over time, the responsibilities of the job can lead to unbalanced and stressful lives; however, recognizing the opportunity the EdD and DiP provided as energy-enhancing tools allowed me to develop key relationships and learning (Sparks, 2007). I have gained clarity about values and purpose and have determined I am on track to serve my community and organization well. Furthermore, my DiP has been shared with numerous stakeholders in my school district. Principals and colleagues having conversations about the role of principal, the need for resiliency strategies, and the various forms of adversity facing school administrators today gives my DiP the credibility it deserves. Numerous recommendations were provided in the DiP for principals, aspiring leaders, school boards, and principal organizations. Time will tell if sanctions take form to improve the role, develop principals, and provide formal and informal opportunities for principals to share their adversity experiences and develop resiliency strategies.

However, Sparks (2007) importantly underscores his belief that almost all schools can benefit from interacting with practitioners and researchers or other sources of outside knowledge and skills. When principals initiate change that encourages sharing of effective practices and demonstrate their appreciation of the talents in their community, staffs are more likely to reach out to other educators and to professional literature for energy and guidance. By my DiP detailing a vision of the desired results and support for principals and grounding the discussions in data and evidence, I am modeling "structural tension" (Fritz, 1989, p. 115). Fritz (1989) encouraged organizations to resolve this tension and move forward closing gaps by creating simple action plans and accessing current data. The success will generate professional learning and energy which breeds more creativity, learning, and success. I feel the energy from the completion of the EdD and DiP and am sustaining the study of professional literature, seeking continuous improvement, and making meaningful connections in and outside the school board. Most importantly, teachers in my school, colleagues in my school board, and those I meet while sharing my learning and research receive this energy and see the passion to bring about change for education.

Participation in the EdD, completion of the DiP, and Sparks (2007) has confirmed that having high expectations for yourself and others brings about organizational creativity, meaningful connections among school communities, continuous development and use of professional knowledge, and judgment. Hearing that future cohorts are thriving and more colleagues are pursuing their EdD and DiP allows for a sense of pride that I may have had an influence on my organization on a larger scale than first imagined. The possibilities for organizations to flourish are truly endless with research practitioners as their school and district leaders!

FUTURE IMPLICATIONS

> At first people refuse to believe that a strange new thing can be done, then they begin to hope it can be done, then they see it can be done—then it is done and all the world wonders why it was not done centuries ago.
> —*Frances Hodgson Burnett (1911)*

Obviously, developing my capacity to lead systemic reform in education was worth the blood, sweat, and tears of the doctoral program and DiP. I have always considered myself a servant-leader (Greenleaf, 1970) and now have earned the academic credibility to be heard on a bigger stage. Reading and quoting research has become my main purpose prior to participating in any initiative. Modeling a thinking process that delves deeper into the need to reflect on why we do things the way we do them. I am asking tougher questions in my organization to those who make decisions impacting students and student learning so they may be held accountable to all our stakeholders for their choices. Most importantly, using my thorough knowledge of the complexity associated with the role of school principal to ensure school boards are using the recommendations suggested from the DiP to improve their leadership development programs, relationships with their administrators, and professional learning for all leaders.

I wonder if I can consider myself a global leader due to the extensive reading, application of knowledge, and universal collegial relationships built through the EdD and DiP. Reilly (2007) offered five considerations when formulating the roles, relationships, and rules necessary to lead in a global society. Reilly lists: be a learner; spend time in the world; value innovation, maintain transparency; and seek the best. Importantly, Reilly expects leaders to reflect upon her considerations for themselves and those they lead. Furthermore, Reilly asks leaders to consider three questions: "What must I know and be able to do to lead in a global society? What must those whose scholarship and learning I guide know and be able to do? How do I, as a leader, prepare a generation of children for a world that I will not see?" (p. 139). To that end, I am seeking opportunities to teach our next generation of teachers. This fall I am teaching in a pre-service faculty which was one of my goals of achieving my EdD and therefore, allowing me to support the development of ideas, creativity, and learning of future school leaders.

Maybe not a fully anointed global leader (yet) but I am further along the continuum thanks to the experiences of the EdD and producing a DiP. I will continue to seek learning opportunities to grow and share leadership with others through the facilitation of courses and presentations to leaders. I have traveled the world on a recent sabbatical and lived abroad but I still require deeper understanding of educational structures in other countries. I have always valued innovation but never been an inventor until the DiP attempted to provide new knowledge on the challenges of the role school principal. I am transparent with my decision-making process, share successes and failures, and am intentional in my choice of professional relationships. I am learning to seek the best from myself and others. Having high expectations of yourself and others is not enough to be on a global level. I must lead change and take immediate action when injustices are revealed, inequities found, or student learning is negatively affected. Clearly, I must continue to grow considering a world beyond the four walls of the school I lead and the borders of my school district to the world community of learning, innovating, and leading change.

Therefore, when sharing the completion of my EdD and defense of the DiP to superintendents and colleagues they express their deep support for my accomplishments. They ask genuine questions about my research and program. They are interested to know if the rigorous program was worth it while handling a full life. I explain that I now have opportunities I would never have experienced without completing an EdD and DiP. I share that school principals have now been given a voice regarding their leadership adversity and resiliency strategies. I share that I get to continue to create a legacy of encouraging, supporting, and inspiring the next generation of school leader to cultivate their belief in education and improve student learning.

In conclusion, now that the doctorate learning cycle of planting ideas, cultivating learning, and harvesting results is completed, this intentional gardener looks even further into the future. Committed to sharing my personal growth and study's results through leadership development opportunities will cultivate the next set of doctoral students and improve leadership in Ontario. This learning will sow seeds validating the need for all educators to address complexities of student learning and school leadership found throughout the world. While gardening is not for everyone, nor an on-line professional doctorate program, they both must be appreciated for their passion, uniqueness, and opportunity to contribute to the human condition.

REFERENCES

Andersen, D. G. (1983). Differentiation of the Ed.D. and Ph.D. in education. *Journal of Teacher Education, 34*(3), 55–58. doi:10.1177/002248718303400311

Bourner, T., & Simpson, P. (2014). Action learning and the pedagogy of professional doctorates. *Higher Education, Skills and Work-Based Learning, 4*(2), 122–136. doi:10.1108/HESWBL-10-2013-0014

Burnett, F. H. (1911). *The secret garden.* New York: Harper.

Deering, T. E. (1998). Eliminating the doctor of education degree: It's the right thing to do. *The Educational Forum, 62*(3), 243–248. doi:10.1080/00131729808984350

Fritz, R. (1989). *Path of least resistance: Learning to become the creative force in your own life.* New York, NY: Fawcett Books.

Greenleaf, R. K. (1970). *The servant as leader.* Cambridge, MA: Center for Applied Studies.

Isaac, P. D., Koenigsknecht, R. A., Malaney, G. D., & Karras, J. E. (1989). Factors related to doctoral dissertation topic selection. *Research in Higher Education, 30*(4), 357–373. doi:10.1007/BF00992560

Kaomea, J. (2001). Completing the doctorate: Reflections of a recent graduate. *Academic Exchange Quarterly, 5*(1), 119–123.

Kouzes, J., & Posner, B. (2002). *The leadership challenge* (3rd ed.). San Francisco: Jossey-Bass.

Kumar, S. (2014). A systematic approach to the assessment of impact in a professional doctorate. *Higher Education, Skills and Work-Based Learning, 4*(2), 171–183. doi:10.1108/HESWBL-10-2013-0020

Mezirow, J. (2000). Learning to think like an adult: Core concepts of transformational theory. In J. Mezirow & Associates (Eds.), *Learning as transformation: Critical perspectives on a theory in progress* (pp. 3–33). San Francisco: Jossey-Bass.

Perry, J. A. (2013). Carnegie project on the education doctorate: The education doctorate: A degree for our time. *Planning and Changing, 44*(3/4), 113–126.

Perry, J. A. (2015). The Carnegie project on the education doctorate. *Change: The Magazine of Higher Learning, 47*(3), 56–61. doi:10.1080/00091383.2015.1040712

Reilly, E. C. (2007). Leadership in a global society: Habits of mind, of heart, and of action. *Educational Leadership and Administration, 19*, 139–149.

Senge, P. (2006). *The fifth discipline: The art and practice of the learning organization* (revised ed.). New York, Toronto: Doubleday Publishing.

Shulman, L. S., Golde, C. M., Bueschel, A. C., & Garabedian, K. J. (2006). Reclaiming education's doctorates: A critique and a proposal. *Educational Researcher, 35*(3), 25–32. doi:10.3102/0013189X035003025

Social Sciences and Humanities Research Council of Canada, Canadian Institutes of Health Research, & Natural Sciences and Engineering Research Council Canada. (2014). *Tri-council policy statement: Ethical conduct for research involving humans.* Ottawa: Interagency Secretariat on Research Ethics. Retrieved from http://www.pre.ethics.gc.ca/pdf/eng/tcps2-2014/TCPS_2_FINAL_Web.pdf

Sparks, D. (2007). *Leading for results* (2nd ed.). Thousand Oaks, CA: Corwin Press.

Tennant, M. (2004). Doctoring the knowledge worker. *Studies in Continuing Education, 26*(3), 431–441. doi:10.1080/0158037042000265971

Western Education. (2016, March 26). *Western education.* Retrieved from http://www.edu.uwo.ca/graduate-education/edd.html

Yates, L. (2004). *What does good education research look like? Situating a field and its practices.* Berkshire, UK: Open University Press.

CHAPTER 19

THRIVING IN WHITEWATER
A Professional Practice Doctorate Experience

Lee S. Barney

Many rivers in the United States' Intermountain West consist of alternating adrenaline inducing whitewater rapids followed by stretches of serene, transparent, refreshing, calm water. When you float these rivers, the roaring whitewater throws itself into the air and tries to tear you and the boat you are on apart. Then come the calm stretches where you can see down to the riverbed and all the life between it and you. These calm stretches draw you in and help you see the natural beauty around you. If you float one of these rivers, the Snake, the Salmon, the Green, the Colorado, or some other, you will experience the danger and thrill of the whitewater and then, as your adrenalin level and your heart rate drops, the beauty of the calm stretches will emerge around you and, if you give them time, they will emotionally engulf you.

Our lives are combinations of whitewater and calm stretches. Sometimes it seems the whitewater in our lives never ends and the calm water, if any, is too short. But if either the whitewater or the calm water was missing, our lives, like rivers without whitewater, would become opaque. Is this why normal, every-day people choose to add more whitewater to their lives? Could this desire for transparency, an aid to self-evaluation and growth, be why a group of people, in the

Exploring the Impact of the Dissertation in Practice, pages 283–296.

283

middle of their careers, would seek out and join a doctoral program that added enormous amounts of whitewater to their busy, complex, and sometimes overwhelming lives?

WHO AM I?

I am a scientist. At 14 years of age I saw the Bohr model of the atom for the first time. It was love at first sight. I decided then and there to devote my life to being a research chemist. To make this happen, I took advantage of every opportunity to study mathematics and science, including two years of chemistry, as I completed Junior and Senior High School.

Unwittingly, as part of this experience, I imbibed a positivistic worldview. Encouraged in this by my teachers, I developed a disdain for knowledge gained in other ways. Not just social sciences fell under my critical view; even statistics, geology, and biology were highly suspect. If evidence didn't come from something that looked like a chemistry experiment or a mathematics proof, I didn't see value in it.

Much later, as a senior at a large university, I finally admitted to myself that I didn't like being in chemistry labs—a huge drawback if you're going to be a research chemist. My world collapsed in on me. Searching for a way to complete my education, I took a few courses in other majors but nothing thrilled me so I dropped out. I needed some time to figure out what to do with my life.

After three years of self-reflection and doing any small job I could find, I was finally ready to try going back to school. My spouse and I considered the sacrifices our family would have to make and decided to make a go of it. We chose a small state university, Southern Utah University (SUU), two hours away from our home. This choice made it possible for me to complete a non-Chemistry science degree and get a teaching certificate in a year and a half. This timeframe was achievable only if I went to school year-round and we made sacrifices concerning our family's togetherness. SUU was over a high mountain pass, so we found a room for me to rent Monday through Friday; weekends I would spend at home.

As I rebooted my university education, any certainty I had in positivistic world views quickly eroded. I tried and failed to apply positivism to diverse areas of study such as art, languages, and history. This failure caused me a great deal of heartburn. Positivism didn't seem to fit but I knew no other perspective and was provided no other in the classes I was taking. I only knew how to search for truth using chemistry experiments and mathematical tools. I was truly and deeply stuck.

Eventually I earned a transdisciplinary degree combining geology, physics, chemistry, and mathematics. In spite of doing well in my courses and being formally recognized by the university for my mathematic abilities, my unease with positivistic proofs and perspectives had grown to the point that I questioned their very foundation. Could it be true that the way scientists and mathematicians view the world is flawed? Could the axioms these areas of study are built be just plain wrong? Without answers, I carried these questions with me to my new career.

I started teaching junior high science, grades 7–9, and closely watched what was happening in my classroom. Because of what I saw, I decided positivism had helped humanity overcome many hurdles, but it simply could not explain or even describe the wonderful young people I loved and worked with every day. Still knowing no other perspectives, I remained adrift and lost in the dark.

After many years of teaching I changed careers for financial reasons. I earned a master's degree in computing and started a new job as a computer programmer. In this job I found, even though at the time I didn't know the terminology, that the computer industry deeply imbibes positivism, atomism, reductionism, essentialism, and pragmatism. Even though computing depends on these philosophies, my time in this job and others I had in the computer industry didn't make me any more comfortable with my positivistic worldview. Instead, it made me less so. I learned and saw how false and fake computer simulations actually are; how models of reality can easily lead anyone astray, especially when they forget models are always flawed and simplified representations of reality.

After working for a couple of tech companies and even starting one of my own, I came across an opportunity to become a fulltime faculty member at Brigham Young University-Idaho (BYU-Idaho) and jumped at the chance. I missed the whitewater of teaching and wanted to once again help students by applying what I had learned from my teaching and industry experiences. This is the point when my hunt for a doctoral degree began.

IN THE BEGINNING...

In August of 2004 I settled into my new position and launched my doctoral program search. Time and again I experienced the same thing—I would find a program that sounded interesting, contact the program director, and hear they'd love to have me. All I had to do was quit my job, uproot my family, and move to be on their campus. I loved the position I had and didn't want to quit in order to get a degree that would qualify me for that same position. To me, that didn't seem a reasonable path forward.

In 2009, as part of my search, I ran across a doctoral program in course and curriculum design for online learning situations. It was available from a small university in a nearby state and sounded enticing. I figured it might be flexible enough to meet my needs so I gave the program director a call. We conversed for about 20 minutes about the program and it sounded great. Then I asked if the courses could be taken online and heard in reply, "Of course not! That's not possible. You'll need to quit your job and move here."

The illogic of that statement struck me hard. How could a program purporting to have instructors who were experts at developing online courses and curriculum not have the wherewithal to use their skills and make their program work online? I explained to the director that their program wouldn't work for me, thanked her for her time, and politely hung up. In despair at the entire doctoral educational system, I started laughing uncontrollably. This experience was the last straw. I gave up and stopped looking.

SOMETHING DIFFERENT

In 2011 the University of Idaho (U of I) began promoting their Ed.D Professional Practice Doctorate (PPD) program at BYU-Idaho. Expecting to hear the same things I heard from other programs, I didn't initially respond. After a while, and because of my spouse's encouragement, I went to an information meeting. What I heard was different from what I had heard before. This new program would draw in professionals from all over eastern Idaho. Some courses would be taught online. Others would be face-to-face and they would be taught after hours on the campus where I worked.

The PPD program director told the potential students in the meeting with me that the program was still being designed. This meant, among other things, it was not completely decided which courses would be part of the curriculum. Those of us in the meeting were informed the program would be built as we experienced it. There was a preliminary plan with preliminary courses in that plan, but change would happen and should be expected. We students would be part of a cohort and the program would adapt as the U of I gathered more information about what the cohort and the program needed. These needs would be balanced with the courses traditionally found in EdD programs; the assumption being that many of the educational, research, philosophy, and other traditional EdD courses would be needed. Three years would suffice to complete the degree since the program would run three semesters a year and we would receive credit for the courses we had completed as part of our existing, individual master's degrees. Using this approach and applying an aggressive calendar meant we would not only complete our coursework in three years, but our dissertations too.

The program director explained to us that the curriculum plan would always be stable for the current semester, almost always for the upcoming semester, and occasionally for the second semester out. This flexibility of design was chosen so the institution could find and schedule instructors for courses, allow the instructors time to design the courses they would teach, and still enable the program to shift as more information was gathered and understood. As students we would periodically be given updated curriculum maps including courses we had completed and what was anticipated for the current and next two semesters.

We were told that within the cohort we would work in teams and our Dissertations In Practice (DiP) would be different than those required of traditional EdD students. They would be team DiPs. Exactly what that meant was, and would continue to be, under negotiation with the College of Graduate Studies. We were told not to worry about this and to begin thinking about topics in our areas of expertise we may want to research.

Cohorts and working in teams were nothing new to me. I experienced these same organizational structures while getting my masters degree. The flexibility of the curriculum schedule didn't concern me. My professional area of expertise, software development, requires a great deal of scheduling flexibility. In spite of feeling comfortable with what I had heard in this meeting, I was still skeptical. It took a great deal of pondering and discussion with my wife and family before we decided to take the chance. I took the GRE, paid my upfront money, and applied to the program.

THE GOOD...

Because I had created a large number of courses from scratch, I knew being part of the first cohort for any program would involve patches of unintended whitewater. Nobody gets program and course designs right the first time out of the box and I went into the program with the idea that, as an adult professional and a student, I could both learn and give back (Knowles, Holton, & Swanson, 2013). This became reality for me in the very first class. As it began, the analogy of building a plane while it is flying was used to describe what we would experience as we developed the doctoral program together. This analogy and the ideas behind it caused stress in some of the students. The idea that everything wasn't completed, tried, and tested ahead of time raised fears in spite of this having been explained to us before. Somehow all the students hadn't understood this ambiguity. Instead of being stressed by this, I experienced excited uncertainty. I knew opportunities always include a risk of failure, but I also knew if I and the other cohort members honestly contributed to the program it would be a great experience. Having already committed to getting the degree, I saw no point in hesitating and dived in.

In a philosophy course taught early in the curriculum, various philosophies were described along with how they could be used as the basis of research; they are, after all, the lenses through which the world is viewed, questions generated, and data interpreted. At this point I finally had ideas to discuss and work with other than positivism. This thrilled me.

As the different philosophies were introduced, it was fun to hear students excitedly say, "That's what I am." They had only heard a brief sentence or two of explanation but they tended to exuberantly wrap themselves in the philosophy of the moment. Then, after a more in-depth discussion of the philosophy and its implications, they would become uncomfortable with the declaration they had made. Then, almost always, they ended up saying something like, "I guess I'm not that."

Eventually, the students stopped declaring themselves as belonging to any single philosophy. Based on my conversations with the other students, they stopped doing this not because of any condemnation or preference by the instructor, but as they gained greater understanding, they ceased to try to fit themselves into preexisting bounds presented by specific philosophies. Instead, most began fitting philosophies to themselves.

As part of this fitting process, students would make "I believe...." or "I think..." types of statements. The professor listened respectfully and would often reply with an assertion indicating which philosophy might match the student's statement of belief. Usually the matching philosophy was one the student had already rejected. Some students expressed exasperation when they had these experiences. I enjoyed them a lot and saw them as opportunities to re-examine my beliefs.

In the out-of-class discussions I tried to help other students see the benefits of this andragogical instructional approach. I explained how they could play with ideas as they addressed the challenges being presented. That they could explore an idea and even advocate for it, and yet not accept it. For example, I found it very fun, as part of the assignments given, to write from the perspectives of different philosophies. I will never forget hearing my voice coming through in an argument applying critical feminism.

I suppose I was able to stand back and have a different experience because, early in the class, and because of my early adoption of and anxiety about positivism, I decided not associate myself with any given philosophy until I had stated an axiology, ontology, and epistemology that I felt described my beliefs. Then I could more rationally evaluate which philosophy or parts of philosophies might work for me. I am no philosopher, so what I arrived at was simplistic and part of it is summed up in these two paragraphs.

> There is only so much we can know or be skilled enough to do. There is insufficient time to know and become accomplished at everything. As an additional handicap, our brains seem designed to forget anything we don't use. I'm a software developer. I trust a plumber to know and be more accomplished than me regarding plumbing. I trust a lawyer to know and do more than me with the law. I trust an architect to know more about building design and be able to create beautiful structures.

> Sooner or later, as humans, we must trust someone to understand the myriad of things we don't have the time or inclination to know or learn to do for ourselves. We must each choose who it is we trust to find, teach, and apply truths in these areas. It may be a single philosopher, a group of philosophers, scientific organizations, peers, friends, political organizations, religious organizations, people who post on Facebook, or God. This trust, that there is another or others that know more and can do more than we do, is faith in that group or individual. We all have to have faith in others. If we didn't we would need to be omniscient. I'm not omniscient nor is any other temporally bound being or group.

Having described this understanding of trust and faith for myself, I listened to and participated in all the discussions of the various philosophies. I also spent many hours exploring and consuming writings by proponents of the philosophies covered by the course. In spite of the broad spectrum of philosophies presented, there were none that included the faith principle, as I understood it. Nor were any that moved me to say, "That matches my experience. That's me."

After completing the philosophy class, I spent even more time exploring philosophies. I discovered most of them by reading published research and exploring the articles' listed references. Among what I found were the works of Gadamer, Kirkegaard, and Kampis. Each provided bits and pieces that resonated with me.

While none of them explicitly expressed trust and faith, as I understood it, the combination of the works of these three philosophers allowed me enough onto-logical and epistemological wiggle room to do what I needed to do. I felt I could combine them and use them as the foundation for my research.

THE NOT SO GOOD ...

Higher Education programs are much more than course lists. Instead, they are contextual, being an amalgam of course designs, course outcomes, students, pro-fessors, administrators, and support staff. As a newly created program, courses were dynamic and varied in relation to rigor and expectations. Specifically, the delivery of the research methods courses was through a social science research lens, which contributed little to my existing knowledge and skills. On reflection being able to choose courses as in the PhD program might be an advantage to many EdD doctoral candidates although I realize that this would then impact the cohesion of the cohort.

The speedy introduction of the EdD program was not without its challenges and though I do not have full awareness of the institutional politics relating to the program I was concerned about the mindset of some faculty. For example when writing iterations of my research proposal I was delighted by the assessment grade but disappointed by the lack of feedback I received from the class professor. For-tunately, this approach was counterbalanced by the ongoing support and feedback I received from my DiP mentor.

OVER AND OVER AGAIN

However, overall the PPD program excelled. We students were able to generate an environment where even from mistakes we could learn, grow, and meet the program outcomes to help us grow professionally. One way we did this was by taking advantage of being able to prepare for writing research proposals and dis-sertations early in the program.

As part of each class we were asked to come up with potential research topics and questions, then explain them to our instructors and other cohort members. This process allowed us, as students, early access to weaknesses in our ideas. By understanding the weaknesses, we could adapt or throw out what we had, and go at it again and again. These early examinations of research topics ended up being a huge advantage to us when we eventually wrote our proposals and DiPs. I personally examined, adapted, and rejected over ten major research topics as I progressed through the PPD program's courses. This amount of iteration was not a waste. It was integral to developing a sense of how to determine if research top-ics or questions are valuable.

As students, we were unaware of questions used to examine research ideas and how to apply them. Does the topic fill an empty niche in the existing body of knowledge? Is the topic neither too specific nor too expansive? Is the research question answerable? Are the research question and sub-questions specific enough to yield usable answers?

As we repeatedly applied these and other questions to our research ideas, we experienced a recursive, discovery process. Throughout this experience I had many wonderful cohort members that uplifted me, challenged me, and caused me to think deeply. They helped me create my best work and my best work was expected by them and the class instructors. This expectation of excellence was not limited to course assignments. Excellence was also expected in our communications as students in and out of the classroom and with others who were not part of the program.

MENTOR ME

One course was on professional mentoring. It included much more than reading and writing about mentors, protégés, and learning what good mentoring is. Instead, we were asked as professionals to evaluate ourselves. We were to examine our professional relationships and communications to see if we were being good mentors. We also were asked to seek out, contact, and develop professional relationships where we could be protégés to researchers in the area of our interest. This encouraged us to begin interacting not just with literature, but communicating directly with others who would become our mentors throughout the DiP/research process and after graduation. My mentors gave me excellent insights and the suggestions they made were always enlightening. Among other things, they helped me see outside my bias boxes and expanded my view of the research space.

They also provided early feedback about the importance of the research I was contemplating and that I eventually completed. When the whitewater seemed impossible to navigate, I could reflect back on their statements to me and gather additional strength. They met Nakamura, Shernoff, and Hooker's (2009) definition of good mentors. They never gave me answers; instead, they helped me find and see paths and possibilities when I could only perceive waterfalls, boulders, and rapids.

LEARNING AS ACTION

In an early semester, I had another value-rich experience. As part of a face-to-face qualitative research methods class, we did much more than read, discuss, and write about the different methods presented. Instead, we were required to perform a small scale research project, which the IRB board determined did not need preapproval. My team ended up needing to plan and perform interviews with outsiders. These interviews were designed to gather qualitative data for our research questions we had back then.

My team of three found some willing participants in Jackson Hole, Wyoming. We scheduled some time with them, drove over, applied the loosely defined interview protocol we had designed, and held a post-interview team discussion of the results. All three of us were very excited to see our learning in action. After getting back home, we coded the qualitative data we retrieved from the audio recordings of the interviews and, with this in hand, produced an improved version of our interview protocol. This experience, coming early in the coursework, removed from all three of us any reservations we had about qualitative research and our ability to be professionals in the research space. We had made it through a small patch of whitewater and found a calm stretch. This continuous improvement process allowed us to shift, adjust, and prepare for creating our final research proposals. Of all of the many wonderful things I learned from being part of the PPD experience, this sifting, examining, filtering, expanding, and focusing process has been the most fundamental to the teaching, designing of courses, and research I do now.

MY DISSERTATION IN PRACTICE (DiP)

When getting a doctoral degree, the DiP is the most dangerous whitewater the student encounters. The boulders, waterfalls, drops, eddies, and standing waves that are committee creation, the proposal and its defense, the research and, most of all, writing of the DiP are thrilling and terrifying. In the U of I PPD program, instead of the traditional approach where students choose and assemble advisors and committees, the U of I found interested faculty that volunteered to help the cohort's research teams by being advisors and committee members. This left the students responsible for finding one committee member, the outsider. Occasionally, but not always, this outsider was someone who was already a mentor.

As part of these volunteers' commitment process, the concept and structure of a PPD three article dissertation (Willis, Inman, & Valenti, 2010) was explained. Even with these explanations, the structure of the completed DiPs varied widely. My DiP's (Barney, 2014) structure included a brief introduction describing what a PPD is and why the DiP's format was non-traditional. Also included were two publishable articles, one by me and one by my teammate.

I added to these articles a white paper for my current employer describing the results of my research and a chapter of reflections about how the PPD process and my research had helped me change personally and professionally. This is in accordance with the PPD principles of dissertation resulting in research contributing to current employment, the student's professional life, and the general body of knowledge (Willis et al., 2010).

It may seem that having others contribute to articles in my DiP made it easier for me. When I compare my experience to those who have done traditional dissertations, I find this is not the case. Working in any team where individual success or survival is determined by the contributions of others is very risky. In the middle of whitewater on a river, if the people on the boat aren't working together, disaster quickly follows. This is also true in DiP teams.

Collaborative DiPs require openness and trust as co-researchers and coauthors work together. My teammate and I worked two distinct sets of research questions as a team. I was a co-researcher and coauthor in his work and he in mine. The process worked well until late into the DiP process when my team hit a horrible patch of whitewater. My teammate stopped progressing. After doing his data collection, he stopped preparing for his defense. Our advisor was unable to energize him. I had known my partner for over two years and worked very closely with him during much of that time. Eventually, he and I sat down and discussed possible outcomes. First, if the present situation continued then neither of us would complete our DiPs within the planned three-year timeframe. Second, he could complete or not complete his DiP on his own but if he chose to not continue to work together as a team then we could no longer share our research since it would be unprofessional and unethical. Fortunately, he decided to step up. At graduation, he and his wife thanked me for helping him get through his personal whitewater.

Not every ending was sunshine and roses. There were two students who left the program in the first year. Another, one of my teammates, became overwhelmed with the whitewater of life, family, work, and the program. He decided to get out of the river and take an Ed.S instead of completing a DiP. The rest of us, 22 in all, completed and graduated with EdD. PPD's. We made it through together, not because the program was easier but because of the determination of the advisors, the committees, our teammates, our mentors, and ourselves.

BEYOND GRADUATION

My team DiP experience pushed me further down a path that I had been exploring in my undergraduate course designs. I had experienced the importance of learning and production teams in industry and saw it again as part of the PPD cohort. I also saw the how, if not designed well, the use of team DiPs could be disastrous. Unlike standard, individualized dissertations, poorly designed team DiP experiences run the risk of punishing all contributors if one or more team member fails.

Strangely enough, generalized punishment is widely accepted in educational situations at all levels but is illegal, and rightly so, when applied to warfare. PPD team DiP experience designs must find ways to avoid this problem. While it is impossible to foresee all situations, plans to mitigate the negative impact of others' choices on their teammates can be created ahead of time.

Over the years prior to joining the U of I PPD program, I tried to plan ahead for these situations by experimenting with various group work assessment schemes promoted by others. These included common approaches such as peer assessment (Topping, 1998) and self-assessment (Boud, 1989). While the promoters of these and other approaches could point to successes, every time I applied commonly used schemes, the final scores assigned didn't reflect the learning of the individual students. In fact, my understanding of the students' learning, developed through my interaction directly with them often varied dramatically from what the schemes generated.

I also found if I assessed student-generated artifacts against rubrics, I got defensible, repeatable results, but the results were once again not in line with my perception of the students' learning. Applying rubrics to artifacts proved to be precise but not accurate. This flummoxed me until I eventually realized I was assessing the wrong learning indicators.

There is no replacement for assessing a primary indicator. Assessing a secondary indicator or a group of secondary indicators does not reliably yield the same assessed values as assessing a primary indicator. Secondary indicators such as tests, quizzes, or assignments indicate how well the taker completed the test, quiz, or assignment. These types of assessment tools are primary measures of work completed, but secondary measures of learning. It is necessary to assess student learning through primary indicators, not by assessing artifacts they submit. Because of my PPD research and creating my DiP, I found, that for me, the most accurate way of assessing students' learning is being a good mentor (Nakamura, Shernoff, & Hooker, 2009). In this situation, good mentoring includes me doing continuous assessment through ongoing interactions with individual students. Most often, these interactions include discussions, answering questions, and helping them achieve their goals. This practice helps me know where each student is in their learning process.

As part of my DiP, I began the development of a rubric that works for me as I mentor my students. It helps me assess two primary indicators of student learning; technical fluency and what the students are becoming. The rubric is a living document that I change and adjust in an attempt to balance clarity of understanding for the student and flexibility for recording my qualitative assessment of their learning. This ongoing conversation between myself, education literature, and the assessments achieved by applying my qualitative rubric has yielded courses that challenge the educational enculturation students have experienced. Without my PPD, I would not have had the philosophical or practical ability to produce, use, and defend qualitative assessments in the highly quantitative cultures of software development and higher education.

While the PPD's impact on my courses has been dramatic, in accordance with the principle of PPD research being applicable to the student's career and work environment (Willis et al., 2010), I invited two deans and the university's lead course design specialist to my DiP defense. I believed they would find my research results not only interesting but informative. Since then, I've met multiple times with one of them, the Dean of Faculty Development and Mentored Research. This dean is responsible, at BYU-Idaho, for encouraging faculty development and to aid the faculty in fostering and mentoring undergraduate student research.

Not only has this dean asked for explanations of my experience in developing myself through the PPD process, but he has held me up to the university at large as an example. One reason he feels strongly enough to do this is while I was doing the coursework for my PPD, I mentored an undergraduate student. This student, by going beyond a learning activity in one of my classes, produced a published article contributing unique knowledge to the mathematics body of literature (Carrión, 2014).

In addition to wanting to help my students contribute and give back, I also desire to give more fully to the body of knowledge for my area of research, the application of complexity theory to learning and educational research. The main article in my DiP was publishable but, due to the DiP writing process, it was not written with a specific journal in mind. To increase the probability of acceptance, I wrote a new, focused article after graduation using my research data (Barney, 2015) that was accepted for publication.

As part of writing this new article, I presented its findings to a small group of administrators including an Associate Academic Vice President. Others attending included those responsible for aiding faculty as they design and create courses. In this meeting, I was able not only to present the results of applying an alternative course design based on agency and risk-taking, but how those principles applied to the university's Student Learning Outcomes (SLO) (Brigham Young University-Idaho, 2013). During the discussion of the information presented, each participant expressed the importance of the research results to the direction of course designs for both face-to-face and online courses at the university. I continue to advocate with administrators and other faculty regarding the importance of agency and risk-taking as course design principles and how these principles help students achieve the university's SLO's.

As part of this advocacy, I have been able to mentor new research team members and help them see the importance of qualitative research methods, processes, and results. One current team member has a Ph.D. in literature and takes a hermeneutic approach to research. Another has a Ph.D. in physics and takes a quantitative, reductionist approach. As part of the PPD experience, I learned how to merge these perspectives with mine, a complexity theory approach, to produce results unavailable otherwise. As a team, we are experiencing the growth provided by leveraging others' philosophical foundations and are able to come to a greater understanding of the whole situation, problem, question, and research results. Without my PPD experience to use as an example, I may not have been able to convince my new teammates to venture into what for them was a realm of whitewater.

INTO THE WHITEWATER

As part of our weekly cohort meetings, the program administrator arranged a trip for us to float a portion of the Snake River in Wyoming. Two cohort members were professional river guides and helped arrange the trip. Together, we enjoyed a bonding experience and afterwards gathered for a light supper and discussion.

For the dialogue's focus, the program administrator and teacher of our first course asked us to ponder what we had just experienced. We were to express any analogies we could draw regarding our trip, learning, and what we expected our PPD journey to be like. Many interesting, valid, and thought-provoking ideas were proposed and talked about. It was obvious to us all that we were going to have a "whitewater doctoral experience." (Carter, 2015)

My whitewater experience involved college graduations, marriages, and births to celebrate, and intermingled with these joyous occasions were painful ones. One of my children lost his job due to major, repeated health problems and moved his young family into our small home for an extended period of time. Others of my children needed help financially or were struggling with the emotional pain of not being able to have the children they desired. My youngest son moved to France, had medical problems and major surgery while there, and then came back home to recuperate.

So was it worth the extra whitewater the PPD experience added to what we already faced in our everyday lives? I would answer with a resounding yes! We grew—and as a part of this growth we faced the huge rapids that make up the personal and educational whitewater found in all doctoral programs. Along with that whitewater came the calm patches in between. There were times of enormous stress and times of joyous enlightenment. There were times of deep despair and times of great hope. There were times of feeling alone and times of deep oneness with the cohort. There were times of opaque self-doubt and times of deep, transparent self-reflection leading to self-confidence (Huber, 2015).

Together we shared stressful, frightening, hard, thrilling, wonderful experiences. We did it with our families; those we found in our homes and the one we built from the PPD cohort. With the support of these families, we didn't just complete our doctoral degree, we became stronger and better people, family members, and educators. We became people who can be a greater blessing to our colleagues, our students, and our families.

We faced the whitewater and didn't just survive, we thrived.

REFERENCES

Barney, L. (2014). *Agency, community, learning-risks, and adult learners* (Doctoral dissertation). Retrieved from http://digital.lib.uidaho.edu/cdm/ref/collection/etd/id/548

Barney, L. (2015). Getting out of the way: Learning, risk, and choice. *Complicity: An International Journal of Complexity and Education, 12*(2), 49–80. Retrieved from https://ejournals.library.ualberta.ca/index.php/complicity/article/view/24198/19190

Brigham Young University-Idaho. (2013). *Student learning.* Retrieved from http://www.byui.edu/Documents/instructional_development/outcomes-assessment/ACA%20Student%20Outcomes%20Handout%2008.22.13.pdf

Boud, D. (1989). The role of self-assessment in student grading. *Assessment and Evaluation in Higher Education, 14*(1), 20–30. Retrieved from https://www.researchgate.net/profile/David_Boud/publication/254219847_The_role_of_self-assessment_in_student_grading/links/56355be508ae88cf81bbdc23.pdf

Carrión, D. F. (2014). *A recursive algorithmic approach to the finding of permutations for the combination of any two sets.* Retrieved from http://arxiv.org/abs/1401.1450

Carter, H. (2015). Tools for the road: Successfully navigating the doctoral journey. *Perspective: Understand Great Teaching, 15*(3), 16–19. Retrieved from http://www.

byui.edu/Documents/instructional_development/Perspective/2015%20Fall/HEATHER%20CARTER.pdf

Huber, R. (2015). Strength and support from a doctoral cohort. *Perspective: Understand Great Teaching, 15*(3), 9–12. Retrieved from http://www.byui.edu/Documents/instructional_development/Perspective/2015%20Fall/RACHEL%20HUBER.pdf

Knowles, M., Holton, E., & Swanson, R. (2013). *The adult learner* (7th ed.). New York, NY: Routledge.

Nakamura, J., Shernoff, D., & Hooker, C. (2009). *Good mentoring: Fostering excellent practice in higher education*. San Francisco, CA: Jossey-Bass.

Topping, K. (1998). Peer assessment between students in colleges and universities. *Review of Educational Research, 68*(3), 249–276. Retrieved from http://rer.sagepub.com/content/68/3/249.short

Willis, J., Inman, D., & Valenti, R. (2010). *Completing a professional practice dissertation*. Charlotte, NC: Information Age Publishing.

CPSIA information can be obtained
at www.ICGtesting.com
Printed in the USA
LVOW10s2326230418
574595LV00008B/39/P